LIVES OF THE
AUSTRALIAN CHIEF JUSTICES
❖

George Higinbotham

*Third Chief Justice
of Victoria 1886-1892*

Lives of the Australian Chief Justices

GEORGE HIGINBOTHAM

Lives of the Australian Chief Justices
J. M. Bennett

New South Wales

Sir Francis Forbes
Sir James Dowling
Sir James Martin

Queensland

Sir James Cockle

South Australia

Sir Charles Cooper

Tasmania

Sir John Pedder

Victoria

Sir William a'Beckett
Sir William Stawell
George Higinbotham

Western Australia

Sir Archibald Burt
Sir Henry Wrenfordsley

Lives of the Australian Chief Justices

GEORGE HIGINBOTHAM

Third Chief Justice of Victoria
1886-1892

J. M. BENNETT, A.M., LL.D.

(Adjunct Professor of Law, Macquarie University,
Sydney, New South Wales)

Foreword
Professor Geoffrey Blainey, A.C.

THE FEDERATION PRESS
2006

Published in Sydney by

The Federation Press
    71 John St, Leichhardt, NSW, 2040
    PO Box 45, Annandale, NSW, 2038
    Ph: (02) 9552 2200 Fax: (02) 9552 1681
    E-mail: info@federationpress.com.au
    Website: http://www.federationpress.com.au

National Library of Australia Cataloguing-in-Publication data:
    Bennett, J. M. (John Michael)
    George Higinbotham: third Chief Justice of Victoria 1886-1892

    Includes index.
    ISBN 978 186287 628 6

    1. Higinbotham, George, 1826-1892. 2. Judges – Victoria – Biography. 3.
    Politicians – Victoria – Biography. I. Title. (Series: Lives of the Australian
    Chief Justices).

347.945014092

Typeset by The Federation Press, Leichhardt, NSW.
    Printed by Ligare Pty Ltd, Riverwood, NSW.

Foreword

By Professor Geoffrey Blainey, A.C.

Higinbotham was neither Prime Minister nor Premier but even today – more than a century after his death – he retains the political fame conferred only on those who held high offices for a long period. Most of his fame comes from his period as a Victorian politician and Cabinet Minister and his six years as Chief Justice, but his political gestures as a judge are now remembered more than his judicial decisions. In the eyes of his admirers, living or dead, he was a giant. Indeed he is one of the few Australian judges to be honoured with a statue, and he stands, fully robed, in a commanding setting. This impressive book is the first attempt to see behind the statue.

This cult-figure was born in Ireland though his surname is of Dutch origin. After studying at Trinity College, Dublin, he worked in London as a parliamentary reporter and studied law before migrating to Melbourne which was then gripped by the gold rushes. While briefly working on the Ballarat goldfield in 1854 he met a household servant, maybe a parlour maid, marrying her in Melbourne a few months later. It was the kind of match which in Victorian society created social difficulties for a professional man. But he did not suffer: it was his wife Margaret who became a social recluse in the comfortable household they set up near the beach at Brighton.

For three years George Higinbotham was the individualist editor of the Melbourne *Argus*, one of the most influential newspapers in the continent. Soon the owner began to wonder whether he really owned his own newspaper, for it increasingly expressed Higinbotham's individualistic opinions. Next the editor became a politician, in that era when most members wore their hats in the Legislative Assembly. His speeches were even more electrifying than his editorials, and his later speech-making in the opinion of

v

that fine orator Alfred Deakin was incomparable. Becoming, in his late thirties, the Attorney-General in the long-lived McCulloch Ministry, Higinbotham was highly influential in the educational debates and during the constitutional deadlocks that were a foretaste of those which brought down the Whitlam government in the Federal Parliament in 1975. Indeed Higinbotham acquired slowly in his own Colony something of the heroic status later given to Whitlam by his most ardent disciples. Nobody else was quite like him in colonial Melbourne; and his deep admirers included Alfred Deakin, H. B. Higgins, Dr H. V. Evatt and others who were very influential in public life.

His capacity for work – he slept often in his office rather than catch the last train to Brighton – and generosity were extraordinary. As a barrister he attracted important cases in commercial and banking law, and part of his income he dispensed to beggars who gathered at his doorway. Few lawyers could reasonably disapprove when he was appointed a Judge of the Supreme Court of Victoria in 1880. Six years later he took the uncommon step of accepting the office of Chief Justice: it was then a principle, founded on valid reasons and applied in most colonies except Tasmania, that promotion should not be given to or accepted by an existing judge. In his new office he pursued certain high principles and flouted or ignored a few others. He refused to accept a knighthood which virtually meant that the other judges newly appointed could not be knighted. He refused to accept the additional salary to which the Chief Justice was entitled and instead of returning it to the Crown, or giving it, as some might have anticipated, to his retinue of beggars, he spent it periodically on lavish banquets for judges and legal practitioners.

He did not believe that a judge should stand aside from political controversy, even in those matters which might ultimately come before his court for a decision. With emphatic language he sometimes said that he saw no reason why a man who had been a serious politician should, after becoming a judge, abandon his politics and instead become what he called "a political eunuch". In the maritime strike of 1890, maybe the first industrial dispute to convulse a capital city, he donated a considerable sum to set up a fund to help the families of strikers and their supporters. In disclosing his gesture to the Trades Hall, he formally used the

Chief Justice's note paper. He did not think so well, however, of a fellow judge who took the same liberties.

Higinbotham's famous intervention in the maritime strike is placed in perspective by the author, who is the first to point out that unfortunate employees whose cases came before him could not always expect sympathy. Higinbotham was rather stern towards injured workers whose negligence had partly caused their injury.

While Bennett has written mainly for legal readers, even those of us whose knowledge of legal history is slender will find it laced with insights into Australia's political history and thought. On Higinbotham's hyperactive mind and unusual blend of views, the book is fascinating. In one phase of his life he was the most ardent of democrats and many of today's republicans admire him: but he was also a constitutional monarchist, an admirer of Queen Victoria, and an upholder of Britain's right to control foreign policy in Australian spheres of influence. He believed in the six colonies rather than a federation; and when he was shown, a year before his death, the first draft of the federal Constitution he was not impressed – with the notable exception of the word "Commonwealth".

Personally religious, so far as can be gauged, he was that oddity, a regular Anglican who admired the Unitarians: or at least he said so when he opened their new church in Melbourne. On religion he held other unwavering opinions. His disapproval of clergymen as a species and of the intense rivalry amongst the various religious denominations was such that today's secularists feel an affinity with him. We all have our inconsistencies and tend either to deny or ignore them: Higinbotham revelled in them. He had the courage of his opinions: some of his opinions required courage.

So far only admirers have written about him at length. His life's work has almost been wrapped in robes of white marble. The long article written by Gwyneth Dow for the influential *Australian Dictionary of Biography* captures part of the magnetic quality of Higinbotham and vividly and accurately outlines his career; and yet her final verdict is perhaps over the top. He is painted as a man without faults: he was "always a scholar", he had "a passion for veracity", and "his probity" was respected even by opponents – a verdict which overlooks the storm which greeted his donation to the strike victims. Those who felt his tongue would hardly have endorsed Mrs Dow's view that he was "personally courteous yet impersonally acrimonious". Writing about him in a book, she felt that he was almost looking over her shoulder. In fact, though long in his grave, his skeleton hand was holding her pen. Such was his power.

John Bennett's book represents massive research: there could be no short-cuts, no easy access to vital clues, for all of Higinbotham's personal papers were burned, soon after his death. The book is the first to study Higinbotham from the vantage point of an observer rather than that of a disciple. It is also the first to meet him on his home ground, the law, and also among the first to glance inside his family life which had been depicted as unduly loving and cosy by his first biographer, E. E. Morris, his own son-in-law. As Bennett has also written the biography of other Chief Justices of colonial Australia he carries a valuable measuring rod enabling him to compare Higinbotham with his peers in other cities. The final verdict, based on the reading of numerous cases, is that Higinbotham is a commanding figure but not the greatest judge of his time.

Melbourne, Victoria **Geoffrey Blainey**
September 2006

Contents

Foreword, by *Professor Geoffrey Blainey*   v

Acknowledgements   x

List of Illustrations   xii

"Dramatis Personae"   xiii

1. "School Life in Those Days was a Rough One"   1

2. "Higinbotham is a Most Estimable Man, But ..."   10

3. "His Short Experience in the House"   35

4. Attorney-General 1863-1868   57

5. "Absolute Political Equality to All"   75

6. "The Destiny of Our Colonies is Independence"   100

7. Puisne Judge 1880-1886   121

8. Chief Justice 1886-1892   152

9. Toy v. Musgrove (1888)   191

10. "Her Majesty's Chief Magistrate in Victoria"   202

11. "Perplexed by Paradox, Stunned by Contradictions"   227

Abbreviations   260

Notes   261

Index   301

Acknowledgements

In earlier volumes I described the evolution of this series of biographies. In the late 1960s, when I was surveying the task ahead as to Higinbotham, I put myself in touch with Gwyneth ("Gwen") Dow, of Melbourne, whose recently published *George Higinbotham: Church and State* (1964) was daunting in many respects. An entire and definitive book had been devoted to an important, yet narrow, aspect of George Higinbotham's career – chiefly his contribution as Chairman of a Royal Commission on Education. There remained the political and judicial aspects of his life, among others, still to be explored. Gwen Dow thought (p. v of the 1964 book) that "the dearth of material on [Higinbotham's] private life make a biography unlikely".

I seek, in this book, to suggest that such a prognosis was too gloomy, and that there is much of human interest and instruction to be drawn from a multitude of scattered sources that have survived. Some of that human interest is due to my good fortune in having, in 1975, located Mr Richard Nixon Higinbotham of London, who held some family papers and made clear the disesteem in which some of George Higinbotham's descendants held him. Richard Higinbotham was the son of Edward (something of a family historian) and thus the grandson of George.

For unstinting assistance in the formative stages of my research, I record my sense of indebtedness to Gwen Dow and to Richard Higinbotham.

More recently I have had the advantage of discussing my research with Professor Robin Sharwood, A.M., for whose advice I am most grateful. Mr Bruce A. Knox, of Melbourne, kindly drew my attention to a number of sources and permitted me to quote from various papers of his published or unpublished.

Research for this book has extended over many years and has taken me to Dublin, London, Canberra, Sydney and, of course on numerous occasions, to Melbourne. For encouragement of the project and assistance in meeting some Victorian research expenses I thank the Victoria Law Foundation and its Executive Director, Professor Kathy Laster. For practical help with overseas travel, and for sustained support of my judicial biographies, I thank the Division of Law, Macquarie University, Sydney, especially the Dean, Professor Rosalind Croucher, and Professor Bruce Kercher, Head of the Department of Law.

For library and archival assistance and advice beyond usual limits, I thank Mr James M. Butler, Librarian of the Supreme Court of Victoria; the Librarian and staff of Trinity College Library within the University of Melbourne; and the Archivist and staff of Melbourne University Archives.

I am particularly indebted to the Honourable Justice Michael Kirby, A.C., C.M.G., of the High Court of Australia, and to the Honourable Marilyn Warren, A.C., Chief Justice of Victoria, for their interest in and material assistance with aspects of this book.

For a legal historian, ever conscious that his work may be seen (mistakenly, it must be submitted) as esoteric and irrelevant by social historians and general readers, it is a most gratifying recognition to have this book introduced by so eminent a historian as Professor Geoffrey Blainey, A.C. I thank him most sincerely for the time and trouble he has applied to embellishing what I have written with his perceptive Foreword, and I thank him also for a number of very helpful suggestions.

The Federation Press of Sydney could not do more to facilitate this biographical series and present it so handsomely and so proficiently. I renew my sense of gratitude to Mr Christopher Holt, Publisher, and to his colleagues of the Press who contribute so much to such an amicable association.

It has been self-evident in the previous volumes in this series that where I have expressed opinions or interpretations they are entirely my own. Given the controversial nature of Higinbotham's character and career, it seems best that I reiterate my position and state that those named in these acknowledgements should not necessarily be assumed to subscribe to my opinions or interpretations.

MITTAGONG N.S.W.   **J. M. Bennett**

September 2006

List of Illustrations

Frontispiece and Dust Jacket

Photographic portrait (undated) of Chief Justice Higinbotham, *Australasian* (Melbourne), 7 January 1893, from the copy in, and by permission of, the State Library of Victoria.

Facing pages 144 and 145

George Higinbotham as a young man, from the original held (1975) by Mr R. N. Higinbotham of London, and reproduced and published with his kind permission. This appears to be the earliest surviving likeness of George Higinbotham and may be assumed to be from a daguerreotype portrait taken in London in about 1853 as a keepsake for his family before he left for Australia. A somewhat similar, but reverse facing, drawing is published in Geoffrey Serle, *The Golden Age* (Melbourne 1968 edn), opposite p. 290, dated "*c.* 1860", but with no other provenance.

"The Head of the Department", *Melbourne Punch*, 22 December 1864 (*see* the text at pp 60-61). The "clerk" facing away from his desk is Sir Redmond Barry.

"St Georgey", *Melbourne Punch*, 7 December 1865.

Drawing of Higinbotham shortly after his appointment as a judge (*Illustrated Australian News*, 31 July 1880 – from the copy held by the Mitchell Library, State Library of New South Wales; by permission of the Library). It captures the written depiction (*see* the text at p. 128) of him as having "an almost boyish face, dimpled in a feminine manner".

At p. 74

"A Case of Great Perplexity", *Melbourne Punch*, 27 June 1867 (*see* the text at pp. 257-258). The cartoon carried the further caption "Hints for further mischief of a novel character will be thankfully received, addressed G.H., Crown Law Offices".

At p. 226

"Mr George Higinbotham, the New Chief Justice of Victoria", from *Town and Country Journal* (Sydney), 9 October 1886.

"Dramatis Personae"

[A brief introduction to the principal actors]

A'BECKETT, Sir Thomas, a Judge of the Supreme Court, 1886-1917.

A'BECKETT, Sir William, first Chief Justice of Victoria, 1852-1857.

ASTLEY, William, journalist (often writing as "Price Warung"): a Higinbotham supporter.

BARKLY, Sir Henry, Governor of Victoria, 1856-1863.

BARRY, Sir Redmond, a Judge of the Supreme Court, 1852-1880.

BERRY, (Sir) Graham, Premier, 1875, 1877-1880.

BRAMSTON, (Sir) John, Assistant Under-Secretary, Colonial Office, 1876-1897.

BUCKINGHAM & CHANDOS, (Richard P.C.T.N.B.C. Grenville), third Duke, Secretary of State for the Colonies, 1867-1868.

CANTERBURY, *see* Manners-Sutton.

CARDWELL, (Viscount) Edward, Secretary of State for the Colonies, 1864-1867.

CARNARVON, (H.H.M. Herbert), fourth Earl, Secretary of State for the Colonies, 1866-1867, 1874-1878.

CHAPMAN, Henry Samuel, M.L.C. 1855-1856; M.L.A. 1858-1859, 1861-1862; Attorney-General, 1857, 1858-1859; temporary Judge of the Supreme Court, 1862-1864.

CLARK, Andrew Inglis, Tasmanian politician and Attorney-General; a Judge of the Supreme Court of Tasmania, 1898-1907; Federation advocate; Higinbotham "disciple".

DARLING, Sir Charles, Governor of Victoria, 1863-1866.

DEAKIN, Alfred, M.L.A. 1879-1900; Solicitor-General, 1883-1886, 1890; Chief Secretary, 1886-1890; M.H.R. 1901-1913; Prime Minister of Australia, 1903-1904, 1905-1908, 1909-1910.

DERBY, (E.H. Stanley) fifteenth Earl, Secretary of State for the Colonies, 1882-1885.

DUFFY, (Sir) Charles Gavan, Premier, 1871-1872; Speaker, Legislative Assembly, 1877-1880.

DUFFY, (Sir) Frank Gavan, Victorian barrister from 1875; a Justice (1913-1930) and Chief Justice (1930-1936), High Court of Australia.

FELLOWS, Thomas Howard, M.L.C. 1854-1856, 1858-1868; M.L.A. 1856-1858, 1868-1872; Attorney-General, 1857; Solicitor-General, 1857-1858; a Judge of the Supreme Court, 1872-1878.

FRANCIS, James Goodall, Premier, 1872-1874.

GILLIES, Duncan, Premier, 1886-1890.

HAINES, William Clark, Premier, 1855-1857, 1857-1858.

HEALES, Richard, Premier, 1860-1861.

HEARN, Professor William Edward, first Dean, Faculty of Law, University of Melbourne.

HERBERT, (Sir) Robert, Permanent Under-Secretary, Colonial Office, 1870-1892.

HIGGINS, Henry Bournes, Victorian Q.C. and politician. A Justice of the High Court, 1906-1929.

HIGINBOTHAM, George, a Judge of the Supreme Court (1880-1886) and third Chief Justice of Victoria (1886-1892), the subject of this book.

HIGINBOTHAM, Margaret, George Higinbotham's wife.

HIGINBOTHAM, Thomas, George Higinbotham's brother; Engineer-in-Chief, Victorian Railways, 1860-1878, 1890.

HODGES, Sir Edward, a Judge of the Supreme Court, 1890-1919.

HOLLAND, Sir Henry, *see* Knutsford.

HOLROYD, Sir Edward, a Judge of the Supreme Court, 1881-1906.

IRELAND, Richard Davies, inaugural Victorian Q.C.; M.L.A. 1857-1859, 1859-1861, 1861-1864, 1866-1867; Solicitor-General, 1858-1859; Attorney-General, 1860-1861, 1861-1863.

KERFERD, George Briscoe, Premier, 1874-1875; a Judge of the Supreme Court, 1886-1889.

KIMBERLEY, (J. Wodehouse), first Earl, Secretary of State for the Colonies, 1870-1874, 1880.

KNUTSFORD, (Sir Henry Holland), from 1888 first Viscount, Secretary of State for the Colonies, 1887-1892.

LOCH, Sir Henry, Governor of Victoria, 1884-1889.

McCULLOCH, (Sir) James, Premier, 1863-1868, 1868-1869, 1870-1871, 1875-1877.

MacPHERSON, John Alexander, Premier, 1869-1870.

MADDEN, Sir John, Chief Justice of Victoria, 1893-1918.

MANNERS-SUTTON, Sir John (from 1869, third Viscount Canterbury), Governor of Victoria, 1866-1873.

MICHIE, (Sir) Archibald, inaugural Victorian Q.C.; M.L.A. 1856-1861, 1863-1865, 1870-1871; M.L.C. 1871-1873; Attorney-General, 1857-1858, 1870-1871; Minister of Justice, 1863-1866.

MOLESWORTH, Sir Robert, a Judge of the Supreme Court, 1856-1886.

MORRIS, Professor Edward Ellis, Professor of Modern Languages and Literature, University of Melbourne, 1884-1902; George Higinbotham's son-in-law; author of *A Memoir of George Higinbotham.*

MURPHY, (Sir) Francis, Speaker of the Legislative Assembly, 1856-1871.

NORMANBY, (G.A.C. Phipps), second Marquis, Governor of Victoria, 1879-1884.

O'SHANASSY, (Sir) John, Premier, 1857, 1858-1859. 1861-1863.

PARKES, (Sir) Henry, Premier of New South Wales, 1872-1875, 1877, 1878-1889, 1889-1891.

PEARSON, Charles Henry, M.L.A. 1878-1892; Minister of Public Instruction, 1886-1890; a Higinbotham supporter.

POHLMAN, Robert Williams, first County Court Judge; Acting Judge of the Supreme Court, 1859, 1871.

ROGERS, (Sir) Frederic (later Baron Blachford), Permanent Under-Secretary for the Colonies, 1860-1871.

RUSDEN, George William, Clerk of the Parliaments, 1856-1882; historian, author of *A History of Australia* (1883); a Higinbotham opponent.

SERVICE, (Sir) James, Premier, 1880, 1883-1886.

SHIELS, William, Premier, 1892-1893.

SLADEN, (Sir) Charles, M.L.C. 1864-1868, 1876-1882; Premier, 1868.

STANHOPE, Edward, Secretary of State for the Colonies, 1886.

STAWELL, Sir William Foster, second Chief Justice of Victoria, 1857-1886.

STEPHEN, James Wilberforce, M.L.A. 1870-1874; Attorney-General, 1872-1874; Minister of Public Instruction, 1873-1874; a Judge of the Supreme Court, 1874-1881.

TURNER, Henry Gyles, historian, author of *A History of the Colony of Victoria* (1904).

VERDON, (Sir) George Frederick, M.L.A. 1859-1868; Treasurer, 1860-1861, 1863-1865, 1868; Agent-General in London, 1868-1872.

WEBB, George Henry Frederick, a Judge of the Supreme Court, 1886-1891.

WILLIAMS, Sir Edward Eyre, a Judge of the Supreme Court, 1852-1874.

WILLIAMS, (Sir) Hartley, a Judge of the Supreme Court, 1881-1903.

WILSON, Edward, newspaper proprietor and editor.

WOOD, John Dennistoun, M.L.A. 1857-1864; Solicitor-General, 1857; Attorney-General, 1859-1860; Minister of Justice, 1861-1863.

WRENFORDSLEY, Sir Henry, Chief Justice of Western Australia, 1880-1883; Acting Judge, Supreme Court of Victoria, 1888.

WRIXON, (Sir) Henry John, M.L.A. 1868-1877, 1880-1894; Solicitor-General, 1870-1871; Attorney-General, 1886-1890.

1

"School Life in Those Days was a Rough One"

Of many 19th century graduates of Trinity College, Dublin, who went on to ornament judicial benches in Australia, George Higinbotham was one of the most conspicuous and most unusual. A man of powerful intellect and fearless independence, he steadfastly followed his own convictions of how society should be ordered and how the law should work. His self-sufficiency enabled him to scorn his critics and, in politics, his opponents.

He tended often to be a solitary figure who seemed to take pleasure in being different from the ordinary run of men. Thus, although he "belonged by religion, education, and upbringing to the Irish Protestant Ascendancy, one of the strictest castes in Europe",[1] he, in later life, would reject many of the tenets of that strict caste. And, although he set very little store on ancestry, he probably took pride in the distinction that, unlike many contemporary lawyers who flaunted or craved lineage from the Norman Conquest, his paternal forebears were Dutch.

Researches by his son, Edward, the family historian, demonstrated that the name "Higinbotham" did not appear in Irish public records before the time of Quartermaster Thomas Higinbotham, who died at "Tullymaglowny", in County Cavan, in 1737. According to George Higinbotham's elder brother, Thomas, the oft-repeated family tradition claimed that:

> three brothers, Dutchmen named Hoogenboom, came over with William of Orange and fought at the battle of the Boyne; that one of them, our ancestor, was aide-de-camp to Schomberg at the Boyne …; that he settled in the north of Ireland.[2]

The Battle of the Boyne, which concluded on 11 July 1690, marked the final defeat of the last Catholic King of England when the Protestant William of Orange (William III of England) defeated the former James II in the field, on the banks of the River Boyne in Ireland. William led his Dutch Blue Guards and mercenaries from several European countries. The commander-in-chief, Frederick Herman, Duke of Schomberg (and an English peer), had been killed in the battle ten days before William's victory.

From perusal of documents dated about 1724, Edward Higinbotham established that "Hoogenboom" had become anglicized successively to "Hogenbotham", "Higenbotham", and eventually "Higinbotham". The relevant ancestor was Quartermaster Thomas Higinbotham whose will was made in July 1731, the signature being "very elaborate and very Dutch in character". A codicil, of May 1736, had a seal affixed bearing a coat of arms believed to have been granted in Holland, especially as it incorporated a blue lion – a symbol of allegiance to William of Orange.[3]

The Quartermaster acquired a considerable estate in County Cavan, extending from Cavan to Coote Hill and north to Ballyhaise. But his principal holding was "Tullymaglowny", some 60 acres, with 4 acres of bog, in Drung Parish, also near Cavan. There he built a substantial house of which only a single stone arch was standing by the end of the 19th century. That property remained in the Higinbotham family for 150 years, being sometimes known by its English name "Nutfield".[4]

Of the Quartermaster's seven children, by his marriage to Anne Nixon of Cranshagh, County Fermanagh, the fifth son, Andrew, acquired "Tullymaglowny". His second son, Henry Higinbotham who, in 1777, married Jane (*née* Verner; widow of James Dobbin) of County Armagh,[5] moved to Dublin, having first purchased "Tullymaglowny" from his younger brother. That Henry Higinbotham died in October 1789, leaving five children, of whom the second son, also named Henry, was the father of George, the subject of this book.

Henry Higinbotham, the younger, was born in the year of his father's death. He inherited "Tullymaglowny", but lived at 4 Mountjoy Square, Dublin, a genteel part of the city. He was a merchant of whom J. L. Forde wrote, that he –

carried on business in Grafton-street, Dublin, opposite the University, and was largely concerned with the "upper", and mostly conservative, classes, living in the fashionable south-east of the city, whose sons were educated at "Old Trinity".[6]

He embraced those conservative views and found little in common in those respects with his father-in-law, Joseph Wilson, the American Consul in Dublin, an avowed admirer of George Washington and of "Liberal" principles.[7] Henry married Wilson's daughter, Sarah, a marriage settlement being executed on 22 May 1812. There were several sons and two daughters of the union, but none seemed much interested in perpetuating the family line. Only two of the sons married and, of them, only George (the present subject) had children.

George Higinbotham was born in Dublin on 19 April 1826. His earliest years remain as if a sealed book, but it is reasonable to assume that they inspired in him a growing spirit of almost rebellious independence, though some saw that as a product of heredity.[8] While his brother Thomas was sent to Castle Dawson School for his early education, George was kept at home where he "received a very careful early training".[9] George, throughout life, set the highest store on the importance of education, but it is likely that his many years of home tuition were oppressive to him.

Aged about 13 he went to the Royal School, Dungannon, County Tyrone, at which "School life in those days was a rough one".[10] The headmaster, the Revd John Richard Darley (later Bishop of Kilmore), nevertheless achieved high educational standards and "laboured not only to impart a knowledge of the dead languages, but endeavoured to instil into the minds of his pupils a spirit of manly Christianity".[11] The headmaster's nephew, Frederick Matthew Darley, was a contemporary but younger pupil at the time Higinbotham was there. By coincidence their later careers took them to Australia where, in the same year, 1886, Higinbotham became Chief Justice of Victoria, and Darley Chief Justice of New South Wales. The matured attitudes of the two could not have been more disparate, Darley being a model of the "establishment" of the Victorian era; Higinbotham a radical in many of his perceptions. Yet they shared Dungannon's qualities of probity, integrity, and concern for the wellbeing of their fellow men. Of them, Sir George Reid would observe that they were "of that splendid type of Irishman of whom more specimens seem to flourish out of Ireland than in it".[12]

F. M. Darley recalled that he entered Dungannon School as "a little fellow about ten years of age" and was befriended by Higinbotham who "then appeared to me to stand head and shoulders over all others in good and manly qualities".[13] Higinbotham made a name for himself as a fighter who would intercede to protect younger boys from bullies. That quality, of looking after the underdog, remained with him for life.

In 1843 Higinbotham won a Queen's Scholarship of £50 *per annum* for five years at Trinity College, Dublin. Headmaster Darley wrote, congratulating him, and remarking that "you have brought me more credit than any boy ever yet did".[14] Higinbotham at first thrived at Trinity, reading with J. Y. Rutledge, later a Fellow of the College, but not, as was then usual, having a "grinder" or coach.[15] Gradually a change came over him as he relished his escape from the strictness he had experienced at home and from the rigours of school. While he continued to apply himself to his studies, his mind became absorbed by more worldly things. He began to question the merits of the "Irish Protestant Ascendancy" and he became increasingly disenchanted with his father's old-fashioned Conservative views. Whereas his father cherished the Dutch ancestry and assumed unofficial arms, incorporating those of Quartermaster Thomas Higinbotham with the loyal motto "*Pro Deo et Rege*", George Higinbotham found such things pretentious and an affectation. His descendants criticized his "negligence", and that of some earlier family members, in failing to "preserve their rights intact" to bear ancient arms.[16]

Nevertheless, Sir Charles Gavan Duffy, Premier of Victoria from 1871 to 1872, who was always loyal to his Irish and Catholic roots, late in life considered Higinbotham to have remained too much attached to the Irish Protestant Ascendancy:

> Mr Higinbotham in manhood was influenced and controlled by the prejudices which an Irish Protestant boy rarely escapes. He had been educated at a school endowed from funds diverted from Catholic purposes, and in a Protestant University endowed with the confiscated lands of a Catholic University; but instead of being impatient to redress such wrongs for other Catholics when he came to power, he was prepared to inflict on them, in Australia, a system not widely different from that which they had endured in Ireland.[17]

George Higinbotham found an outlet for his youthful perceptions in the College's Historical Society which, despite its name, was principally a debating society. He belonged to it, participated in the debates, and was a committeeman for a period. It was the furnace in which his great powers of logical and lucid expression were refined. It would prove to be the true foundation on which his future career rested.

As to formal studies, he was competent and won some prizes, but he disappointed the expectations held of a Queen's Scholar. As George Higinbotham's son-in-law, Professor Edward Morris, would eventually declare, this was "a good university career, though not of exceptional brilliance, but … it did not receive its crown and finish".[18] The expected Classical Gold Medals were not attained. Although, as a "freshman", he would translate "page after page of Greek and Latin historians, poets, orators, and dramatists steadily and literally, without pause or hesitation, just as if he was reading an English author", the fluency faded.[19] He was rather absorbing himself in the writings of Charles Dickens and admiring that author's use of the novel to stimulate social reform. So little was Higinbotham applying himself to the classics that when, in 1847, he went to hear a sermon preached in Latin, as a prerequisite to attaining the degree of Doctor of Divinity, by Hussey Burgh Macartney (eventually Anglican Dean of Melbourne), Higinbotham could grasp only a few fragments of its meaning.[20]

Macartney's sister, Catherine Ann Mona Brougham, widow of a clergyman,[21] lived in Dublin where she had sons of similar age to George Higinbotham and she encouraged their friendship. She held weekly gatherings of College students at which papers in prose or verse were written anonymously by the participants, then read aloud by Mrs Brougham to stimulate discussion. One such paper, by Higinbotham, long survived. It enthusiastically supported the negative of the proposition "Is a strong sense of the ridiculous a desirable quality or not?".[22] His arguments tended to confirm that he had maintained the solemn seriousness that had marked his youth and robbed it of much of the exhilaration normally found in teenaged children. That characteristic continued throughout his life, it being plain that there was "a touch of the Puritan in his make-up, but it was sweetened, not exactly by humour, but rather by generous instincts and a natural humility".[23]

Higinbotham's relationship with Mrs Brougham, who was some 20 years his senior, was remarkable and probably accounted for some lapses in his attention to academic studies. A few months before he died, in 1892, he continued to recall her as:

> the oldest and most steadfast and the most revered friend I had the unmerited happiness to possess in this world. Neither time, nor long separation, nor the known diversity of our thoughts appeared to change her kind disposition to me, from the time I first had the privilege to know her.[24]

What the precise nature of the friendship was will now never be known. She died in the same year as he, first sending him back "with her last message" a ring he had given her some 40 years earlier. His regard for her, and, eventually, his own character as a husband and father in Australia (to be considered later),[25] suggest that his family environment in Ireland was insecure and wanting in warmth and affection.

As to his youthful recreations, little information survives. Physically he found pleasure in rowing and in horse riding – "a spirited horse, or even a refractory one, was his delight".[26] Mentally he not only mastered chess but was attracted to its discipline. "The great glory of chess", he once remarked,

> appears to me to arise from the fact that the game, which engaged to the highest degree the intellectual powers of the players, is altogether under the reign of law, both as to its principles and practice; and therefore the tendency to depart from law and yield to temptations to unfairness is absolutely banished from the practice.[27]

For whatever reason, Higinbotham left Trinity, broke off for a time from his studies, and departed from Ireland for London.[28] He obtained employment as a reporter for the *Morning Chronicle* and, after mastering shorthand, reported parliamentary debates, acquiring an invaluable knowledge of parliamentary procedure that would serve him well in the future. It also gave him the opportunity to hear "all the great speakers, Gladstone, Disraeli, and others" and to enhance his own powers of oratory by studying their technique.[29] It is likely that, on the installation of a new editor in 1848, Higinbotham ceased working full-time for the *Chronicle* and returned to Trinity College to complete his degree. He graduated as a Bachelor of Arts in 1849 and as a Master of Arts in 1853.[30]

Having decided on a legal career, he made no attempt to pursue it through the King's Inns, Dublin, but, at the age of 22, entered as a student at Lincoln's Inn on 20 April 1848.[31] No record seems to survive of the counsel with whom he read. At that time, apart from such empty formalities as dining in hall, the Inns of Court did nothing for students at law. No course of instruction was then available or had been available at Lincoln's Inn since Joseph Chitty delivered some public lectures there on commercial law in 1810. Proposals for reform were ignored until much later in the 19th century.[32] It followed that an inexperienced Higinbotham was called to the English Bar at Lincoln's Inn on 6 June 1853. He did not seek reciprocal admission in Ireland. In the result, he was said by one commentator to have become a lawyer "by accident rather than by bent of natural character".[33] If that were true, which is very doubtful, the accident was fortunate as it under-wrote a career of extraordinary brilliance.

That career, however, would not grow in London or Dublin, where the Bar remained a "closed shop". Without connexions, the chances of a new lawyer's making a living were very limited. There were few ties to keep George Higinbotham in the old countries. His father had died in 1851, following which "Tullyma-glowny" passed to George's eldest brother, Henry, who promptly sold it. Within six months of his call to the Bar, George decided that he must look elsewhere for his advancement in life, and, at the age of 27, he left home for the Antipodes. On 1 December 1853 he sailed from Liverpool in the *Briseis*, a ship of 1141 tons under the captaincy of J.R. Brown, for Hobson's Bay, Melbourne.[34] Higinbotham recalled that "I knew where Victoria was situated on the map of the world … but I knew nothing of its circum-stances or constitution or people".[35] In a slow voyage of over three months, he is said to have studied astronomy, "and of course kept a diary".[36]

The diary no longer survives: it was deliberately destroyed. And the point must here be made that a much clearer estimation of Higinbotham's early years and, indeed, of his whole life, would have been possible had his private papers been preserved. Although destruction of personal records is a feature common to many of Australia's early Chief Justices, such a loss is particularly lamentable in Higinbotham's case.

In 1884 he wrote a "memorandum" containing a request that, on his death, "All my MS books, books and old diaries … all political and professional remains and papers" were "without delay" to be burnt. It was not a testamentary document: it had no binding force. Professor Morris, the son-in-law, nevertheless set to with a will, when Higinbotham died, and "assisted in the burning, knowing that I was destroying material which would have been of priceless value to a biographer".[37]

Morris, who professed humanities, ought to have known better and to have allowed the request to pass unnoticed, so that such important materials might have shed even more light on a luminous career. Did they contain scandalous or embarrassing matter that might have reflected badly on Higinbotham? It is highly unlikely that they did. Yet the modern biographer is left to ponder – what had the Chief Justice to hide?[38] The answer will never be known definitively but, among his descendants, the impression was firmly held that he had wished to conceal the magnitude of his anonymous gifts to public and private charities, made at the expense of his own nearest of kin.[39] The original papers could not all have been concerned with charitable gifts, and would have done more justice to the subject than does the excessively eulogistic and pedantic, yet superficial and discursive, account that Morris offered as a consolation prize in his *Memoir of George Higinbotham.* Being privy to the contents of some of the destroyed sources, he was able to control the biographical field, leaving later writers so much the more handicapped.

A great deal was made of the point at the time. While Melbourne's Anglican Archbishop Field Flowers Goe wrote to Morris that "you have given us a worthy memorial of a very remarkable man", and the *Argus* asserted that "the task of writing a friendly biography could scarcely have been entrusted to better hands",[40] other commentators were more realistically blunt. The *Age* observed that Morris "appears to have lived almost as entirely under the spell of his father-in-law as Boswell did under Johnson". It protested that,

> What we have in … [the] book, however, is neither a memoir proper nor a biography. It is simply a perfervid eulogy, which says a great deal for the author's loyal affection and a great deal against his literary qualification for the task … [We] lay it down with a sense of utter disappointment. We have never got one step nearer

to the subject through the whole of those 320 odd pages … we never see him at play, we never hear him converse, nor are we ever permitted to know any of his private thoughts. The reader is all the time held at arm's length – never permitted to interview the hero either in his study, his chambers, or at his fireside.[41]

The *Australasian* concurred, writing that,

the lesser mind has been dominated by the greater; the biographer worships his hero as a man almost ideally wise and good, and the portrait which he has drawn lacks precisely those contrasts which give so singular an interest to Mr Higinbotham's public career.[42]

How much better it would have been, in hindsight, to have allowed Higinbotham's muniments of his life to speak for themselves.

With those reservations in mind, the present assessment will try, so far as it is possible, to view George Higinbotham, not through the eyes of Professor Morris, but independently.

2

"Higinbotham is a Most Estimable Man, But ..."

"Stripped of Illusions"

Writing in 1851, John Leslie Fitzgerald Vesey Foster (nicknamed "Alphabetical Foster", but who later took the surname Fitzgerald and would become Victoria's Colonial Secretary) cautioned against false hopes of professional success at Port Phillip:

> The lot of young men of education and good family is to be pitied, who have been induced to emigrate without the means of procuring an establishment of their own. For such, until they have acquired a long colonial experience, there is little opening.[1]

Almost overnight, the discovery of abundant gold in Victoria altered those perceptions. On the goldfields good fortune might yield undreamed of riches – bad fortune, despair. Of the victims of the latter, a visiting German musician wrote from Melbourne at the time:

> harsh oppressive need is an implacable mistress and drives thousands upon thousands of discontented people ... to the magnetic pole of gold ... [and] many wretches suffer shipwreck in this distant world, and find themselves in an uninhabited wasteland where every cry for help dies away unheard.[2]

Nevertheless, the gold rush gathered pace and Melbourne's workforce largely dissipated as multitudes tried their luck at the diggings. For a time, the pursuit of windfall riches so diminished Melbourne's commercial stature that the administration of justice and the young legal profession wilted.

When "Mr Higginbotham" – a mis-spelling he would have to endure for some years – disembarked from the *Briseis* in March 1854,[3] he must have pondered very deeply whether he had done the right thing in leaving England. As Sir Archibald Michie recalled of the period:

> The revolution surely is complete when … the son of an English peer is in the police, and ex-Fellows of colleges are in the deep sinkings of Ballaarat. Every man who comes to Victoria is at once stripped of the illusions which mayhap beguiled him in England. He steps on shore at the Queen's wharf … and as the whole city does not come out to feed him, and wrap him in purple and fine linen, he discovers in five minutes that he must work to live.[4]

The question for Higinbotham was – what work to attempt? He arrived without connexions or even, so it seems, letters of introduction. But, for the moment, he was not without means. He must have saved money from his employment as a journalist in London, supplemented perhaps by a legacy from his late father. He had made the sea voyage slowly but economically, the *Briseis* being principally a cargo ship. In Melbourne, he had funds enough soon to take a wife.

Professor Morris claimed that Higinbotham, at first, lived roughly at "Canvas Town", the squalid and unhygienic proliferation of tents on the south bank of the Yarra River, that had not long since been a sheep-walk and, before that, an aboriginal corroboree ground.[5] Dr Serle wrote, of "Canvas Town", that "George Higinbotham and James Service were two who began their distinguished colonial careers there". Yet he concluded the same paragraph with the correct observation that "Late in 1853 when 'Canvas Town' had become the refuge of the shiftless, the criminal and the sly-grogger, it was closed down".[6] Higinbotham did not arrive until three months later, and could not have stayed there, especially as stubborn residents who would not move voluntarily were, at that very time, being physically ejected.[7] After his marriage, mentioned below, he lived at Montague Street, Emerald Hill, a euphemism for the locality that had formerly been "Canvas Town", where new cottages arose phoenix-like, but which was neither green nor elevated. In due time the suburb was called South Melbourne. But Higinbotham did not live, even transiently, in "Canvas Town" itself. It would not, incidentally, have been an auspicious address to be used by an applicant for admission to the colonial Bar, as Higinbotham soon became.[8]

The sequence of events between the certainty of his arrival on 10 March 1854 and his marriage on 30 September 1854 is blurred and, in part, may depend on little more than family legend. Extraordinarily, his admission to the Bar was not reported in the newspapers which, usually, took a close interest in the early legal profession. But the original Bar roll, still held by the Supreme Court of Victoria, gives his admission date as 27 March 1854.[9] The new barrister was not noticed again until 6 May when, as "Mr Higginbotham", he appeared before Judge Pohlman and two assessors in the Bourke County Court. He represented the plaintiff in *Punch* v. *Ainslie*, but without success.[10]

He had discovered that the Port Phillip Bar was as much a "closed shop" as those from which he had fled "at home". Being too independent to try to make a good fellow of himself among Melbourne's lawyers so as to win briefs, he took a different course. His descendants believed that he turned to the gold-fields, along with Michie's "ex-Fellows of colleges".[11] He went to Ballarat, but was deterred by the severe conditions and hard physical labour endured by those seeking riches, while he long remembered the sense of insecurity created by "a considerable number of camp-followers, addicted to indolence and plunder".[12] The only treasure he found there was Margaret Foreman, a young Kentish woman, who was said to be a parlour maid or servant. In his loneliness he became infatuated, proposed marriage, and took her back to Melbourne where they were wed at Christ Church, St Kilda, on 30 September 1854.[13]

Margaret Higinbotham thereafter faded into obscurity. Although she long outlived her husband, she spent all her mar-ried life in his shadow and in purdah. She must have been a loyal, dutiful and subordinate wife in the best middle-class fashion of the Victorian age, and she compensated for his family aloofness in being a loving and devoted mother. But she was rarely seen or heard outside the home, and became a recluse. So much was she his inferior in education and intellect that Higinbotham was des-cribed as a notable example of a man who had married beneath his station.[14] It was not, however, because she was a social misfit that Higinbotham did not move in Melbourne's "society". Seeing it as an affront to his independence, he despised "society" and shunned it, regardless of what it might have thought of his wife.

It must have been even more stultifying to her to find that George encouraged his elder bachelor brother Thomas,[15] not merely to emigrate from London to Melbourne, but, from 1857, to live in the Higinbotham home, then at Emerald Hill, and later in a villa Thomas (who was an engineer) designed for them all at Brighton. George was said to have an "almost idyllic affection for his brother" notwithstanding their strong divergence in politics.[16] In that fraternal domesticity Margaret had no place and was left to concentrate on the household's distaff side, her "closest companion" being the family's governess, a Miss Grant.[17] It is typically paradoxical that George Higinbotham, who would become such a strong public advocate of "women's rights", privately treated his wife as if an item of property devoid of rights. Professor Morris asserted that Higinbotham had a "high and chivalrous appreciation of women":[18] if so, such an appreciation did not apply to Margaret. And it was, surely, perverse that he should write or sanction a leading article in the *Argus*, acclaiming women having "strength of mind and vigor of intellect", while sarcastically ridiculing the suggestion that "a model woman according to a very prevalent conception of the character is little better than an amiable idiot".[19]

"Surpassed by Many at the Bar"

It was another of Higinbotham's many incongruities that his early years at the Bar were undistinguished. Not until he acquired the authority of public office as Attorney-General and later as a judge and Chief Justice, did his distinctive qualities as a lawyer become obvious. As a junior barrister, appearing before judges committed to reaching pragmatic decisions in conformity with inflexible rules and settled court practice, he did not shine. While Sir Arthur Dean assessed him as being "not a great lawyer",[20] that, in fairness, ought to be limited to describing the struggling barrister of the 1850s.

Work, at first, was very slow – a mention here, a minor interlocutory application there. No solicitors came forward to brief him consistently; competitors at the Bar, with whom he did not much fraternize, did little to help him on his way. He persevered, handicapping himself the more, so it has been said, by another of his peculiarities – one that, in later years, would have been thought neither professional nor ethical – only to accept briefs where he felt he could represent a just cause. From the outset he tried, with no great success, to specialize in pleading. Notwithstanding his great powers of oratory, he did not enjoy criminal work; he rarely appeared in the Insolvency (bankruptcy) Court; and he was disinclined to accept cases showing any colour of politics – "Instance after instance could be mentioned in which he refused briefs because he was by no means satisfied with the equities of the case".[21] It typified his approach that when a solicitor briefing him remarked enthusiastically that, "There will be some mud-throwing in this case", Higinbotham at once replied, "Oh, then, somebody else had better be briefed. I am no good at throwing mud".[22]

Sir Samuel Way, when Chief Justice of South Australia, recalled having first become acquainted with Higinbotham in the early 1860s, and having formed the view that

> As a lawyer he was surpassed by many at the Bar in acquaintance with the technical rules of law, but he had a broad grasp of general principles. His great power of expression and his dignified and persuasive eloquence, combined with the rule which he always laid down to never conduct a case the merits of which he disapproved, made his advocacy remarkably influential with juries.[23]

It must be questioned, however, whether Higinbotham misunderstood the law's technicalities. Those were the very issues on which he tried to build his practice, but he did so as a lawyer ahead of his time. And he suffered many reversals for being so. When he could, he challenged the orthodox views, bred of special pleading, that cases were to be won or lost on formal slips or procedural lapses. He tried to argue that justice and the merits of a case ought to prevail over mere practice points. At that stage in legal history he was, in effect, swimming against a strong current. Technicality ruled the law.

On such matters Higinbotham had sometimes sharp exchanges with the judges that left him the more resentful of their literalistic approach to case management. In *Ferrier* v. *Owen*, for example, he appeared for the plaintiff, but could not proceed because his instructing solicitor seemed not to be present.

Williams, J., having ordered that the case be struck out, became irritable when Higinbotham pressed an objection and insisted that he would apply to Chief Justice a'Beckett to restore the matter to the list. Williams, J., said that solicitors had a duty to attend court, no matter what, when their causes were listed, and that he "should take care to instruct [the taxing officer] to make the attorneys pay the costs occasioned by the causes being struck out on this occasion".[24]

Higinbotham later pursued his representations before the Chief Justice and Barry, J., claiming that the instructing solicitor had been present in the court house on the first occasion but, because of the crowded state of the court room, could neither approach the Bar table nor make himself heard. The judges were unmoved, the case remained struck out, its merits were not entertained, and Higinbotham had a harsh lesson in the intractability of old notions of court practice.[25]

On the same day, Higinbotham showed perseverance, if not much tact, in seeking restoration of another case that had been struck out. Again, a solicitor had not been in court at the time of hearing, but had absented himself only briefly, an earlier case having been estimated to run to some length. In fact the earlier case suddenly collapsed taking everyone by surprise. Higinbotham submitted that no-one in the case in which he appeared was at fault, while the other side consented to its relisting. The Chief Justice, displaying that rigid concern for form over substance which Higinbotham so resented, observed that:

> attorneys and suitors ought not to speculate on the length or shortness of a case. It was their business to attend, if their cause was in the day's list ... It would be better for all parties to adhere to the strictest order of the cases on the several lists.[26]

It was one thing for the court to be pedantic as to the inflexible application of its rules of practice. It was another thing for a junior counsel to attempt to influence the court by resort to similarly absurd trivialities inherited from the days of special pleading. In *The Queen at the Prosecution of O'Grady* v. *Melbourne & Mt Alexander Railway Co.* Higinbotham took the heroic point that all the affidavits filed by the defendant were defective, not being intituled "at the prosecution of". He tied up the court with "some considerable arguments, and numerous authorities".[27] But they were too precious for the court to entertain. Chief Justice a'Beckett rejected them as being either conflicting or affording the court no information. The affidavits were allowed.

Higinbotham was driven similarly to resort to tactics that offended his own notions of justice, simply to attempt to survive curial battles. In *Patterson* v. *O'Brien* he represented the plaintiff and took the point that Michie, for the defence, ought not to be heard as, contrary to the Rules of Court, the initiating defence process had failed to specify the number of affidavits to be used and the names of the deponents. Michie was senior enough to be able to argue that the objection was "one merely of form" and that the court should permit an amendment, which the court obligingly did, though mulcting the defendant in costs. The defendant had applied for a new trial on the ground that the original trial had not been set down for hearing within the time specified by the rules. Against that, Higinbotham tried to show substantial compliance, relying on English authority. But his learning did not convince the court. It was held that the rule was peremptory, and failure to comply strictly with it ousted the court's jurisdiction. A new trial was ordered.[28]

Higinbotham must surely have chafed with frustration as the judges persistently rejected his novel views. In *O'Shanassy* v. *Symons*, in 1856, he was given a rare opportunity to advance himself when briefed as junior to T.H. Fellows for the defendant. Higinbotham was permitted to give the leading address in support of a demurrer and also to reply. The demurrer was granted, but Chief Justice a'Beckett was swayed by Fellows' arguments rather than by those raised by "Mr Higginbotham". The case turned on the question whether a covenant, contained in a lease for years, was enforceable after the term had been licensed to a third party without the lessor's consent.

Higinbotham's first argument, that the covenant not to assign, being a collateral covenant, could not run with the land, was rejected by a'Beckett as being "too subtle".[29] As to a related submission, that the covenant touched only personal property – the leasehold interest – a'Beckett was unconvinced by Higinbotham's reliance on English authorities, and dismissed it as "a fallacy".

> On principle ... we cannot see how the doctrine, touching covenants relating to personalty, can have any application to the case of

a covenant relating to land. The fallacy has, perhaps, arisen from confounding the land with the term for which it is demised. The latter is personal property, but the covenant which is contained in it relates to the former, which is the realty.[30]

In *Staughton* v. *Tulloch*, in 1856, he successfully represented the defendant in an odd case, made the more so by its defective reporting.[31] It is surprising that Higinbotham accepted the brief as there was manifest injustice in the working of the old remedy of distress for rent. The plaintiff, who ran a sheep station, loaded wool on a dray and despatched it to Melbourne. On the way, the vehicle passed through land owned by the defendant, but leased to a tenant whose rent was in arrear. The draymen left the vehicle unattended within the defendant's property while they took a meal. The defendant, who seemed to be lying in wait, seized the wool as distress for rent unpaid. The plaintiff, after a false start,[32] brought the present action in trespass to goods, to which the defendant pleaded a right to distrain.

For the plaintiff, Michie put in a replication that attempted to attract English market laws to the Colony. It pleaded that the goods were on their way to the City of London wool market and, by the usage of that market, they were privileged from distraint. It appealed to Higinbotham's sense of colonial "independence" to argue against the application to Victoria of ancient customs of a distant country. In that he succeeded, the Full Court upholding his submissions, on demurrer, that the London market was too remote from the *locus* of the distress, and that the "peculiar circumstances of the Colony" were paramount. That left unresolved the great injustice, wrought by a law of medieval origin, whereby a landlord might seize anyone's property, if it happened to be within the boundaries of his demised land, to satisfy unpaid rent.[33]

Michie, at least, was impressed by Higinbotham's handling of the case and must have been instrumental in securing him junior briefs in a number of cases later conducted by Michie. After two years of determination to persist in the face of setbacks, Higinbotham was, at last, being recognized as a man of promise, though not yet wholly received within the select ranks of counsel whose names were constantly mentioned in law reports, such as the Attorney-General (W.F. Stawell), Solicitor-General Fellows, Michie, R.D. Ireland, H.S. Chapman, Dr R.C. Sewell, Dr George

Mackay, Sir George Stephen, B.F. Bunny, J. Dennistoun Wood and T.W. Whipham. Although "Higginbotham's" name had been mentioned about the Bar in 1856 as a possible candidate for a vacancy in the office of Solicitor-General,[34] with a wife and family to support, he was becoming anxious about his financial position. At a critical moment, an escape from those anxieties miraculously offered itself.

"Biting Their Thumbs at One Another"

One of the most fortunate of Higinbotham's briefs as junior to Michie was in *Harnett* v. *Wilson*, in 1856.[35] It was a newspaper battle in which the proprietors of the *Age* sued Edward Wilson, the principal proprietor and editor of the *Argus* for libel in having published a provocative leading article "The Wickedness of the Age". Michie, Chapman and Higinbotham were briefed for the defence, with substantial success as, ultimately, the jury found for the plaintiffs, but damages of only one farthing were awarded. As the most junior counsel, Higinbotham would have spent much time preparing the case with the instructing solicitors and with Wilson.

In 1848 Wilson had purchased the *Argus* and, for a time, continued its policy of opposing Superintendent (Lt-Governor) La Trobe, Mr Justice a'Beckett and other conservative public figures.[36] The tone of the newspaper gradually softened, though, in New South Wales, Henry Parkes, who formed a close friendship with Wilson, thought him still to be "a Radical of the Radicals".[37] By the mid 1850s, having made much money from the *Argus*, but with his eyesight impaired by the relentlessness of the editorial duties, Wilson was seeking a new editor. The timing of events suggests that the Harnett litigation brought Wilson and Higinbotham together at the opportune moment. Higinbotham's *Morning Chronicle* credentials, his having contributed articles to the *Melbourne Morning Herald*, and his general approach to public issues of the day commended themselves to Wilson. By August 1856, only weeks after the conclusion of the Harnett proceedings, Higinbotham was in the editorial chair at the *Argus* office. His financial concerns were thus resolved, while his name and influence were at once brought into public prominence.

As editor, Higinbotham's first precept was independence. He was in command and would not tolerate interference or opposition by anyone, not even Edward Wilson. It was a precept that worked for a time, but ultimately was his undoing. In his ascendancy he had such dominating self-assurance that he could disregard his critics and generally care not what others thought of him. A colleague depicted him as "a solitary thinker, and not a man of affairs".[38] As will be seen, he was duplicitous in his private and public attitudes to those with whom he differed, particularly as to editorial opinions on politics. One observer wrote of him –

> No man was ever more charitable in private life, but in the realm of politics anybody who differed from him was either a fool or a rogue. He was as chivalrous as Bayard, and as elaborately courteous as Lord Chesterfield; yet he could describe honourable men who differed from him as "plundering banditti", or as pirates who wished to scuttle the ship and throw the captain overboard.[39]

The reservation must here be made, as it will be later repeated, that Higinbotham's private charity did not begin at home.

He was duplicitous too in his approach to those with whom his editorial duties associated him. He could repel written protests sometimes made by Wilson about editorial policy by treating them as mere letters to the editor, to which strong rejoinders would be published. As to journalists, "if [a] contributor differed from his chief upon any essential point the subject was passed on to another writer whose views might happen to be more thoroughly in accordance with those of the editor".[40] Yet he displayed "keen sympathy with any of his subordinates who happened to be in trouble or distress": and he apologized abjectly, and recanted, when those subordinates protested about new conditions of employment he once introduced without notice. If, then, he "inspired a sentiment of affectionate loyalty in the minds of those who worked with him",[41] he did not always inspire the same sentiments in those who paid him.

Some of his contemporaries were not well impressed by his editorial qualities. The *Review of Reviews* acknowledged his "absolutely honest intellect" but thought that rival editors were "shrewder" and had "more versatile pens". It reckoned he was "scarcely a success" as he lacked adaptability and was "hopelessly unpractical".[42] There is substance in those criticisms, as many of Higinbotham's editorial notions were abstract and theoretical. Less compelling is the assessment that he set himself up as intellectually superior to his readers, and wrote over their heads.[43] His style was clear: his ideas commanded attention and, whether agreed with or not, were thoroughly understood by the generally well informed subscribers to the *Argus*.

There were even stronger criticisms of the policies of the *Argus* at the material time. The English author Daniel Puseley, who travelled to Australia in 1854 and again in 1857, in the fourth (1858) edition of his *The Rise and Progress of Australia, Tasmania and New Zealand*, reiterated his view that

> the newspaper press in Victoria is neither impartially nor ably conducted – a truth that applies more especially to the leading organ [*scil.* the *Argus*], which is ever ready to pander to popular opinions, however extravagant or erroneous, without having either the influence to guide or govern them, or the ability to disguise its own subserviency.[44]

Puseley maintained that, editorially, the journal mistook "impudent assurance for power" and "personal abuse for satire".

On the other hand, the journalist William Astley[45] recalled that "a warm friendship existed" between Higinbotham and the principal law reporter for the *Argus*, Moses Wilson Gray;[46] but, curiously, Astley assessed the "tone and policy" of Higinbotham's *Argus* as being conservative, while Gray belonged to "the advanced Liberals".[47] In due course, as a politician, Higinbotham would follow in those footsteps. Dr Geoffrey Serle concluded that Higinbotham "served his political apprenticeship as radical editor of the *Argus*".[48] Against that, it must be suggested that his radicalism, at that time, was much less pronounced than was his idealism.

Higinbotham meticulously reviewed and approved for publication any editorial commentary he did not write himself. It follows that, while every leading article of the time cannot be attributed to his authorship, every one bore his *imprimatur*. Along with day to day commentary, he developed a number of recurring themes – politics, public land policies, public finance, education, constitutional questions, and social welfare among them. Of those issues, only two will be considered in this chapter – Higinbotham's deep-rooted opposition to party government, and his public differences with Wilson as to universal or qualified suffrage. They illustrate Higinbotham's own views, for the relevant editorials were indubitably written by him, not by his delegates or subordinates. Accordingly, his words are here liberally reproduced *verbatim*. They also exhibit his conflicting attributes, such as practicality set against idealism, dignified reason set against stubborn denunciation, and almost arrogantly independent opinion set against caution and prudence.

It may first be mentioned that, as editor, Higinbotham had yet to develop his objurgation of the Colonial Office that he pursued so strenuously when himself in politics. But there were straws in the wind. Complaining, in September 1856, that the Colony had been "very badly governed" in the years before Responsible Government, he maintained that "the mother-evil of ministerial misrule has been a simple one – undue docility to the representative of Downing-street". He further protested that the Colonial Office had subjected the colonists to "a system as primitive and despotic as that which first aroused the lion-hearted Parliamentary champions, who lent such lustre to BRITAIN'S darker days". He hoped that with Responsible Government, Victoria, constitutionally, would enjoy a *tabula rasa* and not be bound by the habits of England, "an old country encumbered by feudal traditions and aristocratic institutions".[49] He would save much stronger expressions for the parliamentary chamber in the following decade.

As to politics, it was a perfect time for him to commence his editorship, with Responsible Government just beginning, somewhat unsteadily and with uncertain direction. He attempted to give it direction, bringing his name so much into the political arena as to seem almost a politician himself. Personalities were not avoided as he hurled barbs, and sometimes a little mud, at those who performed in the arena. One of his earliest arguments was over the formation of political parties. Here was another paradox, of which one writer observed, "Nobody hated party so much as George Higinbotham; but no one else in Australian history ever kindled party conflicts so fierce".[50]

The *Argus*, institutionally, insisted that it was not partisan – "we scorn all party ties" – and that it would not align itself with any transient Ministry, for "it is not usual for the permanent to pander to the ephemeral". It deplored government by mere party machines and, under the headline "Magnanimity", expressed Higinbotham's view that:

> If this country is to keep clear of the vile artifices of intrigue, and the petty plots of party, it cannot do better than fence itself in with such a barrier as this. If it be a duty to oppose Government – if it be a duty to support it – let either be done with magnanimity; but let us make it an established principle to discard everything that is puny, factious, and narrow.[51]

That theme was expanded repeatedly and excitedly over several weeks. Lord Brougham was presented as a witness to the claimed certainty that party government was "absolutely fatal", an opinion said to be shared by "the leading politicians of all civilised nations".[52] Yet Higinbotham perceived that the "deadly influence" of party "forces itself daily … upon us". His solution was to discard party altogether, lest "a drilled and unanimous Ministry might be found mischievously strong, when opposed to an irregular and undisciplined mass, however numerous". That did not postulate closing the door to "co-operation and mutual assistance in politics", but did propose shutting out "factious opposition and factious support, factious disparagement, and factious applause".[53] How such informal co-operation and assistance might be achieved was not made clear, though it was suggested that a substitute for the ties of party could be found by "the greater individualisation of public services". It was then suggested that one consequent benefit "would consist of the distinctiveness of individual outline amongst public men". In other words, they should all emulate Higinbotham's model of independence, and the reforms that were essential "must be *radical*. People must be prepared to go the whole length – if they go any way at all".[54] The words were portentous, but their foundation of practicability was feeble.

It followed that, when members of Victoria's new legislature were observed holding supposedly confidential meetings in order to plan "some sort of opposition policy", Higinbotham condemned the attempt to "play the game of 'party', where no necessity for party, and no sufficient materials for forming a party exist". The very idea of setting up an avowed parliamentary opposition offended him – "Only those who think the present Government so bad that almost any other would be an improvement can be justified in taking measures to bring about a change". The new government deserved a fair trial, and not to be displaced in the absence of complete failure – "Let opposition and change come when opposition and change becomes needful, and not before".[55]

While, on that view, every member, when voting on a resolution, became for the moment a component of an "Aye" or "No" party, the very furniture of the chamber, with benches to the Speaker's right and left, and cross-benches, manifested the uncritically accepted principle that "an assembly should divide itself into parties, which are to remain in permanent hostility to one another – to vote by preconcert, not according to opinion" upon the merits. In Higinbotham's absurdly over-refined and artificial view, the cross-benches were to be preferred to "the settled party opposition" mandated by the disposition of parliamentary seating.[56] While conceding that his views were not winning public acceptance, he would not retract them – "In 'party' we recognise a blight upon the whole constitutional system", and he taunted his critics:

> Now it is the characteristic of this journal, that, moderate as it is in many things, in reforms it is uncompromising. We have no idea of dealing with mortal diseases by superficial applications … We challenge the experience of all countries constitutionally governed, and we denounce party as a damaging and all-pervading taint.[57]

Higinbotham was confirmed in his thesis by the failure of efficient parliamentary government in New South Wales after Responsible Government. Sydney's early Ministries survived for only brief terms, and Governor Denison was convinced that "in these colonies, we had not the elements out of which to form political parties, and that the only party question would be Republicanism *versus* Monarchy".[58] That opinion was astray, for, although formal parties or even informal factions had yet to emerge, a clear fault line existed between members supporting Free Trade and those favouring Protection. Higinbotham railed against the behaviour of the first New South Wales Premier, S. A. Donaldson, and the Leader of the Opposition, Charles Cowper.

> They have suspended the public business of the whole colony with their quarrel, and no man on either side seems able to tell what they are fighting about. They call themselves leaders of rival

parties, but they have not been able even to invent a question to be at issue between them.[59]

Higinbotham's *Argus* loftily deplored the descent of the colonial neighbour into "bitter and causeless animosity" in which the colonists were "splitting themselves up into factions, and biting their thumbs at one another".[60] "Responsible Government", it remarked,

> is in one respect like a penal law, and proves itself to be the more successful the less frequently its extensive powers need to be enforced. Every time a man needs to be hanged it becomes plain that the punishment of death has to some extent failed of its effect; and every time that a Ministry requires to be changed, it is *pro tanto*, an evidence of the ill success of responsible Government – the unquestionable object of which is to get the best men into office and to keep them there.[61]

New South Wales thus supplied a model of how the *Argus* thought colonial parliaments ought not to function. But, to Higinbotham's dismay, the emerging Victorian legislature was equally flawed. Its very genesis was insulting to reasonable people because it followed "the absurdity of the British practice of nomination" under which the future happiness of the entire community degenerated into mere crowd entertainment. Some two thousand idlers were observed braving the winds and cold to hear the Victorian candidates speak to their nominations: the crowd amusing themselves by "howling, groaning, cheering, cracking jokes, whistling, hooting and occasionally blaspheming". Higinbotham's exaggerated sense of solemnity and decorum was affronted.

> Is this a necessary introductory process to a popular election? Or is it not rather a remnant of those barbarous times in political contests in which the form of the thing was allowed almost entirely to supersede more serious considerations.[62]

Coupled with the stump-oratory then on display, Higinbotham's *Argus* damned the nomination system as being an obstacle to the functioning of representative institutions and of good government. Moreover, the electioneering process, in which untried candidates often addressed large assemblies and attempted spontaneously to answer a myriad of questions, encouraged a cynical attitude by voters to inadvertent inconsistencies in policies, and contempt for the integrity of the candidates themselves. It was, said the editor, a system that stimulated deception:

> With the practised and habitual trimmer, the process of winning an individual meeting at the expense of general *prestige* has become a matter of course. It is his cue to promise everything to everybody; and if he can by this course carry a sufficient number of separate meetings with him, he may succeed in his design, and secure the desired post amidst the profound scorn of nearly the whole community.[63]

Such notions illustrated the impossibly pure, almost naive, view Higinbotham took of human nature. To adopt the conclusion drawn by Professor Macintyre, Higinbotham was "dangerously unworldly".[64] The things he criticized were, and always are, at the heart of politics and, like it or not, strenuous political competition, with winners and losers who have attempted to outbid each other in policy promises, must, in a democracy at least, be inevitable.

Again, Higinbotham showed inconsistency in criticizing the contest for the election of the first Speaker, exposing, so he maintained, the "baneful influences" of party spirit, while using the *Argus* to promote the candidature of C. J. Griffith "unquestionably the most suitable for the office".[65] When Francis Murphy was elected, the *Argus* proclaimed its regret, and began to attack his claimed want of competence:

> The House finds itself affirming things it does not want to affirm, and leaving unaffirmed things it wants to affirm, while the Speaker, at once perfectly puzzled and perfectly Parliamentary, contents himself with muttering some Abracadabra about "words proposed to be omitted standing part of the question", and declares the result, satisfied that he has done his duty, and frustrated the intentions of the House.[66]

Higinbotham, who understood parliamentary procedure better than most of Victoria's novice politicians, scoffed at the miscarriage of the early ceremonies. The visitation of the Governor, to be received in the House by the Speaker, was declared to have been "bungled" and made "almost an insult to both". Justices Barry and Williams attended as commissioners to open Parliament, Barry being castigated by Higinbotham for introducing an element of bad manners, especially in his "decided breach of propriety" in failing to stand to read the commission.

The members were ridiculed for their uninformed emulation of the then practice in the House of Commons whereby members might wear hats in the chamber, but with strict rules as to when they were to be taken off. Higinbotham deplored the Victorians' ignorance of English parliamentary usage and their blind adoption of outmoded Westminster conventions in a new legislature.

> It indicated a foolish childish ambition to mimic small parliamentary customs without consideration of whether they were good or bad – to mimic little defects with the hope of attaining to general resemblance – a fatal symptom of real inferiority.[67]

The "No Party" Doctrine

Throughout his editorship, Higinbotham returned again and again to the theme of "party", condemning it as a "delusion" – a "mischievous fallacy" incompatible with "responsible government of an effective kind". He brushed aside all suggestions that his ideas were "crude, wild, theoretical, and calculated to sap the vigour of representative institutions".[68] He took heart from opinions, like his own, lately published in London's *Economist*, and he republished them.

When John O'Shanassy's first "weak and ricketty Ministry" took office in March 1857, Higinbotham discerned in it "mutually hostile cliques" founded on "distinctions altogether unreal and factitious".[69] He then exposed the artificiality of his own views by taking sides and throwing mud – the antithesis of the co-operation and mutual assistance he prescribed for effective politics. Choking over the combination "in one team" of Foster as Treasurer, Duffy as Minister of Public Works, and A.F.A. Greeves as Commissioner of Trade and Customs, Higinbotham's *Argus* asserted that their mere association "would suffice to destroy any Ministry". It exemplified Higinbotham's capacity for harsh personal attack that he could write:

> Mr GREEVES is one of the most notoriously slippery men in Parliament. We never met with a man who had faith in him and we do not suppose that such a faith resides in any one of his new colleagues. What Mr O'SHANASSY could have been thinking about in making this wily bond store keeper head of the Customs department, we cannot conceive.[70]

In the same article, the editor dismissed the stature of the new Attorney-General (H.S. Chapman)[71] and Solicitor-General (J.D. Wood) – men who outclassed him in legal practice – with the words "the Attorney-General is a man generally mistrusted – the Solicitor-General a man generally unknown": judgements that were neither balanced nor fair. As for Charles Gavan Duffy, he "was known as a journalist and political agitator, and at last as a harmless political non-entity. He is now, save the mark! our minister of public works".[72]

Such a team, Higinbotham protested, did not demonstrate that the best men had been selected for portfolios, but rather that the Ministry had "as little cohesion … as among the particles of a rope of sand". He correctly foresaw that they "seem capable of no good effect" – O'Shanassy's government fell in a little over one month after taking office.[73]

The *Argus* was stung by criticisms of its abstract "no party doctrine" and, three days before O'Shanassy vacated the Treasury benches, tried to justify itself. Its doctrine, it wrote, did not advocate "political lukewarmness", it did not require renouncing the journal's right to expose "political follies and political crimes". Party spirit and factional alliances ought, it contended, to be seen as the greatest impediment to parliamentary free speech, importing as they did "the perpetual defence of one's own partisans, right or wrong". Party spirit was said to deprive political comment of its force and value, for each side always saw itself as exclusively right and its opponents as exclusively wrong. The doctrine, then, came down to this:

> that every one ought to speak the truth, and to vote the truth, and to think the truth, as far as he can, upon every question as it arises, and without reference to the secondary question – who asks it?[74]

Higinbotham returned to his theme in June 1858, invigorated by public comments of Earl Grey, former Secretary of State for the Colonies, but then retired and devoting his time to "criticizing the efforts of others".[75] With predictable inconsistency, Higinbotham "entirely dissented" from Grey's contention that "Parliamentary (*i.e.*, party) government derives its whole force and power of action from the exercise of an influence which is at least very much akin to corruption". Higinbotham might have been expected to accord with that statement, but he differed on the ground that parliamentary and party government were not synonymous. His counter-position was:

> Responsible government secures the harmonious action of the various parts of the State. Under it Parliament controls, although it does not directly interfere with, the Executive. It reduces the evil consequences of contests for power; it affords a safe and simple means for the transfer of power; it is the best method yet known for providing, consistently with the preservation of internal peace, fit men to govern the country.[76]

The last was the critical component of that ethereal interpretation of Responsible Government; and "fit men" were to be independent men, not mere party hacks. The colonial ministerial system simply encouraged proliferation of the latter and, at a period where no party traditions had yet taken root in the Colony, was deliberately introducing into the constitution a "dangerous innovation".[77]

He was convinced that Victoria had fallen under the mischievous influence of the United States.

> Thus, in America, where all the subordinate public servants, to the number of many thousands, go out with the President of the day, the violence of party spirit and the excitement at elections increase with the increase of those who are interested in the result.[78]

He deplored emulating such a system and urged that the bond of common interests be diminished in the Colony's Legislature to ensure that party power would be contained. One path to that end, he claimed, would be reduction in the number of Cabinet Ministers and of political officers.

Only a few months before relinquishing the editorship, he was still pursuing his fixation about "party", commenting on similar problems at the Cape Colony, and insisting that party "leads to the constant exclusion from the Executive of a portion of the very few men who are peculiarly qualified for public life".[79]

Those were all engaging ideas, advanced with enthusiastic and vigorous earnestness. But, despite his arguments to the contrary, Higinbotham's "doctrine" was a theoretical one that had no prospect of practical achievement. It typified his eccentricity that he could become so engrossed in an issue that was as academic as his Trinity College debates had been.

"My Dear Sir"

Higinbotham had not been long in the editorial chair when Edward Wilson, who had been a powerful editor, became concerned at the direction Higinbotham's *Argus* was taking. It seems likely that Wilson had held his peace for a time, as he privately viewed the concept of "party" with "the greatest distrust". But, in other respects, he found his opinions and those of Higinbotham rapidly drifting apart.[80] In December 1856 he, as a proprietor, intervened formally by letter to Higinbotham, intending it as a warning shot across the editorial bow and an invitation to change course. Notwithstanding that the letter began "My Dear Sir", instead of the usual "Sir" prefacing letters to the editor, Higinbotham treated it as just another letter for publication.

In a lengthy dissertation, Wilson explained that he had "the ill fortune to differ materially from the views expressed by the *Argus*". He sought to "place you [Higinbotham] and myself in a more proper position relatively than we have hitherto borne", while cautioning against tinkering with "the arrangements for the conduct of a public journal exercising some influence in the community". He took exception to reading, for the first time, at his breakfast table, editorial sentiments with which he repeatedly did not "coincide", and concerning which his friends and acquaintances visited their criticisms upon him as proprietor.[81]

Wilson conceded that a newspaper editor needed, apart from ability and conscientiousness, an independent mind that would "not submit to dictation from any one". While the proprietors remained legally responsible for what was published, the editor, having "supreme control" over the paper, was "morally responsible" for its contents.

The precipitant of the contest had been editorial disapproval by the *Argus* of provisions of a Bill introduced by the first Ministry, led by W.C. Haines, under which any adult male might vote in all the Colony's electoral districts in which he held real property. Having studied the "science of government" and developed strong views on the matter, it affronted Wilson that the *Argus* appeared to champion the principle of absolute electoral equality. He maintained "that we shall never see an even moderately perfect form of representation which is based upon any other principle that that of a representation of interests", and that "manhood suffrage in its integrity would seem to be incompatible with a perfect electoral system". Those were matters for serious reflection, not to be "encumbered by any clap-trap, or by appeals to the prejudices of any section of the community".[82]

Piqued by the reproach, Higinbotham agreed with his employer only on the question of being so editorially independent as not to submit to anyone's dictation. He published a rejoinder that demolished Wilson's arguments by reduction to absurdity. If the community were to be divided into Wilson's "interests", then it would require "many thousand departments into which to distribute them". Thus, although Wilson had identified several categories, and specified property as being a particular interest entitled to carry an extra vote, Higinbotham rejected that as creating injustice.

> Property is but one of many interests, and is itself subdivided into an indefinite number of antagonistic interests. We do not think it is contended that the possession of property should be rewarded with a political bonus: but that is the effect. Yet if you are to make any class a privileged class, the class of educated persons is surely fitter to be so privileged than any other. But here again we should have to classify farther. If you give a man an extra vote for being able to read and write, you should give him another vote for a higher degree of cultivation – you should give him a special vote for a competent knowledge of geography. The highly-prized art of writing Greek hexameters ought not to be overlooked in the distribution of the suffrage.[83]

And so forth. Thus far, in the debate, Wilson was soundly rebuffed and humiliated.

By May 1857 Wilson returned to the contest with two more epistles, again published as if letters to the editor, and again editorially attacked. The first, of 13 May, repeated Wilson's theory that the only true system of parliamentary representation was a "properly adjusted" system of the representation of interests. Giving every man a vote could not, he contended, achieve a "pure, just, properly balanced, and effective Parliamentary system". He qualified his earlier position by proposing that "all *useful* interests ... be adequately represented".[84] Thus parliament would consist of numerous classes "exercising a gentle and healthful check upon each other". The alternative, of simple manhood suffrage, so he insisted, stimulated class legislation and legislative tyranny. In those views, Wilson had become as artificial as Higinbotham was being on the "no party" doctrine. Neither rested on a realistic footing.

Wilson wrote again, on 21 May, stating that:

> Hitherto, under the influence of a perverted liberalism [words pitched directly at Higinbotham], Parliamentary reformers have been contented to stumble along towards the widest possible extension of the franchise, as the *summum bonum* of political happiness. I have tried to show that when this is attained, we shall, perhaps, be no nearer to justice and actual liberty than ever.[85]

Higinbotham had meanwhile responded that the "rooted aversion" of the *Argus* to conceding extra voting rights to special interests had "undergone no modification". He expounded a seminal political thesis –

> the great end of all electoral systems is, as far as possible, to secure justice and good government to every individual; … no amount of wealth gives anyone an extra claim as to these matters; … a community is not a commercial company, in which a man should have a voice potential in proportion to the number of shares which he is able to buy; … and … all men who live a life in a country have so large an interest in its good government, and so equal a stake in it, that their mere pecuniary possessions are but as dust in the balance.[86]

Liberalism and the extension of the suffrage were, in England, he observed, almost synonymous. But he thought that went too far. If the vote were given to everyone, including women, so that suffrage attained its utmost conceivable limits, he considered that "nothing more liberal than adequate representation of the majority" would result, with likely injustice to the minority.

With that unfortunate qualification to his otherwise commanding views, Higinbotham hoped that Wilson's mind would be "sufficiently disencumbered" to appreciate that a scattered property qualification would be "too egregious to be defended". Higinbotham offered an olive branch in conceding that he did not dissent from his employer's opinion that class legislation was objectionable. The difference between them was in the perception, not of the disease, but of a proper remedy. Creating a property based bonus vote would, the editor protested, be a "throat-cutting cure". Property ought not to give extra political claims to its owner, or extra political wisdom.

Wilson had been worsted in the debate,[87] and was then absent from Victoria for about a year. In April 1858 he suddenly re-entered the fray, writing long and vigorous letters over three successive days, all directed to his complaint that, as to representative reform, he "entirely differed from the opinions expressed in the *Argus*". He could not conceive how any intelligent man,

> with history in his hand, can believe in the propriety of starting this country in a headlong career of miscalled democracy, unprovided with any such representation of minorities, or with some other check, of which the history of democratic experiment in all other countries and ages proves the absolute necessity.[88]

He was convinced that democracy displayed a peculiar aggressiveness when associated with a monopoly of power by a numerical majority. Worse, "democracy" itself had become a word "abominably prostituted" – a result due to the American notion of, as he put it, "government by crowd". Instead, he advocated "conservatising" democracy.

Next day, Wilson pursued his ideas in terms seeming almost to replicate Higinbotham's "no party" doctrine:

> the truth is, that the radical basis of the Parliamentary system is vicious in the extreme. Men go to Parliament to vote for the interests of themselves and their order in a spirit which, if accurately examined, amounts to utter corruption. The legislator should be as pure-minded as the judge, and as little biased by any other consideration than that of the right and wrong of the particular subject under discussion.[89]

That being so, he looked upon disregarding minorities in a representative legislature, and vesting political power effectively in the majority, as "one of the most monstrous propositions that ever emanated from mortal man".

In his final word, on the following day, he repeated his principal contentions, but disavowed any wish to be drawn further into controversy with the editor. In that lay another warning to Higinbotham, who was clearly in Wilson's mind when he wrote, "It seems probable that this colony is to be made the victim, I regret to think, to the experiments of men either not predominantly patriotic or rashly theoretical and speculative".[90]

He was as incongruous as Higinbotham himself in conceding that the reforms he advocated could be seen in one light as excessively radical, while, at the same time, he was urging that the Colony's existing Constitution not be tampered with at all. If the two legislative Houses were left untouched, he believed that they would work reasonably well. But, "if in our restless eagerness for change, we must rush upon radical reforms, let them be real reforms, not simply wild and reckless alterations".

Higinbotham responded unrepentantly, though purporting to defer to Wilson's experience and public spiritedness and to agree with him on subordinate points. But as to major issues, it was "startling to find a practical man, with all the experience and acuteness which Mr WILSON possesses, propounding views like these". Higinbotham trusted that the passing of time would convince Wilson that his apprehensions were unfounded and that the Colony would have enjoyed the benefits flowing from the investing of equal political power in all classes of the population.[91]

Wilson was infuriated by Higinbotham's intransigence and, four days after the last editorial rejoinder, he confided to Henry Parkes in New South Wales that, "Higinbotham is a most estimable man, but occasionally wild in his opinions and stubborn in adhering to them".[92] By mid-year 1859 it was plain to Higinbotham that he had completely lost the confidence of his employers, and he resigned. One commentator correctly described him as having been "an editor in the clouds".[93] Another, with equal accuracy, thought the period of editorship to have been one of "ripening" that brought Higinbotham "into quick touch with the life of his adopted country, acquainted him with its problems, changed him from an immigrant into a citizen".[94]

On the one hand, Higinbotham was vexed. He had settled so comfortably and self-assuredly into the editorial office as to regard it as his dominion. He was unused to being, in effect, called to account, and he found it stultifying. There were signs of that in his cold rejection of a farewell gift by his editorial colleagues and staff. Their representative, while assured of Higinbotham's gratification that "mutual respect and friendship" existed between the editor and the editorial staff, was treated to a written homily that seemed to convert the staff into miscreants. Higinbotham had "seized every opportunity" while editor to inveigh against "the common abuse of testimonials". His colleagues ought to have respected his well known views.

I have always regarded it as one of the worst results of the system, that the public are no longer able to judge in any particular case whether a testimonial is a mark of honour or a disgrace to the holder, and I feel that it would be inconsistent with my avowed opinions were I to follow a practice which I have often and publicly censured.[95]

On the other hand, as with taking up the editorship, the timing of relinquishing it was felicitous. His editorial prominence had given a sympathetic boost to his Bar practice: he was in a secure financial position and could devote all his time, if needs be, to the law. He had also been brought so closely in touch with politics that he had come to see it as a matter of civic duty that he should enter the Legislature and try himself to play a part in the Colony's destiny. So it was to be.

3

"His Short Experience in the House"

"The Focus of the Long-robed Gentry"

In 1860, George, Margaret and Thomas Higinbotham moved from South Melbourne to Brighton, a very fortunate decision for George as it would advance his career. The Brighton residence, designed chiefly by Thomas, was called "Warrain" and stood in several acres of land between St Kilda Road and Port Phillip Bay. The house was set back 200 yards from the road and, from that perspective, gave a "pleasant secluded appearance" because of screening trees. Much native vegetation was preserved nearest to the bay to shelter the residence from the "cold-cutting winds" that were prevalent, especially in winter.[1]

Twenty years later, *Melbourne Bulletin* wrote of the property, "a winding gravel path leads us through a delicious garden to a plain-looking but cosy white house, all on one floor". About half the land served the utilitarian purpose of providing food, there being a substantial orchard dominated by varieties of apples, and a vegetable garden presided over by W.H. Kelly who was in service to the Higinbothams for many years. Kelly was a frequent and successful exhibitor at shows by local horticultural societies.[2]

George Higinbotham was very protective of his family's privacy at "Warrain". When the first cautious attempt was made by an intruder to construct a bathing box on the foreshore of the bay, but within Higinbotham's domain, a vigorous clash with the intruder and the local Council saw them both repulsed.[3]

Often "Warrain" was scarcely a home at all for George Higinbotham. With his growing Bar practice and his entry into politics – to be considered presently – he was rarely there. He used his Bar chambers as a residential apartment where he spent most of his time absorbed by his work. It followed that, pleasant and secluded though the matrimonial home might have been, it was little more than a prison for Margaret Higinbotham. Apart from attending church services and functions, she had little contact with the outside world.

Even when George was at home, he cloistered himself in his study for hours at a time. He remained so remote from his own flesh and blood that his children, frustrated by his aloofness, sometimes devised remarkable but unavailing strategies to command his attention. His son Edward, for example, tried to do so by riding a pony through the house into that *sanctum sanctorum*, his father's study. But George Higinbotham merely glanced up from his books, said "Hello Edward" in a matter-of-fact way, and resumed his reading.[4]

Family gatherings of any kind seem to have been exceptional, apart from brief beach visits in the summer, and the journey to Tasmania in December 1873 of "Mr George Higinbotham, Mrs Higinbotham, and family … for the benefit of their health" was the closest they came to a Christmas treat and grand tour together.[5]

Released from the daily demands of journalism, Higinbotham was able to concentrate on making his mark at the Bar. He had his Melbourne chambers at 24 Temple Court, Little Collins Street, West,[6] commonly called Chancery Lane, which an Irish visitor described as,

> the focus of the long-robed gentry; and both it and all the surrounding lanes, alleys, and passages are a sort of legal warren, burrowed by barristers, attorneys, commissioners for taking affidavits, official assignees, law stationers, scriveners, and engrossers, frequented by an ebbing and flowing stream of litigious citizens, as well as isolated lawyers in cracked hats and shiny coats.[7]

By 1857 every privately practising barrister in Melbourne had his chambers there, and it was "the home of the Bar".[8]

That monopoly did not last for long. At much the same time Michie acquired the property 73 Chancery Lane which was converted into additional Bar chambers styled Michie's Building. Higinbotham transferred to that address at some time after 1861 and retained his chambers there when he became Attorney-General between 1863 and 1868, though in that period he accepted no private briefs.[9] He used his chambers, after the English fashion, as the centre of his life, frequently, even when he had a young family, going home only at weekends – if then – during Term time.

Reminiscences of Higinbotham at the Bar made much of his attractive speaking voice and clear diction that won the attention of juries, and of his uniform courtesy. The last was a common enough mask worn by barristers in those days of high decorum and strict formality in conducting court business. Higinbotham's courtesy might well have manifested itself to professional colleagues and the judiciary, but it disappeared in his often successful attempts to break down the testimony of opposing witnesses. His cross-examinations were said to be "deadly enough to make villains tremble".[10] Mr Justice Hodges, in a eulogy following Higinbotham's death, correctly acknowledged that, as a barrister, Higinbotham was motivated by an "obligation to the cause of truth" accomplished by "honest honourable advocacy". Hodges continued:

> Everyone who has practised at the Bar with [him] will know the infinite pains he took to master all the facts of any case entrusted to him, and the law applicable to those facts – how careful he was in forming an opinion, and how stoutly and ably he supported the opinion which he had so carefully formed; they will remember how courageous an advocate he was, and yet how chivalrous a foe.[11]

That, no doubt, was a very fair assessment, though it might equally have been applied to most of the Bar leaders at that time. What was more distinctive was Higinbotham's approach to the work he would accept, as, from the outset, he sought to specialize on the civil side of litigation at common law.

While 1859 had proved to be an auspicious year for him to resume his practice, it was not auspicious for all. Simultaneously the freakish and eventually deranged barrister Thomas Parsons, who had been called at Gray's Inn in 1841 and later migrated to Victoria, started, through newspapers and pamphlets, vigorous attacks on the Victorian legal system. In 1859 he announced his "secession" from the Bar because court practice was so dilatory. He found – was it not ever thus? – too much talk, too much expense, and too many lawyers "trying to appear quick or smart". He blamed the judges for allowing such imperfections, and concluded that:

> This Bar is quite equal to its work, and it will not be its own fault if it become so damaged by its present practice as to be content to indemnify itself for its griefs by its gains.[12]

Higinbotham shared Parsons' abhorrence of the court's equity side, gainsaying the memory in old age of the Melbourne solicitor Theodore Fink who claimed that Higinbotham was "a member of the Equity Bar".[13] No record in Wyatt and Webb's Reports shows even an appearance by Higinbotham in the Equity Court before he became Attorney-General. Similarly, he rarely appeared before the court's Insolvency, Ecclesiastical and Matrimonial side. Instead, his *forte* was common law. In, for example, the first volume of Wyatt and Webb's Reports at common law there were just over 100 reported cases. After disregarding criminal matters, Higinbotham appeared in about one-third of the remaining 90 or so cases. He thus had a very large share of that practice, especially when mentions and unreported actions are taken into account. He had as well a large uncontentious practice, his advice, particularly in local government law, being constantly sought.[14]

The extensive range of common law matters in which he acted invites review of the suggestion that he would accept briefs only when satisfied of the merits of his client's case or that he was engaged in a just cause. That suggestion has enlivened another Higinbotham myth.[15] There were too many matters to be so assessed and, of course, the merits often would not appear until the evidence had been entered into on both sides. The suggestion probably rested on a misunderstanding of Higinbotham's determination to limit his litigation practice to civil matters. Beyond that there is little surviving evidence that he was a purist in his selectivity.

Nor was he so unworldly as to ignore the realities of having to work to live. He jocularly admitted that a discussion with a colleague about immigration policy had "brought a light to his mind" when it was pointed out that "every man, woman, and child that comes into Hobson's Bay [is] an additional chance of a brief for you or me".[16] But some cases, even though slight, disclose that he was driven by the desire to vindicate a principle without any thought as to his remuneration.

Robinson v. *Bonfield*, in 1862, enabled Higinbotham to pursue his notions that statutes should be construed strictly, and that the public revenue should be protected, while showing his contempt for the frequent shortcomings of magistrates.[17] In an appeal from Flemington Petty Sessions, he represented the appellant, keeper of a toll gate at Flemington. The respondent, as Keilor pound-keeper, while taking his pound receipts to the Melbourne Treasury office, was denied the use of the road at Flemington unless he paid the toll. He paid under protest but, claiming to be on government business, he sued the toll collector and recovered judgement before the Flemington magistrates.

The pound-keeper did not appear at the hearing of a Supreme Court appeal in which Higinbotham argued that an exemption under the *Road Act* did not apply to the pound-keeper because he had no personal obligation to deposit his receipts at the Treasury office and so was not "in the service of the Government" at that time within the meaning of the exemption. The court accepted the argument and allowed the appeal, but marked its disapproval of having to entertain so minor a case by declining to award the appellant costs. Higinbotham, who doubtless appeared without fee, nevertheless derived satisfaction from the result: justice had been done.

The most striking instance of his taking a brief outside his normal sphere of practice, was in representing the wife in proceedings for alimony *pendente lite* in preliminary stages of the *cause célèbre Molesworth* v. *Molesworth*.[18] Those proceedings appealed to Higinbotham's ideas of fairness and of consideration for the position of women. Mr Justice Molesworth, of the Supreme Court, petitioned for divorce on the ground of his wife's adultery. Meanwhile he expelled her from the matrimonial home and physically assaulted her when she sought to return or to request maintenance payments. The case attracted much prying interest and was the talk of Bench and Bar for years. Ultimately judicial separation was ordered by the Full Court following a jury finding that Mrs Molesworth (who denied it) had committed adultery with a person unknown.[19]

Higinbotham, in the interlocutory proceedings, succeeded in obtaining a fair award of alimony.[20] His courage was evident as he feared not that, by crossing Molesworth, his prospects at the Bar might be prejudiced should the judge become vengeful.[21] It was further in character that, when the ultimate decree was pronounced by the Full Court, Higinbotham, then Attorney-General, wrote to Molesworth suggesting that he no longer sit in matrimonial causes. While protesting against such a "singular communication", and urging Higinbotham to mind his own business, the judge quietly acknowledged the wisdom of the suggestion and rarely sat in divorce cases thereafter.[22]

Another instance of Higinbotham's self-assurance, suggesting that he cared not what others thought of him, was his acceptance of a junior brief for the appellants in *Matthews v. Muttlebury*.[23] The respondents were the prominent firm of solicitors Muttlebury, Malleson & England, and the appeal, in a dispute as to costs, was dismissed. Higinbotham might not afterwards have been a preferred counsel in that firm's books.

Higinbotham prospered financially at the Bar, and the greatest of his peculiarities must surely have been his attitude to money. He seemed almost to resent it. His habit of striking out fees marked on his brief and substituting a lesser sum was renowned.[24] Theodore Fink recalled that, as an articled clerk, he was sent – a boy on a man's errand – to remonstrate with Higinbotham that a client felt that the brief fee charged was so low as to cast doubt on the quality of the advice given, and to request a reconsideration. Fink, who was "in fear of having his head bitten off", remembered the experience as –

> one of the most interesting interviews I have had in my life ... [Higinbotham] expressed his astonishment at such a request being made, and [said] that Counsel were the sole judges of the value of the amount of their fees in each particular case.[25]

On one view that seems plausible enough, he could well afford to take that position as he was reputed to have a princely unearned income of "about 1500£ a year arising from shares in a mining company".[26]

Reference is made on later pages to his habit, at the Bar, of receiving beggars at his chambers, to whom he would distribute largesse, while leaving his family to complain.[27] Melbourne's *Weekly Times* confirmed the incongruity of his character – his outgoing concern for the less privileged, coupled with his disdain for ordinary social diversions:

His pocket helped many, and not a few were the recipients of his "silent charity". He lived a very quiet and retiring life … He had no particular hobby or amusement. He did not affect lawn tennis or bicycling … He seldom frequented the theatre.[28]

On appointment as Attorney-General, on 27 June 1863, in McCulloch's first Ministry, Higinbotham, by convention, ought to have become *ex officio* leader of the Bar. But his relationship with the Bar, while he was in office, was characteristically unorthodox. Despite being an ardent monarchist, he would not accept the dignity of Queen's Counsel which, as first Crown Law Officer, was his entitlement. And he demonstrably abdicated the Bar leadership to Michie, Q.C.

A notable instance was a meeting of "the Bar" held, not at the Attorney-General's chambers, but at Michie's, on 1 September 1864.[29] Those attending debated at length "the state of the Bar" and appointed a committee to examine the matter further, determine what changes were needed to the Bar Rules, and furnish a written report. The committee members were "Lawes, Wood, W. Stephen, Fellows, Moore, Michie and Higinbotham". The Attorney-General was neither named as such nor placed at the head of the list. The ensuing report was obviously important to him – he might well have been a principal author – as a copy was one of the few documents to have escaped burning by Professor Morris and to have survived in the Higinbotham family.

The report, of 20 October 1864, would have been momentous had its recommendations been implemented. It regretted the encroachments on the domain of the Bar by attorneys acting as advocates in the County Courts, as it deplored the converse position on the goldfields where barristers were seen to "engage in or superintend business of a merely clerical or semi-mechanical nature". It proposed assimilating the "government of the Bar" to that in England, the Inns of Court being replaced by "a body to be styled the Council of the Bar …, which should have the same authority as regards Barristers and students as is possessed by the Inns of Court". It was to be a body independent of the Supreme Court, and was to be the creature of the Legislature by special Act. The court's powers of admitting, suspending or disbarring barristers would, so the proposal ran, be removed from its Act and vested in the Council under the new Act. The Council would regulate Bar etiquette and ethics, and would require candidates for admission who did not hold an approved university degree "to pass a legal examination" and attend Supreme Court sittings during the four Terms immediately preceding their admission.[30]

The report appears to have come into collision, not only with the Supreme Court Judges, but also with the strong, and ultimately successful, campaign to amalgamate the Victorian profession. Although it failed in its principal purpose, the report remains instructive in showing that, when Attorney-General, Higinbotham saw himself, not as the Bar leader, but as a leader equally with others.

Higinbotham went out of office when McCulloch was defeated in May 1868 and, although the intervening Sladen Ministry lasted for only two months, Higinbotham declined the Attorney-Generalship in McCulloch's second Ministry which commenced on 11 July. The reasons will emerge later. He served instead as Vice-President of the Board of Land and Works, but resigned and returned to the backbench on 1 February 1869.

From May 1868 Higinbotham resumed his Bar practice. Being rusty, he found it hard at first to re-establish himself, and had to make do with some minor briefs and even an occasional appearance in equity. But, by 1870, he was back into his stride, with constant matters before the court on its common law civil side. That was the work that appealed to him and in which he specialized. Again, nothing supports the suggestion that he acted only in cases where he was satisfied of the merits.

He did not enjoy a consistent run of successes in court at that time. Yet solicitors remained very loyal, and his lack of success in many complex cases reflects the trust solicitors reposed in him to do the best that could be done with a difficult brief. He appeared frequently in leading commercial cases, particularly those involving banks, in cases requiring the interpretation of contracts, and in real property matters.

The conspicuous exception to that class of litigation was Higinbotham's representing, without fee, the Irish barrister turned journalist, Gerald Henry Supple, on a special case stated to the Full Court on Supple's conviction of having murdered John Sesnan Walshe.[31] Because of poor eyesight, Supple had abandoned Bar practice and become an editorial employee of the *Age*. Although he would never admit to unsoundness of mind, he certainly was not in his right mind when he became outraged at the indifference to Irish questions of the *Age's* editor G.P. Smith, and resolved to kill him. Following Smith into the street, he fired at him with a revolver. Weak vision frustrated the object and he merely wounded Smith in an arm. But Walshe, a bystander, rushed forward to try to stop the attack, and, in the ensuing struggle, was fatally shot.

Higinbotham argued that, as the jury at trial had found that the shot was accidental, Supple could have had no felonious intent to kill Walshe. "It cannot be said", he submitted, "that under such circumstances this discharge took place while the prisoner was in pursuit of his murderous intent against *Smith*". The Full Court disagreed and upheld a capital conviction, remarking that –

> the felonious intention is, from the verdict, legitimately connected with the event which followed. The struggle may be regarded as one continuous struggle by the prisoner in furtherance of his felonious object.[32]

A great deal of Irish based sympathy for Supple resulted in petitions and representations for clemency. After extraordinary intervening proceedings, his sentence was commuted to life imprisonment from which he was released after six years.[33]

"The Most Commanding Influence of Any Public Man"

More important than the character of his practice was Higinbotham's legacy to a number of younger, able and rising lawyers who were sometimes described as his "disciples" or even "passionate admirers".[34] They were attracted to his approach to the law and the legal system as also to his political and social principles. Among that band of followers was, in the first instance, Henry John Wrixon, a fellow Dubliner and Trinity College man. Although only 13 years his junior, he regarded Higinbotham as a mentor, and their political ideas in the 1860s brought them into a natural association.[35]

Wrixon originally shared Higinbotham's contempt for the self-appointed "upper classes" in Victoria. The words could well have been Higinbotham's, when Wrixon wrote, in 1868:

> There is with us, as elsewhere (though we have rather more than our fair proportion), a class of permanent non-contents, who rather enjoy taking everything ill. They simply say that the cause of all our troubles is democracy … What they want from politics is profit, not

principles; and their real inmost aspirations are to make as much as possible out of the institutions they direct.[36]

Wrixon was Solicitor-General in McCulloch's brief third Ministry from 1870 to 1871, and was Attorney-General in the enduring Gillies Ministry (or Gillies/Deakin coalition) from 1886 to 1890. The presence in that Ministry of Gillies as Premier, Deakin as Chief Secretary, Wrixon as Attorney-General, and C. H. Pearson as Minister of Public Instruction, created a group of supporters committed to seeing Higinbotham appointed Chief Justice when the occasion presented itself in 1886. Unlike Higinbotham, Wrixon in later life became much more conservative. He had married well, his Bar practice was prosperous, and he found, with wealth and property, that many of his views came to merge with those of the "upper classes".

William Shiels, another Irishman by birth and barrister by profession, became Premier in 1892 for a short term. Also inspired by Higinbotham's ideals, he followed that example as a "proponent of women's rights", pressing for revision of the *Matrimonial Causes Act* and the *Married Women's Property Act*, and for reform of the divorce laws.[37] Shiels did not condone the wealthy "upper classes" as Wrixon came to do, and remained steadfast in asserting the social conscience Higinbotham and others had awakened in him.

Henry Bournes Higgins was yet another Irishman to come under Higinbotham's spell from his arrival in Melbourne, aged 18, in 1870. He evidently had an introduction to Higinbotham and secured his support as a referee of fitness for admission to the Bar. On one adulatory account, Higgins, from that time, felt himself "initiated into the life of Victoria by the aid of the man whom he most revered, and whose aims, so far as he understood them, he was prepared to accept as his own".[38]

Established at the Bar, and interested in politics (he was a Member of the Legislative Assembly from 1894 to 1900, and a Member of the House of Representatives from 1901 to 1906), Higgins has been variously described as an "advanced liberal ... [and] uncompromising democrat", as driven by "protectionist radicalism", as one who had "followed British politics with the keen interest of an ultra-Radical and a Home Ruler", and as a man of "unflinching devotion to doctrinaire principles".[39] His work as a Justice of the High Court, from 1906 to 1929, including his Presidency of the Commonwealth Court of Conciliation and Arbitration, enabled him to superintend at a national level great social achievements that Higinbotham had not been able even to contemplate for Victoria. The master would have been proud of his pupil. In due time, Mr Justice H. V. Evatt, High Court Justice, later Leader of the Federal Opposition, became a fervent admirer of Higinbotham and of Higgins.

The only contemporary "disciple", among those considered here, who was not an Irishman, was Alfred Deakin. After an indifferent Bar career, he involved himself in journalism and Victorian politics, going on, after Federation, to be thrice Prime Minister of Australia. Higinbotham was "one of his boyhood heroes" and continued to influence Deakin's political philosophy and practice.[40] Deakin's effusive testimonials praising Higinbotham did much to elevate the latter to the status of the Victorian paragon. Deakin saw him as –

> The greatest of Australian orators and of Australian Liberals, the noblest nature and the most refined, George Higinbotham was at the same time the most ardent of imperialists in policy … His manner in its simple dignified courtesy surpassed that of any man in Victoria or Great Britain no matter how high his station or important his office … His influence was more magnetic, his thoughts – political, religious and social – more radical, and his will more dominating that Morris's *Memoir* describes.[41]

Deakin concluded that Higinbotham "possessed the most commanding influence of any public man in Victoria".[42]

Deakin was a powerful journalistic writer. While much of his assessment of Higinbotham is well founded and has inspired the reverence in which Higinbotham's name is still remembered in Victoria, the biographer is put on guard by the frequent use of unqualified superlatives. That will be considered further in the concluding chapter. Suffice it here to foreshadow that much of Higinbotham's greatness lay in his ability to encourage others to follow in his footsteps and to succeed where he had sometimes failed.

"A Defiant, Independent Tone Upon the Hustings"

In 1861 chance delivered to Higinbotham the opportunity to enter Parliament, an ambition of his since the *Argus* days of armchair politics. He had dabbled a little in electioneering in 1856 when his friend James Service pressed him to nominate Fellows, Solicitor-General in the old Council, for election to the new Council. Higinbotham accordingly addressed a gathering of 400 at Emerald Hill, but with little enthusiasm. Fellows repelled the electors by speaking down to them, and was humiliated when they rejected him.[43]

Higinbotham, just installed at the *Argus*, turned upon Fellows, who was then seeking a Legislative Assembly seat, and wrote or approved editorials doubting Fellows' political ability, hoping that he would "devote his life rather to making law better than to making money out of its abuses",[44] and ridiculing his Emerald Hill speech:

> Coriolanus himself was not a worse electioneerer. A defiant, independent tone upon the hustings, when unlimited concession was the fashion of the hour, certainly seemed like a new road to success, if a road to success at all.[45]

When his own time came to solicit the support of voters, Higinbotham did not practise what he preached to Fellows, who, despite the setback, won an Assembly seat and served in Parliament for many years, often in political opposition to Higinbotham who had shown that he could never be relied upon as a whole-hearted political ally.

In May 1861 ill health compelled Charles Hotson Ebden, who had been Auditor-General for a brief term before Responsible Government, and Member for Brighton from 1857 (during which he was Treasurer from 1857 to 1858), to resign the seat. At a by-election, Higinbotham was returned unopposed. It was an odd result for two reasons. On the one hand, Ebden's conservative views tended to reflect those of "the superfine local grandees of Brighton",[46] whereas Higinbotham's political tenets were never conservative. And, on the other hand, given that he faced no opposition, Higinbotham's address to electors, at the Devonshire Arms Hotel, was eccentric. An ordinary political candidate, in those circumstances, would have dwelt upon the local issues he would pursue if elected. But Higinbotham was no ordinary candidate. He delivered a long manifesto that ignored local issues, developed his own political creed, and at times seemed like a lecture on political science.

He touched upon great public questions that would remain paramount in his mind throughout his political career – "the operation of representative institutions" in Victoria, public education, immigration from England, and the land laws and the squatters whom he so opposed. Above all was his quaint notion that Parliament should be free of party.

> I say you have not the materials of party, and unless you have the materials, if you attempt to construct a Parliamentary party, you simply succeed in creating a faction – a faction which has no motive except its own interest to pursue, or its own animosities to gratify.[47]

Therefore he would not join any organized opposition to a government that commanded parliamentary confidence or at least was tolerated by the majority of the House. He would be careful not to support votes of censure on an incumbent government if he perceived the object to be merely to displace that government and substitute another. He would not, however, refrain from joining in censure of any individual member whose unparliamentary conduct deserved it. The Brighton voters were left in no doubt that they would elect an independent. Higinbotham was remarkably lucky not to have been challenged by an advocate of local issues who almost certainly would have beaten him. But, as it turned out, the district was preoccupied with the Brighton races held on the same day.[48]

He pursued his stated course from his entry into Parliament on 17 May 1861, with disastrous consequences on facing re-election when Heales' crumbling second Ministry secured a dissolution in July and barely scrambled back into office. Higinbotham, however, was spurned by the Brighton electors who had not warmed to his abstract independence and pursuit of questions of parliamentary principle during his two months as their representative. At the poll, the Heales faction nominated J.G. Burtt, a ship's ironmonger and, in politics, a Chartist who had been gaoled in England. Much more radical than Higinbotham, he trailed the field. The other and successful candidate was William Adams Brodribb, a pastoralist – one of the class of "squatters" Higinbotham so despised. The *Argus* considered that Higinbotham's erratic behaviour in his parliamentary votes, and the existence of a triangular contest, had deprived him of "what was one of the surest seats in the colony".[49]

Higinbotham's proposer commended his public spiritedness, his ambition "to do good to the country", and his character as "a gentleman at once erudite, energetic, honest, and faithful". Higinbotham then launched a frontal attack on Brodribb's squatting interests, reminding voters that Brodribb had said nothing on that subject and probably had something to hide. In an act of political suicide, he criticized the other candidates' promises of doing great things for the district, whereas,

> he could not promise them universal roads and the abolition of tolls; and he was not one of the Jack Cade school of politicians, who were ready to make promises which could never be fulfilled. If they returned him as their representative, he would not promise to do more for the district than it was justly entitled to.[50]

Such naivety ensured his decisive defeat. He too might have taken a lesson from Coriolanus!

His self-assurance was undoubtedly deflated, but his principles stood fast. He concentrated on his Bar practice while seeking to repair his electoral image by making himself more visible in Brighton affairs. He joined the Brighton Volunteer Rifle Corps as a private, being outranked by Sergeant Kelly, his gardener.[51] He became a founder of the Brighton Free Library, lending and eventually donating substantial sums to help construct a building for Brighton Mechanics' Institute where a large collection of books was soon acquired. It was not well sited and eventually the building was sold and new premises obtained for "The Brighton Library and Reading Room", of which Higinbotham was President.[52]

Chance again interposed when, in March 1862, Brodribb resigned the Brighton seat to take his family to the Exhibition in England. Higinbotham contested the ensuing by-election against William John Clarke, nominee of John O'Shanassy's second Ministry then in office. The contest was carried on "with considerable energy and spirit by both parties, … [and] the roads in the municipality presented a lively appearance with carriages, cars and other vehicles, dashing to and from the different polling places". Higinbotham was politically organized this time, with an active committee and a sudden awareness of local issues, including proposals to reduce road tolls, to endow municipalities with grants of land, and to extend local self-government. There were only hints of such wider issues as a national system of education, and "free trade, but a revision of the tariff".[53]

That redeemed his position and he triumphed by a large majority, to the crowd's loud cheers and "cries of 'Higinbotham, Higinbotham'". There were more cheers when told the crowd that he was proud of his success, not so much on his own account as on behalf of the district. He denied that he was a committed opponent of the government, and maintained his independent principles while reprobating "influences which had been used by the opposite side".[54] He took his seat in the House on the same day.[55]

"A Member of the Collective Legislature"

From the outset of his parliamentary term in 1861 Higinbotham adopted the role of monitor of the conscience and privileges of the House. With his great command of Westminster practice and conventions, he was constantly urging his colleagues to aspire to the same elevated standards. Yet those colleagues did not warm to his homiletics and they despaired of his aloof independence.

> The man who sees all sides of a question, and who speaks with a candid mind, has rarely the ear of Parliament, which likes rather to listen to strong reasons for a straight vote. Mr Higinbotham was no more lucky than [most] independent members, and was equally regarded by both sides as very much of a nuisance.[56]

His penchant for propriety brought him sometimes into conflict with other members, particularly, in the early years, with Charles Gavan Duffy. In December 1862, for example, Premier O'Shanassy was called to order by the Speaker for depicting the speech of a member as a "violent tirade". During a vigorous dispute over the ruling, Higinbotham interposed to say that the proper question was not whether the words were disorderly, but whether the Speaker's authority was to be maintained –

> And he would respectfully urge upon the Chief Secretary, that in his position as leader of the House, if he did not set the example of cheerful and instantaneous submission to the Speaker's ruling on a question like this, the business of the House could not be properly conducted.[57]

Duffy, amidst expressions of approval, dismissed the criticism, although its validity could not reasonably be impugned. Duffy contended that, while there was a duty on members to accept the ruling of the chair, "there was a more important duty still, namely, to maintain the free speech of Parliament", and the calling to order of O'Shanassy was therefore irregular, so he claimed.[58]

In March 1863 it was proposed that a select committee be appointed to inquire into charges of misconduct against Dr Callan, health officer at Point Nepean Quarantine Station.[59] Callan was Duffy's brother-in-law and Duffy, at the time, was President of the Board of Land and Works. There were suggestions that patronage had aided Callan's appointment. Higinbotham condemned as unparliamentary Duffy's attempts to speak to the motion and vindicate Callan's reputation. At the same time, Higinbotham opposed the motion because not even a *prima facie* case of misconduct had been put to the House, and because he distrusted select committees –

> The very constitution of select committees rendered them improper tribunals to deal with delicate questions affecting private or professional character. Five or seven gentlemen were appointed to serve on a committee, but how many of them attended the meetings of the committee regularly, or took the trouble of acquainting themselves with the whole of the evidence given … ?[60]

The character of public officers, he insisted, was not committed to the superintendence of Parliament, but to the government. The proper constitutional course was for the government to discharge its duty.

Even when he supported a colleague he sometimes was so ambivalent that it was difficult to gauge where his conviction lay. Within a fortnight of being sworn in, in May 1861, he spoke to a motion that, if carried, would have unseated James Frederick Martley, Member for Maldon. Martley, a fellow barrister from Ireland, was one of those who had introduced Higinbotham to the House. Martley had been Solicitor-General from March to November 1860 in the Nicholson Ministry and had received the fees, at the annual rate of £1500, prescribed for that office. The objection was then taken that, having accepted an office of profit under the Crown, he had vacated his parliamentary seat.[61]

The motion failed, as did an amendment that the matter be referred to a committee for inquiry. It was a provocative attempt to turn past or present Crown Law Officers out of the House by attacking Martley as the weakest link rather than the incumbent and powerful Attorney-General R.D. Ireland. Higinbotham, who might have been expected to give unqualified support to a friend, was more interested in denouncing the attack as manifesting "the influence of party spirit".[62] He would not support the motion because its consequences would be that every officer paid for doing government business must forfeit his seat in the House. In principle, he did not see that payment of any ministerial salary should lead to such forfeiture, but, on the other hand, he could not agree "that the law officers should stand on different grounds from other Ministers of the Crown, and should receive fees which other Ministers were not allowed to receive".[63]

Higinbotham's most significant remarks on propriety, before he became Attorney-General, were in May 1863. The erratic medical practitioner Louis Lawrence Smith, Member for South Bourke, was "worked to a pitch" by reflections on him in the House by J.D. Wood, Minister of Justice. They were in response to controversial remarks by Smith in addressing the chamber. Later, in the refreshment room, Smith demanded an apology of Wood, who replied "I will see you d—d first". Smith then struck Wood and was removed by police.[64]

Ireland moved that Smith be committed to the custody of the Sergeant-at-Arms for a breach of parliamentary privilege.[65] Higinbotham was typically equivocal. He deprecated Smith's conduct, yet considered that, when Smith was addressing the House, he had been provoked by government members in disregard of their duty to have called him to order. It was difficult, Higinbotham said, having allowed the matter so to develop in the chamber, to assess on which side lay the greater degree of provocation. Both sides were to blame: Smith for not calling Wood to order in the House but pursuing his grievance afterwards: the government for permitting disorderly conduct among its own supporters. But the air had been cleared –

> it would have the effect of checking the unlicensed liberty of speech which was too often heard in the House (hear, hear), and which, he regretted to be compelled to add, from his short experience in the House, generally proceeded from the Treasury benches.[66]

Smith survived to enjoy an intermittent parliamentary career that endured until 1894.

Related to Higinbotham's views about parliamentary conduct were his views about how the legislature ought to work. When the June 1861 no-confidence motion upset the Heales Ministry, Higinbotham used the debate to advance his peculiar ideas. He spoke, he said, neither as a supporter nor as an opponent of the government. For him, the question "really was, whether it was expedient or best to pass a vote of censure upon the Government". He thought it was not, for, although the government had been feeble and disunited, there was no prospect of finding a better alternative. Suggestions of a coalition had been mooted, but he saw no merit in them –

> In coalitions there was an element of weakness, because the strength of a Government usually consisted in the subordination of the various members to one commanding mind; and when an attempt was made to combine various members of different principles in one Ministry, the result had been that divisions very soon arose.[67]

He felt that no "urgent and strong reasons" had been advanced to displace the Heales Ministry which should be permitted to continue with its legislative programme. The majority thought otherwise.

As one who proposed such novelties in ordering the political system, Higinbotham might have been expected to embrace contemporary English suggestions for electoral reform, not least the proportional representation scheme devised by Thomas Hare. Higinbotham, however, would have none of it, declaring that the existing composition of the Legislative Assembly allowed all aspects of any question to be entertained in a manner reflecting community opinion – including minority opinion. The Hare system, he maintained, would produce the undesirable result of representing sectional interests rather than the broadest range of opinion. And, with cautious conservatism, he demanded, "why should they attempt a novel principle which had not yet been shown to be successful elsewhere?".[68]

Meanwhile, the no-confidence motion against Heales had resulted in a dissolution which, it was understood, Governor Sir Henry Barkly had promised unconditionally to grant even if the government's Appropriation Bill could not first be carried.[69] The Opposition won Assembly support for an address of protest to

Barkly and for amendment of the Bill. Barkly suggested that the amendment be withdrawn, the matter being within his prerogative powers. Higinbotham asserted that, as the Bill would have to be presented for royal assent, the Governor was entitled to make suggestions for its alteration without thereby infringing the privileges of Parliament.[70]

Further asserting that the expenditure of public money by those who controlled it, after a dissolution but before the granting of supply, was "highly unconstitutional", Higinbotham had the following noteworthy exchange with fellow barrister and journalist George Samuel Evans, LL.D., Member for Avoca:

> *Higinbotham* – … For what purpose is it sought to deprive the Governor of the power of exercising the prerogative of the Crown?
>
> *Evans* – To bring the Governor under the control of Parliament.
>
> *Higinbotham* – I am not aware that the Governor is placed under the control of Parliament.
>
> *Evans* – The Governor here is the same as the Queen.
>
> *Higinbotham* – I am not aware that it is the right of Parliament, or that it is in the power of Parliament to attempt to bring the Governor of this colony under its control in such a sense that Parliament shall interfere with the exercise of the prerogative vested in the Governor.[71]

On another occasion he advanced some preliminary thoughts on the Governor's constitutional position – a matter on which he would have strong opinions later in his career.

> the Governor of a colony stood in a totally different position with regard to his Ministers to that which a Sovereign of the United Kingdom held in relation to her Ministers. The Governor might virtually be a constitutional Sovereign with regard to internal matters; but with regard to matters of Imperial concern, and not of mere local import, it would clearly be the duty of a colonial Governor to resist the advice of his responsible Ministers in case that advice should be inconsistent with the instructions he had received from home.[72]

Over the ensuing 30 years, Higinbotham would refine his position to contend that the Governor did stand in the position of a local "sovereign", while his prerogative powers were at once subservient to the will of the Ministry; and that royal instructions to the Governor were illegal.[73]

True to his word, Higinbotham disdained notice of legislation of direct importance to his constituents, and limited his parliamentary involvement to policies of concern to the whole Colony. He revealed his inveterate loathing of Parliament's class structure. Although Victoria had won the concession in its Constitution (denied to New South Wales) of an elected rather than a nominated Legislative Council, that electorate was limited largely to those with money, property or both. Higinbotham despised the squatters whose acquisition of valuable landed estates was due to getting in first, enjoying good luck, and twisting the land laws by ingenious evasions so as to accumulate ever expanding landholdings. From the outset, he lost no opportunity to complain about the injustice of the system. He even proposed that the government repossess land of those who had acquired it "unjustly".[74]

In November 1862 he protested that the squatting class had already devised schemes to circumvent Duffy's *Land Act* of that year which had sought to preserve 10 million acres for the use only of agriculturists. He criticized the government for not disclosing what steps it would take to prevent further evasion. And he pursued his odd notion that the legislature ought to be united in decision on the subject, not riven by party spirit. It was no answer for a Member to say that he had voted against the Bill, because –

> there was a distinction between his responsibility as an individual member of the House, and his responsibility as a member of the collective legislature … [The] defects in the Act were discreditable to them all as a Legislature … [because] the collective Legislature of the colony had committed one of the greatest and most mischievous blunders which had ever been committed by the Legislature of any country.[75]

His remedies, which could have won him no friends in the Council, were to create open competition in the acquisition of public land, and to deter speculators by imposing a land tax on all land whether improved or not.[76]

The government later offered some suggestions for preventing future evasion of the Act, but Higinbotham thought them ineffectual. He urged that the Act be amended, such amendment not being construed as a want of confidence in the government which ought to "look rather to the merits of the amendment than to the side from which it came".[77] Although his remarks received Opposition support, they came to nothing. He had, moreover, to meet constant criticism that, while hostile to the principles of Duffy's Act, he had voted for its third reading. He looked back on his action "with extreme regret" but, having been returned for Brighton only the day before that reading, he felt that there was community support for the Bill. There was self-assurance to the point of arrogance in his explanation:

> I felt unwilling to oppose myself to the opinions of the majority of members on the question. I believe I committed a great mistake in permitting the prevailing opinions and hopes of the country to act as a substitute for opinions of my own.[78]

Early in 1863 he moved to amend the Local Government Bill by striking out a proviso exempting Crown pastoral tenants from being rated at more than one-third of the annual value of the land they occupied. He could see no reason why they should not pay rates at the same level as everyone else – "and he cared not what the consequences might be elsewhere [*scil.* in the Legislative Council]".[79] The amendment failed.

Immigration was one of the broad issues that attracted his attention. He objected to any legislation designed to bring out English migrants selected by agents or commissioners in England – "The system was a bad one, and he was arguing against it because it had the tendency to introduce a class of persons to the colony who would be useless anywhere". He also opposed the policy of introducing labour to private employers at public expense.[80] Then there was education, as to which he proclaimed his belief in "a sound system … in common schools provided for all classes alike", and he deplored a suggestion of paying teachers by results –

> such a system would produce evil results; and it would lower the salary of the teacher and render it uncertain. That would be followed by lowering the social position of the teacher; and by so doing they would lower the character of the article in which he dealt.[81]

He occasionally offered suggestions in the field of "lawyers' law", urging, for example, reconsideration of a Bill to alter the law of partnership which appeared to create a novel regime that would take the lead of the law in England. He propounded a "general rule" that, in legislation of that kind, they should "follow the track of English legislation rather than attempt to precede it". By doing so, the Colony would have the advantage of being guided by decisions of the English Superior Courts on such new enactments.[82]

Higinbotham had little opportunity to introduce Bills as a private member. Other things aside, he had so few allies in the House that he could count on no assured support. But he persisted with a Conveyancers Bill, giving notice on 14 November 1862, that he would introduce the measure to enable conveyancers to be admitted as attorneys, solicitors and proctors of the Supreme Court.[83] Its object was to offer relief to the existing conveyancers, nine in all, "whose profession had been seriously injured by the passing of the Real Property Act".[84] His Bill would require those seeking admission to pass an examination and pay a fee of £50. The Law Society did not oppose the Bill, but lawyer members of the Assembly did. Ireland and Wood combined to urge its postponement because so few applications had been made to bring old system titles under the *Real Property Act* that conveyancers had "received no injury to complain of".[85] Nevertheless, the second reading passed.

Some amendments were made in committee and Ireland again "objected altogether to this kind of legislation" and vowed to oppose its third reading, as he did.[86] He maintained that the measure was premature and that "the barriers of the legal profession ought not to be broken down, and these [conveyancers] placed in a position they had no right to claim. The bill inflicted an injustice, and was a bad example of hasty legislation". O'Shanassy's Ministry voted against the third reading, but it was carried by one vote: on the motion that the Bill pass, there were some changes of heart and it was lost by one vote.[87] Higinbotham tried again, in February 1863, and the Bill passed on the technicality that, a division having been called, only one teller could be found for the "Noes".[88]

The measure was rejected by the Legislative Council, giving Higinbotham additional reason to wage war against that body when he came to power as Attorney-General on 27 June 1863.

4

Attorney-General 1863-1868

George Higinbotham held office as Attorney-General for five years, a tenure (since Responsible Government) not exceeded before or after until Isaac Isaacs became first Crown Law Officer in September 1894. Some able men had preceded Higinbotham, among them Stawell, Fellows, Michie, Chapman and Ireland. As to the administrative functions of the office, Higinbotham's contribution did not outshine that of his predecessors. Two works of supererogation distinguished him. He personally undertook a consolidation of the Colony's scattered and fragmented statutes, and, in 1866 and 1867 he was Chairman of a Royal Commission on education. Those good works will be examined in the final chapter.

Were the administrative duties severed from the Attorney-General's political functions, Higinbotham's term would have been commendable for efficiency and diligence. The same cannot be said for his political career which was unorthodox and incongruous. Higinbotham had grand views of the "nation", Victoria, functioning as a mature entity under the blessings of Responsible Government. With moderation, attaining those visions might have won him the laurels of a statesman. Instead, his impatience, intolerance of dissent or criticism, loathing of alleged "interference" by the Colonial Office, and contempt for the squatter-dominated Legislative Council, diverted him into a state of perpetual animosity. His opinions became unyielding and obsessive. In the major political contests of the day he lacked tact, diplomacy or any sense of compromise. He readily and repeatedly admitted the fact, as when, in 1868, he said in the Assembly, "A compromise has been talked of. Sir, I heard the expression, and I confess I did not like it. I do not know what this House has to compromise".[1] In short, he was, as Sir William Stawell described him, "a dangerous politician".[2]

Much of Higinbotham's time at the Attorney-General's desk was devoted to writing legal opinions and often to drafting important government documents such as Cabinet memoranda and, under Governor Darling, despatches to the Secretary of State. That Higinbotham's legal opinions were not always sound will emerge from following pages. Yet he had an overweening confidence in his own infallibility that was prone to lead him astray. A typical if minor instance was recalled by J. A. Gurner who, as Parliamentary Draftsman, assisted with statutory consolidation. Higinbotham feared that the Act constituting the Court of General Sessions had been repealed but, inadvertently, not re-enacted in consolidated form. Gurner, who later confirmed that he was not mistaken, tried to direct Higinbotham to the volume containing the re-enactment, but " 'Pardon me', said he, 'I have satisfied myself that what I say is correct', and he laid a restraining hand upon mine. No more was to be said".[3] On greater public issues, Higinbotham's opinion once formed was similarly irreversible and its truth maintained inflexibly.

An analysis will be made later of the myths surrounding Higinbotham's career as Attorney-General, and of some strong expressions of praise or denunciation of him over the years. It will suffice, at this point, to mention some of Higinbotham's actions or ideas that seem unsound legally or constitutionally. Controversial though the views of historian H.G. Turner may be, he was surely correct in writing that,

> when [Higinbotham] assumed the responsibilities of office it was quickly apparent that he was an extremist in action, and an unflinching devotee of his own views. And he had an exceptional power of forcing the adoption of his views upon the majority of those who came under the spell of his oratory.[4]

In the Assembly, Higinbotham was conscientious in attendance but often retiring in debate. Unless on major issues, when he could speak with passion and at length, he preferred to leave discussion to others. But he was astute to see that everything was done decently and in order. He overawed the House with his command of parliamentary procedure and, in brief interpolations, acted as if a supervisor of procedural decorum. He would constantly insist that members defer to the Speaker's rulings, make suggestions about expediting the order of business or manner of bringing it forward, and explain why proposed measures or amendments would not work as a matter of law or of practical administration.[5] A curious example was his apology for not noticing a drafting error in an Electoral Law Consolidation Bill whereby,

> the right of voting had been conferred on females quite inadvertently ... Speaking for himself, he thought that females should be entitled to vote; but the privilege should not have been conferred upon them inadvertently. It should have been done with deliberation.[6]

As to his portfolio, he generally declined to discuss in Parliament "the departmental arrangements of his office",[7] but he was concerned to see that those within the superintendence of his Department were not subjected to idle criticism. In April 1866, he rebutted suggestions that Crown Prosecutors were "more anxious to secure convictions than to do justice".[8] He hoped that they would perform their duties in proportion to the anxiety of defence counsel to secure acquittals, and he believed that they did so with efficiency and moderation. While he agreed that the decisions of honorary magistrates were generally "far less satisfactory" than those of Police Magistrates, and decisions in remote areas sometimes "wholly inexplicable", he insisted that "there was hardly a district in which a magistrate had sufficient to do". He was examining the possibility of deploying itinerant Police Magistrates. Meanwhile, honorary justices had it within their own hands to place themselves in a better light.

> If these gentlemen would attend the benches in the districts where they lived, and if they would not flock to benches on particular occasions, they would save themselves from suspicions which, though they might be unfounded, were, nevertheless, created by their own act.[9]

He was impressed by the possibility of saving expense and securing greater efficiency by reorganizing the Colony's coronial system.[10]

He was actively involved in proposals for the erection of a new Supreme Court House in Melbourne, the most favoured site for which was then "at the west end of the town, and near the Exhibition Building". Work on the project had, he thought, been delayed too long, and he could only agree with the "flattering opinion" of Sir Alfred Stephen, Chief Justice of New South Wales, on a recent visit, that "the only building which was not a credit to the city, or rather, was an actual discredit to it, was the Supreme Court".[11]

As to the legal profession, he was less than dynamic as *ex officio* leader of the Bar. Asked, in 1865, to introduce a Bill regulating the admission of barristers, he felt unwilling to give it priority over more urgent legislation. Yet he opposed the attempts of a private member to introduce such a measure.[12]

Apart from his numerous Statute Law Consolidation Bills, he did not take a prominent part in introducing legislation, and was not always successful when he did. His initiatives largely concerned "lawyers' law", such as reforming the laws as to imprisonment for debt, trade marks, and the land laws[13] – as to the last of which he became even more hostile to the claims of the squatters. A more defensive measure was his resolution, in May 1866, after a Select Committee on the working of the *Real Property Act* reported serious irregularities in the Land Titles Office. He tried awkwardly to explain away the clear lack of control over that office and sought to protect himself by moving the House approve of defining the duties of Titles Office staff and that "the commissioner should devote himself solely to his judicial duties".[14]

"He Spoke of Leaving Victoria"

An early instance of setting obstinacy against diplomacy occurred in January 1864.[15] It was an instance where Higinbotham was technically right but tactically wrong. The senior puisne judge, Sir Redmond Barry, then described by the *Age* as "supercilious and insolent",[16] and still smarting at not having succeeded Sir William a'Beckett as Chief Justice, proposed to take leave to visit Sydney and Brisbane. He reported his intentions to Governor Sir Charles Darling who so advised Higinbotham, stating "I presume the Judges have a legal right to take [this] step".

In Higinbotham's practical view, such matters came within the authority of the Attorney-General's Department. It would be absurd to suggest that English judges arranged personally with the Queen the mundane matter of taking leave. It was similarly absurd that colonial judges should bring those matters before the Governor. Diplomacy might have suggested that Higinbotham wait upon Chief Justice Stawell and reach an amicable agreement about colonial procedure for future like applications.

Instead, Higinbotham returned an inflamed reply to the Governor. Its terms would re-echo to his disadvantage down the years –

> the Attorney-General cannot permit any officer in his Department – no matter how eminent the position of the officer may be, or however independent the law may have made him in the exercise of his official functions – to place himself outside the limits of the system of responsible government, and communicate with the Attorney-General on an official subject by means of letters addressed to the Governor in person.[17]

There followed a battle between the judges, the Governor, the Attorney-General and the Cabinet, in which the judges claimed that their rights were being infringed. All possibility of compromise was lost. The Executive Council directed that all "official communications" by the judges as to the "rights, privileges, or duties of their offices" were to be directed only to the Attorney-General.[18] Higinbotham hinted that judges who did not comply might be suspended or removed form office.

That raised the question of the judges' security of tenure and again set the Bench against the Executive, with even greater animosity on both sides. The judges accused the Attorney-General of using his consolidation of the statutes to introduce into the *Supreme Court (Administration) Act* 1852 provisions relating to the judges' position and powers that had never been enacted. Stawell sought the Secretary of State's intervention but was rebuffed on the ground that Responsible Government placed it beyond the adjudication of Downing Street. A petition by the judges to the Queen was treated similarly. But their position was saved by the Legislative Council which struck out the contentious provisions of Higinbotham's consolidating Bill.

He had thus another score to settle with his intractable enemy, the Council. In the end, the honours were evenly divided. The judges were, for the future, unable to deal directly with the Governor. But the attempt to make it easier to remove them from office failed. In 1865 yet another clash with the Supreme Court put Higinbotham in an untenable position. The first Law Officer traditionally shielded the judges from unreasonable criticism. Yet, in the "Urquhart Scab Case",[19] Higinbotham, as Attorney-General, himself used parliamentary privilege to attack most viciously Mr Justice E.E. Williams of the Supreme Court. If the Attorney-General, in his official capacity, had a just complaint about a judge, protocol would have suggested that it be pursued, in the first instance, with the Chief Justice. Higinbotham preferred direct action.

The facts of the case are of little present importance. George Urquhart, a former Member of the Legislative Council, owned a station on the Lower Murray and went about buying sheep at such low prices as to suggest that they were afflicted with scab. He was proceeded against, before country magistrates, and fined for having scabby sheep and, through his agent, having impeded a government inspector attempting to examine the sheep. He tendered cheques in payment of the fine: they were dishonoured. The magistrates, being doubtful what to do next, took the exceptional step of seeking the Attorney-General's opinion. He took the exceptional step of offering them advice with the caution that "the magistrates will be prepared, I have no doubt, to deal with the cases on their own responsibility".[20] The magistrates then consulted solicitors who wrote to Higinbotham, as if a public legal adviser, inquiring whether their clients should sue on the cheques, the risk of levying execution on Urquhart's flocks being too great given their diseased condition. Higinbotham obligingly volunteered that the magistrates had a good cause of action on the cheques and, if willing to undertake the perils of litigation, should be represented by their own solicitors. The magistrates would not undertake those perils: the fines were remitted.

The *Argus* then published two articles claiming that Urquhart had "evaded his sentence and defrauded the Magistrates' court", and "by grace of our Attorney-General, he is enabled to snap his fingers at the administrators of the law".[21] Urquhart sued Edward Wilson and Lauchlan Mackinnon, proprietors and publishers of the *Argus*, for libel, the case coming before Williams, J., and a jury, between 1 and 3 March 1865.[22] A verdict was entered for the defendants. Williams, in charging the jury, suggested that, as the defendants must have known that the fines had been imposed but effectively remitted, the defendants were "almost justified" in their publication. He deprecated the Crown's irregular course.

> I think that the manner in which this case has been dealt with is likely to establish a very dangerous precedent. I think it will be a very dangerous thing if a decision which has been sanctioned in open court is set aside in a room.[23]

In the Assembly, George Collins Levey, Member for Normanby and proprietor of the Melbourne *Herald*, mischievously moved for appointment of a Select Committee to inquire into those observations of "an officer in the Attorney-General's department".[24] He secured a much more newsworthy scoop for his paper than he could well have foreseen. Higinbotham's frenzied response must have been unique in the annals of the Crown Law Office. He rounded upon Williams, accusing him of having directed "extra-judicial and improper remarks" to the jury, and declaring, in terms he would have done well to recall later in his own career, that,

> If a Supreme Court judge dealt with political questions, he should be asked to descend from the bench, and if he did not come down from the bench, it was quite right that his remarks should be met in a deliberative assembly … These things sprang, he believed from the political feeling which … was not absent from the minds of the judges – a political feeling embodied in a strong and intense desire on the part of the Bench to disparage the Government and exalt the judges.[25]

His reflections on the judge were outrageous and unwarranted. Williams had said nothing political, but was unable to refute the accusations. The suggestion that, in effect, the entire Bench was corrupt, was the more reprehensible coming from an Attorney-General. Yet Higinbotham insisted that he was at liberty to criticize Williams for making remarks that were "indecent in character".[26]

The *Argus*, which protested that it was really the target, complained that "the office of Attorney-General, as it is at present conducted, is one of the most dangerous anomalies in our system".[27] It declared that Mr Justice Williams had never interfered in political matters, and it deplored Higinbotham's "pretensions" to exercise the functions of "a superintendent of the judges". His reflections on Williams

> deserve all the epithets which he himself employed in regard to
> the Judge's observations … "indecent" in a high degree were such
> remarks emanating from an Attorney-General, whose duty it is
> to uphold the law and those who dispense it. The pettishness,
> unjustifiable resentment, and cowardliness, involved in these
> animadversions, are conspicuous. No man with a particle of mag-
> nanimity would have permitted himself to defame a judge, who, by
> his position is utterly unable to reply.[28]

Higinbotham had left himself open to just such a censure.

Despite the uncompromising way in which he met the
judges in these contests, he was evidently bruised by them. J. L.
Forde recalled that, after such experiences, Higinbotham

> felt some reluctance to resume practice before the judges with
> whom he had been so lately in collision. He spoke of leaving
> Victoria and settling in New Zealand.[29]

"The Liberty of the Press Must be Suppressed"

As self-appointed custodian of the conscience of the House,
Higinbotham was alert to any breach of or departure from the
rules of parliamentary privilege. Sometimes the matters he raised
were relatively trifling. In August 1863, for example, he moved
that it was a breach of privilege for the Government Printer to
alter a Bill after its first reading and distribution without the
authority of a parliamentary officer. Alterations had been made to
a Bill at the direction of someone at the Crown Law Office, a
practice Higinbotham condemned as "incredible".[30]

An odd case occurred in 1866 when Edward Cope, member
for East Bourke Boroughs, complained of having been served
with a subpoena to give evidence in a Supreme Court action. He
moved that such service was a breach of privilege, as compliance
would disable him from discharging his parliamentary duties.
G. C. Levey then moved that Cope be given leave to attend on the
subpoena, sarcastically adding that "he presumed the next thing
would be to make service of a writ upon an honorable member
for a debt which he might owe, a breach of privilege".[31] Cope
protested that he wanted an exemption not leave. Higinbotham
interposed that, privilege having been raised, Levey's motion was
improper unless with notice or special permission.

> Usually subpoenas were not treated as breaches of privilege. But if
> [Cope] objected to attend, the best course would be for him to bring

forward a motion, asking the protection of the House, and permission from the House not to attend.[32]

There were numerous other such minor matters.[33]

More important were tests of strength between the privileges of Parliament and claimed privileges of the press, particularly the *Argus*. Higinbotham had come to despise the policies of the newspaper he had once edited and, more broadly, the influence of journalism. He observed, in 1866, of English prints –

> the papers which have been most severe in their censures have been the most blundering in their comments on the acts of the Government … that portion which is opposed to us is distinguished above the rest by the numerous errors into which its writers have fallen. I … will not be guided by the opinions of the press.[34]

The first round of a battle between George Dill, then proprietor and publisher of the *Argus*, and the Legislature had ended before Higinbotham became Attorney-General.[35] The Assembly deemed an *Argus* editorial, critical of a member, a "scandalous breach" of privilege, to which Dill rejoined with a more provocative column. Summoned to the bar of the House, he failed to appear, was arrested for contempt under the warrant of Speaker Sir Francis Murphy, and committed to detention by the Sergeant-at-Arms for one month. Failing in *habeas corpus* proceedings, Dill sued the Speaker and the Sergeant-at-Arms for trespass and false imprisonment, but without success. Newspaper publishers were thus on notice.

In March 1866 Hugh George, then editor of the *Argus*, published the assertion that an Assembly speech by McCulloch "bristled with falsehood". McCulloch moved, and Higinbotham seconded, a motion that the publication was "a scandalous breach of the privileges of this House".[36] The motion met some opposition because the bounds of reasonable comment had not been breached, and similar items published with impunity by other newspapers were adduced as proof of government partisanship.[37]

Higinbotham rebutted that opposition on the ground that the Premier had been publicly defamed. He could not "conceive how it is possible to assert that such an imputation is not a breach of the privileges of the House". The term "falsehood" was especially offensive, he said, and it could not be dismissed as an ordinary journalistic irritant:

> I am quite habituated to the use of such terms as "chicanery", "lawlessness", "revolutionary", and so forth whether applied to this Ministry or to any other; for it has become the habit of the degraded press which now exists in this colony.[38]

The motion being carried decisively, Higinbotham moved that George be committed to the custody of the Sergeant-at-Arms, exclaiming that, if the *Argus* were to be so conducted, "I say, the liberty of the press must be suppressed".[39] He admitted that the power of the House "was a very absolute power indeed, and I [once] thought that possibly it would be wise to abandon the privilege altogether".[40] On reflection he considered that "this is a matter which depends upon the individual feeling of each member … I hold that individual members have a perfect right to demand the protection of the House where they feel that their personal honor is affected".[41] Levey, who edited the Melbourne *Herald*, thought George's incarceration to be "such a monstrous piece of injustice that I am astonished that the Attorney-General – a statesman, a lawyer, and an old journalist – should propose it".[42]

After a week, McCulloch was minded to relent, and proposed George's release subject to payment of the fees of the Sergeant-at-Arms.[43] George, who reckoned that martyrdom sold more newspapers than did meek compliance, would not pay. In retaliation, he was denied access by visitors and given very basic meals. Higinbotham virtually admitted that those changes had been at his suggestion, for he thought that George "had been allowed a degree of liberty which certainly seemed to be wholly inconsistent with the position of a prisoner of this House". Yet Higinbotham maintained that the Sergeant-at-Arms alone must bear responsibility for any suggestion that George was mistreated.[44]

After three weeks the Assembly capitulated and George was released. As Rusden said, "The country press teemed with denunciation of the tyranny of the Assembly, and Mr Higinbotham's views did not receive public sympathy".[45] Parliament had made itself seem ridiculous, and the adverse press achieved exactly the opposite of maintaining the stature of the House.

Higinbotham was much to blame. Although he said he had acted with regret against George "whom I have the pleasure to call my personal friend",[46] might not mediation have preceded condign punishment? An informal discussion with George might have settled the whole matter: perhaps even an apology might have been negotiated. Moreover, Higinbotham's stance rested on double standards. Nathaniel Levi[47] complained of a recent *Leader* article accusing him of being supported in Parliament by "disreputable traders", and of having attempted in Parliament "to drag reputable people into the dirt" and of having acted in the House "with peculiar cunning".[48] If it were a breach of privilege to state that the Premier's observations "bristled with falsehood", how could the imputations against Levi be any less a breach?

Higinbotham pooh-poohed the suggestion. Levi had allowed a fortnight (during much of which, incidentally, the House stood adjourned) to elapse since the publication complained of, and was being dilatory, so Higinbotham claimed, to ride on the coat-tails of McCulloch's motion concerning George. Such a procedure, said Higinbotham, would "render the proceedings of the House farcical",[49] though he gave no reasons. Some sanity was introduced into the debate by Ireland who opposed the course pursued by McCulloch, contending that,

> he [Ireland] had entered his protest against the arbitrary exercise of the unlimited powers and privileges possessed by the House in dealing with the public press … He regarded it as most unfortunate that such a precedent should have been set.[50]

Higinbotham's judgement as to parliamentary privilege and the press might have been very pure in theory, but it was lamentably defective in practice.

"Piratical Enterprises Against the Citizens of a Friendly Power"

On the eve of Australia ("Anniversary") Day in January 1865, as the American Civil War reached its climax, the (southern) Confederate States Steamer of War, *Shenandoah*, arrived in Port Phillip Bay.[51] Its commander sought and was granted Governor Darling's permission to undertake repairs and take on provisions and coal. Victoria being a neutral state, so much could be permitted. Thus began a complex sequence of events that cannot be pursued in detail here. They demonstrated that Higinbotham's advice in matters of admiralty and public international law was insecure, and that Darling was misled by it.

So far from departing within 24 hours as the rules of neutrality prescribed, the vessel lingered for nearly a month, the officers and crew being received as honoured guests at grand social occasions from Melbourne to Ballarat, with reciprocal entertainments on board ship. Howls of protest came from William Blanchard, the United States Consul in Melbourne, who then wrote to Darling, in furtherance of "his duty to urge upon Your Excellency the greatest caution", recommending that the *Shenandoah* be detained.[52] Darling would have done well to heed the warning and to examine the legitimacy of the vessel's claim to the rights of a belligerent,

> lest, under flimsy pretences of necessity, the ports and coasts of Her Majesty's dominions be not unguardedly thrown open to afford lawless and unauthorized marauders cover and bases for new and piratical enterprises against the citizens of a friendly power, their lives and property.[53]

Presciently, Blanchard warned also of the risk of "new claims and additional and serious complications" arising between the United States and British Governments.

Darling turned to Higinbotham who, jointly with Michie, gave a perfunctory reply on special pleaders' grounds – no evidence was placed before them that the *Shenandoah* was a pirate.[54] Blanchard rejoined with affidavits and another long letter manifesting a powerful command of British law, citing precedent British cases and insisting that "this vessel is not a legal cruiser of the so-styled Confederacy".[55] Further, the vessel was believed to have been recruiting crew in Melbourne, including at least one British subject contrary to the *Foreign Enlistment Act* 1819 (59 *Geo. III c.* 69). Blanchard went on –

> I have confined myself to a view taken from imperial law. I have urged nothing from a consideration of the law of nations, nor from the obligation of treaties. These, indeed, doubtless Her Majesty's Neutrality Proclamation and Foreign Enlistment Act only illustrate and enforce. Nor can they be interpreted apart without manifest injustice.[56]

Higinbotham, to whom those representations were referred, ought to have recognized that he was dealing with a Consul who knew much more about maritime and international law than he did. Instead, he curtly advised Darling that there were "no grounds … for an alteration of the views … already submitted".[57]

Not only was Higinbotham's advice wantonly superficial but it was slanted to advance his warfare against the Colonial Office. He maintained a false pretence that, just as the Imperial Government, in his view, had no right to give advice or directions unsought as to the conduct of colonial affairs, so the Colony had neither right nor duty to obtrude on Westminster its views on such imperial matters as the *Shenandoah* case. Darling, taken aback at the lack of substance in Higinbotham's advice, sought guidance from the Executive Council. Although the matter was considered only at special meetings or at the close of other business at ordinary Council meetings, "these were full meetings, more fully attended than usual, and the members definitely and repeatedly tendered advice as a Council".[58]

Yet, years afterwards, when Britain had lost a case for damages, assessed at U.S. $15,500,000[59] by a Tribunal of Arbitrators at Geneva, for destruction of United States vessels and commerce by *Shenandoah* after departing from Melbourne, Higinbotham persisted in the implausible contention that, in January 1865,

> Her Majesty's ministers for this country absolutely ceased, in reference to every thing that occurred with regard to the *Shenandoah*, to hold the place of responsible Ministers of the Crown at all … Sir Charles Darling thought proper to ask the opinion, counsel, and assistance of those Executive Councillors who happened then to be nearest to him … But … whatever advice was given … was given not as Ministers of the Crown.[60]

As Professor Bailey pointed out, that was an "idle" contention made the more so for want of explanation of the "other and undefined capacity" in which the Ministers purported to act.[61] More recently it has been put that "The executive councillors could not easily divest themselves of responsibilities as ministers of the crown because the matter was of international import".[62] Such divestiture would have been at odds with their oath of office. Their collective judgement was at fault in not recognizing that they had a duty to give the best advice that they could to the Crown, whether in England or in Victoria, and not to allow themselves to be led by the nose to gratify the Attorney-General's idiosyncratic notions.

Darling had been let down by Higinbotham's careless and shallow advice. But the Governor was not blameless.[63] Common sense alone would have recommended him to detain the *Shenandoah* until the pleasure of the Colonial Office could be ascertained. He would have lost nothing, and would have protected himself from criticism, if he had.

"The Conscientious Member of the Administration"

The incidents already described were minor skirmishes when contrasted with Higinbotham's fierce campaign against the Legislative Council, waged chiefly between 1864 and 1868. Investing Victoria with a bicameral Legislature imported prospective conflict should the Houses disagree. W. F. Stawell, principal architect of Victoria's Constitution, in explaining his object, wrote, "it is extremely desirable that by means of an Upper House a safety valve should be opened against hasty or unduly considered legislation".[64] That power of review has been an incident of most Australian State Parliaments and of the Commonwealth Parliament, often creating tensions, but leading to the sensible result either of stimulating compromise or of leaving a resolution to the electorate. The tensions, during Higinbotham's Attorney-Generalship, showed him willing rather to fight to the death than to compromise: and the Legislative Council responded in kind.

The fall of O'Shanassy's third Ministry, in June 1863, brought James McCulloch to power as Premier in the first and longest of his four Ministries: he retained office until 1868.[65] Higinbotham, as McCulloch's Attorney-General, was characterized by G. W. Rusden as "a theoretical enthusiast, steeped in a mixture of the ideas of John Stuart Mill and the French iconoclasts of 1789",[66] and the deference shown to his views as Attorney-General was depicted as "Higinbotha-mania".[67] Higinbotham's conduct in the matters of present relevance over the ensuing few years lent some credence to those acidic assessments.

Higinbotham fired the first shot of his campaign by introducing a Bill to amend the *Electoral Act* passed at the instance of O'Shanassy's Ministry in the same parliamentary session.[68] Most of the amendments went to procedural matters, particularly the inadequate time allowed for making up electoral rolls. But Higinbotham's real grievance was that O'Shanassy's Act had covertly taken away the right of voting by secret ballot. "If", he said, there had interposed "an alteration of a portion of the law which was generally regarded as a fundamental part of the Constitution, then the Parliament and the country had just ground to complain of not being informed of such intention".[69] Otherwise he was willing that the Act, which he thought had several objectionable provisions, be tested by experience. The Legislative Council agreed to the Bill subject to amendments which the Assembly conceded.[70]

Then there was Duffy's 1862 *Land Act*. Higinbotham, who thought its wording so defective as to have encouraged evasion by the squatters,

> did not believe that the squatters of this colony were a more degraded, selfish, and unprincipled class than any corresponding class in any other country who possessed an interest antagonistic to the public interest. He freely admitted that they were not better, but he disputed that they were worse.[71]

He attacked the views of O'Shanassy, who resisted: and there were similar clashes with Duffy.[72]

There was little time for legislating, as Parliament was prorogued by Darling immediately after his assuming office as Governor on 11 September 1863. Sittings did not resume until 26 January 1864. Little was achieved even then, as the session expired in June and general elections commenced in August. Higinbotham succeeded with some Consolidation Bills, but otherwise the sittings were, as H.G. Turner described them, "brief and colourless".

> Heales brought in a Bill to amend the Duffy Land Act, which afforded a jaded discussion for a couple of months, and then went to the Council to meet the fate which had befallen a similar effort in the preceding session.[73]

Higinbotham offered an unconvincing explanation of the government's reluctance to negotiate informally with the Upper House as being "not consistent with the dignity of the Government, or the independence of legislators".[74] He foreshadowed the possibility of the government's resigning or seeking an early dissolution on the question. Yet, almost in the same breath, before the Council's rejection of the Bill, he was telling the Assembly that he had the reasonable hope that the House would bring pressure to bear upon deliberations in another place, who, seeing that the bill was founded on an equitable principle, conserving existing claims [of squatters], and endeavouring to promote the real interest of agricultural settlers, might be induced to allow it to become law.[75]

The Council was not so induced, and Higinbotham concluded that "the public would look with some degree of care and scrutiny into the conduct of those who had rejected the bill".[76] The Council thus presented McCulloch's Government with an attractive platform on which to go to the electorate – comprehensive land law reform, and more radical reform of the composition and powers of the Upper House. The government was returned overwhelmingly at ensuing elections.

Higinbotham did not face his Brighton constituents until October 1864 and, in a preliminary address, cast off his appeals to abstract principles, giving one of the most political public speeches of his career. He was grateful that no-one from his electorate had tried to influence his views on public questions, and that requests to support local objects or to assist individuals had been moderate and reasonable. He explained that, while zealous in his regard for the Brighton electors, he relied firmly on the strength of his own opinion as to the right course on any issues.

> I believe a public man always makes a mistake when he permits the opinions of others to stand in the place of his own; and a still greater mistake if, having formed opinions, he permits himself to be driven from them.[77]

He turned to the land question, asserting that it should have been settled within the first year after Responsible Government. He favoured abandoning the 1862 *Land Act* and dealing with the issues afresh, but had felt constrained because the Act was originally "a contract of a kind similar to many other contracts which we have seen made in the old country between different classes and interests". The squatters, however, had obtained the chief benefits of the contract – "they gave up nothing and they have received much". And they had given only "tacit agreement that they would no longer be political intriguers or social slanderers to overthrow any Government that dealt with the subject".[78]

As the Legislative Council had been obdurate, he believed that the "political contract" with the squatters had been rescinded such that the *Land Act* could fairly be overhauled. There was a stronger reason, given that many Councillors owned runs such that "in voting on this question, [they] are not to be regarded as independent and impartial judges". They were rather the representatives, partners and agents of the pastoral tenants. If, then, they remained unwilling to embrace reform:

> I do not hesitate to aver that, if the proposition of the Government is rejected by the Legislative Council, I will be no party to any further compromise or delay. I will not be a party to any bill that does not propose to totally and immediately repeal the Land Act of 1862, and provide for the disposal of the pastoral property of the country by auction.[79]

For good measure, the government would propose a comprehensive reform of the Council, particularly to enlarge the constituency (then only one-eightieth of the whole community) by which members of that House were elected – "if such an institution existed in the mother country it would be called an oligarchy … [and one] of the most dangerous description". The existing Council was dangerous, he said, because its membership depended on wealth that conferred power enabling the Council to be a permanent obstruction to wise legislation and "a standing menace to all Governments".[80]

Although he insisted that he did not wish to hurt anyone's feelings and did not believe in threats, he reprobated the Council's membership and looked forward to reform that would make it more representative. To prolonged applause, he uttered another unforgettable aphorism, that the effect of the reform "will be to strike a blow at a very dangerous class – the wealthy lower orders of the community".[81]

He hoped, in sum, to be re-elected so as to ensure the creation of "a permanent Government". The *Argus* remarked cynically on Higinbotham's appeal to his constituents having been deferred to the very end of the electoral process –

> It can scarcely be set down to chance that the conscientious member of the Administration was only let loose when two-thirds of the elections were over, and a large working majority already secured for the Government. A little earlier, and the honest man might have spoilt the game.[82]

Taking the squatters' side, it condemned the speech as characteristic of the speaker, "ludicrously insufficient and ineffective", with its "mixture of guileless candour, of ingenious sophistry, of professional acuteness, with a sort of child-like simplicity of mind and transparency of motive". It considered his "theories" about the squatters and the Council as "worse than absurd".[83]

The Legislative Council needed no stronger apologist than the *Argus* as then conducted, and thus were the battle lines drawn.

A CASE OF GREAT PERPLEXITY.

5

"Absolute Political Equality to All"

"The One Dominant Desire For Victory"

In December 1864 Higinbotham began his attack by insisting that the government's legislative programme, so resoundingly endorsed at the recent elections, be honoured.

> If general elections were not to indicate the opinion of the country, of what use were they? The country was put to considerable expense, and what for but to enable the people to elect representatives whose opinions on leading questions were the same as theirs, and who should carry into law that of which the country approved.[1]

The Legislative Council, to whom those remarks were particularly addressed, although chastened by the election results, still held its ground. A Bill from the Assembly, to reform the Council, was tied on its second reading, whereupon the President, who had used his deliberative vote in its favour, in effect used a casting vote to declare it lost.[2] There was thus another score Higinbotham wished to settle.

Then came consideration of the promised overhaul of Duffy's *Land Act*. Introduced by J. M. Grant, President of the Board of Land and Works, in November 1864, the Opposition rump assailed it in the Assembly, inviting the same response from Higinbotham, that "the Government did put distinct issues before the country, and that the country had pronounced upon them".[3] The Legislature thus had a duty to implement those pronouncements. The Opposition tried again, in committee, to alter fundamental principles of the Bill. Higinbotham angrily rejoined:

If [the Government's] attempts to obtain justice for the agriculturists failed – if the bill were again rejected in another place – he
was perfectly prepared to treat the Land Act of 1862 as revoked by
the consent of both parties.[4]

The Bill was pushed through to its third reading in January
1865 whereafter "it was further amended by the Legislative Council, and sent backwards and forwards several times, until finally a
conference between the Chambers adjusted all difficulties, and it
became law on 28th March".[5] That significant outcome suggested
that, with good will and reasonableness on both sides, the
legislative business of Parliament could be carried on.

Instead, those compromising qualities were extinguished
when fiscal legislation was proposed. It need not have been so.
The Council, late in January 1865, was most accommodating in
passing a Consolidated Revenue (£560,000) Bill through all stages
at one brief sitting.[6] It was a Supply Bill that enabled the government to draw from the Treasury £60,000 in arrear for 1864, and
£500,000 for the current year. Before the funds could be released
an Appropriation Bill would need to specify the particular
disbursements required. The interests of the Colony would have
suggested that such an Appropriation Bill go to the Council and,
almost certainly, be there passed.

The perpetual clash between Protection and Free Trade
intervened and was aggravated by Higinbotham's foolish attempt
to coerce the Council to yield to the Assembly's fiscal policies.
The Council supported Free Trade. Privately, so did Premier
McCulloch and his Crown Law Officers, Higinbotham and Michie. Higinbotham, from his first appearance on the hustings had
proclaimed Free Trade, and persisted until the government's
monetary policies diverted him.[7] There was much "trimming" by
the Ministry to accommodate public opinion, at the polls, that
local manufactures and industry ought to be protected against
competition from imports.[8]

Although McCulloch lost supporters from the Treasury
benches, and a Free Trade Association was formed to resist him,
his Ministry resolved to adjust the incidence of duties so as to
satisfy popular opinion.[9] A new tariff schedule was prepared,
reducing duties on such staples as tea, sugar and molasses, but
imposing duties on items previously tax free, such as salt, salted
provisions, vinegar, doors and window sashes, articles made up

from specified fabrics, and a host of household items. The export duty on gold was reduced by one-third. The result was estimated to generate no higher revenue than before, but to distribute the taxation burden more equitably. Those intentions had been foreshadowed by Governor Darling when announcing the government's programme on opening Parliament in November 1864.[10]

The Treasurer, G.F. Verdon, presented his budget on 19 January 1865, disclosing the new tariff rates. Collection of duties at those rates commenced forthwith. Ordinarily the tariff provisions would form part of a Customs Bill. But, evidently to Higinbotham's design, the Assembly resolved on a mischievous and ultimately dissipating strategy in dealing with the Council which, it expected, would reject such a Customs Bill. Section 56 of the *Constitution Act* 1855 enabled the Council to reject Money Bills but not to amend them. Darling reported on the next phase, an exercise in legislative "tacking":

> It soon became an article of belief with the majority of the Assembly, but based … upon information derived from personal sources, that the Legislative Council would … reject the Tariff. The Ministers … avowed their intention to support what they maintained to be the constitutional right of the Assembly practically to control the taxation of the country … by combining the Tariff with the Clauses of Appropriation, which have hitherto constituted in Victoria a separate Bill.[11]

A Customs and Excise Bill had been introduced in the Assembly in February 1865. It contained over 500 sections and the scheduled tariff. Next month, McCulloch bluntly announced that the Bill would not proceed, but the tariff provisions would be "tacked" to the Appropriation Bill for submission to the Council.[12] Some members resisted that course, while the Speaker Sir Francis Murphy (a supporter of O'Shanassy in Opposition), declared it unconstitutional.[13] Higinbotham, adhering to his "no party" policy,

> would rather appeal to the House, not as a body of opposing parties, but as a body having common interests and common rights. He did not think, in dealing with a question of this kind, hon. members ought to range themselves on different sides of the House, or that votes should be given with regard to the attitude assumed by hon. members towards the Government.[14]

He eloquently defended the "tack" and his argument had some plausibility. He maintained that Bills of Supply and of Appropriation, being of like genus, could be amalgamated. His argument broke down over a theory he had long maintained, but only he could discern, that the *Constitution Act* provided a complete constitutional Code for the Colony.

> If they were to admit that the Constitution of the country was within the limits of the Constitution Act, he would ask what objection there could be to tacking bills of all kinds? There was nothing in the Constitution Act to prevent that being done; and, therefore, he argued that they were entitled, so far as regarded that Act, to resort to tacking whenever they thought proper to do so.[15]

He relied on two House of Commons precedents from the 17th century.

His initial premise was false. The Colony's Constitution was not found exclusively within the words of the *Constitution Act*. Parliamentary practice and usage, in particular, depended heavily on inherited custom. It was irrational, too, that an Attorney-General committed to statutory consolidation should subscribe to wholesale legislative tacking with its risk of hiding significant provisions within quite unrelated enactments. But, as matters turned out, the dispute about "tacking" became otiose.[16] Instead, the question became one of the propriety of presenting to the Council a conglomeration of Bills dressed up as a single Money Bill.

The two Houses appointed committees to examine the Assembly's proposals, the Council finding them unconstitutional, the Assembly maintaining the contrary. Meanwhile the Bill had been so burdened by provisions that were not cognate that the Council derisively labelled it the "Customs Import Duties, Gold Export Duty Act Amendment, Appropriation, Bill",[17] declared that its component parts could not be severed, and "laid aside" the whole Bill without report to the Assembly. The Bill had effectively been rejected.

The year drifted by, almost to the end of July, with nothing accomplished as to fiscal matters save the collection of new duties on the bare resolution of the Assembly, and the granting of supply in January. As Darling noted, in frustration, money allocated for the year was "overflowing in the Treasury" with no means to appropriate it to the necessary purposes of colonial administration.[18]

"Simply for the Sake of Further Triumph"

On 27 July 1865, Darling, who hoped vainly that an early con-ference between the Houses might have been negotiated, reported to the Secretary of State that those Houses were "now in a state of antagonism of which it is very difficult to foresee the result; and which will probably lead to much perplexity and embar-rassment".[19] The Assembly, provocatively and unreasonably, declined to sever the components of the conglomerate Bill.

Next day suspension of salary payments to government em-ployees was gazetted. Rusden colourfully remarked, "it was not obscurely threatened that the convicts in the gaols would soon be let loose upon society in order to terrify the Council".[20] It was an appalling position. The government had supply. There was no indication that the Council, in its more conciliatory humour, would resist a conventional Appropriation Bill.[21] Making civil servants pay for parliamentary warfare was reprehensible.

Petitions from both Houses urged the Governor to intervene to uphold their respective positions. Petitions from the rival supporters of Free Trade and Protection flooded into Parliament. Some half-hearted attempts at negotiation between the Chambers failed. It was Responsible Government at its most irresponsible. McCulloch, on 29 July, tendered his Ministry's resignation. It was declined.[22] Darling, who was supine in the contest, must have longed for the autocratic powers exercised by his uncle, Sir Ralph, when Governor of New South Wales in the 1820s.

After posturing and the assertion of "rights" had run their course,[23] Darling exulted that he had "succeeded in making tem-porary and provisional arrangements for meeting the inevitable pecuniary liabilities of the Government, in the present emer-gency" and that those arrangements were of "a very simple nature".[24] On the contrary, they were inimical to constitutional principle, most cumbersome in practice, and conducive to a logical outcome in which Parliament would need no formal sanction either for supply or appropriation.

Six Melbourne banks, with which the public revenue was deposited, were invited to

> make advances equal to the amount at the credit of the Colony, upon no other security than the pledge of the Government that the amount advanced would be repaid under the Governor's authority

whenever the existing dispute between the Council and the Assembly should be arranged.[25]

Five of the banks, "acting in concert" so Darling alleged, declined the invitation on legal advice that the proposal was illegal. The London Chartered Bank, of which Premier McCulloch was local director, accepted it, exposing both to a prospective conflict of interests.[26]

The ruse did not end there. Funds were advanced incrementally by the London Chartered Bank from 5 September. At once, creditors, including the bank, sued the government which allowed default judgement to be entered against it, on sighting a certificate of which the Governor would sign a warrant for payment directly from consolidated revenue, in pursuance of the *Crown Remedies and Liabilities Act* consolidated by Higinbotham and passed in May of that year. The Governor also obtained from the Audit Commissioners certificates confirming that the respective judgements were proper claims upon the Treasury.

Asked by Darling to give a confirmatory opinion as Attorney-General, Higinbotham was typically terse – "Her Majesty's Local Government has legally the power to enter into contracts binding on the Crown for purposes of a public nature, and necessary for carrying on the proper functions of Government, including contracts, to borrow money for the payment of existing legal public liabilities".[27] Given the seriousness of the emergency, and the contentious nature of the issues, such an *ex cathedra* pronouncement, without a single reason for or measure of its conclusion, was at best unhelpful.[28]

By October 1865 Darling was beginning to wilt under a constitutional dilemma that was too much for him. He lost patience with the Council when it requested him to submit to the Queen its petition seeking, in effect, imperial intervention "for maintaining in this Colony the Constitution as by law established".[29] Most pertinently, as to the bank accommodation, the petition, which was largely the work of Fellows, pointed out:

> 20. There is no Act in force in this Colony empowering the Governor, either alone or with the advice of the Executive Council, to borrow money without the sanction of the Legislature.

> 21. The confession of judgment for debts incurred without the authority of the Legislature, and for the purpose of applying the

consolidated revenue without the concurrence of this House, appears to us to be not only collusive but unconstitutional if not revolutionary.[30]

They were incontrovertible statements, but Darling attempted to traverse "this indictment" in a despatch of 61 numbered paragraphs prepared, no doubt, by Higinbotham.[31]

Darling castigated the Council for acting "simply for the sake of a further triumph" that "without any regard to their public responsibilities" would "see the Colony plunged into [further] confusion and difficulty".[32] The Assembly, on the other hand, in Darling's view had acted with moderation when provoked, and had worked so harmoniously with him that "the whole House" had presented him with an address of thanks for his support of its measures.[33] He also was "satisfied with the advice of the Responsible Law Officers of the Crown [Higinbotham and Michie]".[34] He ought not to have been. He was obviously committed to the Assembly rather than to the Council when he perceived that the motive behind the latter's petition was "to induce Her Majesty to pass a severe censure upon my conduct, if not to recall me from [my] high office".[35] He would have done well to have reflected further upon that possibility in ordering his future actions.

By November the tariff component of the conglomerate Bill had been passed by the Assembly as a discrete measure, sent to the Council, and again rejected. Darling noted that "the collection of duties under the higher rates fixed by the Resolutions of the Assembly immediately ceased, and the amounts received under them since they first came into operation will be refunded".[36] On 20 November he urged the Executive Council to ensure that the Assembly cease "to embarrass the Executive Government" and that there be either a new Appropriation Bill or a dissolution of Parliament. McCulloch signed a reply, assuredly of Higinbotham's composition, re-asserting the Assembly's position, and standing ready to face the people on the understanding that they be asked to determine "if, in future, their Representatives shall control the public finances".[37]

The Secretary of State visited unmixed censure on Darling, declaring that all steps taken to impose the tariff without full parliamentary sanction, and the contrived funding of colonial administration by unauthorized dealings with a bank, were improper and that "you have departed from the principle of conduct announced by yourself and approved by me – the principle of rigid adherence to the law". That departure had created a "continued violation of the law, with the concurrence of the Queen's representative".[38] Darling was instructed "to conform yourself strictly to the line of conduct which the law prescribes". An even stronger censure followed in January 1866, the draft of which was written by Cardwell himself in his tidy small script.[39]

The result, by the end of 1865, was that, through stubbornness on all sides, the business of the Colony had been allowed to suffer, and all the combatants, though bloodied but unbowed, equally protested constitutional propriety and concern for the wellbeing of Victoria. The new year would bring even more remarkable developments.

Interest meanwhile turned to the Supreme Court where, on 1 September 1865, five cases by numerous plaintiffs against the Crown were heard together.[40] Instituted by petition, they claimed recovery, as a debt, of duties paid under the new tariff but, so it was put, unlawfully imposed. The Crown pleaded "never indebted", and a specific plea that one of the privileges and powers of the Commons was to pass resolutions, charging customs duties, operative until the end of the then session of Parliament unless since incorporated in an Act, and that that privilege was inherited by the Victorian Legislative Assembly. The petitioners demurred to the specific plea as being bad in substance.

After hearing numerous counsel, not including the Crown Law Officers, the Full Court delivered its unanimous decision on 14 September. It found that the recovery of duties pursuant to resolution of the Assembly alone did not come within the privileges of that House. It was a privilege never claimed by the Commons in England, and it violated the established principle that "no tax can be imposed save with the full assent of the three estates".[41]

In October, the Legislative Council's petition to the Queen asserted, of the court proceedings, that the Supreme Court "had decided" that the collection of duties under the new tariff "was not warranted by law; but nevertheless the Governor still allows the pretended duties to be collected as if no such judgment had been pronounced".[42] Higinbotham, with more regard for beating the Council than for the public revenue, loftily advised that the government, as represented by the Assembly, could not "allow the decision of the Supreme Court ... to stop the collection of the duties". The Assembly's claimed privilege having been rejected by the court, the government could not "accept this decision as final on a question so vitally important to the collection of the revenue".[43] Application would be made to appeal to the Privy Council. Pending that, the government would treat the matter as still *sub judice* so that collection of duties must continue.

That position was not wholly unreasonable and did not warrant the conclusions of Sir Frederic Rogers at the Colonial Office that it was "perfectly disingenuous"[44] or that Darling was at fault "because he persisted in acting on the opinion of his L. Off^{rs} *after an adverse judgment of the Supreme Court*".[45] Nor did it betoken anarchy.[46] Darling was incautious, but the Colonial Office seems not to have seen the judgement or realized that the proceedings were interlocutory. The demurrer to the specific plea had succeeded, but the "never indebted" plea remained for determination. Until the court pronounced upon it, the ultimate position remained doubtful.

In December the Crown unsuccessfully sought to nonsuit the petitioners on the ground that they had no claim under the *Crown Remedies and Liabilities Act*, there being no express contract, and a contract with the Crown created by the wrongdoing of the Crown's agents could not be implied. The Full Court observed that, "the cause of action essentially arises out of contract – a contract implied by the law to repay that which it would be inconsistent with equity to retain".[47]

The force of those pronouncements was to some extent over-borne by the dissolution of Parliament that had already occurred on 11 December.

"Is This Dispute to Last Forever"

The new year 1866 saw McCulloch again resoundingly returned to power with a mandate from the *un*wealthy lower orders to pursue Protection. Michie, who, as Minister of Justice, had been an unlikely coadjutor with Higinbotham as a Crown Law Officer, lost his safe seat of St Kilda. He was punished for abandoning his allegiance to Free Trade. So was Higinbotham at Brighton where he faced strong opposition from J. W. Stephen (later a Supreme Court Judge) supported by the Free Trade Association.

At the hustings, Higinbotham depicted Stephen as – "only a pawn pushed forward on the chess board of politics and moved by unseen figures" – a man with no parliamentary experience. Reverting to his old conviction that Members of Parliament should be independent, he could not understand how Stephen "reconciles it with a sense of self-respect to receive assistance from any party for the purpose of sending him into Parliament". Here was a purely artless and unpractical form of politics. But Higinbotham persisted that voters must ask themselves:

> whether the representative House of Parliament shall in its jurisdiction have the right to legislate for the general body of this community, or whether particular classes and particular interests shall have the power year after year to excite Parliamentary dissension, to turn out one Government after another, for the purpose of procuring delay or overthrowing legislation in the interests of the body politic, to maintain it in the interests of a class or clique.[48]

As to this and other questions of the day, he declared: "My own opinion is fixed and I will act upon it".

He was lucky to be able to do so, as the electors received Stephen favourably and, of 746 votes cast, Higinbotham secured a majority of only 46.[49] The new parliamentary session commenced on 12 February 1866 as if nothing had changed. A tariff identical to that for 1865 passed the Assembly without division as a schedule to a Customs Bill submitted to the Council. It was there rejected on 13 March on the grounds that it "imperilled" the Civil List, improperly incorporated provisions as to duty on gold exports, and contained an unacceptable preamble.[50] The last, fought for by Higinbotham in the Assembly, tried to entrench his view that the Assembly alone granted supply to the Crown. He said:

> It is not pretended by any one that it was the original intention of the framers of our constitution that in financial matters the other House should have co-ordinate rights, for co-ordinate they are if you merely give to the Assembly the right to introduce money Bills and give to the Council an equal right to reject them.[51]

A preamble asserting the Assembly's pre-eminence in such matters would, he claimed, "serve as a perpetual reminder to this House of its own rights".

Denying that there had been any parliamentary "crisis",[52] he noted ominously that, should the Customs Bill be rejected by the Council, "then, looking at the decisive verdict pronounced by the country … I am very much mistaken if a real crisis does not come which will astonish those who provoked it"[53] – as if he were a mere bystander! While he hoped that he was mistaken, he added, "Is there any tribunal we can refer the practical question to, except the people? and, if not, is this dispute to last forever?".[54]

It seemed that it would. On the Council's rejection of the Bill, McCulloch resigned. O'Shanassy having withdrawn from the Assembly because of illness, Darling invited Fellows of the Council to form a new administration – an extraordinary manoeuvre as the two were as if political enemies. Fellows was willing to nominate members of a new administration if the Governor would guarantee passage of supply until the end of the necessary elections. That condition could not possibly be met. Darling turned back to McCulloch, suggesting that his Ministry remain in office, or that he construct a new Ministry, or nominate some other member of the Assembly to do so.[55] The Cabinet returned a lengthy "minute", clearly of Higinbotham's drafting, indicating their willingness to continue on the same path sanctioned by "the strong public opinion" of the recent elections. It was for the Council to yield, and make "such concessions as may render the continuance of Government according to law possible".[56]

McCulloch then tried to reintroduce the Customs Bill, but Speaker Murphy ruled that it could not be brought forward twice in the same session. Darling prorogued Parliament on 10 April and ordered a new session to commence next day.[57] The Bill sprang back to life, passed all Assembly stages immediately, and went back to the Council. Before the Council could consider it afresh, there intervened, *deus ex machina*, news of Darling's recall.

The Colonial Office, while considering Darling's management of the various crises to have been inept,[58] was careful not to displace him on that ground. He was popular in the Colony, and the predicaments he had faced were unusual. But he had opened the way for his own removal by prejudicial comments to the Secretary of State when forwarding an address by 22 past or present Executive Councillors (the name of Fellows second among the signatories), complaining about Darling's conduct.[59] He accused them of having wilfully suppressed "every material fact" in their "conspiracy", and he hoped "that the future course of political events may never designate any of them for the position of a confidential adviser of the Crown, since it is impossible their advice could be received with any other feelings than those of doubt and distrust".[60] Darling had, in effect, signed a warrant for his own execution.

"It is your own act now", replied Cardwell, "which leaves me no alternative; you force me to decide between yourself and the petitioners". It was the duty of the Queen's representative to stand aloof from all personal conflicts, but "in the present instance you have rendered this impossible". It was equally impossible, because of his "personal antagonism" to the petitioners, that Darling could "with advantage continue to conduct the government of the Colony".[61] For his part, Darling entertained "a deep and poignant sense of the unjust and cruel decision by which that retirement has been produced".[62]

The Council responded to the shock by proposing that there be a conference between the Houses, comprising seven representatives of each. It was held forthwith and the sticking points were resolved, enabling Supply and Appropriation Bills and a Customs Bill with scheduled tariff to pass all stages and be assented to by 18 April. Absent, for the second time, from the Assembly's representatives was Attorney-General Higinbotham because, as even Professor Morris had to admit, "he was not prepared to make concession".[63]

It was remarkable that, in Higinbotham's absence, accord was reached so promptly. It gave the lie to the portrayal of him, over the years, as the consummate politician of his age, and as the driving force of McCulloch's Ministry.[64] Much of the distress caused in 1865, and which yet lay ahead in 1866, was due to his intractability. Darling had paid a heavy price for acting "at every step … with the encouragement and advice of the most powerful figure among his ministers, Higinbotham".[65]

Apart from mortification at the plight of the Governor – "a wounded and ruined man"[66] – Higinbotham was unrepentant, turning his anger upon the Colonial Office, which he would continue to do for the rest of his life. He foreshadowed his approach, in February 1866, when he accused Cardwell of being "subject to the influence of insidious and designing persons", and continued:

It is hardly to be required that either the Government or the public men of this colony should bow their judgments implicitly to the opinion of a gentleman fifteen thousand miles away, a gentleman who does not possess by virtue of his position a right to control the acts of [such] public men … We have a constitution, and it is no part of that constitution that members of the Government should be responsible to the Secretary of State.[67]

By May, Higinbotham was heaping fuel upon the flames, telling the House:

I decline to enter into a justification of any of my acts, or of any advice I have tendered His Excellency the Governor, in consequence of any criticism which the Secretary of State may have been pleased to make. I am not responsible to the Secretary of State. It is in that gentleman's power to recall the Governor; it is not in his power to censure the Government. I deny his authority to criticise my acts.[68]

No doubt the Secretary of State had as much right as anyone else to criticize colonial politicians: it is in the nature of politics that it attracts criticism. The *Ballarat Star* remarked that, "Our Attorney-General may be a law unto himself and may have been, for a time, a law to the Governor, but he will not be a law to Downing-street, nor even to Mr Cardwell alone".[69] Cardwell's criticisms went further than idle censure. He was properly concerned that Victoria's Governor was being advised to act beyond limits authorized by law. Higinbotham's perpetual battle with the Colonial Office thereafter is considered in later chapters.

"The Very Vilest Faction"

On 7 May 1866 Darling quit the Colony amidst the acclamations of thousands. Public indignation at his treatment evoked a multitude of petitions to the Queen supporting him. He transmitted many of them before he left: Brigadier-General Carey, as Administrator, sent more. They might as well have been raindrops falling in the ocean, making no impression at the Colonial Office and receiving the briefest acknowledgements. Darling was fortified, however, by an address to the Queen from the Legislative Assembly acknowledging his service and proposing, as colonial regulations precluded his receiving any gratuity, a grant from Victorian funds of £20,000 to Lady Darling.[70]

At Downing Street, Cardwell had been succeeded as Secretary of State by the formidable Earl of Carnarvon who seemed to think that Darling was damned without redemption, not least because of his costly mishandling of the *Shenandoah* difficulties. The ex-Governor spent weeks after returning to London writing stultifying letters to Carnarvon appealing for some financial compensation, whether as a pension, or half pay since relinquishing office, or by acceptance of the Victorian grant.[71] Dismissed with brutal cussedness, his pleas were curtailed with the words "Lord Carnarvon regrets that you do not agree in the grounds of his decision, but cannot undertake to continue the discussion".[72] Even a request that the English Government not oppose a petition for relief Darling was minded to submit to the Westminster Parliament was rebuffed. It was "not expedient … to involve Her Majesty's Government in any pledge on the subject".[73] Dismayed and in despair, Darling resigned from the colonial service on 17 April 1867.

The new Victorian Governor, Sir John Manners-Sutton (from 1869 successor to the title Viscount Canterbury), was gradually drawn into a continuation of the war between the Houses which had smouldered since Darling's recall.[74] In March 1867 a Customs Bill, with scheduled duties, passed the Assembly in a form devised by Higinbotham to re-assert that House's primary power over Money Bills. It was returned by the Council with amendments. Committees of the Houses disagreed on resolving the disagreement, while Higinbotham, who would never surrender, pressed for reintroduction of his preamble, abandoned in the compromises of the previous year.

Those diversions were overtaken by news of Darling's resignation, interpreted, in Victoria, to mean the Colonial Office had no further ground for opposing Lady Darling's grant.[75] On 17 July McCulloch signed a minute advising the Governor "that provision be made upon the Estimates for the grant of 20,000*l*. (twenty thousand pounds) to Lady Darling". The Governor, without disclosing his own opinion, was "prepared at once to act upon the recommendation": while confidentially acquainting the Secretary of State that privately he thought the grant "liable to very grave objections on ground of general policy".[76]

In the Assembly, a number of members, led by Ireland, held a similar opinion when supplemental estimates, including the grant, were presented. Ireland denounced Darling's administration as incompetent, leading the supposedly mild-mannered Attorney-General to retort that the grant should have been passed unanimously and in silence.

> I rejoice that this vote will brand the enemies of Sir Charles Darling who pursued him while here, and who do not desist from that pursuit now. I will tell those honorable members that I have always considered the faction to which they belong as the very vilest faction by which this country has been cursed.[77]

The government otherwise contributed little to the debate, allowing the Opposition's fiery speeches to pass unheeded. McCulloch, however, insisted that Lady Darling's grant be a component of the Appropriation Bill, not a separate measure. In that form, after decisive passage through the Assembly, the Bill went to the Council and was rejected, not only because it incorporated the grant in general appropriation clauses, but also because "the grant itself is unconstitutional and highly mischievous, and calculated to produce corrupt practices in every department of the state".[78]

Thus the war of attrition resumed, and, for want of appropriation, there were no funds to conduct the business of government. The Colony returned to the financial impasse of 1865. Manners-Sutton trod precarious ground when he began to sign warrants to satisfy judgements against the Crown, obtained again under the *Crown Remedies and Liabilities Act*. He had sought Higinbotham's advice and been given the Delphic opinion that the power under the Act "ought not to be denied in any case except for clear and most cogent reasons" while, at the same time, the power was not "legally obligatory" and the Governor could decline to exercise it without assigning reasons.[79]

McCulloch recommended that Manners-Sutton follow Darling's example and prorogue Parliament briefly so that a new Appropriation Bill might be passed and presented to the Council.[80] The Governor declined. McCulloch, who was becoming adept at the manoeuvre, tendered his Ministry's resignation. Manners-Sutton sent a "memorandum" to Fellows inviting "the advice of those by whom the [Appropriation] Bill has been rejected".[81] Fellows felt it "improper for him, on the present occasion, to assume the position of the Governor's legal adviser" but noted that no attempt had been made by anyone "to bring the two Houses into harmony".[82]

The Governor went back to McCulloch who insisted on a prorogation followed quickly by a new session. Manners-Sutton yielded and announced, on reopening Parliament, that "I rely upon your making adequate provision for the requirements of the public service". But he soon perceived that "the respective positions of the two Houses … might, perhaps be regarded as remaining unchanged".[83] There was no need for "perhaps": by November the deadlock, as it was commonly called, caused Parliament to stand in abeyance so that all animosity might be concealed during the visit to Melbourne of Prince Alfred, Duke of Edinburgh.

Meanwhile, a new Secretary of State (the Duke of Buckingham), to Higinbotham's fury, lectured the Governor about the mischief done by the Assembly in attempting to include "in the Appropriation Bill a grant [to Lady Darling] exceptional in its character and notoriously obnoxious to a large portion of the Upper House, instead of sending up that grant in a form in which it might have received a full and deliberate discussion".[84] It was understandable, at Downing Street, that the Council should regard the stratagem as a form of coercion. Only on reflection did the Secretary of State recognize that the overwhelming majority of the Assembly, representing a like majority of the community, wished the grant to be made, and, in a *volte-face* one month later, he gave a broad hint that the Council ought to reconsider its position.[85] The Council did not. Parliament was dissolved on 30 December 1867. At the ensuing general elections, the McCulloch Government was emphatically endorsed and, in Brighton, Higinbotham increased his majority.[86]

In those most abnormal of times, Higinbotham delivered one of the momentous public speeches of his career that prompted Deakin to proclaim him "the great Liberal Orator".[87] It was late in 1867 when, as Turner recounted, "demonstrations in the form of public meetings were manifold and vehement", and, at one of them,

> Mr Higinbotham declared to a huge gathering that all that was required for good Government was a representative of the Crown and the representatives of the people. The third estate which they

had foolishly created was an oligarchy of wealth, insolently claiming to be the principal of all three.[88]

Higinbotham's oratorical magnetism was at its most powerful, and cemented his place more firmly in the popular mind as the champion of the ordinary citizen, supposedly oppressed by the Legislative Council and the Colonial Office. As Frank Gavan Duffy would sum up Higinbotham's standing among the citizenry – "My name was once the people's battle-cry".[89]

Attention returned to the Supreme Court where, between 3 and 24 December 1867, the action *Alcock* v. *Fergie* was entertained.[90] Alcock, who owed money to Fergie under a loan agreement, was one of those who had a default judgement against the Crown, for furniture sold to the government. It was alleged that Alcock, having obtained extended time for payment from Fergie in consideration of assigning to him the benefit of the judgement, was nevertheless sued by Fergie for full recovery without any extension of time.

Nutt and Murphy, solicitors of Melbourne, submitted to Higinbotham, on 29 November, a brief to act for Alcock, given that "the present action raises the important question of whether a judgment by default against the Crown is valid". Higinbotham declined to support the procedure to which he had been so enthusiastic a party, and returned the proffered brief and its covering letter without reply.[91] Instead, Alcock was left with Billing and Harris of the Bar representing him against a daunting team for the defendant – Ireland, Q.C., Dr Mackay, Fellows and Dr Hearn.

It was obvious why Higinbotham stayed away – Billing was given a grilling. To the contention that the Prothonotary's certificate of signing judgement enlivened power to charge consolidated revenue, Barry retorted –

> Then the Parliament has extinguished itself by Act of Parliament? You seem to be of opinion that all the acts alluded to can be done without the necessity of an Appropriation Act.[92]

Stawell added that, "a ministry might not call Parliament together for a whole year, and spend the whole revenue of the colony as they thought fit".[93]

Nevertheless, the plaintiff enjoyed substantive success. Although the court found no precedent enabling the government to enter into contracts binding the state without parliamentary authority, and held that taking legal proceedings merely to recover a debt neither conferred any power nor validated any act, it concluded that the plaintiff's judgement had to stand because no defence had been pleaded in those proceedings. Such a judgement could then be signed consistently with the *Crown Remedies and Liabilities Act*, and thus far, the plaintiff's judgement was valid and assignable.[94]

That enactment did not repeal by implication the *Constitution Act* or the *Audit Act*, nor was it in substance an *Appropriation Act* permitting a special appropriation of the revenue to satisfy all judgements against the Crown. So the plaintiff's original judgement, although valid, was incapable of being satisfied until Parliament voted money for the purpose. "It is left to Parliament", said Stawell,

> to determine whether the judgment obtained ... should be satisfied or not. It is possible, we do not say probable, that this judgment may never be satisfied; but it is in our opinion regular, and we deem it a valuable security.[95]

The Governor and his advisers read the judgement with feigned surprise. Higinbotham all but sneered at it, telling the Assembly that it was no more than "an expression of opinion" by the judges extra-judicially. Being, on that view, mere *obiter dicta*, Higinbotham,

> communicated that opinion to the Treasurer, with the remark that, although it was an opinion deserving of respect, ... it was not binding upon the Government, and that it rested with Her Majesty's advisers to decide whether they would or would not give effect to it.[96]

Fortunately those other advisers kept their own counsel and spared the Colony another bruising contest by recommending that the Governor abandon authorizing payment directly from consolidated revenue of money due under judgements against the Crown. For good measure, the Colonial Office, always opposed to avoiding the want of an *Appropriation Act* by conceding default judgements against the Crown, warned Manners-Sutton that he acted at his peril. While the law empowered him to refuse a warrant for direct disbursement of public funds without parliamentary sanction, "Her Majesty's Government are unable to relieve you from the responsibility of deciding for yourself" how to act constitutionally.[97]

Buckingham's despatch, regretting the Assembly's attempt to coerce the Council, was received in Melbourne on 6 March 1868. Manners-Sutton sent a copy to McCulloch who responded with a minute, having all the attributes of Higinbotham's authorship, that "deeply … regretted that Her Majesty's Government should have seen fit to depart from their former determination – 'that the controversy must be locally decided'". As the government held the latest election results to have been "absolutely conclusive", it would not "take any course, submit to any condition, or offer any advice inconsistent with that decision". The Governor replied that he was bound by his instructions: the McCulloch Ministry resigned.[98]

Manners-Sutton was relieved to be able to rely on those instructions. He had scrupulously maintained his impartiality in public despite his private aversion to grants like that proposed. It was deceitful for Higinbotham, years later, to represent him as

> a Governor who came to this country for the purpose of giving the Legislative Council a victory over the Legislative Assembly, and who did it. And the representative not of the Crown but of the foreign nobleman who is at the head of the Colonial Office will do it again if any question arises between the two branches of the legislature. He must do it in obedience to his instructions.[99]

For one who was supposedly so outstanding a lawyer and politician, where were Higinbotham's initiatives when the ship of state was becalmed for nearly a year in a Sargasso Sea so largely of his making? Had he not been so headstrong and proud, he might, for example, have proposed that a key to the deadlock be found in petitioning the Parliament at Westminster. Victoria's *Constitution Act* was a creature of that Parliament which still could legislate concerning it by paramount force. When apprised of the Council's defiance of the repeatedly expressed will of the electorate, the Westminster Parliament might well have reckoned that the original plan for a nominated Council, as in New South Wales, should be reinstated. Although also imperfect in many respects, it had worked well enough in the neighbouring Colony, and supplied an effective brake on deadlocks by actual or threatened "swamping" of the Upper House into submission. But Higinbotham would not parley with Downing Street, and offered no other solution to the problem than that of complete capitulation by his opponents.

After great difficulty, during which Victoria's government was paralysed for many weeks, the Governor persuaded Charles Sladen of the Council to form a Ministry from 6 May.[100] It survived only for two months, but that marked the end of Higinbotham's political power. To his dismay, Fellows, his arch-enemy in the Council, had taken the Assembly seat of St Kilda in March, and was Sladen's Minister of Justice. The Darling deadlock was meekly resolved, not in Victoria, but in England. Darling negotiated a settlement under which, on his waiving all claims for his wife or himself to a Victorian grant, he was permitted to withdraw his resignation from the colonial service, and was then retired on a small pension.[101]

Out of office, Higinbotham was enraged by that outcome. In the House he belligerently maintained the right of the Assembly to combine appropriation and taxation measures. As to the Darling grant, "the country" had spoken such that it was,

> the imperative duty of honorable members on this side to insist upon the grant by all means in their power, and, in defiance of all consequences, to assert that the grant must be paid, so long as a Government exists in this colony.[102]

Given that, in his view, Victoria's future was cloaked in "great darkness and doubt",[103] he renewed his attack on the Secretary of State, and the inappropriateness, as he saw it, of that Minister's control, by instructions, over the Governor, notwithstanding that Victoria had Responsible Government. He perceived demons everywhere. The collective mind of the House of Commons had been poisoned by former residents of Victoria then living in London, "gentlemen who were exceedingly anxious to attach themselves to the draggled skirts of English society", who were "reviling, and falsifying, and vilifying the country to which they owe all they have and all they are". If the poison worked upon the Commons, then "it would be as necessary for the people of this country – if they wish to preserve their privileges – to resist the House of Commons just as they have resisted and are determined to resist the Colonial-office".[104] He would therefore proclaim "disloyalty to Downing-street rule", while professing "sincere loyalty" to the English throne and the British connexion.

> We are entitled to demand that the Governor of this colony shall either obtain from Downing-street a distinct claim of interference in

our affairs, or a distinct avowal of the right to interfere in our affairs. We cannot deal with Downing-street, we can only deal with the agent, or rather the person who is most improperly treated as the agent of Downing-street, who tells us that he has received instructions he cannot depart from; and we have merely to tell him that these instructions cannot be allowed to interfere with our liberties … I believe it will be … well worth our submitting to a far greater amount of privation than we have yet undergone, in order to settle once for all a question so important as this.[105]

His colleagues and constituents were less anxious to endure further privation. McCulloch, returning as Premier in July 1868, was disposed to make political concessions Higinbotham would not tolerate. He declined to continue as Attorney-General, but served as Vice-President of the Board of Land and Works only until February 1869. There was a lingering twilight in 1869 when he seemed scarcely able to comprehend that he no longer held the reins of power. His "resolutions" directed against the Colonial Office are considered in the next chapter.

"My Views are at Present so Desponding"

The case of Hugh Glass is noticed at greater length in a companion volume.[106] A former squatter of immense wealth, Glass, and an associate, were summoned to the bar of the House to answer charges of contempt and breach of parliamentary privilege in having promoted a fund from which bribes were offered to Members of Parliament. Always concerned about alleged corruption, Higinbotham maintained that the House alone should protect its privileges and not leave such matters to the courts.[107]

Accordingly, he was exercised when Glass, having confessed his wrongdoing, and been gaoled indefinitely pursuant to the Speaker's warrants to the Sergeant at Arms, applied to the Supreme Court by *habeas corpus* for relief. His counsel submitted that the warrants were void for failing to particularize the offence for which Glass was imprisoned, and for being issued with no seal affixed. The Full Court accepted that the warrants failed for want of particularity.[108]

In the House, Higinbotham condemned the judgement. It had been pronounced by Stawell – the very architect of the Constitution – whose professed aim in the 1850s had been to ensure that "the Legislative Assembly should represent the House of Commons in England, and should be possessed of all the powers and rights in regard to Victoria that the House of Commons possesses in respect to England".[109] Counsel for Glass had conceded that a warrant in the form issued in respect of Glass would have been valid if issued by the Commons. In Higinbotham's view, there could be no rational basis for a different interpretation in Victoria, and the Assembly had:

> good reason to complain of [the Supreme Court's] decision, and not merely of the decision itself, but of the manner in which it was given, the circumstances under which it was given, and, above all, I will say the quarter from which it proceeded.[110]

He protested that inadequate notice of the court proceedings had been given to the Attorney-General, and the decision reached with unseemly haste. He censured Stawell for a claimed miscarriage of justice – "the present Chief Justice is responsible – personally responsible – for the failure of our Constitution to give effect to our claims, if there has been such a miscarriage in the attempt to give effect to those claims". Stawell ought to have consulted his own memory as to drafting the Constitution, not sought to have construed it as an abstract form of statutory language, because "the framer of a law is likely to know better than anyone else what was his intention in framing that law".[111] Higinbotham paid a glowing tribute to Stawell when formerly in office as Attorney-General,[112] but thought the Colony had suffered a loss when so able a man "was removed into the splendid obscurity and comparatively insignificant sphere where he has since been"[113] – (an ungracious and undeserved conclusion). Higinbotham hoped, in short, that the House would defy the court's decision.[114]

In written form the address appears typically reasoned and assertive. Its strictures upon the judges were hedged about with assurances that no personal slight was intended: but things needed to be said frankly in protection of the privileges of the House. The language, though emphatic, did not support the conclusion of the *Argus* that it constituted "a most vindictive speech";[115] nor did it amount to "a passionate spate of words".[116] Stripped of the *argumentum ad hominem* visited on Stawell and the judges, it was a persuasively argued address.

The Supreme Court declined to rescind its decision. The Assembly, after considering the report of a committee, appealed to the Privy Council where Higinbotham's views were substantially vindicated. The Board held that the Assembly inherited in 1855 the Commons' privilege of committing for contempt "of the House generally, without specifying what the character of the contempt is".[117]

The Brighton electors were becoming increasingly disenchanted with their Member, now politically powerless and pursuing, not their interests, but his own doctrinaire notions. Brighton capitalists must have pondered on his celebrated pronouncements in discussing the land question in 1869:

> In that struggle of capital against those who have no capital, whom it is desired to endow with a portion of the advantages resulting from the public possession of the lands, capital is always sure to gain the victory ... those who are eager to obtain land, and are willing to obtain it by unjust and fraudulent means, if assisted and backed by capital, will always succeed in getting it.[118]

In 1870, though he declared himself weary of the long conflict between the Houses, he foresaw that war must continue until the Council yielded, prompting the *Australasian* to write that he had "gone much too far".[119] It hoped that, for his own reputation, "he may long continue in the position of a private Member", not that of a Minister.[120] But, even as a private Member, his days were numbered. In the 1871 elections, he offered his Brighton constituents more of the same – defiance of the Colonial Office; the assurance of another deadlock; sympathy for Protection if the majority wished it, though his allegiance was still to Free Trade; and concern for public education. Local issues were ignored. As to the emerging debate on Australian Federation he saw no merit in it. He all but invited the electors to look to another representative:

> I do not feel at all sure that the course I may take in Parliament will be one that will render me a representative deserving of your continued support in that position. I own to you that my views of public affairs are at present so desponding that I do not know what other course I can take as a politician than simply to wait.[121]

His constituents took the hint and dumped him.[122] Some of the press rejoiced that he would no longer be in the House as "the rallying point of the Adullamites", and thought his retirement beneficial to all – "He needs rest. Above all he needs to be freed from that irritating sense of unredressed wrong which is consuming his heart".[123] Thereafter he drifted politically until winning the seat of East Bourke Boroughs, at a by-election in May 1873. But politics had no future for him and he quickly became frustrated by his relinquishment of power and by his impression that Parliament had become little more than a debating society. As he told the Assembly:

> We suffer shame and humiliation in the feeling that we are called night after night to sit and discuss public measures when we know that the whole of our discussion is fruitless, and that our talk is idle, aimless and purposeless.[124]

The successive Ministries of Francis and Kerferd survived respectively for two years and for one year, until Graham Berry came to power in August 1875. It was his first Ministry and, being in a minority, it lasted only for a little over two months, being unpopular in the House because of Berry's plans for a harsh land tax.

When the House rejected his measures, Berry sought from Sir William Stawell, then Acting Governor, a dissolution that was refused on contentious grounds, and made the subject of detailed reports by Stawell to the Secretary of State.[125] McCulloch was invited to form a new Ministry and did so – his fourth and last – with effect from 20 October 1875. Higinbotham fulminated in the House about Stawell's sending his reports to Downing Street to "a foreign authority … to be judged of by a person who had as much right to interfere in the affairs of this Colony as one of the Parliamentary doorkeepers has".[126]

That was the breaking point. As Turner summarized the outcome:

> Suddenly Sir James McCulloch turned upon [Higinbotham] and delivered a scathing indictment, charging him with being the cause of all the disorganisation that had ever arisen in the Assembly, and declaring that … he trusted Mr Higinbotham would be careful to sit in direct Opposition, for [McCulloch] would give no countenance for any scheme for embroiling the colony with the Imperial Government.[127]

Until resigning his seat in January 1876, Higinbotham generally opposed McCulloch, but he had become even more disenchanted with Berry's tactics which prompted him to complain that, "We have nothing else to do now but to criminate one another. We have become like common scolds in this House".[128] With the erection of the Berry "stonewall" of filibuster and technical obstruction, Higinbotham resigned in disillusionment, unsure whether it was "a right step or a wrong step, a wise step or an unwise step".[129] But he had been unable to agree to "using the forms of the House even to effect an object which I anxiously desired to effect" – to obstruct passage of the McCulloch Ministry's Budget.[130] It was an odd ground for resignation by one who had so repeatedly used the forms of the House to try to have his own way when Attorney-General. He departed, with renewed reprobation of party politics, and a typical epigram –

> I have always been of opinion that the two principles which ought to lie at the root of all government and all legislation in this country … are these – absolute political equality to all citizens before the law, and as a consequence of political equality the absolute supremacy of the majority in the deliberative council of the nation.[131]

6

"The Destiny of Our Colonies is Independence"

"Really Governed By a Person Named Rogers"

Higinbotham never forgave the Colonial Office for its treatment of Darling and, implicitly, of himself. To adapt an expression much used of a Federal Ministry somewhat similarly placed nearly a century later, he resolved to, and did, "maintain the rage" in a manner equally petulant and unmeritorious. His simmering resentment at times boiled over, especially when he became Chief Justice, as will be seen later.[1] Meanwhile, he inveighed against the Colonial Office's "vindictive displeasure" visited upon Darling as "a crime … yet unavenged", and he sought to avenge it.[2]

A *Westminster Review* article, "Democratic Government in Victoria", concluded that Darling had been "a mere puppet in the hands of his Ministers" and had aided them "in doing violence to the law". It urged the Legislative Council to stand fast, and, in terms of present relevance –

> Let the colony, if it chooses, separate from the empire altogether. But until it does so, it is our duty to insist that at least the constitution which it has made for itself shall be respected – that it shall rule itself according to the law which is its protection – that it shall not claim to have all the privileges of a separate State without incurring the obligations of independence.[3]

With such sentiments in the air, the House of Lords entered on a debate, in May 1868, that canvassed inconclusively the extent to which British control should be maintained over the colonies.[4] In the assessment of Dr Alpheus Todd, "leading statesmen, on both sides of the House, adverted to the constitutional position of a Colonial Governor, and on his duty to protect the Crown, if need be, against the proposals of his Ministers".[5] When he discovered what had happened, Higinbotham seethed. Observing that very few members participated in the debate, he protested that:

> Six of them … denied the existence of responsible government in this colony, and four out of the six have been either Secretaries of State for the Colonies or Under-Secretaries. The seventh – the only member … who asserted on behalf of these colonies the right of self-government, and traced to its full and legitimate conclusions the effect of those rights – was the Lord High Chancellor [Sir Hugh Cairns].[6]

That was not wholly accurate. Cairns had spoken in support of the Duke of Buckingham, then Secretary of State, who had delivered, in the view of Carnarvon, his predecessor, an "extremely bad" speech.[7] The majority, however, deprecated the recent constitutional excesses in Victoria: Carnarvon and the Marquis of Salisbury promoting the need for continuing imperial control throughout the Empire.

In speaking to the series of parliamentary resolutions he advanced in 1869, Higinbotham poured scorn on the Lords majority, attacking them one by one with sarcasm and personal insult, particularly ridiculing Carnarvon[8] – who had repelled Darling's appeals. Higinbotham seems to have treated the matter almost as a cruel game. He played to his Victorian gallery, catching their attention by his darts and barbs (many of them ill-founded), parading himself as if a player on a world stage and closely acquainted with his British counterparts (none of whom he had met), and caring not whose good name he besmirched. Once again, it was little more than scoring points as if in an undergraduate debate at Trinity College. There would, however, come a day of reckoning when he would reflect with embarrassment on what he had done. Carnarvon, visiting Australia in 1887, dined cordially with "the fiery & violent Higinbotham whom I well remember of old … I was very glad of the meeting. I believe he had said previously to Sir H. Loch 'I hope Ld. C does not remember my old speeches'".[9]

Higinbotham did not learn of the Lords debate until 1869, the year in which he drifted to the backbench of the Victorian

Legislative Assembly, having resigned from the Executive Council, and declined to retain the courtesy title "the Honourable". Early in November, when the MacPherson Ministry was briefly in office, Higinbotham, on a pretext of no present concern,[10] moved in the Assembly for the adoption of five resolutions of considerable constitutional import. Those of immediate moment consisted, first, of a protest against "any interference, by legislation of the Imperial Parliament, with the internal affairs of Victoria" unless by consent.[11] Second, and more significantly:

> That the official communication of advice, suggestions, or instructions, by the Secretary of State for the Colonies to Her Majesty's representative [the Governor] in Victoria, on any subject whatsoever connected with the administration of the local government [with a presently immaterial exception], is a practice not sanctioned by law, derogatory to the independence of the Queen's representative, and a violation both of the principles of the system of responsible government and of the constitutional rights of the people of this colony.[12]

Finally, and most significantly, there was a resolution that the Assembly join in measures to put "an early and final stop to the unlawful interference of the Imperial Government in the domestic affairs of this colony".[13]

Those three resolutions had about them a sense of harmony and consistency sharply at odds with yet another resolution expressing the desire of the Victorian community to "remain an integral portion of the British Empire".[14] The propositions were mutually exclusive, but a suggested explanation of Higinbotham's approach is offered below.

There was no substance to the resolution that sought to strike down Imperial *legislative* interference in Victoria's internal affairs. No such interference existed or was in prospect. So long as Victoria remained a British Colony, the Westminster Parliament retained power to legislate by paramount force on Victoria's constitutional position and on matters of common concern, such as copyright and merchant shipping laws, that benefited from identical legislation throughout the Empire. The Parliament at Westminster otherwise made no attempt to legislate for Victoria's domestic purposes.

Putting aside, for the moment, the position of the Governor, Higinbotham's greatest concern was developed in his last resolution that sought to stop Imperial interference in Victorian affairs. Speaking to it, he attacked in turn the Colonial Office as an institution, various Secretaries of State for the Colonies, and successive permanent Under-Secretaries. His remarks, occupying more than an hour, revealed a remarkable lack of tact, a remarkable want of understanding of the workings of the Colonial Office, and an egregious distortion of constitutional principle.

He began with the generalization that:

> We all know, though we don't like to say it, that responsible government does not exist [in Victoria]. We don't govern ourselves, and we know it. We are all ashamed of it, though we don't dare to say it.[15]

The claimed want of Responsible Government was, he said, due to usurpation by the Secretary of State of powers properly reposing in the Victorian Cabinet. He believed, falsely, that most Secretaries of State for the Colonies had little or nothing to do with the office over which they presided – "there is not a department of the English Government which is controlled with less knowledge than the department of the Colonial Office". He contended that, because those Ministers rarely visited the colonies, they knew nothing about them, and that the functioning of the Colonial Office was one of mindless delegation.

> An ignorant Minister, and a transient Minister, quickly supplanted by the changes in party politics, certainly point to one conclusion, and that is that the permanent officers of the department are the real governors. I believe, myself, that it is not the Secretary of State for the Colonies, who appends his name to the despatches, who is the real author of them, but his clerks.[16]

He then made an unguarded remark, that would later be visited against him with censure, asserting that, since Responsible Government, the Australian Colonies had been "really governed during the whole of that time by a person named Rogers"[17] a reference to Sir Frederic Rogers (later Baron Blachford), Under-Secretary for the Colonies since 1860. Higinbotham protested that Rogers had a settled policy of inculcating in each Secretary of State all the inflexible traditions, practices and ways observed in the Colonial Office for generations.

Those statements, delivered in excited oratory, swayed an audience that was as ignorant of the workings of the Colonial

Office as was Higinbotham himself. His representations were unsound and unfair. The staff, over whom the Under-Secretary presided, collectively had a vast knowledge, not necessarily augmented by personal visitation, of the whole colonial Empire. Many of them were experienced lawyers: all were experts in their field. The surviving minutes, so carefully maintained and laboriously handwritten, that were appended to every despatch or other communication to the office, testify to the competence of the Colonial Office clerks – who were all senior officers, not merely administrative staff – and to the professional quality of their work. Matters requiring a decision or a written reply by the Secretary of State would pass through several hands, with cross-references made to previous or related files, comments (sometimes very serious, and sometimes very droll) on the issues and personalities involved, with a recommendation for action and, usually, a draft despatch for the Minister's approval. At the higher levels the drafts would undergo rigorous review and, often, reshaping.

When placed before the Secretary of State, the minutes and related documents would ordinarily be scrutinized in detail. Sometimes further alteration of the drafts would be called for by the Minister to reflect government policy or to pursue a different strategy. It was never the case that the Secretary of State acted as a mindless and mechanical signatory to documents prepared at the direction of the Under-Secretary.

The personal attack on Sir Frederic Rogers was unworthy of a man in Higinbotham's position who knew virtually nothing of the subject of his criticism. As Mr Knox has put it, "had Higinbotham known the mind of his *bête noire* he might have found him tolerable after all".[18] Rogers, who succeeded to a baronetcy in 1851 and was later created, successively, K.C.M.G. and G.C.M.G., was an able lawyer who, after a brilliant academic career, and a successful Bar practice, was a legal adviser to the Colonial Office before succeeding Herman Merivale as permanent Under-Secretary in 1860.

A much more reliable prophet than Higinbotham ever was, Rogers had no aspirations to impose the Colonial Office and its perceptions on the burgeoning Empire. He foresaw that its component parts would gradually go their own ways, but, as he hoped, in a spirit of accord and mutual respect. He was the last

man to be ramming down an unwilling Victorian throat any unpalatable form of government.

Rogers, when acting as legal adviser to the Colonial Office,
had looked philosophically, though with some sadness, on the
Constitution Bills for New South Wales and Victoria that yielded
Responsible Government. In 1854 he wrote privately that the Bills
were –

> little less than a legislative Declaration of Independence on the part
> of the Australian colonies … What remains to complete colonial
> independence except command of the land and sea forces, I don't
> quite see … It is a great pity that, give as much as you will, you
> cannot please the colonists with anything short of absolute inde-
> pendence, so that it is not easy to say how you are to accomplish
> what we are, I suppose, all looking to – the eventual parting
> company on good terms.[19]

He reiterated that position late in his term as Under-Secretary:

> I had always believed … that the destiny of our colonies is inde-
> pendence; and that, in this point of view, the function of the
> Colonial Office is to secure that our connexion, while it lasts, shall
> be as profitable to both parties, and our separation, when it comes,
> as amicable as possible.[20]

Being unaware of those views, Higinbotham's public attack not
only hurt the Under-Secretary personally but caused Rogers great
anxiety how to contain such inflammatory proposals should the
Victorian Government act on them, as further considered below.[21]

"Strike It in the Face With the Back of Your Gloved Hand"

Two matters call for comment. First, it is scarcely credible that
Higinbotham should have committed himself to such public
denunciations of personalities and of the Colonial Office, relying
only on his imaginings and suppositions. Nothing suggests that
he maintained a correspondence with anyone in Britain who
might have lent colour to his wild surmises. Had he acquainted
himself with the facts, he would have found that, at heart, his
position was not greatly at odds with the conciliatory policies of
Rogers. Had he advanced his proposals for change with diplomacy and tact, Higinbotham might well have reached a cordial

resolution with the Colonial Office. But, as repeatedly noticed, qualities of that kind were foreign to Higinbotham the politician.

Secondly, it is in character that Higinbotham did not act, when in power as Attorney-General, immediately after the Darling *contretemps*, but stood by until he no longer had the parliamentary and ministerial authority to press home his proposals. It was as if he did not really want to see his resolutions applied. They were a bluff. Throughout his life he lacked incisiveness, preferring to dwell on issues in the abstract and on merely theoretical courses of action that were open, rather than to see them carried into effect. He recognized that as an argument against his 1869 resolutions, conceding that political colleagues might fairly ask – "You were five years in office; you profess to have strong opinions on this subject; why did you not take the course which you ask us to take?". His lame answer was that he had only recently become aware of the 1868 debates in the House of Lords.[22]

Such hesitancy suggests that Higinbotham, the powerful demagogic orator, while able to inflame feelings by his rhetoric, and to commit his spoken thoughts to equally powerful writing, lacked any commitment to see those thoughts translated into deeds. It might well have suited him that his 1869 resolutions captured attention without his having to do more. Perhaps he realized that, had they been implemented to the extent further mentioned below, Victoria would have suffered commercially and in many other ways. So he was well content to huff and puff demonstratively without having the will or intention to blow the house down.

The thrust of his resolutions went far beyond personal abuse. He advocated a policy which, if literally adopted, would have turned Victoria into a republic: something he clearly did not want.[23] He wished to preserve the imperial and monarchical ties on condition that the English Government kept itself at arm's length. Nevertheless, the Victorian governments of the day saw in the resolutions the seeds of revolution, and abandoned them.[24] Higinbotham later angrily recalled that the group of resolutions,

> after a lengthened and animated discussion, in which every prominent politician who was a member of that House of Parliament took part, was passed by a majority of two votes to one. But this debate took place after public opinion, clearly expressed at repeated general elections, had sustained a decisive defeat through the

action of the Colonial Office. The resolution of the Legislative Assembly was disregarded, and the community, then disheartened, quickly became, and has ever since continued, profoundly indifferent.[25]

He had made his intentions plain enough in 1869 when he described his resolutions as being a threat – "the only language that an Englishman, in his coarser nature, can understand".[26] He wanted to retain the imperial connexion, not to create a republic.[27] He was convinced that the Colonial Office would yield, and was discountenanced when it did not. But that did not make him a republican. The opinion, in the *Oxford History of Australia*, that "George Higinbotham's uncompromising anti-imperialism remained a source of republican inspiration", is misconceived. Higinbotham always regarded the British Isles as "home": his support for the Queen and for the Empire (if freed of the fetters of the Colonial Office) has been noticed often in these pages. Republicans could have derived no comfort from his views, for he wrote, at the close of his life:

> There is no immediate danger of Republicanism. It were to be wished, indeed, that it could be raised in some one or another of these Colonies as a question of practical politics, for as soon as a government & the people came to understand the necessary consequences of the adoption of a Republican system in one or all of the Australian Colonies they would assuredly regret it.[28]

The violence of Higinbotham's threat emerged when he urged the Victorian Assembly to stop "very quickly and simply … this whole system of illegal interference" by Downing Street. At the cost of a sheet of paper and a mail delay of three months, the Victorian Premier ought, he said, to write to the Secretary of State, offering to communicate directly with him on any matters of mutual concern, but telling him that,

> after a day to be named, no official communication addressed to Her Majesty's representative [the Governor] on any subject relating to Victorian affairs, except the reference of Bills home, would be entertained by Her Majesty's advisers, would be received by them, would be permitted to have official publication in this country, or would be laid on the table of either House of Parliament.[29]

Even if that resulted in suspension of diplomatic relations between the two countries for a period, he believed, with arresting naivety, that Victoria would "suffer absolutely nothing" from it.[30] He maintained that the English government, as to such matters as trade and commerce, would be the first and greater loser. He also asserted, without having any basis for doing so, that, if Victoria set the example, the other Australian Colonies would follow. That, at a time when Australian Federation was gathering pace, was an unrealistic assumption. He concluded that the Colonial Office system was:

> a mere straw image of official intrigue, and unlawful arbitrary interference. If you reason with it, you degrade yourselves. If you go to it, and strike it in the face with the back of your gloved hand, you will see it tumble in a heap at your feet, and the morrow after you have done so you will be establishing in this country a government which has never yet existed.[31]

The colour of his language ensured transitory support, and the resolutions passed to the committee stages without opposition. But his charges against the Colonial Office and its personnel have been well described as "extravagant to the point of absurdity".[32]

Victoria's Governor, Viscount Canterbury, reported those proceedings to the Secretary of State with considerable misgivings. At Downing Street, the Colonial Office clerks and Rogers himself shared that concern.[33] In Victoria, however, Higinbotham's initiative had petered out. The MacPherson Ministry lasted only until April 1870. Although it had time enough to act on the resolutions, it had lost interest in them. So had the third McCulloch Ministry and its immediate successors. Nevertheless, the Colonial Office, although considering Higinbotham's threat to be no more than that, for more abundant caution, treated it seriously.

"Secret Agents of an Irresponsible Authority"

Higinbotham's remaining resolution of present concern touched upon the office of Governor, another subject about which he maintained an obsessively irrational position for the rest of his days. He relied on the premise, which he, as an intelligent and well read lawyer, must have known was impossibly false, at least at that period of colonial development, that Victoria was a "sovereign State" and the Governor its "sovereign".[34] Victoria never was, is not, and (absent secession from the Australian

Commonwealth) never will be a sovereign State. At the material time it was a self-governing colony under the Crown within the British Empire. So far from being a local "sovereign", Victoria's Governor in the 19th century was not even a "Viceroy" in the strict sense of one who was not merely the Crown's local representative, but one who governed a country in the name and by the authority of the Crown as supreme ruler. So much was stated succinctly in Sir Charles Tarring's *Chapters on the Law Relating to the Colonies*:

> The Governor of a colony (in ordinary cases) cannot be regarded as a Viceroy; nor can it be assumed that he possesses general sovereign power. His authority is derived from his commission and limited to the powers thereby expressly or impliedly entrusted to him.[35]

The Colony of Victoria, for that purpose, was an "ordinary case".

Higinbotham would have been fully acquainted with the 1835 statement of principle by the Judicial Committee of the Privy Council in *Cameron* v. *Kyte*:

> If a Governor had, by virtue of that appointment, the whole sovereignty of the colony delegated to him as a Viceroy, and represented the King in the government of that colony, there would be good reason to contend that an act of sovereignty done by him would be valid and obligatory upon the subject living within his government, provided the act would be valid if done by the Sovereign himself … But if the Governor be an officer merely with a limited authority from the Crown, his assumption of an act of sovereign power, out of the limits of the authority so given to him, would be purely void.[36]

Higinbotham would also have known that, in 1841, the Privy Council, in *Hill* v. *Bigge*, had advised that:

> If it be said that the Governor of a colony is *quasi* Sovereign, the answer is that he does not even represent the Sovereign generally, having only the functions delegated to him by the terms of his commission, and being only the officer to execute the specific powers with which that commission clothes him.[37]

Those were the leading decisions of the day in the field of colonial government and, coming from the Privy Council, were not merely persuasive but absolutely binding on the British Colonies. Higinbotham, who prided himself on his command of

English judicial decisions, must have been well aware of them. It followed that his resolution, as to the Governor's instructions, rested on illegality, and his advocacy of it was not merely sophistical but wilfully deceptive.

Pursuing the deception, he asserted that "the Governor of Victoria, in 1855, became … an independent sovereign in and for Victoria". From that falsehood he argued that the Colonial Office either ignored the Governor's proper status or "interfered" with it by circumscribing the Governor's powers through the instructions issued to him. Higinbotham told the Legislative Assembly that:

> If the proposition I have submitted to the House be well-founded in constitutional law [which it was not], these instructions, except so far as they are authorized by terms of express legislation, are beyond the power of the Secretary of State to give. He has no right to give them.[38]

On the contrary, the Secretary of State had an indubitable right to give instructions that were not standing instructions. The essential source of the instructing power was found in the royal prerogative.[39] Professor Keith pointed out that, over the years, an abbreviated procedure was adopted by which, instead of the Secretary of State advising the Crown and obtaining a formal instrument under the sign manual and signet in respect of instructions other than standing instructions, the Secretary gave such instructions directly in the name of the Crown, though "the Secretary is nothing *per se* but merely as an expression of the will of the Crown".[40] The instructions about which Higinbotham complained were either standing instructions that had nothing to do with the Secretary of State but were issued formally by the Crown in exercise of the prerogative: or they were occasional instructions validly issued by the Secretary. In that context, the *Constitution Act* 1855 was irrelevant.

In 1924 Mr Justice H. V. Evatt of the High Court (as he became in 1930) wrote a thesis "Certain Aspects of the Royal Prerogative" for the degree of Doctor of Laws in the University of Sydney. Published posthumously, it devoted a chapter to "the doctrine of *Musgrave* v. *Pulido*". Tarring had relied on that authority, a Privy Council decision delivered ten years after Higinbotham had put forward his resolutions. While it and the earlier cases cited above were good law for the remainder of the 19th century, the Privy Council to some extent reconsidered its position in 1916.[41] Dr Evatt concluded that, by the 1920s, "any shreds which may remain" of the "Musgrave" doctrine had been destroyed by legal decisions and learned commentary.[42] However that may be, the circumstances of the British Empire following the Boer War, World War I, and the *Statute of Westminster* 1931, could not have been foreseen in 1869. The earlier Privy Council cases then continued to direct the law, and the Victorian Governor was not then a sovereign in any sense of the word.

Higinbotham had weakened his case by overstating it. As will be noticed presently, in Canada, Edward Blake, Q.C., when Minister of Justice, achieved what Higinbotham failed to achieve, by putting his arguments at a lower level than that of claiming sovereignty in the Governor-General. As Dr Alpheus Todd summarized the result:

> The authority of the Crown in every colony is suitably and undeniably vested in the Governor. He possesses "the full constitutional powers which her Majesty, if she were ruling, personally instead of through his agency, could exercise".[43]

On that view, the Governor properly remained an "agent" not a principal or "sovereign" in his own right.

While the gubernatorial instructions, as they existed in 1869, had not been modified for years, and some of them were demonstrably stale, Higinbotham maintained that they contained "most offensive and unconstitutional directions".[44] But they were, for the most part, of so little practical consequence that no-one but Higinbotham was at all concerned by them.[45] He came close to admitting the point when telling the Legislative Assembly that, "I really do not like to press upon the House views which may appear abstract, but which I confess seem to me to be connected intimately with the practical interests of our daily lives".[46]

He propounded, as an example, the claimed degradation of the Governor in his being obliged to send monthly reports on the Colony to the Secretary of State – "he is made to feel, month by month, that he wears the livery of the Colonial Office" and that he was the mere servant of the Secretary of State.[47] Governors, on appointment throughout the Empire, understood it to be their duty to make such regular reports, as well as annual ones. In days of still primitive and delayed communications, it was entirely reasonable that the Colonial Office should be kept aware of the condition of the Empire through intelligence conveyed by the various Governors. No Victorian Governor appears to have cavilled at discharging that duty, or to have subscribed to Higinbotham's assessment that they were "only the secret agents of an illegal and absolutely irresponsible authority, the English Secretary of State for the Colonies".[48]

Although not borne out in Victoria, the experience of some other colonies would demonstrate that, in these concerns, Higinbotham had a valid ground for anxiety. In 1875 an instance occurred at the Cape Colony.

> A Governor in a colony possessing responsible government was expected to aid the Secretary of State in overcoming any opposition due to suspicion of Imperial motives or to political motives. When Sir Henry Barkly at the Cape seemed luke-warm about Lord Carnarvon's confederation proposals, Lord Carnarvon wrote an exposition of his views of a Governor's duties. He complained that Barkly had lent him little support, and had not used "the moderating influence and the personal explanations which Governors of experience, ability and position such as yours can and do often interpose in cases like these". Moreover, he added, "it is to the Governor … that the Minister in England must look to remove misapprehensions, to smoothe difficulties, to reassure as to the intentions of the Home Government and in fact to prevent such a collision of opinion as has unfortunately here occurred".[49]

Had Victorian Governors been so importuned there might well have been a sense of degradation. But, at the time Higinbotham raised the matter, it was of no consequence there.

As to his insistence that the royal instructions to the Governor were illegal, his highly literal construction of statutes, (much in evidence when he became a judge), did not serve him well. He claimed that, there being no express power in the *Constitution Act* 1855 as to the giving of instructions, the Crown was powerless in the matter.[50] That was wrong. The draft Bill for the *Constitution Act* submitted to Downing Street by Victoria contained a clause that would have authorized the Queen-in-Council to give instructions to the Governor as to assenting to Bills, disallowing them, or reserving them for the royal pleasure.[51]

The proposed section was struck out by the Colonial Office, not to abrogate the royal instructing power, but because the draft appeared to fetter that power. The Colonial Office preferred, as Professor Bailey put it, to rely on "the usages and the understandings which clothed the system with life and regulated its growth".[52] The result, to adopt the words of Professor Keith, was that "there can be no doubt, despite Mr Higinbotham's plea to the contrary, that [the Governor] is bound to obey his instructions";[53] and their legality was beyond question.

"Not at All an Honest Arguer"

Rogers, on receiving Canterbury's despatch reporting the resolutions, was defensive. He regretted that the subject had been reduced to personality and that he had become Higinbotham's principal target.[54] While he did not respond in kind publicly, he had already formed an unfavourable opinion of his critic, noting, despite reports of Higinbotham's "high character ... as an honest politician", that:

> He struck me at the time of the Darling controversy as not at all an honest arguer – prepared to support reckless measures by arguments (in law) which a clever man must have known to be bad.[55]

That was a fair and well justified comment: as were Rogers' later observations that Higinbotham's ultimate mark was the Victorian Legislative Council which he "naturally hate[d] worse than the Col[onial] Office", and which he hoped to "grind to pieces".[56]

Rogers therefore was on guard. He saw such a large majority vote in the Assembly as a precursor to, and a virtual endorsement of, the separation of Victoria from the Empire. He reckoned that Higinbotham's tactics might well be to provoke another deliberate quarrel with the Council over Appropriation Bills, call on the Governor to authorize expenditure of public money in defiance of the Council on the certain defeat of the Bills in the Upper House, and, on his refusal, turn upon the Colonial Office "and to press for independence – not that friendly independence wh. mt be conceded if really wished for by the Colony – but independence with & thro a quarrel".[57]

That disregarded the fact that, as a backbencher, Higinbotham no longer enjoyed true political power. But Rogers committed much time and effort to preparing a counter-attack on paper and, on one view, "this was the moment at which George Higinbotham came as close as anyone could to precipitating a crisis that might well have ended in the partial dissolution of the ties between Britain and her self-governing colonies".[58] As things resolved themselves, the counter-attack was not needed.

One of Rogers' proposals, overruled by the Secretary of State, was to send a voluminous despatch to the Victorian Governor so that he might point out to his Ministers "how completely the policy of this country has been that of non-interference", and that it would be preferable "that the imperial connection would remain until there was a federal union of the Australian colonies" rather than that Victoria should first go its own way.[59]

Lord Carnarvon, who, in his first term as Secretary of State for the Colonies in 1867, had regarded Victoria's then "crisis" as so serious as threatening to become a "revolution",[60] was one who championed the preservation of the Empire and who pursued that aim in his second term from 1874 to 1878. In a paper "Imperial Administration", he insisted that the great colonies endowed with "free and responsible self-government" still derived much value from the imperial connexion:

> It is perfectly true that those great colonies deal, and deal, as I think, admirably, with the questions which concern themselves, their local institutions, and the sphere of their internal life; but there also arise great constitutional questions which can only be settled, I will not say at home, but at all events with the help of the Home Government, and questions also with which the relations and interests of foreign nations are interwoven.[61]

Carnarvon, incidentally, was, "in England, … practically alone in his optimistic view of the future empire".[62] Higinbotham, to some extent, was unfortunate that his demands for constitutional reform came at a period when the shifting sands of English Government policy favoured imperial cohesion: a position that had fluctuated markedly and unpredictably during Queen Victoria's reign.[63]

Meanwhile the distinct lack of enthusiasm for Higinbotham's resolutions, as successive Ministries came and went, demonstrated that reality had taken hold.[64] The imperial connexion was of the essence for Australian trade at that time. If Victoria withdrew from the Empire, bankers, merchants, business houses and many other commercial undertakings would have transferred their activities to those Australian Colonies maintaining the more certain economic climate assured by the links to Great Britain. Given the rivalry between those colonies, the result almost certainly would have secured a windfall benefit to the others at Victoria's expense. There were abundant practical reasons, on sober reflection, why Victoria should not go it alone – the likely suspension of appeals to the Privy Council among them. They were reasons Higinbotham had overlooked or discounted in his abstract enthusiasm.

In the end, although Rogers' proposed counter-attack came to nothing, he remained committed to his long-standing view that self-government had worked as a declaration of independence for the colonies, and that the cause of Empire was all but lost. He wrote, resignedly,

> As to the colonies *becoming* republics, they *are* republics. The difference between them and the U.S. being … that instead of a principal magistrate … elected directly by the people whom he governs under the name of President, they have a principal magistrate appointed indirectly by the people of this country under the title of Governor. As to their *becoming* independent, they *became* independent when they received responsible Government. Responsible Government once established, the dissolution of the Empire becomes a matter of time.[65]

"Politics Without Compromise"

Higinbotham's futile contest with the Colonial Office, in 1869 and later when he became Chief Justice, has led to his having been portrayed as a hero figure in terms as exaggerated as they are unsound. Thus, in an obituary, Higinbotham's unstinting admirer and myth-creator, the journalist William Astley, wrote:

> The battle of Constitutionalism against an oligarchic officialdom had been fought in New South Wales; the conflict of which it was the precursor and which was still more tremendous in its intensity and in its scope because it attached an indelible character to the democratic institutions of Australia, was naturally fought in the younger province. Wentworth was the animating soul of the one; Higinbotham, a greater Wentworth – the phrase is measured and advised – that of the other.[66]

That was newspaper hyperbole. By the time Higinbotham arrived in Australia the great battles for Responsible Government had been won. The single-minded determination of Wentworth and others such as Robert Lowe and James Martin in New South Wales, and Stawell and Foster in Victoria, achieved practical results Higinbotham never attained. Lowe and Martin, particularly through the columns of the *Atlas*, had assailed the Colonial Office and Lord Stanley, then Secretary of State, much more sharply than Higinbotham did concerning the incumbents of later years.[67] Higinbotham's theories, while not always without merit, did not approximate even to a shadow of Wentworth's achievements for New South Wales and for Victoria as well.

(Sir) Frederick Eggleston, in 1933, wrote of Higinbotham that he was "one of the most attractive products of Australian democracy, but his political usefulness was marred by his idea that politics could be carried on without compromise". Eggleston concluded that "Victoria had a statesman in George Higinbotham … who could put the Australian point of view with force and precision" (though, he might have added, with a breathtaking lack of success).[68] It is difficult to see how the prolonged and abrasive pursuit of a private vendetta against the Legislative Council and the Colonial Office was statesmanlike, attractive or democratic. Higinbotham's methods of personal abuse and invective mixed with unyielding confrontational attack lacked the essential qualities of statesmanship and, in the long run, achieved virtually nothing for Victoria.

Professor (Sir) Kenneth Bailey confirmed that conclusion when he described Higinbotham's life as "full of disappointments" – scarcely to be wondered at given Higinbotham's aggressive and combative disposition – but praised him as "the exponent of a definite logical theory of responsible government".[69] That must be questioned. Save for the element of bluff, there was no logic about Higinbotham's resolutions that insisted on the one hand that Victoria remain attached to the Crown and the Empire, while at once seeking to destroy the very links that bound Victoria to the Empire.

In fairness to the distinguished lawyers whose interpretations are here discussed, it should be said that access in Australia to the full range of original source materials was very limited at the time when they wrote. The insights provided by records now readily available justify a reappraisal of those interpretations.

Whereas Higinbotham so antagonized successive Secretaries of State for the Colonies that he was dismissed as eccentric and his ideas were discredited, some of his notions came to have effect, but only through a side wind. Here the matter can be touched upon only in outline.[70]

Since the passing of the *British North America Act* 1867 (Imperial), an Act dictated by "Canadian not British policy",[71] it was the Canadian view, expressed by Edward Blake, Q.C., Minister of Justice, that, in seeking further constitutional reforms for the confederation, including revision of the Governor-General's commission and instructions,

> the peculiar position of Canada, in relation to the mother country, entitled her to special consideration, and that the existing forms, while they might be eminently suited to other colonies, were inapplicable and objectionable in her case.[72]

The Colonial Office agreed generally, permitting Canada to take the lead in achieving reforms. Other colonies, in due course, would have to be content to draw upon the Canadian model.

Yet there was a distinctly Australian impetus for change, impeded rather than advanced by Higinbotham's declamations, and originating chiefly from New South Wales. In 1868 that Colony's Governor, the Earl of Belmore, who was tested by a variety of constitutional issues,[73] raised with the Secretary of State the extent to which the gubernatorial instructions conceded unfettered discretion to the Governor to exercise the royal prerogative of mercy in the remission of sentences. He was advised that he "would be bound to allow great weight to the recommendation of his ministry" but otherwise was to exercise an independent judgement.[74]

Belmore's successor, the headstrong Sir Hercules Robinson, became enmeshed in an argument with the Premier, Sir Henry Parkes, and his Ministers, on the same question. In a Higinbotham-like approach, Parkes' Cabinet insisted that, in a Colony enjoying Responsible Government, the Governor, as to the prerogative of mercy, ought to take and accept his Ministers' advice: otherwise no such advice should be given.[75] After an impasse, a compromise was reached whereby applications for remissions of sentence were to be submitted to the Governor, with a recommendation, by one responsible Minister. That course was approved by the Secretary of State, but, almost simultaneously, there was colonial uproar when Robinson, of his own motion, though with the falsely claimed support of Chief Justice Sir James Martin,[76] released the notorious bushranger Frank Gardiner, being held under a long term of imprisonment.

The details cannot be pursued here,[77] but they led to an immediate review of its position by the Colonial Office, and the issue of a circular despatch to all Governors of Australian Colonies, in May 1875, reiterating that, in exercise of the prerogative of mercy, they must, as to capital cases be advised by their Executive Councils; and, as to lesser cases, be advised by one or more responsible Ministers; but, in all cases, they were ultimately to decide for themselves. Lord Carnarvon declared that "a Governor may (and, indeed, must, if in his judgment it seems right) decide in opposition to the advice tendered to him … [If he] by acting in opposition to the advice of his Ministers, has brought about their resignation, [he] will obviously have assumed a responsibility for which he will have to account to Her Majesty's Government".[78] That produced a result of little satisfaction to anyone. But the issues raised were analysed carefully by Edward Blake in Canada.[79]

A more able lawyer and a much more astute politician, Blake nevertheless had many characteristics in common with Higinbotham. Blake was reputed to be "the outstanding Canadian Liberal" of his generation,[80] matching Higinbotham's Victorian reputation. And Blake, "like many brilliant men",

> was unstable by temperament: aware of his abilities and morbidly suspicious of any fancied slight; arrogant and inconciliable in nature; subject to alternate moods of exultation and depression; intensely ambitious, restless, and independent. Yet withal he was urbane and high-principled, a man who could display great social charm if he were so inclined.[81]

Higinbotham was cast in much the same mould.

Blake, however, had qualities and advantages Higinbotham did not possess. Although he went to England very unwillingly to negotiate the reforms he sought, Blake persisted.[82] By checking his temperamental nature, he secured in person results Higinbotham could not possibly achieve by acrimonious speeches from afar. Blake also put up with the torments of the Colonial Office while it played with him, as would a cat with a mouse, hoping, in his case, that he would go away. He was kept preoccupied by high social engagements he could not diplomatically decline and which were intended to distract him from his purpose. Official appointments were too numerous but too brief to achieve much, and the real issues were constantly deferred.

> Blake … would talk, propose, and go home to await decision … There were endless requests for supplementary drafts, for revisions of his memoranda and suggestions as to new bills … He was to be fittingly entertained, he would wait and write in the intervals, and he remained the outsider from Canada on the fringe of great concerns.[83]

During those intervals, if not already aware of them, Blake must have become aware of Higinbotham's 1869 resolutions, and have studied and adapted them to his own advantage.

At last Blake's perseverance was rewarded. Carnarvon, then Secretary of State, who, according to Rogers, "was friendly to everybody",[84] warmed to Blake's persuasiveness and yielded most of the reforms sought.[85] The result was a reflection of Higinbotham's aims that local control should be asserted over local affairs, without British supervision or intrusion. As to Canada, that was accomplished in 1876 by modifying the Governor-General's commission and instructions "so that in future that official would no longer be encouraged to think of himself as an independent representative of the imperial authority in Canada".[86] Victoria, meanwhile, had made no progress on such issues.

As if deliberately to snub Higinbotham's demands for attention, the first concessions to Australia came as an altered standing commission and instructions to Governor Sir William Jervois on his appointment to South Australia in April 1877. Apart from omitting obsolete provisions, the instructions were "necessarily more restrictive in character than those … framed in reference to Canada", and retained several clauses that offended Higinbotham.[87] Similarly worded instructions were not issued for Victoria until February 1879,[88] and would become the subject of yet further onslaughts on the Colonial Office by Higinbotham when he became a judge and then Chief Justice.

Speculation is of no help to the study of history. But, given the cordiality of the meetings between Carnarvon and Higinbotham in Melbourne in 1887, and again in Sydney in 1888, one cannot but reflect on what might have been. Carnarvon recorded of the then Chief Justice that

> I had afterwards a very long and interesting conversation with him ranging over all kinds of questions … He was very mild & reasonable & once when he indulged in an old piece of forensic rhetoric on my restating the case he recognised the justice of the correction & said very frankly that he retracted his words. It was a very interesting talk.[89]

Had Higinbotham been able to emulate Blake, and to have had a similarly interesting talk with Carnarvon and with Rogers in the 1870s, his grand design of Responsible Government might have come to something. Instead, it failed – at least, in his lifetime.[90] His resolutions stand as a memorial only to a voice crying in the wilderness.

7

Puisne Judge 1880-1886

"The Example Which I Shall Set"

After the appointment of William Foster Stawell as Chief Justice (*vice* Sir William a'Beckett), in February 1857, the composition of the Supreme Court remained unchanged for 15 years. The puisne judges were Sir Redmond Barry, Sir Edward Williams and Sir Robert Molesworth. In 1872, in pursuance of an Act increasing the Bench to five, T. H. Fellows was so appointed and, in April 1874, J. W. Stephen took the seat vacated by the retirement of Williams. Stephen, incidentally, was Attorney-General in the Francis Ministry and was elevated by virtue of holding that office.

E. D. Holroyd was first offered the place taken by Fellows in 1872, but unwisely declined it. Holroyd, who would take silk within a few years, appears to have been more attracted to lucrative Bar fees than to a fixed judicial salary. He did accept elevation to the Supreme Court in 1881, but that capped his ambitions as he had been overtaken by Higinbotham, and thus lost a reasonable prospect of succeeding Stawell on his retirement as Chief Justice in 1886.

It seems that the 1872 appointment had been hawked about the Bar with little success. It was offered to, but declined by, Higinbotham, because, so Professor Morris claimed, "the offer had been made by a Premier who had grossly insulted his brother [Thomas Higinbotham]".[1] That explanation is unconvincing. More credible is the newspaper account that:

> It was for long an open secret at the bar that [Higinbotham] was averse to accepting a judgeship, mainly because of the attitude assumed towards him in the course of his practice by particular members of the then bench.[2]

To be more precise, the Bench retained the keenest memory of Higinbotham's treatment of them as "officers in his Department", when he was Attorney-General; and the prospect of working as a brother judge, with Barry in particular, must have been too daunting even for a man of Higinbotham's independence.

Eight years later, different considerations applied, and Barry's death would soon close that chapter.[3] James Service was Premier between March and August 1880: J.G. Francis was a Minister in his government. Service and Higinbotham had been good friends since their days as pioneer residents of Emerald Hill. "From that time onward", Service recalled, "our intimacy … went on increasing. There was no man, probably, with whom I have exchanged ideas so confidentially on other subjects than those of politics".[4] Higinbotham regarded Francis, a fellow Minister in McCulloch's first Ministry, as an "old colleague and friend".[5] Shortly after taking office, Service invited Higinbotham to call and, at that confidential meeting, asked him whether he would accept appointment as a Judge of the Supreme Court if formally offered it.[6] A vacancy had existed since the death of Fellows in 1878. The second Berry Ministry had not succeeded in filling it and, about two months before the fall of the Service Ministry, the legal profession formally petitioned that the Bench be brought to full strength.[7] Hence the confidential meeting, at which, no doubt to the Premier's surprise, Higinbotham responded almost queru-lously.

Service's first Ministry did not long enough survive to achieve anything of consequence, and hindered itself the more by introducing a Reform Bill.[8] Such a measure was anathema to Higinbotham. Relevantly it contemplated widening the franchise, subdividing electorates, and reducing tenure of political office. More importantly, it proposed a practical solution to Upper and Lower House deadlocks. If a Bill were passed by the Assembly at two consecutive sessions and each time rejected by the Council, the Governor might order a double dissolution. If, in the new Parliament thereafter, the same measure should pass in the Assembly, but not in the Council, there was to be a joint sitting of the Houses and, should the majority there pass the Bill, the Governor was to assent to it. "This", wrote Henry Gyles Turner, "was converting the absolute veto, which the Council possessed under the Constitution Act, into a suspensive veto, which, it was reasonably contended, was a sufficient safeguard against ill-considered legislation".[9]

Higinbotham might have been expected to embrace the measure as a step towards disempowering the Council. Yet, with typical perversity, he would have none of it, and thought it would have the opposite effect. He told Service, at their interview, that the pending Bill would create an "insuperable difficulty" in the way of his accepting a judgeship.

> I regarded it as a proposal subversive of the foundations of our Constitution, … and I could not accept this [judicial] office or any other distinction at the hands of a Government which was trying to pass, or which should succeed in passing, into law a measure in my opinion so mischievous.[10]

There had been three previous attempts at such reform, all of which had failed because they were seen, on one view, to propose "the absolute extinction of the Upper House, and [creation of] another Constitution". Higinbotham, however, would have shared Berry's opinion that the Service measure would be calculated to degrade the popular chamber, annihilate manhood suffrage, and make the Council impregnable.[11] Service, though taken aback by Higinbotham's response, invited him to a second discussion at which Francis also attended.

By that time the Reform Bill had been defeated in the Assembly by two votes and, as the government seemed minded to abandon it, that obstacle had been removed from Higinbotham's path. But he volunteered another. If he were appointed a judge, he would regard it as his duty, judicially and personally, "to resist always and by every lawful means, the illegal interference of Her Majesty's Imperial Government in the domestic affairs of this Colony".[12]

It was an arresting assertion, and a prejudicial one coming from a prospective appointee to the Supreme Court Bench. It is not in the nature of Australian judicial appointments that they should be subject to conditions other than those of impartiality contained in the judicial oath. It was the reverse of the *contretemps* that would occur in 1913 when A.B. Piddington was offered appointment as a Justice of the High Court after disclosing to the Federal Government, at its request, that he was in sympathy with preferring the supremacy of Commonwealth over State powers.

So strong was the adverse reaction of the legal profession that Piddington resigned before taking his seat.[13] If it were inappropriate for a government to canvass the views of a prospective judge on potentially sensitive issues, it was equally inappropriate for a prospective judge to prescribe terms on which he would be prepared to sit, as Higinbotham purported to do.

Asked to specify the ways in which his views would "practically affect [his] conduct as a Judge", Higinbotham's formidable complaints of illegality dissolved. There was only one real sticking point. He insisted that the Governor had no power, under the imperial instructions, to require a judge to report to him all cases in which sentence of death was pronounced, and to attend before the Executive Council on consideration of the report – notwithstanding that the practice was of long standing. It could only be a legal practice, he insisted, if the Governor were advised so to act by the responsible Ministers in Victoria. If appointed, Higinbotham would "officially and openly refuse to comply with the requirements contained in the so-called instruction" unless those requirements were conveyed to him by "Her Majesty's Advisers for Victoria".[14]

He conceded that his response was "somewhat ungracious" and he was reconciled to the likelihood that it would weigh against his appointment to the court. Lest there be any misunderstanding that, if he were to be appointed it must be on his terms, he added condescendingly that,

> I shall regard the fact that I am not deemed to be disqualified as gratifying proof of the progress amongst influential politicians of rational and just views respecting public law, and I shall ever cherish the hope that the example which I shall set in this matter as a Judge of the Supreme Court may have its weight with those who shall hereafter be called upon to advise the Crown in Victoria.

He further insisted that the contents of his letter to Service should not be constrained by confidentiality.[15]

G. B. Kerferd, then Attorney-General, interposed to take "a prominent part in inducing Higinbotham to accept the office".[16] Service also gave ground and reckoned (mistakenly as it would turn out)[17] that Higinbotham's reports on capital cases could be sought from the judge as "an officer in his Department" by the Colony's Attorney-General, without troubling the Governor.

Higinbotham accordingly received his appointment in July 1880, a little over a fortnight before the first Service Ministry was granted a dissolution by the Governor and, to its chagrin, was defeated at the ensuing elections. Service had not allowed propriety to stand in the way of friendship in preferring Higinbotham. The conduct of the latter, when Attorney-General, in seeming to defy the Supreme Court's decision that condemned the 1867 ruse to govern without supply, might well have militated against his appointment to that court.[18] And it was plain that, in any proceedings in which he might be called upon to adjudicate, where questions of public law arose, particularly questions of constitutional law and the relations between the Imperial Crown and the Colony, Higinbotham might bring to court preconceptions, prejudices and a closed mind. What he would do, if faced with legislation like Service's failed Reform Bill or other measures about which he held strong political views, could not be foreseen.

In her sometimes fanciful and romantic *My Recollections*, written in old age, Lady Stawell, widow of the incumbent Chief Justice at Higinbotham's appointment to the Bench, claimed that Stawell "strongly advocated Mr Higinbotham's elevation to the judgeship, for, although he considered him a dangerous politician, he believed he would be a most fearless and conscientious judge".[19] In a companion volume, *Sir William Stawell*, the present writer suggests that the expression "strongly advocated" was infelicitous and that "tolerated" would have been more realistic.[20] The fact was that Higinbotham had laid it down as a condition of his appointment that he would not abandon political views. He persisted with that position, writing to Richard Richardson, M.L.A., thanking him for his congratulations on entering "the narrower but yet honourable sphere of judicial duty", but adding,

> I shall never cease to be a politician, in the sense in which you and I have understood the term, to my life's end, and as a Victorian politician I shall continue to watch your course in Parliament with close attention and interest, and with the warm sympathy which springs from feelings nearly identical, I believe, in reference to matters of the highest concern.[21]

Sometimes that warm sympathy would obtrude upon Higinbotham's judicial perceptions.

"The Appointment is Said to be a Good One"

On Monday, 19 July 1880, a *Gazette Extraordinary* was published at night announcing that Higinbotham was made a judge. He had been sworn in, as the sixth puisne judge to be appointed in Victoria, at an Executive Council meeting on the same afternoon.[22] Veiled in secrecy, his elevation took the community by surprise, but the news was well received by the press. The *Argus* declared the appointment to be "one of those acts of administration about the merits of which happily there is no difference of opinion … and the applause consequent upon [this] will be general, spontaneous, and hearty".[23] As if to hark back to Higinbotham's *Argus* ideas about party government, that journal praised the Service Ministry for putting "Victoria in the first place and party in the second". The *Age* agreed:

> The appointment is one that would bring popularity to any Ministry, and the only question that is likely to be raised over it is whether the Service Ministry were justified in making it under the circumstances in which they are placed …, [but] the appointment has so much to recommend it that the disposition will be not to look too critically at the way in which it has been made.[24]

How the *Age* measured "popularity" did not emerge. The general community was not much interested in who occupied the bench of the Supreme Court, and there is no reason to suppose that this appointment differed in that respect from any others. Public attention, in Victoria, was then much diverted by the fate of the bushranger Ned Kelly.[25] The *Age* cautioned, however, that patronage ought not in future to be exercised in such a fashion by a defunct government: and it concluded that the appointment had been right, but the method of making it wrong. Similar views were echoed in provincial newspapers.[26] The *Illustrated Australian News* declared that Higinbotham's acceptance of the office "was a surprise in many respects, but the public generally were satisfied that the appointment was the very best that could have been made".[27] *Melbourne Punch* could not contain its superlatives, proclaiming that "the new judge is thrice welcome", first, because of "his acknowledged ability in his profession"; second, because "in addition to being a lawyer, he is a law-abiding man"; and, third, "because he has saved us from the national disgrace of witnessing a 'party blunderer' sitting upon the judicial bench".[28] Such ceremonious assessments were well and good, but those who made them were not to know that Higinbotham had prescribed conditions on which he would occupy the judgement seat.

The Governor, Lord Normanby, reported the news to Downing Street, without comment. The Colonial Office noted it without enthusiasm, John Bramston minuting the file "An appointment made by the outgoing Service Ministry hoping to make it impossible to give it to Sir B. O'Loghlen". The Secretary of State (the Earl of Kimberley) was more charitable, writing, "That was I believe the object but the appt. is said to be a good one in itself".[29]

The Colonial Office's information was not entirely accurate. Bryan O'Loghlen had succeeded to an Irish baronetcy in 1877, was prominent at the Victorian Bar, and was active in Victorian politics. Because he wished to further his political career – he became Premier in 1881 – he declined the offer by the second Berry Ministry (in which he was Attorney-General) of the judicial vacancy caused by the death of Fellows.[30] Through inertia, the vacancy remained until Higinbotham accepted appointment. The *Argus* considered that: "It was in no sense a political appointment, as the promotion of Sir Bryan O'Loghlen, whose claims as a lawyer were insignificant, would have been".[31]

The new judge first took his seat in a temporary court room in Swanston Street, converted from premises formerly used as a dining room for gaol warders. An unusually high bench was accessible only by climbing steep stairs. J.L. Forde recalled of the occasion that Higinbotham,

> robed in silk gown and wearing a plain wig, … gathering his skirts about him proceeded to ascend the stairs leading to the bench. At the fourth or fifth step he stumbled, but, with a smile, quickly recovering himself, he presently gained the bench, and, bowing deeply, took his seat, and was congratulated by Mr J. L. Purves on behalf of the Bar.[32]

A journalist, writing in 1882, presented an engaging pen portrait of the new Mr Justice Higinbotham. He was "this quiet little gentleman in black", habitually seen, with his umbrella, walking between the court house and the Brighton train. As the writer observed him:

> The countenance is singularly placid – an almost boyish face, full and rounded, but with the paleness of the student and ascetic, and

dimpled in what one calls a feminine manner. His thin and closely cut hair is white; so is the mere suspicion of a whisker, the little "sideboards", which fringes his visage. He is always pensive, and looks as if about to sigh. His very light blue eyes catch ours for a moment, as he bows in a furtive nervous way.[33]

Alfred Deakin, who was a Higinbotham "disciple", wrote later in very similar terms.[34]

Despite the emergence from that time of an ever expanding myth that attributed extraordinary qualities to the man, Higinbotham was not entirely successful as a puisne judge – though, as will be seen, he served with distinction when elevated as Chief Justice in 1886. But, as a puisne judge, he was not incisive. His preoccupation was with law books, precedents, and taking detailed shorthand notes of legal proceedings, so that he might dwell on the issues and not rush to judgement. That put him at odds with his judicial colleagues who were no-nonsense lawyers, concerned only to get to the essence of the one case and move on promptly to the next.

Because he preferred to take time to consider his decisions, and to write independent judgements, he frequently delayed the course of business in the Full Court. At first instance and at *nisi prius*, where he did not have the luxury of reflection, he did not always shine. On several occasions he admitted to having committed procedural errors or given wrong directions to juries,[35] and there were a number of successful appeals from his decisions, particularly in the year or so before he became Chief Justice.[36]

While his law more often than not was sound, he was much criticized for his dilatoriness in dispensing it. "As a judge", wrote the *Leader*,

> his conscientiousness was so acute as to approach the morbid. He spared himself no labor in mastering the details of every case before him ... In addition to his court business, he spent half his nights and all his holidays in consulting authorities ... He had a tendency to pursue an abstraction to its final conclusion.[37]

He irritated the Bar by his fastidiousness in duplicating the work of the court reporters and keeping such excessively detailed notes, so that "he held the balance so fairly between the parties before him, and weighed every point so nicely, that notwithstanding the time he saved by taking his notes in shorthand, it took him twice, and even thrice, as long to hear a case as one of the other judges".[38]

Younger members of the Bar were inclined to make fun of his methods. The most conspicuous example was Frank Gavan Duffy's "A Dream of Fair Judges", written in 1892, the year in which Higinbotham died. Duffy became Chief Justice of the High Court in 1931, but in the 1880s he was a frequently briefed junior in the Victorian Supreme Court. His satirical poem did not mention Higinbotham by name, but it was obvious to whom he referred in a stanza depicting Higinbotham's distinctive voice and his often complex pronouncements:

> His firm tones fell like strokes of silver pure,
> Tones to my weary ear familiar long
> In laboured judgments lucidly obscure,
> Perspicuously wrong.[39]

Higinbotham was said to have resented bitterly those reflections on him but, during his term as puisne judge, at least, they were often accurate.[40]

On Higinbotham's death, the then Premier, William Shiels, a barrister and Higinbotham "disciple", confirmed, in a panegyric that praised many of Higinbotham's other qualities, that "We have had greater advocates at the bar, we may have had sounder and quicker judges on the bench".[41] Alfred Deakin was similarly frank, but explained away Higinbotham's shortcomings in decidedly eccentric terms –

> His practical career whether at the Bar or on the Bench was never an unqualified success in the ordinary acceptation of that term. His standards were too high, his temper too unbending, his scrupulousness too indiscriminating to render him a colleague whom it was easy to co-operate with or to understand.[42]

The conclusion, that Higinbotham was "too great for the great positions he filled",[43] verges on the bizarre, and all but invites the further conclusion that he was too good for this world. Thus was the myth made all but indestructible. It will be further considered in a later chapter.[44] For present purposes, as to his career as puisne judge, the myth had no valid foundation. Higinbotham was but one among equals in a strong Bench. Stephen, Williams and Holroyd were not his inferiors as lawyers, while Higinbotham made no unique contribution to particular fields of law as

Molesworth most notably did to mining law. As will emerge in more detail, Higinbotham's most conspicuous part as a puisne judge was more provocative than constructive.

"Laws are the Decrees of the High Court of Parliament"

Some earlier writers have regarded Higinbotham's accession to the Bench as meritorious above others, and portrayed him as a giant among men – "the outstanding legal figure of colonial Australia" – heroically resisting "the forces of reaction".[45] On that view, he and Chief Justice Stawell represented extremes of judicial ideology. While Stawell "stood for judicial power against the parliament and the executive", Higinbotham championed "parliamentary supremacy and an expansive view of executive power".[46]

A different position will be taken here. Stawell and all his judicial colleagues between 1880 and 1886 (Barry, Molesworth, Stephen, Hartley Williams, Holroyd, Kerferd and Webb), all that is except Higinbotham, were pragmatists. They were not lawyers of the schools, but practical men nurtured in the law through experience and hard knocks. Their common purpose was to administer justice as swiftly and accurately as possible without digressing into nice studies of ancillary principle. They sought to resolve doubts, particularly about the meaning of statutes, by a common sense, practical and just interpretation. If there were a contest of ideology, it was not one between Higinbotham and Stawell. It was Higinbotham *contra mundum*. With his affected intellectual superiority and his capacity to create conflict by insisting that he alone was right, he was, in these exceptional matters, at odds with all his colleagues.

That Stawell was on a crusade, to make the court the most "supreme" of the three arms of government, does not emerge readily from a reading of his decisions,[47] and appears to rest largely on assumptions that are unsound. Thus it is assumed that, before 1880, Stawell so controlled his coadjutors that all conformed to his supposed policy of asserting court dominance – for which there is no evidence. And it is assumed that the Supreme Court was a court of last resort, able to compel Parliament to yield to its will; whereas the final arbiter, if invoked, was the Privy

Council. Nothing suggests that the latter had or countenanced preconceived policies that subordinated the Victorian Legislature to the Supreme Court.

Higinbotham's advocacy of parliamentary supremacy is found only as asides in very occasional decisions. His "High Court of Parliament" analogy, referred to below,[48] was the most egregious instance, and was demonstrably misplaced. In a practical sense, the Legislature was always supreme, with or without Higinbotham's indulgence. Especially was that so in the field of statutory construction, where Parliament could alter enactments to neutralize a curial construction of which it disapproved. But, in colonial Victoria, the Legislature seemed generally well content with the Supreme Court as its interpreter.

Higinbotham, at first, moved unobtrusively in his new judicial company. Following the sense of caution with which he customarily began his great parliamentary speeches, giving little hint of the dynamics ahead, he caused few introductory ripples. The Full Court's habitually concurring judgements continued so in most cases, though Higinbotham was quietly engineering a change. Liking to be seen to be different, he began to insist on delivering independent, though concurring, judgements. Stawell was no longer able always to hand down the leading decision with which his colleagues would merely agree.

By December 1880, Higinbotham began a career of dissent from the majority which, while not excessively pursued, shattered the court's former character as one united in opinion. It also began, for a short time, a new method of judgement-writing in which Higinbotham's detailed attention to precedent cases sought to move the court away from its pragmatic style.[49] All the judges found that they had to apply themselves to the law with a detail equal to Higinbotham's or be made to appear superficial. That created court delays on a scale that had been less common in the past. In 1882, for example, the majority of the court in *McVea* v. *Pasquan* were so concerned at the course Higinbotham had disclosed he would take in dissent that they wrote a contrary opinion that expanded to 12 pages in the Law Reports and caused judgement to be reserved for 3 months.[50] As will be seen, Higinbotham, as Chief Justice, generally abandoned his preference for detailed judgements.

A clash between the two jurisprudential positions, in which the pragmatists prevailed, occurred as early as December 1880, in *Mitchell* v. *Watson*.[51] In essence, the question was one of agency – whether the appellant had so authorized his foreman to purchase farm machinery from the respondent as to confer discretion as to the place and manner of delivery. Stawell held that the foreman, on the evidence, stood no higher than an agent by implication, having no powers beyond those necessary to complete the purchase. Stephen, agreeing, held further that there was no relevant contractual writing or part payment to constitute an acceptance and receipt of goods within the Victorian equivalent of the *Statute of Frauds*.[52]

Higinbotham, with the assistance of nine English precedents and *Story on the Law of Agency*, reached the opposite conclusion, holding that, as soon as the machine was delivered for despatch by rail, it had been "delivered to, and actually received by" the appellant. Relying on remarks of Erle, C.J., and Bramwell, L.J., his statement of principle was:

> Any dealing by the buyer with the goods as owner, will justify the inference that the buyer has accepted the goods. So, any act of the buyer which amounts to a recognition of the contract between the parties, will warrant the conclusion that he has "accepted" the goods. In the present case, the buyer's agent, having authority to buy and accept a reaper and binder, selected and approved a particular machine, and directed the vendor to send it to Kyneton, within a time named. This direction as to time and place of delivery, is, in my opinion, sufficient and strong evidence of acceptance.[53]

Stawell, conceding that there was merit in Higinbotham's approach if the circumstances were otherwise, properly rejoined that "had the defendant [appellant] himself been present, and made the contract, the matter would have been different".[54] But the appellant was not present at any relevant stage of the transaction.

It must not be thought that Higinbotham was perpetually or vexatiously in dissent. More often than not the court continued as of one mind even if by different reasoning processes. But a series of his decisions from September to December 1882 marked, not only a divergence of judicial attitudes, but the beginning of a temporary shift in the court's methodological centre of gravity.[55]

Whether in accord with, or differing from, his colleagues, Higinbotham found a number of areas of the law of such interest to him as to warrant their special exploration and analysis. For present purposes, they may be grouped under the headings of statutory interpretation, negligence and, of greatest significance, the extent to which Victorian statutes might lawfully have extraterritorial operation. Those areas of interest will be examined below.

It will be necessary, in that examination, to remember that the cases discussed represent only a tiny proportion of all those pronounced upon between 1880 and 1886. They are, by and large, unusual not typical cases. It is inappropriate to use them to support the view that Stawell and the pragmatists were systematically "reading down" and otherwise manipulating statutory language to confer greater power on the court itself.

On the other hand, Higinbotham's sometimes abstract, almost academic, notions on the Bench as puisne judge were reminiscent of his less than practical views when editor of the *Argus*. Thus any claims he might have had for parliamentary "supremacy" *vis-à-vis* the court, rested on the fallacy that:

> Laws are the decrees of the High Court of Parliament, and if the Supreme Court should allow itself to judge of the competence of Parliament to enact this or any other law, the inferior would be sitting as a court of appeal from the superior court, and, by refusing to administer, would in effect unmake or repeal the law.[56]

The reasons of history that invested the Parliament at Westminster with curial powers were never received into the Australian court system, whether before Federation or after.[57] In the 21st century the function of the High Court of Australia, in determining upon the constitutional validity of Commonwealth or State legislation, is so familiar as to be unremarkable. The Supreme Court of Victoria had comparable powers in respect of Victorian legislation in the 1880s. To suggest that the court was the inferior of a supposed parliamentary court was plainly wrong. Higinbotham's theories about parliamentary "supremacy" in that sense have never been adopted in Australia and must be discounted accordingly.

In the end, there were only two substantial changes Higinbotham would have made, had his colleagues permitted him, in his term as puisne judge. One was his passion for seeking, not merely the chief precedent authorities to support his reasonings, but to trace the development of the common law to bedrock if necessary in order to elucidate the law in his day. The other was his insistence, further considered later,[58] that the court was entitled to instruct itself, by any proper source (not merely the face value of statutory words), what was the legislature's intention in enacting any particular provision. Although energetically resisted by his contemporaries, and later little pursued by him, those precepts came increasingly in the 20th century to be followed in all courts; but that was not directly due to him.

Interpretation of Statutes and Other Instruments

The great canon of statutory construction, where an enactment is clear and unambiguous, that it be given its ordinary and grammatical meaning,[59] was accepted as common ground by all the judges during Stawell's Chief Justiceship. That set an objective test, sometimes confounded by disagreement whether the statutory meaning was indeed clear and unambiguous. If it were, then it followed that the court would apply the Act's provisions literally even if the result seemed unjust or inconvenient, though not if it produced absurdity.[60]

The differences arising from Higinbotham's determination to satisfy himself about Parliament's real intentions exposed subjective shades of interpretation and left the court open to the perennial risk that individual judges might "put their own ideas of justice or social policy in place of the words of the statute".[61] In a dissenting judgement, in *Oakden* v. *Gibbs*, for example, Higinbotham came close to that position in holding, of a remedial statute,

> for the purpose of advancing the remedy provided by Parliament and rendering it effectual, we ought to be prepared, if it were necessary, to compel the language of the Act to yield a meaning in accordance with its remedial policy.[62]

The problem with subjective interpretations was their inconsistency, with right and reason sometimes seeming to be with Higinbotham, and sometimes with the pragmatists.

The modern reader may well be attracted to Higinbotham's carefully detailed approach to the construction of legal instruments. His colleagues, on the other hand, often applied a broad-brush to such matters, relying heavily on elementary principle and their impressions of the court's settled practice. Higinbotham developed his contrary method in *Renison* v. *Keighran*, where the meaning of "having property for her separate use" in the *Married Women's Property Act* 1870 fell for determination. In one of his more important dissenting judgements he observed,

> where, as in the present instance, a leading phrase occurring in an Act of Parliament is of doubtful meaning, and the Legislature has omitted to remove the doubt either by interpretation or recitals, it becomes necessary to examine the history of the law.[63]

For that purpose, he said, the judge might look to "all sources of information from which he can derive enlightenment in any degree, great or small". At a time when it was unsettled whether the court might inform itself by referring to parliamentary debates, records and papers, Higinbotham had no doubt that the court was not merely at liberty, but under a positive duty, to do so.[64] He accordingly referred to reports of an English Parliamentary Committee on which the corresponding English Act was based. That Act had operated experimentally for 12 years and then been revised without altering the meaning of "having property for her separate use".

Higinbotham then traced the legislative history of the Victorian enactment, showing it to have been almost entirely borrowed from the first English model. He could find no indication of any legislative intention that that Victorian measure "should have a wider scope and operation than could be claimed for any of its principal component parts", nor could he construe such an intention from the structure of the Act itself. Because the Act enumerated specific kinds of "separate property" in its various sections, it had to follow, he said, that a married woman was not to be considered a *feme sole* in respect of every kind of property whenever acquired, held for her separate use.[65]

The majority judges (Stawell and Holroyd), in a joint judgement, found that methodology too precious and "plainly contrary to the spirit of the Act". They thought Higinbotham's conclusions would require the court "to bend the literal reading to the plain intendment of the Legislature, but to adhere to the letter against a merely conjectural intention". On that basis, the long standing "distinctive meaning" of "separate use" would be applied unless any contrary indications could be found in the Act. There being no such indications, the Act was to be taken to mean exactly what it said on the surface. "After all", they concluded, "the reasons of the Legislature, when undisclosed in any way of which the law allows judges to take cognisance, are too conjectural for judges to rely upon".[66]

Here, accordingly, was a result in which neither side could be said to be objectively right or objectively wrong. The pragmatists were unwilling to go behind the words of the statute to develop its meaning. Higinbotham, on this occasion, was not willing to accept the Act at face value, but was prepared to go where his colleagues would not. Lawyers of later generations would have no difficulty in following his course.

As to statutory history, in *Fitzroy Local Board of Health* v. *Howell*,[67] the appellant Board issued a notice under the *Health Amendment Act* requiring the respondent to drain and pave a lane on his land, the condition of which was a public health risk. The respondent failed to comply. The Board prosecuted a complaint at Petty Sessions, which was dismissed by the magistrates for failure of the notice to stipulate specifications and levels for the work. The Full Supreme Court, by majority (Higinbotham dissenting), dismissed an appeal.

The effect of s. 62 of the Act was that, where a Local Board directed that an act be done but it was not done, the defaulter "shall be deemed guilty of an offence". The section further prescribed a penalty for offences under the Act where no penalty was otherwise fixed. The subject default was such a case.

Stawell and Stephen considered themselves bound by an earlier Full Court decision (which they were at liberty not to follow)[68] that s. 62 was not to have a dragnet operation, and that non-compliance with a statutory notice was not an "offence". Where the Act prescribed penalties, they said, it did so commensurately with the relative offences it created. Its silence as to statutory notices was deliberate, and the legislature, being aware of that prior decision, had acquiesced in it.[69]

Higinbotham, on the other hand, traced the legislative history of s. 62 back to English antecedents, and then construed it as making every breach of the Act, including disobedience of orders, notices and by-laws, an offence if not made so by other sections. He also deprecated the magistrates' decision that the notice was vitiated by failure to specify full details of the works required.[70]

Stawell was earlier in unaccustomed dissent in *Playford* v. *Brown*[71] where, on appeal from the County Court, the appellant gave the Registrar as security a bond instead of money. Stawell held that the Registrar had no authority to accept a bond: Stephen and Higinbotham held otherwise. Again, Higinbotham followed legislative history and found s. 120 of the *County Court Statute* (Vic.) to be based on the English Act 13 & 14 *Vict. c.* 61, as later amended to recognize the legality of giving security by bond. The Victorian *County Court Rules* said nothing as to the form of security, and the words "give security" in s. 120 were, Higinbotham held, to be construed according to their natural and plain meaning to embrace security in any form of which the Registrar approved.[72]

Precedent and practicality were with Higinbotham in his dissent in *Harding* v. *Board of Land and Works*.[73] That case, tried before him and a jury, concerned the assessment of compensation for land injuriously affected when portion was resumed for railway construction. Here, a public road traversed the relevant land. By the *Lands Compensation Statute* 1869, s. 35, a jury, in so assessing compensation, "shall take into account the value of the adjoining land belonging to the person to whom compensation is to be made". Higinbotham, at trial, was asked to direct the jury as to the meaning of "adjoining", but declined to do so.

On appeal, Stawell and Williams disapproved of his refusal, holding that, as "adjoining" could create difficulty in the "non-professional mind", the jury were entitled to assistance. The majority further held that, giving the statutory words their ordinary and natural meaning –

> Land separated from other land by a public road, the legal estate in the soil of which is in another person, cannot ... be said to adjoin the latter land – it is separated.[74]

Relying on much English authority, Higinbotham insisted that "adjoining" had "no legal meaning, and admits of no legal interpretation". It was popularly understood, on the one hand, to imply "contiguity" – a physical contact or continuity of ownership, but, on the other hand, it was understood to mean "adjacent" or "neighbouring". The same line of English authority led him to prefer the latter usage. He resisted the suggestion that he had failed to explain "adjoining" to the jury. He had been asked by counsel to direct them in specific terms, which he considered to be wrong, and, if adopted, to have resulted in a misdirection.[75]

While his interpretation of "adjoining" was persuasive, the case demonstrates Higinbotham's want of incisiveness as a trial judge. It was not for the jury to construe an equivocal word used in a statute; and it was not correct that the word could admit of no legal interpretation. Counsel's request, that the jury be directed as to the meaning, was reasonable enough, but it was within the judge's discretion how to frame his direction. Had he done so, an appeal might have been avoided. But he lacked flexibility and without having time enough to research the point at the trial, the judge himself was insecure.

When, however, English judicial authority was itself in an uncertain state, as it was concerning part of the model from which the *Stamp Duties Act* 1879 (Vic.) was drawn, Higinbotham, in *Davies* v. *Herbert*, insisted that the colonial court ought to make up its own mind:

> I apprehend that it is the duty of the Court not only to interpret every part of this, as of other Statutes, in accordance with the plain and natural meaning of the terms used by the Legislature, but also to take due care that the public revenue shall not suffer loss by the uncertain construction or the lax application of a revenue law which may operate with unexpected severity in particular cases.[76]

An action that exposed the divergent judicial attitudes was *Brown* v. *Board of Land and Works*. It produced an extremely harsh decision in negligence. The plaintiff, who was employed by the Board to drive steam locomotives, formally reported to his superiors, fellow servants of the Board, a material defect in the locomotive he was assigned to drive. Left unrepaired, despite the plaintiff's further complaints, the defect caused a collision in which he was seriously injured. He sued the Board, recovering damages of £2000 – a very large sum.

The Board sought, and was granted, a non-suit on the ground that the demonstrable negligence was not due to it, but to the plaintiff's fellow servants (acting in one common employment – that "most nefarious judicial ploy")[77] by whom the defect had not been made good despite the plaintiff's complaints. The majority in the Full Court (Stawell and Williams) held that, by continuing to drive the locomotive, knowing of the defect, the plaintiff had voluntarily contributed to his injury. His only recourse was against his fellow servants – men of no financial substance. Higinbotham dissented strongly.

Part of the problem was that, as yet, there was in Victoria no governing statute to be construed. The English *Employers' Liability Act* 1880 was a remedial statute that abrogated the fellow-servant doctrine and made employers much more accountable for injuries suffered by their employees while so employed. No such measure had yet been introduced in Victoria. Stawell and Williams felt "compelled" to adhere to the common law's severity as it existed before 1880.[78] They could sympathize with the plaintiff's predicament, but offer only the relief (of no benefit to him) of alerting Parliament to the need for reform:

> Our obvious duty … is to endeavour to expound the law as it is, not to strain it as we may possibly wish it had been. Some benefit may perhaps result from this case. The attention of Parliament may be invited to the subject, and it may see the necessity for devising some well-considered measure, protecting alike the interests of employers and employed.[79]

Higinbotham, on the other hand, would not have ordered a non-suit. Citing many cases, he contended that the principles of the English Act of 1880 could be adopted by the Supreme Court of Victoria even though that Act did not apply there. While his research could detect no "rational and just principle" to support the fellow-servant doctrine, there ought, he maintained, to be a "reading down" of that doctrine to effect justice:

> while we are bound to administer this law (discredited as it may seem to be), so far as it has not been altered by Parliament, we are bound also to maintain and apply those limitations of the law which are a part of it, and which serve to mitigate, in some degree, its severity in application.[80]

He would have sheeted home liability to the employer as being bound, not only to supply a locomotive in sound working order, but to maintain it so.[81] In this case, he considered that the Board had failed in discharging a duty that had been made clear in previous court decisions, to ensure that its machine would not become dangerous, especially where the Board, through its servant supervisor, was on notice that it had become dangerous.

The old chestnut, of applying the 1828 *Australian Courts Act* (9 *Geo.* IV *c.* 83) tests for the reception of English law in Australia, arose in *McHugh* v. *Robertson* in 1885 where it was held that the *Sunday Observance Act* 1780 (21 *Geo.* III *c.* 49), s. 1, which prohibited the taking of money for admission to entertainments on Sundays, was in force in Victoria.[82] It seemed a case likely to fire Higinbotham's interest in many ways, and he appeared to be rising to the bait when he asked J. B. Box of counsel in argument, "Do you say that this case is to be decided according to the circumstances of New South Wales in 1828, or of Victoria now?". Box replied, correctly:

> The Act [9 *Geo.* IV] was introduced to New South Wales once for all, and it is for the Court to say whether it could at that time be reasonably applied to the colony. This colony was then part of New South Wales, though it was not settled upon by Europeans for seven or eight years afterwards. But all the laws in force in New South Wales at the time of our separation from that colony were declared to be in force here.[83]

Higinbotham rested content with that and mildly concurred, without further comment, in the decision of Molesworth, A.C.J., that the *Sunday Observance Act*, s. 1, was in force in Victoria, with the rider that "when public opinion changes so as to call for a change of the law, I suppose it will produce that change".[84]

Another "chestnut" that troubled most Australian courts in the 19th century was the interpretation of "timber". In *Campbell* v. *Kerr*, in 1886, the question arose before the Full Court in construing, not a statute, but a covenant in a lease, prohibiting the cutting of any "timber" on the demised land, except necessary domestic firewood for use in the leased premises. The defendant, who had been sued for breach of the covenant, contended that "timber" was to be understood in its common law sense, that is, as oak, ash and elm, and other northern hemisphere trees incorporated by later usage. On reservation of the point to the Full Court, Higinbotham gave the leading judgement.

> Not only have we no proof of the common law having been introduced here, but legislation has never recognised that meaning … I think … the word "timber" applies to all trees living or dead, and is not restricted to those which are fit, or ordinarily used, for building purposes.[85]

The clash of opinions revealed in some of these cases magnifies their importance far beyond their true relationship to the vast bulk of decisions in which the court was of one mind. While Higinbotham's methods grew in stature in after times, those of the pragmatists retained authoritative support, and he himself embraced them when he became Chief Justice. But, as will be seen, so firmly entrenched were those methods at his death, that his successor, Sir John Madden, resisted submissions for the creative construction of an Act, with the words,

> We are not here to administer abstract justice, but merely to act according to law. We must not assume the position of law-makers, and we cannot redress grievances contrary to the intention of the statute law … So far as statute law is concerned we have no right to act except according to well-known canons of construction.[86]

Negligence

It has been put, on high authority, that Higinbotham's judgement in *Fergusson* v. *United Steamship Co. of New Zealand, Ltd* was "progressive in outlook".[87] With the greatest respect, it must here be suggested that his decisions in that case and in a number of others relating to the law of negligence were extremely severe and demonstrative of little more than a slavish adherence to old technicalities that worked hardship and injustice upon plaintiffs.

Higinbotham was long cited with approval for his aphoristic summary of principle in *Fergusson's Case* when he said:

> Negligence consists in doing that which a person ought not to do, or omitting to do that which he ought to do, in disregard of the rights of another.[88]

The principle was sound, but its application, in concurrence with the judgements of Stawell and Williams in that case, seems much astray. The plaintiff leased a steam ferry that carried passengers across the Yarra, propelling itself along chains which, when not in use, rested on the river bed. The ferry was constructed and operated in accordance with the *Boroughs Statute*. The defendant owned river steamers that plied along the Yarra even when the water level was so low that they scraped the bed of the stream.[89] In doing so they severed the ferry chains repeatedly.

The plaintiff recovered damages in a Supreme Court action against the defendant, but the latter, in the Full Court, sought a non-suit for want of evidence of negligent navigation. The jury had accepted evidence that the ferry's chains did not so obstruct the river channel that steamers could not, when navigated with due care, avoid striking them. The Full Court granted a non-suit on the ground that the Yarra, as a public navigable river, was to be treated as if a public road.[90] Using the steamers at all hazards, virtually to plough their way through at low water, on their view, was not an unreasonable use. The jury's findings were displaced.

Relying on numerous English authorities that seemed little related to rivers liable to silting, as the Yarra was, Higinbotham acknowledged no cause of action in negligence, but hinted that there might have been one in trespass had it not been that the *Boroughs Statute* authorized only the operation of a cross-river ferry, not the use of chains. He rejected the plaintiff's argument that "a vessel which has not complete floatage has no right of navigation. Such a doctrine would be a dangerous infringement of an important public right".[91]

It is difficult to regard those conclusions as either progressive or just. The defendant's vessels were not merely at risk of, but were in fact, "smelling the ground", as maritime usage had it.[92] In those conditions the vessels could lose steerage, become unmanageable, cause collisions, and block the "highway" channel if grounding on the river bed. There must have been an abundance of evidence of negligence fit to be put to the jury, and the plaintiff was very unfairly deprived of the damages award.

Likewise, for a judge supposedly inspired by forward-looking and humanitarian notions, Higinbotham could apply the laws of the steam age with extraordinary harshness. In *Tobin* v. *Melbourne Corporation*,[93] for example, a young girl, while walking along a public road, passed a steam roller being used by servants of the defendant. A shower of sparks, emitted from the roller's opened firebox, struck the plaintiff's eye causing permanent injury and disfigurement. She sued the defendant in negligence and, at trial before Higinbotham and a jury, was awarded £350 damages as claimed. The defendant, on technical grounds, obtained a rule *nisi* to enter a non-suit. Thereafter the plaintiff amended her claim to allege trespass rather than negligence and, by majority in the Full Court, a new trial was ordered and the rule for a non-suit was dismissed.

Higinbotham, in a dissenting judgement that appeared clouded by formality and excessive analysis of precedents at the expense of justice, would have granted a non-suit. Even during argument he showed no sympathy for the plaintiff.

> HIGINBOTHAM, J. Persons using a street must accept the numerous risks ordinarily existing there.

> *McFarland* (of counsel). Fire is not one of them, any more than a wild beast.[94]

In judgement, Higinbotham was even more strongly against the plaintiff, saying that the evidence showed only that the fireman on the roller opened the firebox door whereupon sparks flew out. That, he insisted, "disclosed no negligence in the user or management of the roller". He continued:

> Actionable negligence has been defined to be the omission to do something which a reasonable man, guided by those considerations which ordinarily regulate the conduct of human affairs, would do; or the doing of something which a prudent and reasonable man would not do. I do not think that there was a single fact which, if unanswered, would justify men of ordinary reason and fairness in affirming the existence of either of the two kinds of negligence which the plaintiff undertook to prove.[95]

The only significant "answer" by the defendant was to assert that the steam roller belonged to another Council. But the pleadings themselves contained an admission that the machine was in fact the defendant's.

A prudent and reasonable man, in the position of the defendant's employee, would not have opened the firebox without first keeping a lookout for passers by, especially children. There was no hint of Higinbotham's going beyond the supposed purity of the law books to the reality of the plaintiff's having suffered permanent injury through no fault of her own. A different approach might well have been expected of a "progressive" judge.

Nor did the sometimes grotesque disposition of 19th century law to favour a master at the expense of his servant evoke much reforming protest from Higinbotham. A notable exception was *Brown* v. *Board of Land and Works*,[96] considered earlier. But in *Litton v. Thornton* the plaintiff was employed by the defendants to work a pile-driving machine.[97] When it broke and injured him, he sued his employers in negligence, alleging that they knew, but he did not, that the machine was unsafely constructed of defective materials. At trial, before Stawell and a jury, the judge directed the jury that the plaintiff ought to have been observant enough to discover the defect for himself and, as he was not, he took the risk upon himself. The jury accordingly found for the defendants.

On a rule for a new trial on the ground of misdirection, the Full Court (Stawell, Stephen and Higinbotham) found no misdirection. Stawell held that "the circumstance of the person injured having been acting as servant of another, does not exonerate him from the necessity of using reasonable exertions to avoid danger".[98] Higinbotham took the position even further –

> Even if a servant has a right to give up his contract of service on discovering danger in the machine he is working, I do not think he is relieved from the obligation to use reasonable means of obviating danger from its imperfect construction; he must make reasonable efforts to avoid danger, otherwise he may be held to contribute to any injury resulting from the defect.[99]

They were perilous days in which to be an employee: and Higinbotham seems not yet to have refined his view, expressed in *Brown* v. *Board of Land and Works*, that an employer was bound to supply and maintain an essential workplace machine in safe working order.

Two cases heard together in 1882 (*Smith* v. *Robertson*: *Anderson* v. *Robertson*) illustrated the gulf between some 19th century concepts of negligence and those of later times.[100] Today it would seem scarcely imaginable that such cases could be defended at all, let alone successfully at first instance as one was. The defendants operated stage coaches between Melbourne and its suburbs, conveying fare-paying passengers. One coach, when proceeding rapidly down hill between Kew and Melbourne, lost a wheel and overturned, injuring several passengers two of whom sued the operators in negligence.

There was conflicting evidence whether the coach was licensed to carry 36 or 38 passengers, and whether, as the plaintiffs alleged, the coach was overloaded, conveying at least 40 passengers. The defence, in effect, was that if there were overloading (which was not admitted) the defendants had only to face a statutory penalty, and that was not to be "twisted into negligence conducing to the accident": the only reasonable explanation for

George Higinbotham photographed c. 1853

THE HEAD OF THE DEPARTMENT.

(ACCORDING TO HIS OWN INTERPRETATION.)

Higinbotham's assertion that judges were officers "in his Department"

ST. GEORGEY.

A SCENE FROM THE LATEST BURLESQUE.

As depicted by Melbourne Punch

HIS HONOR MR. JUSTICE HIGINBOTHAM.

Drawn at the time of his appointment as judge – July 1880

the loss of the wheel was the poor road surface over which the defendants had no control: and that "we are not insurers, and we only undertook to do our best to carry you to the end of your journey".[101]

At trial, before Stawell and a jury, damages of £10 were awarded to the plaintiff Smith, but, in Anderson's case, Stawell later conceded that he had called for "an exactness of proof, more than was required", telling the jury that "they must be almost coerced by the evidence given to find that the overloading did not conduce to the accident".[102] The jury found for the defendants who obtained a rule *nisi* in Smith's case to enter a non-suit "on the ground that the negligence proved by the plaintiff had nothing to do with the accident":[103] while the plaintiff in Anderson's case obtained a rule *nisi* for a new trial on the ground of misdirection of the jury.

In the Full Court (Stawell, Higinbotham and Holroyd) the rule for a new trial in Anderson's case was readily granted. In Smith's case the judges agreed that the verdict should stand. Higinbotham, incomprehensibly, thought the nexus between the overloading and the accident involved "a conjecture highly improbable, and difficult, indeed, to understand". He preferred to rely on a broader principle –

> The accident itself is a fact from which reasonable and fair men might infer negligence, and the burden of proving absence of negligence, by proof of due care on his part, is cast on the carrier.[104]

In the field of local government, in which he had practised much at the Bar, Higinbotham developed a strong aversion to the abuse of their powers by local government authorities. He carried that to the Bench, particularly as to the responsibility of those authorities to maintain public roads made by them. He saw their liability for any neglect of such responsibility, not merely as strict, but almost as absolute.

In a long but concurring judgement in *Scott* v. *Collingwood Corporation*, in 1881, he reviewed many earlier decisions, especially those relating to the distinction between misfeasance and non-feasance, and, in holding that the distinction had no application to the subject case, concluded:

> The obligation to keep a formed road or street and every part of it in repair and in a condition reasonably safe for use by the public,

arises the moment the road or street is formed; and when once it exists the council, as the caretakers and managers of the road or street, never can divest themselves of it.[105]

He dissented strenuously from the inclination of his colleagues to require that, in negligence proceedings against local authorities for failure to repair road damage, whereby injury was caused to users, a reasonable time must elapse between the disrepair and the injury to enable the authorities to become aware of the danger. In *O'Connor* v. *Hotham Corporation* he propounded his view of the strict liability attracted:

> The [authority] has the means, through their officers, of informing themselves of the facts. Having the duty laid upon them to repair the defect in the street, they are presumed by law to have notice and knowledge of all the facts occurring within the local limits of their jurisdiction, out of which that duty arose.[106]

Had that been the majority view, it is difficult to see how most local authorities could possibly have met such an artificially high standard, and that at a time when perfection in maintaining public roads of often poor quality was financially unpractical.

Higinbotham did agree that such an authority would be under no liability, at common law or by statute, to maintain or repair roads that had been dedicated but not formally made, and over which merely informal tracks had been developed by usage. As he put it in *Dodds* v. *Berwick Corporation*:

> So long as a surveyed, proclaimed, or reserved road remains in the condition in which it is left by nature, the only duty of the council is to open it … and to keep it open and free from such obstructions as will wholly prevent the public from using it.[107]

Higinbotham's views about negligence sometimes varied according to the chance of his sitting alone at first instance, or of his taking more time to deliberate when sitting in the Full Court. In *Atkins* v. *Walsh*, one of a series of successful appeals in 1885 from Higinbotham sitting at trial without a jury, the plaintiff's property had been destroyed in a vehicular collision.[108] The defendant, who was engaged to level a hill, employed contractors to remove some of the soil. One of them, the plaintiff, provided his own horse and dray managed by his servant. Other soil was removed by trucks running on a tramway operated by employees of the defendant. While crossing the tramway, the plaintiff's horse and dray were struck by a truck, the horse being killed and the dray destroyed. Higinbotham awarded the plaintiff damages of £41, held that the fellow-servant doctrine had no application, found the defendant negligent in failing to place warning signs at the crossing place, and exonerated the plaintiff and his servant of contributory negligence.

The Full Court (Williams, Holroyd and Cope) unanimously allowed an appeal. Williams pointed to evidence by the plaintiff's servant that, in crossing the tramway he had looked one way but not the other, as an admission of contributory negligence – "That one admission that in broad daylight he had failed to look both ways, nonsuited him … [He] was to all intents and purposes asleep; he was driving a dray with his eyes shut". Higinbotham's attempt to place the onus of disproving contributory negligence on the defendant was held to be "diametrically opposite" to a line of English authority.[109] Holroyd agreed that "if the plaintiff's servant whom he had instructed to use caution had simply used his eyes there would have been no danger at all".[110]

In this field of the law Higinbotham did not have "the future with him" and, as puisne judge, left the law very much as he had found it.

Colonial Extraterritorial Legislation

While Higinbotham, generally speaking, did not allow his latent political interests to obtrude upon his judicial perceptions, this was one area in which he sometimes tried to use cases to advance his political philosophy that, since the *Constitution Act* 1855, Victoria was a sovereign entity. That area was whether the Victorian Parliament could legislate validly with extraterritorial effect.

In September 1880 the first opportunity arose for him to comment generally on the matter. In *R. v. Pearson; ex parte Smith*[111] the question was whether the *Passengers, Harbours, and Navigation Act* 1865 empowered the Executive Council to make Regulations operating beyond the limits of a port. The outer limits of Port Phillip were defined by such a Regulation to extend from Point Lonsdale to Point Nepean. The master of a vessel was convicted by magistrates for not flying the usual signal for a pilot, as required by the Regulation, when at sea within five leagues of the Port Phillip entrance.

Stawell held the Regulation to be *ultra vires* in purporting to operate beyond port limits.[112] Barry concurred, as did Higinbotham but in a separate judgement in which he doubted whether the legislature had conferred power enough to enable the Regulation to operate extraterritorially. But he impliedly recognized that the legislature itself had that power. He said,

> I do not think the Governor-in-Council could accomplish the object under the power to define the limits of the port, unless the Act were expressly to give him power to such extent; for an Order in Council is a nullity, and will not be enforced by the Court, if it exceeds the limits of the authority given by law.[113]

In a rare interjection, Stawell remarked: "I quite concur in that observation".[114]

There was no such cordial meeting of minds in *In re Victoria Steam Navigation Board; ex parte Allen*[115] which arose out of the striking of a submerged rock, near Cape Jaffa in South Australia, by a steamship proceeding from Adelaide to Melbourne. The ship's master reported the accident to the Board which, on conducting an inquiry, found that he was at fault in not having followed Admiralty sailing directions while rounding Cape Jaffa. The master, by counsel, objected that the Board had exceeded its territorial jurisdiction. The Board dismissed the objection and purported to suspend for three months the master's certificate, which had been issued by the Board of Trade in England. In the Full Supreme Court the master sought prohibition. The majority (Stawell and Stephen) granted it for excess of jurisdiction. In a very long judgement, Higinbotham dissented.

In his view, the *Merchant Shipping Act* 1854 (Imp.), as amended in 1862, authorized the investing in local tribunals of a power to suspend or cancel a master's Board of Trade certificate after inquiry revealing his misconduct or incompetency. In the case of Victoria, the colonial Board was the authorized tribunal in pursuance of the *Passengers, Harbours, and Navigation Act* 1865 (Vic.), s. 77 of which defined its powers, including a general authority "to do all such acts, and exercise all such powers as are mentioned in or are conferred by" s. 242 of the Imperial Act. In Higinbotham's opinion:

> These words, which create the general jurisdiction of the [Board], are words which contain no limitation of the local extent of its

jurisdiction. There is no reference to territorial limits. It is a court of inquiry only. It is not a court or tribunal in the proper sense of the word.[116]

He must well have known, as Stawell would hold, that extraterritorial efficacy could be conferred under the Victorian statute only by express enabling Imperial legislation.[117] Section 242 of the *Merchant Shipping Act* was confined to specifying the circumstances in which a master's certificate, issued by the Board of Trade, might be cancelled or suspended, and penalties imposed for maritime offences. Higinbotham's attempt to extract enabling authority from that Act by reference to the general procedural "catch all" words in s. 77 of the colonial Act, failed a fundamental test of construction – *generalia specialibus non derogant* – in other words, an earlier specific enactment is not constrained or affected by a later general enactment. All the more so, in this case, where the earlier statute was an Imperial one: the later statute merely an ingredient in a colonial one.

If the Higinbotham position were adopted, as Stawell pointed out, the jurisdiction of the Victorian Board could become boundless, and it might "hold an investigation into some charge of incompetency that may have occurred in Great Britain or in any other part of the British dominions". Higinbotham's first experiment in seeking a platform on which to construct a Victorian "sovereignty" thus failed. "Such a course if taken", declared the Chief Justice, "would have been in violation of powers conferred by the Constitution. The local Act applies [only] to local certificates".[118]

In *R. v. Pearson; ex parte Smith*, mentioned above,[119] Higinbotham had made a controversial statement again predicated on the absolute sovereignty of the Victorian legislature, a constitutional condition it did not enjoy in the 1880s. In reference to the making of Regulations operative beyond Victorian waters, he asserted that,

> it may not be doubted that, if [the Victorian] Parliament thought fit so to legislate in excess of its powers, a duty would be cast upon the Court to obey and give full effect to the enactment.[120]

He relied on an observation of Cockburn, C.J., one of the majority in the celebrated English case *R. v. Keyn (The Franconia)*:[121] a case completely at odds with the circumstances of Victoria, because of its attraction of relations between the British Empire and foreign states – relations that Victoria was not competent to influence or regulate. Dr W. Anstey Wynes put the position (as it stood after the passing of the *Statute of Westminster*) thus:

> According to international law it is not competent to Parliament [at Westminster] to enact laws, for foreigners outside Her Majesty's Dominions and beyond the jurisdiction, or for vessels on the high seas, but if such a law is passed, English Courts, no less than those of the Dominions, are bound to apply and administer it, it being left to the [United Kingdom] Government to justify its action with other States.[122]

The United Kingdom Government was so displeased with the majority decision in *R. v. Keyn* that it nullified its effect by the *Territorial Waters Jurisdiction Act* 1878 (Imp.), which conferred maritime jurisdiction only to "such a distance as is necessary for the defence and security of [the British] dominions".[123]

It was mischievous of Higinbotham, in 1880, on notice of the statutory reversal of the majority in *R. v. Keyn*, to look to that case to suggest that the colonial Supreme Court was bound to give effect to a colonial extraterritorial enactment that lacked Imperial sanction. The obvious course for the colonial court to have taken, if that contingency arose, would have been to pronounce the colonial enactment *ultra vires*, leaving aggrieved parties to pursue their claims before the Privy Council.

Yet, in 1881, Higinbotham adhered to his thesis in *R. v. Call; ex parte Murphy*[124] – a case going to the power of Victorian magistrates to "endorse" or "back" warrants issued out of Victoria. Stawell, in holding that *mandamus* would go to compel a Victorian magistrate to endorse a warrant from New South Wales, indicated that the power operated only within the limits of Victoria, and that the court's duty was

> to assume that Parliament will not lightly attempt to exceed its territorial limits, and that should such an effort ever be made, the Legislature would in justice to all those who are concerned in the administration of justice give utterance to their intentions in plain and unmistakable language conveying distinctly what its meaning and intentions are.[125]

Higinbotham, while agreeing with the issue of *mandamus*, was exercised by Stawell's remarks and rejoined with his "High Court of Parliament" simile previously discussed.[126] He tried to support it by the strong injunction of the great English judge

Willes, J., against courts making laws instead of administering them, and thereby being, not judicial, but autocratic. "Are we", Willes had asked rhetorically, "to act as regents over what is done by Parliament, with the consent of the Queen, Lords and Commons? I deny any such authority exists".[127] However exalted its language, that pronouncement had little application to the constitutional circumstances of the Colony of Victoria.

Within a month before his elevation as Chief Justice in succession to Stawell, Higinbotham presided, with Williams and Holroyd, at the hearing of questions reserved for the Full Court's consideration in *Hartle* v. *Campbell* and *Miller* v. *Campbell*.[128] The *Post Office Act* 1883, with the object of suppressing horse-racing sweeps, purported to prohibit the registration or delivery of specified postal articles. The question arose whether it operated extraterritorially to empower the defendant Postmaster-General to decline to register or cause to be delivered letters posted in Victoria to the Sydney address of a known promoter of sweeps.

Williams and Holroyd disposed of the matter unhesitatingly. The object of the legislation, they said, was to suppress sweeps, lotteries and the like when conducted in Victoria.

> we legislate only for those amenable to our jurisdiction; for legislation is intended to be effective; and what effect could legislation of this or any other colony have in compelling Frenchmen, or Germans, or Italians, or South Australians, or New South Welshmen to refrain from this act, or to do that act.[129]

It followed that the Postmaster-General had no authority to decline to register and deliver the relevant letters addressed to a person in New South Wales.[130]

While agreeing, under "considerable difficulty, which is not yet entirely removed", with that conclusion, Higinbotham saw in the Act another instance of competent extraterritorial legislation:

> I do not assent to the argument that, *prima facie*, the Legislature is to be deemed to be legislating, in an Act like [this], for Victoria only. This Act authorises the making of arrangements with the Government of other countries.[131]

With obvious reluctance, he had to admit, however, that power to prohibit postal delivery beyond the limits of Victoria could not be inferred from the wording of the Act.[132] Extraterritoriality was a subject to which he would return when occupying the office of Chief Justice.[133]

8

Chief Justice 1886-1892

"The Judge Was Making a Great and Unnecessary Fuss"

On 24 September 1886, the Executive Council accepted the resignation of Sir William Stawell from the office of Chief Justice he had occupied with distinction for nearly 30 years. His robust health had begun to crumble in 1881, significantly enough at the very time when Higinbotham, as judge, had begun his unsettling course. Compelled to take long leave in 1884, Stawell was not physically equal to resuming judicial duties in June 1886. Realizing, in August, that his concentration had lapsed during a trial, he submitted his resignation to take effect after he had delivered some reserved judgements.[1]

As early as 18 September 1886, the *Argus* was reporting the resignation (while also running a column "ought we to have lady lawyers in this colony?") and noting that "Mr Justice Higinbotham has now practically signified his willingness to accept the vacant position".[2] Sir Redmond Barry, who, as incumbent senior puisne judge, had aspired to the Chief Justiceship on the resignation of Sir William a'Beckett in 1857, would have been mortified. Since the grant of Responsible Government it had been almost unheard of in mainland Australia for judges once appointed to be promoted.[3] The only previous instance had been the elevation of Mr Justice Lilley to be Chief Justice of Queensland in 1879.

Higinbotham's advancement, at that period, was not only unconventional, but as paradoxical as the man himself. Through death or retirement, the Supreme Court had lost Barry, Stephen and Molesworth between 1880 and 1886, and Higinbotham was suddenly senior puisne judge at an auspicious moment. If he cherished any ambition to succeed Stawell he did not reveal it in the usual fashion of demonstrating outstanding legal ability, of being uncontroversial and detached, and of being noticed only in the most favourable light. On the contrary, he had gone out of his way, in an almost churlish manner, not only to remind the second Service Ministry, in office from March 1883 to February 1886, of the conditions he had prescribed for his acceptance of judicial office, but to seek to enforce those conditions uncompromisingly.

Although Higinbotham took his fair share of criminal trials, that was not a field in which he had practised much at the Bar, and, while he performed the duty competently, he did not relish it. Once in 1884, and again in 1885, he was obliged to pronounce sentence of death in capital cases: and that posed the question – would he fulfil his promise "to officially and openly refuse to comply with the requirements" of reporting to the Executive Council on the exercise of the royal prerogative of mercy.[4] He lost not a moment in answering "Yes".

On 10 May 1884, from the "Supreme Court" at Warrnambool, he addressed a letter of prodigious length to the Attorney-General, G. B. Kerferd. It reported that, on that day, Higinbotham had for the first time been obliged to pronounce a death sentence: it was in the case of Henry Morgan found guilty of murder. The judge resolved upon a pre-emptive strike, writing:

> I beg respectfully to request that the wishes or commands which the Crown may be pleased to convey to me in reference to the case of this condemned man may be transmitted to me in accordance with the English practice, through you or through some other responsible adviser of the Crown in Victoria, and not through any other channel whatsoever.[5]

He set out the imperial "instruction" to the Governor, of 21 February 1879, under which a sentencing judge in a capital case was to report to the Governor and, if required by him, to attend before the Executive Council to give advice and produce his trial notes. That instruction, Higinbotham complained, was in terms identical to those given to the Lieutenant-Governor of the District of Port Phillip, and had "ceased to be warranted" since the operation of the colonial Constitution in November 1855. It followed, he maintained, that, apart from reserving Bills for the royal assent,

> it is not competent for the Crown, and it is still less competent for any of the Crown's Imperial advisers, to give instructions to the Crown's representative with respect to any question connected directly or indirectly with our local affairs.[6]

With that air of artificiality that had distinguished so many of his *Argus* editorials, he then lapsed into hyperbole, claiming that "the constitutional rights of the people" were being threatened, causing anxiety to Victoria's politicians (could not they speak for themselves?). He criticized the Secretary of State and the Colonial Office for "unabated interference" in the Colony's domestic concerns at a time when, "so far as Victoria is concerned, it cannot any longer be contended that the Imperial Government is unacquainted with our public laws and violates them in ignorance".[7]

The judge therefore, as a member of the colonial community alive to the privileges and responsibilities conferred by the Victorian Constitution, reiterated his determination "to resist by every means the arbitrary and wholly illegal intervention of the Imperial Government in our domestic affairs, which has introduced, in my opinion, very grave and widespread evils into our political system".[8] He insisted, again, that he had a right to make his letter public.

Kerferd denied the latter right, but yielded some gratification to Higinbotham with the news that, for the future, the attendance of judges upon the Executive Council in capital cases would be at the invitation of Victorian Ministers of the Crown. The dire dangers and evils said to be attributable to Imperial "interference" were not admitted.

> I am directed to thank you for the expression of your valuable opinion, and to inform you that the matter is one, as you will readily admit, for the consideration of Her Majesty's Government, as affecting the proper and constitutional control by Parliament, through responsible Ministers, over every act of the Executive, and upon which I can therefore express no opinion to you.[9]

An exchange of some ten letters was then spread over as many days, in which Higinbotham querulously teased out having to comply with the request that he furnish his notes and attend before the Executive Council concerning Morgan's case. At length he capitulated, having created a ferocious storm in a teacup to produce only a minor procedural change. A few unofficial and diplomatic words would probably have achieved a better result more promptly. But diplomacy was a concept foreign to Higinbotham.

Kerferd, with a keen sense of the incongruous, repaid in kind Higinbotham's reference, when himself Attorney-General, to judges as "officers in his Department". Kerferd, as Attorney-General, declined to notice any representations by the judge made as a private citizen. But Higinbotham's prevarication, as judge, in complying with the government's requirements concerning the prerogative of mercy, was visited with a polite but pointed censure:

> it would be disastrous in the extreme if a Government allowed *any officer of the state, however highly placed*, unasked, to indicate to the Government its duty, or to request an assurance that it had adopted a specific course.[10]

Stawell, as Lieutenant-Governor, then administering the Colony after the departure of the Marquis of Normanby and before the arrival of Sir Henry Loch, submitted the correspondence confidentially to the Secretary of State, commenting only that "as the views of the Attorney-General were clearly presented I did not think it necessary to intervene".[11] At first blush, the Colonial Office was perturbed by the matter as it seemed to raise "a question vitally affecting our relations with the Colony". But, on reflection, Higinbotham's extravagant representations produced rather "the general impression … that the Judge was making a great and unnecessary fuss over a point of no immediate moment".[12]

Sir Robert Herbert dismissed "this old 'fad' of Mr Justice Higinbotham's" and reprobated its being raised at a time when Stawell was administering the government, probably with the intention of embarrassing him. Herbert was minded to seek the advice of the English Crown Law Officers.[13] Under-Secretary A.E.M. Ashley, however, could see "nothing to consult the Law Officers about" and criticized Higinbotham's observations as "so diffuse and hazy that some parts of his statements are susceptible of an entirely different construction from that of other parts".[14]

The Earl of Derby thought it best that the Law Officers be consulted, and draft instructions to them were prepared. But they were "suspended" when the Colonial Office staff disagreed about what specific advice was to be sought. As Stawell's despatch was confidential, it was thought best to ignore what had happened, and the file was "put by".

Higinbotham did not like being ignored, and he was irritated that the Colonial Legislature had not acted to correct the constitutional enormities he had exposed. But he waited patiently until he had next to pronounce sentence of death. That occurred in December 1885 when Freeland Morrell was convicted of murder. Higinbotham wrote again to Kerferd, recalling their earlier exchange of pleasantries, forwarding a copy of his trial notes, and laying down his proposed future course. He would adopt the rule of the English judges and "withhold my personal attendance from any meeting of the Executive Council called to consider a capital case, and I shall decline to communicate, by report or otherwise, with that body". He insisted, again, on a right to publish his views, and he did so.[15]

He must surely have antagonized his friends in the Service Ministry so much that, had Stawell's resignation occurred while Service remained in office, Higinbotham's appointment to succeed as Chief Justice would have been unlikely. But the Service Ministry fell in February 1886 and was replaced by a durable coalition between Duncan Gillies and Alfred Deakin – the former representing "conservative" interests and the latter the "liberals". Deakin was a dedicated Higinbotham admirer, and the Ministry included others who supported him, particularly H. J. Wrixon, the new Attorney-General, and C. H. Pearson, the Minister of Public Instruction.

As with his appointment as puisne judge, the fortunes of politics again smiled upon George Higinbotham when Stawell eventually retired and, in Professor Morris' exuberant words, "the Coalition … hesitated not an instant to appoint him Chief Justice".[16] The reality was otherwise. Early in May 1886, the government had invited Higinbotham to become Acting Chief Justice. In reply he recalled his correspondence with Kerferd in 1884 and 1885 "on the subject of illegal instructions issued to the Representative of the Crown by the Imperial Government". He said that his position was unchanged and that, if appointed Acting Chief Justice, it would be my duty to use the increased responsibility and possible large opportunities of that position to secure the independence of the Queen's Representative in this Colony, and to expose and resist the illegal interference of the Colonial Office in our domestic affairs.[17]

At that time his response was viewed with such concern by the Ministry that Molesworth was appointed to act in Stawell's place.

By September, Cabinet decided to give Higinbotham a second chance, and Wrixon extended the invitation to become Stawell's successor, noting how gratifying it was "to communicate the offer of this high office to one from whom I have received so much kindness, personal, professional, and political".[18] But, on this occasion, the feeding hand was bitten, and Higinbotham again tempted fate by prescribing the terms on which he would be prepared to accept appointment. He reminded Wrixon of what he had put to him in May, and of what he had earlier put to Kerferd; expressed his determination to abide by that position; and proposed that Cabinet reconsider, during which time the offer to him should be regarded as one "still unmade".[19]

The Ministry nevertheless adhered to their offer and so advised Sir Henry Loch. Troubled by Higinbotham's stubbornness, Loch sought advice from the Attorney-General whether appointing Higinbotham would constitute a direct or indirect admission that the judge's contentions were correct. The answer was that it would not: but Loch disagreed.[20] More challenging, and left undecided, was whether, in the light of Higinbotham's views, his name could be included in the dormant commission to act as Lieutenant-Governor or Administrator in the Governor's death, incapacity or absence.[21] Loch decided to accede to Higinbotham's judicial appointment, but to refer to the Secretary of State the other matters, including the latter's "views upon some matters of Imperial concern unconnected with the judicial functions of the office of Chief Justice".[22]

As the appointment required swearing in, not in court as in other jurisdictions, but before the Executive Council, Higinbotham attended before that body, on 24 September 1886, to take the oaths.[23] The *Australasian* thought the appointment "could not have been improved upon".[24] In Sydney, the *Australian Town and Country Journal* discerned "but one opinion across the border" as to the appointment, and "that opinion has been unanimous approval".[25] Dr Madden, on the Bar's behalf, congratulated Higinbotham when first taking his seat as Chief Justice, though, according to *Melbourne Punch*, Higinbotham "was particularly severe in some of his remarks when replying to the congratulations".[26]

Deakin left a pen portrait of the new Chief Justice in terms strikingly similar to others quoted earlier, depicting Higinbotham's profile as

> cameo-like in its delicacy, refinement and finish; his full face judicial, broad-browed and square-jawed; his blue eyes clear, still calm and far-seeing when not ablaze with passion. There was a mildness and sweetness in his manner, tone and carriage which were cherubic.[27]

Frank Gavan Duffy confirmed that impression, writing of Higinbotham as a man,

> With dome-like brow, a sweet mouth firmly set,
> Features clear cut as newly minted gold,
> And eyes of calm regret.[28]

"The Judges Must Maintain the Proper Administration of Justice"

W.F. Stawell was said to have experienced a religious conversion when of mature age. Higinbotham, on becoming Chief Justice, appears to have undergone a judicial conversion. Its most remarkable feature was that he embraced and pursued the style and methods of his predecessor so completely that it seemed almost that the "Stawell Supreme Court" had continued uninterrupted. Higinbotham had suddenly become a pragmatist.

While the new Chief Justice still liked to be seen to be different, as shown in his refusal of a knighthood and in other eccentricities noticed in a later chapter,[29] his judicial attitudes became constrained by the exalted responsibilities of his office. From the outset he reverted to the Stawell preference for brief judgements in the Full Court in which, more often than not, he delivered the unanimous decision of the Bench. He was conscious of new obligations falling on him to see that the court was functioning efficiently and keeping pace with the pressure of litigation. Discursive judgements and nice analysis of precedents became the exception not the rule. He was rarely in dissent, and rarely were his first instance judgements successfully appealed. No more could Gavan Duffy fairly criticize him for delivering "laboured judgments lucidly obscure, perspicuously wrong". Moreover, a detailed reading of his judgements between 1886 and 1892 reveals that hardly ever did he allow his personal political views to obtrude upon his decisions. No evidence supports the opinion that "as Chief Justice, Higinbotham still saw himself as a liberal politician who should exploit any legal case that furthered responsible government".[30]

The one great exception, that has coloured later assessments of his term as Chief Justice, was his dissenting opinion in *Toy* v. *Musgrove*, to be considered in the next chapter. Apart from that, he did return to some of the themes he had pursued when puisne judge, but much more succinctly. In managing the course of proceedings, particularly in entertaining counsel's submissions, he was similarly Stawell-like in his capacity to command and direct. Thus, when counsel was struggling over a contention that a landlord's right to distrain for rent was an interest in land, not a merely personal right, Higinbotham halted the argument with the remark "If you cannot find an authority to show that it is an interest in land, you may fairly conclude that it is not".[31] Again, on an application for an order compelling magistrates to receive specific evidence in a prosecution still proceeding before them, counsel's submissions were demolished when the Chief Justice said:

> There is no precedent for such an application as the present. If it were allowed it would make the Supreme Court a court of appeal on the hearing of a prosecution at every stage during the hearing, and before the justices decided whether they would commit for trial or not.[32]

In *Warburton* v. *Alston*, a successful appeal from the hapless "journeyman judge" Sir Henry Wrenfordsley,[33] a brilliant team of barristers for the plaintiff (Dr Madden, H.B. Higgins, and Leo Cussen) outsmarted him. They showed that Sir Henry had overlooked commission of fraud by the defendant. Higinbotham was emphatic:

> We think it clearly wrong to permit a failure of justice of this kind to stand, and … a new trial ought to be granted, and we have no doubt whatever that we have power to grant it.[34]

At the same time Madden was called upon to explain his misuse of English authorities, and the Chief Justice showed much sympathy for events that had displaced them:

> Since those cases the Court has shown a far stronger disposition in the interests of real justice between the parties to amend errors and correct slips between the parties.[35]

Sometimes Higinbotham would interject in argument to draw attention to a leading case, but no longer in the didactic style he had cultivated as puisne judge to show that he knew of more precedent authorities than did counsel.

He rose particularly to the duties of his office in protecting the authority of the court itself. The Supreme Court House in William Street opened in February 1884, at first to entertain criminal proceedings.[36] For years it was commonly known as Central Criminal Court. In 1887 Higinbotham's patience became exhausted, when presiding at criminal trials, because of constant loud hammering from an adjacent workshop that manufactured wooden notice boards. The noise was "frequently so overpowering as to drown out the voices of witnesses, and to make it extremely difficult and almost impossible for me to hear and record their evidence". Court officers were sent to request abatement of the noise, but the occupier, T.E. Dakin, claimed that he had done all that was possible to mitigate any nuisance.[37]

On 22 August 1887 Higinbotham signed and caused to be served an order directing Dakin and his employees to "forthwith cause the said noise to be stopped and do stop the same": but it continued on the following day. Higinbotham then signed a much longer order stating that "the business of the said court now being carried on … is still disturbed and impeded by the said noise", and requiring Dakin to appear two days later to show cause why he should not be committed to gaol for contempt.[38]

On the return day Dakin was represented in court by a strong team of counsel, Madden, Box and Hodges. Proceedings began testily after the associate inquired if Dakin were present.

> *Box* – He appears here under protest.
>
> [HIGINBOTHAM, C.J. I will hear that from Mr Dakin himself. Is he here?]
>
> He is in Court, but appears under protest. (Dakin then rose in Court and stated that he appeared). It is desired at the outset to know who is the prosecutor, or person moving in this matter.

[HIGINBOTHAM, C.J. Do you ask that question of the Court?]
Yes.
[HIGINBOTHAM, C.J. The Court has no answer to give.][39]

Counsel then sought an adjournment to prepare a response, which was granted on Dakin's undertaking "to abandon his contempt, and abstain from further disobedience".

Four days later, before the Chief Justice, counsel for the Attorney-General indicated that affidavits had been served on Dakin by the Crown Solicitor, the matter being of public concern "as the noise interfered with the Crown business". Madden, in a belligerent humour, objected to the Attorney-General's participation, argued that he had no standing, and submitted that the only remedies were for the Crown to institute proceedings against Dakin in nuisance so that the issues might be tried by jury, or to seek an injunction. "The Attorney-General", he complained, "has no right to shelter himself behind the protection of the Court".[40]

Higinbotham noted the objection, but declined to notice a protest advanced by Dakin himself. The precedent was being followed, he said, of *Skipworth's Case* in England where Lord Chief Justice Cockburn approached the Attorney-General, "as head of the legal profession and also as representing the Government", so that affidavits could be considered by the Crown and be the subject of such further action as might be advisable.[41]

Madden, however, raised the stakes by submitting that the Chief Justice's original order was in excess of jurisdiction, informal in not being sealed or made in pursuance of a rule of court, and therefore unlawful.

> So long as a man acts within the ordinary scope of his calling and does not disdain or flout the Court, no person has any right to interfere with his business. In this present case there is no evidence of any design to interrupt the Court, nor is there any evidence to connect or identify Mr Dakin with it. There is no clear definition of what is contempt of court.[42]

In sum, the order was claimed to be too wide in seeking virtually to prohibit Dakin from carrying on his business for all time.[43]

Higinbotham handed down a long written judgement on the following day. Expressed with great conciliation, out of regard for the consequences to Dakin's business, it contented itself with admonishing him "that he cannot and will not be allowed to disturb the business of this Court in future". Were it otherwise, his private business would take precedence over the administration of justice, so that the court, being unable effectively to conduct its hearings, might as well close its doors.[44] A nominal fine of £1, with imprisonment until payment, was imposed.

The court's summary power, to protect its proceedings against interference, rested he said on necessity. *Skipworth's Case* was further authority for the proposition that the court and its judges were under a duty to interfere summarily to prevent things having even a tendency to obstruct the ordinary course of justice or prejudice a trial.[45] He cited several supporting English authorities.

It was essential, he continued, that judges, being charged with that duty, should resist the "very strong temptation" not to perform it.[46] Concepts of natural justice militated against a judge's being seen in such cases to be prosecutor, judge and jury. However, those high discretionary powers were unlikely to be misused by judges who were exposed to parliamentary scrutiny, answerable to the Executive Council, and rendered liable to suspension for misbehaviour.

Higinbotham rejected the suggestion that the only remedy open was to institute a prosecution in which the complaining judge would effectively become the accuser. "If it should appear in the prosecution", he said,

> that one of the judges had instigated such a prosecution, and without any other apparent ground for such instigation than a desire to relieve himself from the necessity of performing a disagreeable duty, there can be very little doubt indeed that the accused person would be shortly and quickly dismissed from the bar.[47]

Dakin appealed to a Full Bench (Williams, a'Beckett and Holroyd) who unanimously dismissed the appeal. In a powerful judgement, Holroyd described the Chief Justice as having "acted with the greatest circumspection and deliberation, and with even more formality than was necessary".[48]

The suggestion that Dakin be prosecuted for a nuisance was, Holroyd thought, a "ridiculous farce" because it would defeat the imperative object of attaining a prompt resolution. Dakin's trade might or might not have been a nuisance in the legal sense, but that was by the way. It impeded the business of the court: it represented a lawful trade being conducted in an unlawful manner. Dakin had mistaken his remedy, said Holroyd. He could address his complaint to Parliament, which, having fixed the site of the court house, could recompense him if he made good his case. Meanwhile:

> Until some other place is provided by the Executive Government wherein the business of the Criminal Court in Melbourne may be carried on, the judges must maintain the proper administration of justice within the building which Parliament has provided, and by the only means in their power – the exercise of their summary jurisdiction.[49]

Dakin, who was merely a tenant of the workshop premises, no doubt transferred his business to an industrial site. He was fortunate, given the aggressive manner in which he had tried to maintain an impossible position, not to have been dealt with more severely by the court. But the important principle had been vindicated that the court's summary jurisdiction was potent, and that a contempt of court could be committed even though not "in the face of the court" itself.

In 1889 two cases (*In re Daly*; *In re Winter*) came before Higinbotham sitting alone, in which the Crown sought to have committed for contempt of court a solicitor who had published prejudicial letters in Melbourne newspapers, and the proprietor of the *Herald* which had published prejudicial matter about pending trials of persons charged with perjury.[50] A.D.J. Daly, the solicitor for some of those already tried before Williams, J., but before the trials of others had been completed, wrote to the *Argus*, the *Age*, and the *Daily Telegraph* (Melbourne), letters that were published alleging that four of those tried had been undefended "and were consequently practically judicially slaughtered without being able to say a word in their own defence". The letters contended that "a fearful and awful mistake has occurred on this one-sided investigation".[51]

The Chief Justice held that Daly had "wilfully and designedly" sought to interfere in the even and ordinary course of justice, and had committed "a grave offence against the administration of justice" and "an aggravated contempt" of the court's authority.[52] Daly was fined £25 (a significant sum) and sentenced to imprisonment for one month and indefinitely thereafter until the fine was paid.

The imputation in Daly's letters had been that innocent men had been tried "in some wholly unusual and improper manner", whereby they were unjustly condemned to undergo wrongful imprisonment. "The Court and all these juries", said Higinbotham to the prisoner, "are jointly charged by you … with an odious and shameful dereliction of their respective duties", in circumstances where the charge could not be met or refuted. The contempt had been aggravated by Daly's submitting an affidavit seeking to justify his letters and his right to publish them. But the affidavit adduced no evidence to show that the representations in the letters were true. The Chief Justice accordingly held that their publication had probably achieved Daly's "evil design" of poisoning alike the minds of the community and jurymen in the remaining trials.[53]

The case of Winter, for permitting publication in the *Herald* of statements that were "strictly and literally inaccurate" in relation to the same trials, was less serious. The Chief Justice conceded that Winter and his reporter had been misled by their undisclosed source, and had published the statements in question with no intention to prejudice the administration of justice. Yet, however innocent the intention, the publisher was strictly liable for what was published. The principle was:

> Where the facts connected with such a case may be stated they must be truly stated, and actual facts must not be stated in such a way as to instil a false prejudice or create a wrong bias. The publisher must verify at his own risk the facts which he chooses to communicate to the public.[54]

To remind the defendant of "the strict but necessary obligations which devolve upon the Press", a fine of £5 was imposed.

Higinbotham, however, was left as the dissentient in *In re Ebsworth; ex parte Tompsitt* in 1891.[55] H. T. Tompsitt had moved the Full Court for an order that A. M. Ebsworth, printer and publisher of the *Age* and the *Australasian*, be attached for contempt of court in permitting prejudicial articles to be published in those journals. Tompsitt had sued Ebsworth in defamation: Ebsworth pleaded the tender of an apology and payment into court of £25 as damages. The trial judge entered judgement for Ebsworth, with costs, Tompsitt being at liberty to take the money paid in. Tompsitt moved for a new trial on the ground of misdirection of the jury.

A new trial was ordered but, before it came on, the *Argus* and the *Australasian* published the articles complained of. The former was in general terms and to the effect that the Supreme Court of Victoria was lagging behind overseas approaches that recognized greater freedom of commentary by the press, and was a captive of "the relics of an odious special demurrerdom, which it was the main mission of the judicature system to purge out of existence". It trusted that the day was at hand "when our judges will seek to apply to newspaper libels [a] liberal and progressive interpretation of the law".[56] The *Australasian* wrote to similar effect, protesting against the harshness of the existing law and perceiving an "urgent necessity for a revision of its principles by the Legislature, and of a more generous and modern interpretation of those principles by the courts".[57]

In the Full Court, the majority (a'Beckett and Hood) declined the motion for attachment. a'Beckett thought that the articles neither misrepresented the facts of the case nor commented on them unfairly. Their only mischief was to present in a favourable light one side of the question still pending between the parties.[58] Hood considered that a mere tendency to prejudice a fair trial would not suffice: there must be a reasonable probability that injustice might be done to one party. Where prospective jurors might read and be influenced by the newspaper articles, the effect on their minds, at a trial estimated to be at least two months away, would be so likely to have faded as to be inconsequential.[59]

Higinbotham, on the other hand, found the articles to be prejudicial to a fair and impartial trial, and thus in contempt. While the newspapers might have published their opinions freely after the litigation had ended, the course they had taken before that event was unacceptable to him.

> it is the natural and necessary intention of these articles ... to reverse the positions of the plaintiff and the defendants in the judgment of the public ... [They] represent the plaintiff as a person who has no meritorious claim, ... while the defendants are made to appear as innocent persons, whose legitimate rights are neglected by the Legislature, and are harshly judged by the judges of this Court.[60]

The influence such articles might have on the minds of future jurors could not be assumed to be extinguished within two months and, in any event, "a wrongdoer [should not] be allowed ... to fix arbitrarily a limit of time after which he shall not be held responsible for the probable consequences of his wrong".[61] In those views Higinbotham appeared a very conservative judge *vis-à-vis* his coadjutors.

Courts, Judges and Related Matters

Higinbotham was astute to see that the court's jurisdiction was respected. In *R. v. Strickland; ex parte King*, the complainants were employees of Riley whom they sued for wages in Sandhurst Court of Petty Sessions.[62] Riley took out a cross-summons against them, returnable before the like court at Huntly, and applied to the Sandhurst magistrates to transfer the hearing of the complaints to Huntly which was convenient to him but very inconvenient to the complainants. In the Supreme Court they sought *mandamus* compelling the Sandhurst magistrates to hear and determine their complaints, which relief the Full Court granted. Higinbotham was unpersuaded by the submission of Dr John Quick, for Riley, that the Full Court, being properly a court of appeal, could not issue the prerogative writ. The Chief Justice declared that "the Full Court has jurisdiction, if it think fit to exercise it, in everything in which the 'Court' has jurisdiction".[63]

Jurisdiction, furthermore, was a precise concept: it was not something that could be conferred on a court merely by consent of the parties. In *Fleming* v. *Essendon Borough* an appeal had been taken to magistrates against the quantum of a municipal rate levied by the defendant. The magistrates said they had no jurisdiction to entertain it as it was brought out of time. On an application to the Full Court for an order that the magistrates be directed to hear the appeal, counsel submitted that the Borough had waived compliance with the statutory time limit. That was the end of the application for, as the Chief Justice concisely pointed out – "It is a question of jurisdiction, and consent cannot give jurisdiction".[64]

As to the jurisdiction of courts and quasi-judicial tribunals, Higinbotham held, in *Ellis* v. *Bourke*, that it was open to litigants to object to the jurisdiction sought to be assumed by a court, but not to invite the court to "determine that it is not a court at all" – that making such a submission assumed the very existence of the court itself.[65] That conclusion turned, however, on the pleadings involved in the case. Other remedies might have been available in the circumstances.[66]

Several decisions raised questions of jurisdiction, natural justice and transparency in court proceedings. In *R. v. Fitzgerald* the prisoner, charged with perjury, was tried before Kerferd, J., and a jury. After deliberating for some hours, the jury sent a message to the judge, who had left the court house, seeking advice about an issue being tried. Without discussion with the prisoner or his counsel, Kerferd returned, through the sheriff, a written answer that reiterated exactly what he had said to the jury in his directions in open court. On convicting the prisoner thereafter, Kerferd, by request, stated a special case to the Full Court on the question whether the communication between judge and jury, in the absence of the prisoner and his counsel, rendered the trial a nullity.[67]

A Full Bench (Higinbotham, Williams, Holroyd, Kerferd and Hodges) decided by majority that the trial was avoided so that the conviction must be quashed. Even Kerferd agreed that he had been wrong in following an informal course as the jury's question related to "a matter pertinent to the issue".[68] Higinbotham was the sole dissentient. It was of the essence of the criminal law, said Williams, that the entire trial proceed in open court. To hold that the communication that had occurred was legal,

> would have the effect of destroying all confidence in the administration of justice, and would be breaking down that most wholesome principle, that the trial of prisoners shall take place in open court, for a redirection to a jury before they have given their verdict is clearly part of the trial. I think the private communication objected to in the present case was clearly an illegal act, and that there has been no trial, and that the so-called trial is a nullity.[69]

Holroyd, while unprepared to differ, was "not sure that a private communication is more than an irregularity" – the court practice on the point being regulated neither by statute nor the common law. Hodges, however, loftily declared that, but for the Chief Justice's view, "I should have thought the question raised in this case was beyond the region of debate". It was, he said, "absolutely unlawful" that there be any private communication between judge and jury after the latter had retired.[70]

Higinbotham alone resisted the suggestion of Fitzgerald's counsel that "a hard and fast rule should be laid down preventing any communication between judge and jury in the absence of the prisoner". That, Higinbotham pointed out, would create a logical dilemma – "If that rule be carried to its full length you have no *locus standi* here now. This Court [could] not deal with any application in the absence of the prisoner".[71]

In a dissent that was again remarkably Stawell-like, Higinbotham drew upon the previously unbroken practice of the court. And relying also on English authority he held that the Full Court was powerless:

> Our jurisdiction is limited as on a writ of error to inquire whether the conviction is good or bad, and if the conviction presented in the special case be either a question of practice or a mixed question of practice and of law, we cannot in this proceeding review the discretion exercised by the judge at the trial.[72]

It would, he contended, be "unreasonable and also dangerous" to constrain that discretion. Reduced to an absurdity such constraint would require the attendance of the prisoner, his counsel and the jury in open court so that a juror might request a glass of water, or that the jurors might inspect a particular document in evidence. The settled practice, of not requiring a prisoner to attend at the argument of points of law, would have to be abrogated.[73]

Where, at trial, Kerferd had merely reiterated in writing exactly what he had already told the jury in open court, Higinbotham reckoned that:

> the Court is assumed to have a discretion varying with the facts and necessities of each case to allow or not to allow the exercise by a prisoner of his undoubted legal right. In the present case I think the judge had to determine a mixed question of law and practice. He had to determine in the exercise of a judicial discretion allowed to him by law and by the practice of the Court whether the question put to him by the jury had such an intimate and material connection with the issues as to render it right that the prisoner should hear the question put in open court; and if the question appeared to the judge not to have such connection he was at liberty … to give an answer to the question in the prisoner's absence.[74]

Accordingly, the Chief Justice maintained that the Full Court lacked jurisdiction to determine whether the trial judge had been right or wrong.

The result was unsatisfactory. Had Kerferd adhered to his original decision, and had Holroyd reflected further on his doubts, the majority might well have been with Higinbotham. The Chief Justice's conclusions were practical and posed no threat to the administration of justice.

A case raising somewhat similar principles about openness in the conduct of court proceedings was *R. v. Casey; ex parte Lodge*.[75] Judge Casey of the County Court heard a case at Stawell, reserving a point of law for further consideration. He announced in court that judgement would be entered either for the plaintiff or for the defendant in the light of that consideration, and that he would post his decision to the Registrar who would record judgement accordingly. Neither party then objected, but the defendant, finding judgement entered against him, sought prohibition in the Full Supreme Court, restraining the County Court and the Registrar from proceeding further on the judgement.

The Chief Justice spoke for the court in observing that a judgement expressed in the alternative was no judgement at all. Likewise the so-called judgement was a nullity for not having been pronounced in open court. The County Court Judge might, however, redeem himself by delivering his considered judgement on a later day.[76]

A related point was the character and correct use of the Supreme Court's seal.[77] Under the court's founding Act (15 *Vic. No.* 10), s. 9 prescribed the form of its official seal. It was, however, an unwieldy device, to be impressed in wax, that was inconvenient to use for ordinary court purposes. Under the *Supreme Court Rules* of 1853, a smaller seal, in the form of a metal or rubber stamp, was authorized, and its use was confirmed by the *Common Law Practice Statute* 1864. In the Court of Insolvency a bankrupt's application to expunge a proof of debt was granted on the ground that the judgement on which the proof was founded did not bear the Supreme Court's formal wax seal, and that the stamp seal appeared, not on the face, but on the back of the document.

The Full Supreme Court reversed the expunction. Higinbotham found the Insolvency Judge to have erred in assuming that the rubber stamp seal could not be recognized if its imprint were produced in any other Victorian court than the Supreme Court itself. Any Supreme Court judgement might be proved in any Victorian court by the production of the appropriate instrument bearing the Supreme Court's "working seal" under the 1853 Rules. The seal might appear anywhere on the instrument and, although there was evidence of a practice followed since 1853 to place the impression of the seal on the front and back of the document, that, in Higinbotham's view, was surplusage:

such double position of the official seal is by no means necessary to verify the judgment. Wherever the official seal is affixed, whether on the face or back of the instrument, it is the official seal of the Court, and proves that the judgment was signed.[78]

A question of judicial tenure may also be noticed here. Robert Le Poer Trench, Q.C., was appointed a County Court Judge in 1880, his tenure being at pleasure.[79] By an Act of 1884,[80] he and five other County Court Judges were confirmed in that office but on the footing of tenure during good behaviour. By that time Trench was aged 70. The *Administration of Justice Act* 1885, s. 5, stipulated that:

> Every judge of a county court who shall have attained the age of 70 years … may be called upon by the Governor-in-Council to retire from such judgeship, on a retiring allowance.

By Order-in-Council of December 1885 Trench was called upon to retire on 1 January 1886, and he was so advised by departmental letter. He protested that the peremptory call to retire was "fraught with most grievous injustice to me", and he instituted proceedings under the *Crown Remedies and Liabilities Statute* 1865.[81] At first instance, Higinbotham stated a case for the opinion of the Full Court. There Dr Madden submitted that Trench had been given no direct notice of the Order-in-Council or any opportunity to show cause why he should not be removed. He might, it was put, have shown that, although aged 70, he was still competent to discharge his duties. For failure to observe principles of natural justice, the Minister's discretion was claimed to have been exercised capriciously and so miscarried.[82]

The Chief Justice, in delivering the principal judgement, that offered no relief to Trench, held that s. 5 of the 1885 Act applied to all County Court Judges no matter when appointed or under what statute. That was apparent in the Legislature's use of the expression "every judge". The section's stipulation of the attainment of 70, as itself a sufficient ground to require retirement, did not import any right to show cause or advance contrary reasons –

> it is clearly not desirable that an officer, who is called on to retire on the ground of age, should be invited, or should be allowed the right, to take part in the consideration of the question.[83]

The correspondence in evidence sufficiently showed that Trench was well aware of the terms of the Order-in-Council affecting him.

Thus Trench's judicial career ended, though he lived for a further ten years with the benefit of the retiring allowance awarded to him.

Statutory Construction

A number of cases arose concerning the interpretation of Acts, Regulations and Rules, though few of them involved major questions of public law. In *Whitney* v. *Footscray Justices* the plaintiff was manager of a company that manufactured ammunition.[84] In May 1889 the company obtained a Crown lease at Footscray for the purpose of constructing an ammunition factory. Under the lease the company was to supply the Victorian Government with large quantities of cartridges, and it was permitted to manufacture ammunition for general sale. The *Ammunition Factory Act 1889* ratified the lease, and the company commenced its operations.

At that time the *Explosives Act* 1885 prohibited the manufacture of ammunition except at a factory licensed by Regulation: and, by the *Explosives Act* 1890, such factory could not operate unless licensed under its provisions. The factory in question was not licensed under either of those Acts nor had it obtained the assent of Footscray Municipality to its operations. An over-zealous government inspector prosecuted Whitney, as manager, for failure to comply with the 1890 Act. At Footscray Court of Petty Sessions he was fined five guineas and ordered to pay costs. He appealed to the Court of General Sessions which quashed the conviction, but the Chairman of the court stated a case for determination of the Full Supreme Court. There it was unanimously held that the conviction had been rightly quashed.

In the leading judgement, Higinbotham regarded the case as one where the provisions of a general Act must, so far as inconsistent with them, yield to the provisions a of special Act. The express intentions of the Legislature had been made plain in the 1889 Act. Accordingly,

> a lease when thus ratified, must be regarded … as a parliamentary licence to the lessees to carry on this hazardous business exempt from the necessity of obtaining for the leased site the assent of the municipal council or a licence from the Minister.[85]

It was not, he said, a case where the court ought to speculate on parliamentary intentions: it was simply a matter of construing the language used in the 1889 Act.

There were, however, some special circumstances where different canons of interpretation applied. In *Levey* v. *Azzopardi* the Full Court was called upon to interpret a provision in the *Rules of Court*.[86] The plain intention of the Rule was to delay the signing of final judgement for 14 days to give the unsuccessful party time to take any appropriate steps. Instead, the Rule *ex facie* limited a period of 14 days "within" which judgement might be signed. In argument, the judges made plain their impression that "within" was an inadvertent slip that subverted the real object of the Rule; during which Hodges of counsel, who argued for the contrary, had teased Higinbotham for his well known literalism:

> *Hodges.* The Court cannot construe this clause so as to give no meaning whatever to an important word therein. The Court cannot say that an Act of Parliament does not intend what it says.
>
> [HIGINBOTHAM, C.J.] Such an interpretation may be put upon a word, if it be opposed to the plain meaning of the Act itself. That was decided in *Becke* v. *Smith per* Parke, B. [(1836) 2 M. & W. 191 at 195; 150 E.R. 724 at 726].[87]

The Chief Justice therefore held that the parties could not intentionally have agreed to adopt a form of words that led to manifest absurdity.[88]

The word "within" in the *County Court Act* 1890, s. 134, caused difficulty in another context exposed in *Watson* v. *Issell*.[89] The objection was raised that the defendant, being dissatisfied with a judgement against him in an action on a contract, had failed to appeal "within seven days" after the judgement as stipulated by the section. The objection relied on an interpretation that reckoned time as including the day on which judgement was given and also the day on which the appeal was lodged. The Chief Justice held, and his coadjutors agreed, that the English authority of *Lester* v. *Garland* must be followed under which fractions of a day were disregarded in computing time.[90] In the result time ran from the end of the day of delivering judgement, but included the day of lodging the appeal. On that basis, the appeal in the present case had been initiated on the last permitted day after excluding the day on which judgement was given.[91]

Another instance of what appeared to be a slip in legislative drafting arose in *R. v. Morton*.[92] The prisoner moved the Full Court to grant *mandamus* to compel the Chairman of General Sessions to reserve for the opinion of the Full Court questions of law that had been raised at trial. Under the *Judicature Act* 1883, s. 70, power was given to compel a Supreme Court Judge to reserve points of law raised at the trial of a criminal case. Under Higinbotham's second consolidation of the statutes, that section became s. 485 of the *Crimes Act* 1890. In that form it recognized a similar power of compulsion directed to a judge, but made no reference to the Chairman of General Sessions who would ordinarily be a barrister, not a judge. The Crown submitted that, in those circumstances *mandamus* would not lie.

Higinbotham conceded that the new s. 485 had been awkwardly placed in the statutory consolidation; but he concluded that the law had not been changed:

> the alteration in the collocation of that section does not make any alteration in its legal effect. The application of the section then was, and now is, to cases where the Supreme Court, represented, no doubt, by a judge who presides in that Court, refuses to reserve a question of law.[93]

Mandamus was refused.

The old and self-defeating remedy of imprisonment for debt still lingered in Victoria, and questions arose as to construction of the governing Act. In *R. v. Henson; ex parte Bond*, the Fitzroy magistrates purported to make an order in pursuance of the Act that the debtor, having the means to pay a debt for board and lodging, must pay it to the complainant.[94] On hearing an application to quash the order, the Full Court readily did so. Higinbotham's leading judgement held, first, that an order under the Act that money be paid directly to the complainant was void – payment into court or to the Clerk of Petty Sessions was the only procedure recognized by the Act. Then the Act required that the debtor had the means and the ability to make the payment. Explaining that "means" and "ability" were not synonymous, the Chief Justice observed:

> "Means" to pay the debt points to the debtor having property out of which the debt might be paid. "Ability" to pay points to the capacity of the debtor to apply that property to the purposes for

which it is his duty to apply it. A man may have property in such a form that he cannot at any particular time, or may not be able during a continued time, to realise it and apply it in payment of his debts.[95]

Here, the magistrates had evidence before them of the debtor's means that were sufficient to pay a debt of under £8, but no evidence of his ability to pay. It was therefore impossible for the Full Court to know whether the magistrates had reached any conclusion as to ability. The magistrates were reprimanded for their "very grave negligence indeed". Higinbotham expressed concern for the victims of injustice in the administration of a law directed to a particular purpose only. The court, he said, had often warned magistrates of their responsibilities under the *Imprisonment for Debt Act*.

> It has had occasion repeatedly to call attention to the fact that justices appeared to use the Act as a means of enforcing payment of debts. This is an entire misapprehension as to the meaning and effect of this law. This law is one intended to punish persons who act in a criminal manner by dishonestly withholding payment of a debt which they are able to pay, or dishonestly incurring a debt which they ought not to have incurred. And to use it as a means of enforcing payment of ordinary trade debts is a gross abuse of the intention of the Legislature, and involves a very great injustice to individuals.[96]

Declaring that the law does not attach a penal effect to non-payment of debts, and that magistrates generally were on notice of the court's interpretation of the Act, the Chief Justice gave a warning that, if future such cases came under the court's notice, it might be necessary "to visit upon the justices the consequences of the injustice they have inflicted on individuals" and render them personally liable in costs for their negligence. Had the Fitzroy magistrates been joined as parties in the subject proceedings, such a costs order would have been made against them.[97] Their order was quashed.

The Chief Justice's sympathy with the "underdog" was also plain in his dissenting judgement in *Murphy* v. *Lee*.[98] Under the *Police Offences Act* 1890, the City of Ballarat made a by-law intended to prohibit itinerant street vendors from loitering. It proscribed the use of "any fixed stand", and required such a vendor to "keep moving along such street on the side thereof situate on his left hand at a reasonable walking pace of not less than one mile per hour". The defendant was observed by a constable to be standing beside his fruit cart at a street corner, conversing with passers by and selling fruit to at least one of them. He remained there for 35 minutes. Magistrates dismissed an information against him for breach of the by-law. On an order *nisi* to review their decision, the majority of the Full Court (a'Beckett and Molesworth) set aside the magistrates' decision and ordered a rehearing. a'Beckett considered that the by-law required reasonably constant movement, and did not allow a vendor to mark time for 35 minutes and then walk one mile in 25 minutes.[99] Molesworth thought the evidence of the defendant's spending time conversing to be fatal to his position: he might have stopped to sell fruit, but not to have a yarn.[100]

Higinbotham, on the other hand, began with the premise that the defendant was going about a lawful business and that the by-law supplied the entire test by which that business was to be governed. If a hawker traversed one mile at a reasonable walking pace within one hour he was not in breach of the by-law. The true test, he thought, was found less in the literal construction of its words than in establishing the intention of the city corporation. On that basis:

> The object of the regulation was to prevent itinerant vendors of commodities from taking up a fixed stand in any street and from unduly delaying therein, and thereby causing obstruction of the street. It was not intended that the vendors or hawkers should keep in perpetual motion. Such a regulation would be altogether unreasonable, and would prevent such persons carrying on their lawful trade.[101]

There were numerous interpretation cases turning on old-fashioned technicality that would be tiresome to notice here. But one instance, that raised the perpetual problem of construing statutory words according to their plain and natural meaning (if it could be discerned), was *Hickling* v. *Todd*.[102] The *Stamp Duties Act* 1879, s. 51, imposed duty on promissory notes which it defined as "any document or writing, except a bank note, containing a promise to pay any sum of money".

The plaintiffs, share brokers, arranged the sale of shares to the defendant and issued a bought note indicating how the purchase money was to be paid, portion being payable "at any time on or before the 19th August, 1888". It was not so paid. The plaintiffs, in the County Court, proceeded against the defendant, putting the bought note in evidence. The defendant objected that the document was a promissory note and, not bearing the requisite stamp duty under the Act, was inadmissible. The judge overruled the objection and found for the plaintiffs. The defendant appealed to the Full Court.

There the majority (Kerferd and a'Beckett) dismissed the appeal, holding that the generality of s. 51 had to be curtailed, otherwise "scarcely any contract would escape taxation as a promissory note" if full effect were given to the section. Relying on English authority precisely to the point, they "read down" the expression "promissory note" to mean a document the contents of which consisted substantially of a promise to pay a definite sum of money, and of nothing else. The brokers' note was not such a document.[103]

Relying also on English authority, Higinbotham reached the opposite conclusion on public interest grounds. He thought that his colleagues' reasoning invited evasion of the Legislature's "distinct intention" and would work "to the detriment of the public revenue". It was not good enough, he said, to construe a fiscal statute merely to overcome supposed inconvenience and uncertainty.

> The desire is a natural one, but I take leave to doubt if it be admissible for the purpose of influencing judicial opinion in the interpretation of terms in an Act of Parliament not ambiguous on their face. The uncertainty was anticipated by the Legislature; commercial convenience was consulted, and facilities for determining doubts in all cases have been provided by means of an application to the Comptroller of Stamps … I think that we ought to apply the terms of the 51st section according to their plain meaning, and without the addition of an arbitrary limitation to the facts of each case.[104]

Local Government

The Supreme Court's consideration of statutes that prescribed the powers of local government authorities concerning roads, represents a specialized extension of the issues of statutory construction that have just been considered. In this area Higinbotham's policy of preferring literal interpretations, even at times at the expense of justice and reason, was at its more extreme. He did not disguise his view. In one of the earliest cases he heard as Chief Justice he stated that "a law …, however unjust it may seem to us to be, must be upheld and applied until it is altered by the Legislature".[105] In that inflexibility he was anything but a liberal or progressive judge.

The Law Reports were strewn with cases about roads, some of the decisions being at odds with others. It is unpractical to attempt to review them all here. But confusion resulted when the *Local Government Act* 1874 conflated relevant provisions of the *Boroughs Statute* 1869 and the *Shires Statute* 1869. Previously the responsibilities of boroughs and shires in relation to roads had been different.

Borrowed from English local government usage, but without the same extensive powers, "borough" was adopted in early colonial Australia to designate a well populated urban area, later styled a municipality. Shires were rural or less populated areas. Boroughs, and shires that had passed relevant by-laws, were obliged, under the *Local Government Act*, to prepare plans of intended road works, exhibit them to the public, and entertain ratepayers' objections, rejection of which could be the subject of appeal. When works so notified injuriously affected adjoining property, compensation was payable. Shires that had never been boroughs and had not passed the relevant by-laws were not liable to take any of the steps just described.

The first of a *catena* of cases to occur during Higinbotham's Chief Justiceship was *McDonald* v. *Shire of Coburg*.[106] The plaintiff owned premises fronting a major road that had been metalled, kerbed and guttered, and remained so for over 10 years. During that time the plaintiff piped roof rainwater and kitchen waste water into the road gutter. Without notice, the Council raised the level of the adjoining footpath, cutting off the plaintiff's pipes, and causing flooding and structural damage to the plaintiff's home. The amenity of the home was further affected because its elevation was lowered relatively to the street, and access was rendered awkward. Before the issues of fact were tried, points of law were referred to a Full Court (Higinbotham, Kerferd and Webb) which, although of one mind, directed that the case be argued before the court *in banco*, as it appeared likely that a long-standing decision of the court would be challenged.

The result was a feast of technicality in which the plaintiff, despite all the preliminary stages, was substantially put out of court because his pleadings were held to be inadequate to cover the relief he sought.[107] Difficult and conflicting statutory provisions were construed strictly against him by all of the judges except Williams.

Coburg Shire, never having been a borough or passed relevant by-laws, claimed exemption from the *Local Government Act* provisions relating to boroughs. In argument, counsel for the Shire submitted, and the court accepted, that:

> in sparsely populated districts it is unnecessary to provide means for fixing the levels of roads. In a shire where the inhabitants are few and scattered it may be inexpedient to permit the council to fix the level of any road. Were it fixed, circumstances might change, and with increase in population a subsequent alteration of level might become indispensable; and that might involve the payment of a large sum for compensation.[108]

It followed, in the Chief Justice's view, that, as the defendant was not a borough, it possessed unlimited discretionary power to raise or lower the level of roads and footpaths, without compensating any person claiming to be injured thereby, and that the *Local Government Act* was to be so construed.[109] All the other judges, except Williams, concurred. While the plaintiff could have had no right, prescriptive or otherwise, to drain water from his premises on to the roadway, his other claim of loss of amenity was different. Williams considered that the preliminary words, "subject to the provisions of this Act", to the operative part of the Act, did not confer absolute and unconditional authority on shires, but imported the obligations, of notice and so forth, set out in the sections relating to boroughs.[110]

For the Chief Justice, as for the majority, the plaintiff's interests were to be subordinated to legal principle and dry statutory construction. As Higinbotham put it:

> The doctrine that no action will lie for doing that which the Legislature has authorised, if it be done without negligence, although it occasions damage to anyone, is … now thoroughly well established … [Hence] although the form in which the power is given is permissive only and not imperative, the donee of the power will be protected by the statute in the exercise, without negligence, of the power in such a manner as to interfere with private rights.[111]

It followed that a Shire Council could alter the levels of streets or footpaths in its absolute discretion, whether or not injury to property or loss to individuals resulted.[112]

The court seemed to have before it no evidence, other than the quoted submission of counsel in argument, why the Legislature would place residents of shires in a worse position than residents of boroughs in those respects. The literalistic view of the majority, however binding, reflected a narrow and illiberal approach to statutory construction, and a disregard for the practical merits of a case in which the plaintiff was treated most harshly – whether or not his pleadings were to blame.

In *Brett* v. *Slater* the plaintiff was more successful in proceedings against, not a local authority, but his neighbour.[113] A Council drained a road, causing water to concentrate on the plaintiff's land. He erected an obstruction that diverted the water on to the land of the defendant who destroyed the obstruction. In the County Court the plaintiff recovered judgement and damages against the defendant who appealed to the Full Supreme Court. The appeal was unanimously dismissed. Declaring that the plaintiff had "an undoubted right" to prevent injury to his land by an artificial concentration of water, Higinbotham said that the defendant could look only to the Council for redress. As to the extensive powers given to Councils to undertake radical drainage works associated with road-making, he added:

> that power must be exercised ... under such conditions that the owner of private land will have the water not merely thrown upon his land, but carried through his land, and shall receive compensation for the drain by which that water is carried through his property.[114]

Holroyd and Kerferd concurred.

Then came *Bailey* v. *Port Melbourne Corporation*.[115] It seemed to suggest that the court's sympathy was beginning to swing behind ratepayers whose properties were adversely affected by roadworks. But that result turned only on particular provisions of the *Local Government Act*, of which Holroyd was to complain, "no more difficult Act to interpret has ever come under my notice ... It is full of inconsistencies, full of difficulties of language and conflict of arrangement. It is impossible to construe some sections without doing violence to the language of others".[116]

The plaintiff sought damages from Port Melbourne Corporation for injury to his land occasioned by the raising of the level of two streets adjoining it. He claimed, and it was accepted at first instance, that the streets had been already levelled or paved before the passing of the *Local Government Act* in 1874. The Corporation appealed to the Full Court against the award of damages to the plaintiff.

The appellant sought to argue that *McDonald's Case* was in conflict with earlier Supreme Court decisions. Higinbotham rejected that, pointing out that the earlier decisions related to boroughs, *McDonald's Case* to a shire: and the court had to distinguish between the authority Parliament had given to the one local authority but not to the other. Construing the Act, he concluded that:

> wherever a street within a borough can be ascertained to have been in part levelled or paved according to the general meaning [previously] assigned to those words by the Court …, it is assumed to be the act of the council or its predecessors, and the act or series of acts by a council or its predecessors, in levelling or paving, is equivalent to fixing the level.[117]

Williams and Holroyd agreed, though with some doubts. It followed that the appellant, not being a shire, had no discretionary authority to alter the level of the subject streets which were to be treated as already levelled or paved, and the plaintiff had been entitled to recover damages.

Another tortuous and unsatisfactory piece of litigation, concerning the liability of a local authority for injury suffered by a person using an unmade road, was *Hitchins* v. *Borough of Port Melbourne*.[118] It came before the Full Court in 1888 and again in 1889. The plaintiff's husband, a Melbourne solicitor, while walking at night along a proclaimed but unmade public highway, fell into a huge excavation in the roadway: he sustained severe injuries that precipitated gangrene from which he died. Years before, another public authority created the excavation: neither it nor the Borough Council had filled it in afterwards. The Council, sued by the widow in negligence, pleaded that it had neither made nor formed the road but that, if there were negligence, the deceased had been guilty of greater contributory negligence, he being intoxicated at the time.

Before Webb, J., and a jury, the judge found that the death was caused by the consequences of the deceased man's fall while lawfully using a public highway; that the Council had not made or formed that portion of the highway; and that the deceased was not guilty of contributory negligence. The judge reserved for the Full Court's opinion the question whether, on such findings, the Council was negligent.

Williams and Holroyd considered that the Council ought to be liable for the injuries. That liability arose, they said, not for failure to repair a road not formally taken over by the Council, but for standing idly by when aware that excavating had begun, and for not fulfilling its duty to attempt by injunction or otherwise to prevent the trespass and nuisance being caused. Higinbotham, on the other hand, thought that the Council was not negligent. He relied on a very strict reading of the governing statute, under which he held that the Council was not compellable to remove "any obstruction in a highway caused by the act of a stranger not being an adjoining proprietor or occupier", and therefore not liable for any damage caused by such obstruction.[119]

The majority conceded that, within the limits of the question asked by the trial judge, the answer must be that the Council had not been negligent. But they advised that amendment of the pleadings ought to be permitted to disclose that the excavation was made with the Council's knowledge, and that the Council had failed to prevent it. Leave to amend being given, the case came to a new trial before a'Beckett. Perversely, he flatly refused to apply "a new rule, for which I find no warrant in the Statute prescribing the council's duties". He gave judgement for the Council, because its omission to proceed against those who made the excavation conferred no right of action on the plaintiff. He would adhere to the "old rule" –

> that the council had no active duties with reference to a road until it had accepted responsibility for forming the road. I am not prepared to adopt the qualification that it has the duty of proceeding against any stranger whom it may find intermeddling with a road before formation.[120]

In case there should be an appeal from his decision, he said he would have awarded compensatory damages at a very low level having regard to strong evidence "as to the drunken habits of Mr

Hitchins, and his consequent impecuniosity". That overlooked the state of destitution in which the widow and six children were left.

There was an appeal, of the most unsatisfactory kind, to a Full Bench of four (Higinbotham, Williams, Holroyd and Kerferd) who were equally divided in opinion. The appeal was dismissed according to the usual practice whereby, in those circumstances, the Chief Justice's decision prevailed.[121] Williams and Holroyd adhered to what they had said before, though Williams resisted the Chief Justice's assertion that:

> The proposition that a municipal corporation having knowledge of the unauthorised act of a stranger which does damage to the natural surface of a highway within its jurisdiction which has not been formed or made, is liable in damages to a person injured through the act of a stranger because it has not prevented nor attempted to prevent that act, is a proposition now advanced for the first time, and is wholly unsupported by judicial decision.[122]

Williams insisted that that was "emphatically *not* the proposition" previously stated by Holroyd and himself, and he criticized the trial judge for having made no findings on the material questions raised by the amended pleadings.[123]

The decision of Kerferd, J., thus swayed the outcome through his constricted reading of the *Local Government Act*, and his conclusion that Parliament, had it intended to cast on Councils a duty of preventing damage by strangers to roads in an unmade or natural state, would have said so in the legislation; but it had not. The result, neither just nor fair, stands as a memorial to an era where strict and literal reading of statutes took priority over humanity and often common sense – a practice in which the "progressive" Chief Justice was all too often a participant.

Then there came another turn of the tide, this time in favour of landowners,[124] though Higinbotham was not for turning. In *Carslake* v. *Caulfield Shire Council*,[125] in 1891, an appeal was taken from a decision of Webb, J., to a Full Court comprising Higinbotham, a'Beckett and Hodges, who were in such disaccord that they ordered the case to be re-argued before the whole Bench, excluding Webb. The result was simple enough, that a Shire Council had no statutory authority to drain a street so as to concentrate water on, but not to conduct it through, adjoining land. Attaining that result, which affirmed Webb's decision, split the

Bench: Higinbotham and Hood dissented from the judgements of a'Beckett, Hodges and Molesworth.

The majority conclusion had reason and justice on its side. a'Beckett pointed out that a Council's statutory power to make roads gave no express authority to make drains. Implied authority was insufficient, in his view, to permit Councils to create an artificial nuisance by concentrating drainage water on private land without any liability to compensate for consequential injury. Hodges was unwilling to yield to "a very harsh statute" under which

> a man may be compelled as a ratepayer to contribute to the making of a road which is to do peculiar and permanent injury to, and which may even ruin, the very property in respect of which he is rated.[126]

He could find in the governing statute neither express words nor necessary implication to authorize the trespasses complained of. He further justified his conclusions by reference to legislative history[127] – a subject on which Higinbotham had become somewhat subdued since becoming Chief Justice, except, as will be seen, in *Toy* v. *Musgrove*.

Molesworth was content to hold that the Council had no right to remove a nuisance from a road on to a ratepayer's land, and that what had been done in this case could not be justified under the Act.

At first instance Webb, having also directed attention to the inconsistent state of the court's prior decisions, determined to follow *Brett* v. *Slater* to reach a conclusion like that of the majority on appeal.[128]

In dissent, Higinbotham delivered one of those "laboured judgments lucidly obscure" that had been typical of him as a puisne judge. He considered that *Brett* v. *Slater* had been misconstrued. He denied that it had overruled earlier Victorian decisions, based on English authority, that laid down the principle

> that where an Act of Parliament gives power to make roads, it gives, by necessary implication, the power to construct the works necessary for the drainage of the roads, and that an action will not lie for consequences hurtful to individuals resulting from such works.[129]

He therefore disagreed with the liberal reading down of the "harsh statute" by Hodges. Higinbotham considered that Parliament could not have been unaware of the legal and other problems caused by the volatile state of the law concerning road drainage: so he concluded that,

> we must assume, ... although the hardship [earlier cases] seemed to involve may sometimes have caused murmurs, and even doubts, they have not been overruled or modified either by the Court or by any of the numerous Acts relating to local government which have since been passed. We are called upon, therefore, I think, to uphold them to the fullest extent, and not to suffer their authority to be weakened unless we are compelled to do so. They are ... founded on the principle long established, and now quite indisputable, that where Parliament has expressly, or by necessary implication, required or authorised an act to be done, the doing of that act, without negligence in the design or execution of the works necessary for accomplishing the act, is lawful, and furnishes no cause of action to anyone who has suffered damage from the act.[130]

When a similar set of facts, occurring in Victoria, came before the High Court of Australia, in *Aisbett* v. *City of Camberwell* in 1933,[131] Higinbotham's strict interpretation was not favoured. Starke, J., said of *Carslake's Case* that:

> It is too late now to canvass that decision. It has stood for forty years and been frequently followed, and has to some extent been recognized by the Legislature.[132]

Dixon, J., with whom Rich, Starke, Evatt and McTiernan, JJ., concurred, traced the progression of the Victorian Supreme Court decisions, but held that the Legislature could not be taken to have "adopted a form of expression" intended to permit Councils to pour water indiscriminately on to land adjoining roadways.[133] McTiernan, J., further thought such cases to be governed by the presumption that public bodies are not authorized to create nuisances or otherwise affect private rights unless compensation is provided.[134]

Negligence

As if to make amends for his frequently severe approach to statutory construction, Higinbotham's was sometimes a dissenting voice for humanity in the field of torts, particularly negligence. At a time when the common law was generally applied on the basis that individuals were responsible for their own acts, and, if they suffered injury through acting incautiously, the fault was their own, Higinbotham at times tried to introduce a measure of reform. He was rarely successful.

A striking example was *Slade* v. *Victorian Railways Commissioners*,[135] where Williams and Holroyd, who had tended to resist Higinbotham's narrow view of statutes, prevailed over his opinion, in this negligence action, to produce a monstrous result. The plaintiff, a boy of 10, sued, by his representatives, for damages in consequence of permanent injury suffered while playing on Port Melbourne railway pier. The defendants permitted the public access to the pier on Sundays. One Sunday the plaintiff and other boys were playing on a machine that travelled on the railway lines and, when not in use, was anchored by clamps. Some of the boys managed to release the clamps; the machine moved forward and crushed the plaintiff's foot.

At the trial, before Williams, J., and a jury, a verdict was given for the plaintiff with substantial damages of £1000. Williams, however, reserved questions for the Full Court whether, on the facts, the defendants could be liable in negligence. There, Williams and Holroyd had no doubt that the defendants were not liable. According to Williams, the plaintiff at best was a mere licensee to use the pier for recreation and, in order to succeed under the law, "the plaintiff has to establish the fact that he … occupied a higher position than that of a bare licensee". On the contrary, the evidence showed that in being on the machine (which was not "dangerous in itself") the boy was a trespasser, and, with his playmates, "mischievous trespassers". He was therefore in an even worse position than ordinary members of the public walking on the pier who did so at their own risk.[136]

Holroyd considered that the plaintiff "as one of the public, was using the pier by the tacit permission of the defendants, but nothing more". The boy had no right so much as to touch the machine, let alone meddle with it "and if he had not mounted [it] the accident would not have occurred". Accordingly, one trespasser was injured by the acts of other trespassers, for which the defendants could have neither liability nor responsibility.[137]

Aside from attributing to young boys, out for an innocent prank, a level of judgement and maturity in decision far beyond their years, the injustice of that view of the law is arresting, though it was all pervasive in the late 19th century.

Higinbotham, in dissent, introduced a much more modern element of the duty of care owed to invitees. He said:

> The plaintiff was on the pier as one of the invited public … He was entitled, therefore, to expect that the defendants would use reasonable care to prevent damage from any unusual danger on the pier which they knew or ought to have known.[138]

The evidence showed that the machine could be dangerous if set in motion, and the fact that no system was in place to fasten the clamps so that visitors could not move it, was in itself a sufficient ground to show negligence by the defendants. Neglect to take those precautions was "the primary and substantial cause" of the accident.

In another railways case, further curiosities of 19th century attitudes to negligence were revealed. In *King* v. *Victorian Railways Commissioners* a passenger in a train late at night put his head out of the window, for what reason was not known, and was struck and killed by an open door of a train passing in the opposite direction.[139] The administrator of his estate sued the Commissioners in negligence in having permitted the passing train to travel with an open door. The Commissioners denied negligence and alleged contributory negligence. At a trial before a'Beckett, J., the jury found that the passenger had not acted negligently in putting his head out of the window, and that the door which struck him had been left open through negligence of the Commissioners' servants. Judgement was entered for the plaintiff though with damages of only £200. The Commissioners appealed to the Full Court and moved for a new trial on the ground of misdirection of the jury.

By majority, the Full Court dismissed the appeal and declined to order a new trial. Perhaps unsurprisingly, in those *laissez-faire* days, the majority (Higinbotham and Holroyd) agreed with the finding that the passenger had not been guilty of contributory negligence. Higinbotham rejected out of hand some American authorities propounding the daring notion that voluntarily allowing any part of a passenger's body to protrude beyond the limits of the carriage was negligence in itself. He preferred English authority that "looking out of the window … was not an improper act", and that placing one's self beyond the carriage limits might be necessary in an emergency. In the end, it was not a matter that would detain him – "negligence on the part of a defendant, and contributory negligence on the part of an injured person, are questions of fact and not of law".[140]

Holroyd was satisfied that, except perhaps for an implied requirement that a passenger keep his body beneath a train's roof, there was no legal condition attached to the contract of carriage requiring passengers by train to remain wholly within the train itself.

> Our Victorian first-class carriages are generally so constructed that passengers can put their heads or lean their bodies out of the window, or sit with their elbows protruding, and there is nothing about them to indicate that those who do so will incur any danger … A hard and fast rule, turning a railway carriage into a prison van, seems to me contrary to common sense.[141]

On the other hand, the majority conclusion of Higinbotham and Holroyd was that carriers of passengers for hire were under a duty of care to see that everything under their control was in "full and complete and proper order".[142] Permitting outward opening doors to remain open when a train was in motion breached that duty.

Williams, however, could not discover "any duty on the part of the defendants to take precautions for the safety of a passenger who voluntarily projects part of himself outside the carriage". He did not dispute that a passenger had a "right" to lean out of a train window if he pleased, but if he did so, it would be at his own risk. Williams rejected submissions that the contract of carriage permitted a passenger to make any reasonable use he pleased of the carriage in which he travelled. Such a user, he said, might be an implied term of the contract as to the interior of the carriage, but could not be extended to an act done outside the carriage, or done partly inside and partly outside.[143]

Williams, incidentally, observed that "the point raised in this case appears never to have been decided by any English court".[144] He agreed with the conclusions, but not the reasoning, of those daring American decisions that seemed much more attuned to public safety and the efficient operation of public transport than was the Anglo-Australian common law.

A case that raised the question of contributory negligence by a servant in the course of his employment was *Davidson* v. *Wright*.[145] The plaintiff, a fitter, was required by his employer (the defendant) to move to a different position a bolt securing a chain pulley that lifted heavy weights. He failed to fix the bolt securely, so when he next went to use the pulley it fell and injured him. He brought his action under the remedial *Employers' Liability Act* 1886, and the question was whether that Act limited the common law doctrine as to contributory negligence. In the County Court the trial judge held that it did, and he declined to put to the jury the question whether there had been contributory negligence by the plaintiff. Damages were awarded to the plaintiff.

On appeal, the Full Supreme Court unanimously held that the Act had not touched contributory negligence, and that, in this case, the plaintiff was properly to be seen as the author of his own wrong. According to the Chief Justice the relevant provisions of the *Employers' Liability Act* put an employed workman in the same position as a member of the public so far as contributory negligence went. Here, the plaintiff had given evidence that his attention had not been drawn to the insecure state of the bolt: if it had been, he would have recognized the potential danger, but he "did not think it was dangerous". That was enough, in the Chief Justice's opinion to raise the presumption that the plaintiff knew of the defect and failed to inform his employer. Thus, on his own evidence, there was enough to go to the jury on the question of contributory negligence, and the trial judge had erred in declining to put that question to the jury.[146]

In the following year, 1887, the court returned to embracing hoary old concepts of contributory negligence by a servant. In *Collins* v. *Munro* the plaintiff was employed by the defendant who had contracted to construct the new Prince's Bridge in Melbourne.[147] The plaintiff was required to oil the wheels of machinery that moved on a staging to which no ladder or other simple access was supplied. The plaintiff had to scramble as best he could over beams and scaffolding. While doing so he was struck by a travelling winch and seriously injured. In the County Court the trial judge submitted questions for the opinion of the Full Supreme Court, the most material one being whether it was the duty of the defendant to have supplied the plaintiff with safer access to the place at which he had to work.

To modern minds it would seem axiomatic that a safe system of work was a paramount requirement. But to the Full Court in 1887 it was not. In a terse common decision they declared that:

> if the insufficiency of means of access was an obvious fact, it would not be the duty of the defendant to have supplied to the plaintiff safer means to obtain access … than he has supplied.[148]

To reinforce the plaintiff's predicament, Williams, J., in argument, suggested that he was caught by the maxim *volenti non fit injuria* (in other words, he was a volunteer):[149] and Higinbotham added:

> May not this be the distinction, that knowledge of the facts is an element of contributory negligence, but knowledge not merely of the facts but also of the risks constitutes "*volens*", and knowledge of the risks as well as of the facts makes the maxim applicable.[150]

The court then gave its advice, as *obiter dicta*, that:

> If before the happening of the accident the plaintiff had full and perfect knowledge, not merely of the facts, but of the risks attendant upon the performance of that portion of his duties in the performance of which the accident occurred, the plaintiff cannot recover.[151]

That was a monstrous miscarriage of justice, but it was all too typical of the inhumanity of much contemporary law.

A concluding example of unreasonableness was *Helms* v. *Munro & Co. Ltd*[152] in which the Full Court, guided by notions derived from the old forms of action, seemed more interested in debating whether the plaintiff had sought the right remedy and the right defendant than in considering the merits. The defendants, as contractors to construct a railway, cut down a wire fence on land the Railways Commissioners had purchased from the plaintiff. The fence continued on land still owned by the plaintiff but, without the support of the section that had been cut, it collapsed. The plaintiff's cattle then strayed and were lost. In the County Court at Ballarat the plaintiff sued the contractor for trespass and negligence and was awarded damages only to the extent of reimbursing him for erecting straining posts on his land to reinstate the collapsed fence. The trial judge declined to receive in evidence a provision in the contract between the Commissioners and the contractors requiring the latter to fence all land acquired from private owners, with liability for all damage arising from failure to do so.

On appeal, the Full Court disposed of the matter perfunctorily. As to the rejection of the contract in evidence, the Chief Justice held that "this action is not brought against the Commissioners for not erecting a fence, it is brought against the contractor, and the contractor has not been shown to be under any obligation whatsoever, except to the Commissioners".[153] Hodges similarly failed to understand "how any contract between the Commissioners and the defendants can give rise to any claim on the part of persons who are strangers to that contract".[154] Webb could not see "any right of the plaintiff to recover at all", and he was not aware "of any right of an easement of tension which an owner of land, fenced with a wire fence and who sells half his land has against his purchaser".[155] Altogether it was a most peculiar result under which, without possible equitable or prerogative relief, the plaintiff, who had no contract as to fencing with the Commissioners, appeared to have no remedy at all.

The cases here discussed do not cover the whole spectrum of issues considered by the Supreme Court in the 1880s. Many that exposed developing (and now generally antiquated) principles of real property law, corporations law, divorce law, commercial law, and so forth, have been discarded here. There were relatively few cases going to major matters of public law. Moreover, Higinbotham's term of only six years as Chief Justice was a very short one in Victorian judicial history, and was eclipsed by Stawell's three decades, and Sir John Madden's 15 years, in that office. Higinbotham's greatest legacy as Chief Justice must surely be in having pursued and furthered the steady course of judicial excellence that had been established by his predecessors.

9

Toy v. Musgrove (1888)

The Adventures of the "Afghan"

It is unfortunate that, in common estimation, *Toy* v. *Musgrove* is thought to have brought out the greatest of Higinbotham's achievements as Chief Justice. Instead, the case was exceptional in every way and did not sustain the judicial qualities described in the preceding chapter. It was almost the only instance, during his Chief Justiceship, in which, in court proceedings, Higinbotham cast aside detachment and yielded to his *idée fixe* about supposed constitutional wrongs done to the Colony by the Colonial Office.

As earlier observed, the generality of cases then before the Supreme Court touched few issues of public law. The fact that *Toy* v. *Musgrove* not only did so, but afforded a pretext to denounce the Colonial Office's misdeeds, was so providential to Higinbotham that he could not resist seizing its opportunity. Many of those denunciations were not germane to the case itself and, much as they may appeal to more modern minds, they were gratuitous and of little practical consequence in their day. They, along with related constitutional propositions propounded by Higinbotham, have rather been described as "prophetic".[1]

By the late 1850s the magnet of gold had attracted fortune hunters to Victoria in vast numbers, particularly from China. Tens of thousands of Chinese descended on the gold fields, living in virtual ghettos isolated from most other, generally European, miners, causing disputes by their methods of working the fields, and often creating great racial disharmony.[2]

Even after the richest pickings had been won from the gold fields, Chinese migration continued unabated, and the governments of Victoria and New South Wales set out to curb it by legislation. The *Chinese Immigrants' Statute*, passed in Victoria in 1865, was strengthened by the *Chinese Act* 1881. Apart from Chinese who were British subjects, or Chinese leaving the Colony temporarily and holding an exemption certificate, the Acts permitted entry to Chinese immigrants only on payment of poll tax, £10 per head, by the master of the vessel conveying them. A formula, related to the tonnage of the vessel, regulated the number of immigrants who might be carried to the Colony. Even so, their entry was popularly resented and there were lively exchanges of opinion between the Australian Colonies and the Colonial Office.

In April 1888, the *Afghan*, a British ship that plied between Hong Kong and Australian ports, arrived in Hobson's Bay, having on board 268 Chinese immigrants. Under the tonnage formula it was entitled to convey only 14. Some passengers carried naturalization certificates which, on inspection, proved to be false. The master, who would have been liable to a fine of £100 for each of the 254 passengers carried in excess of the limit, indicated his willingness to pay the poll tax for all of them but, under ministerial direction, the defendant Collector of Customs declined to accept payment.

Instead, the master was offered a compromise – that, if he desisted from seeking to land his passengers, the Victorian Government would waive recovery of the fine to which he had become liable. He sailed on to Sydney where, a comparable legislative scheme operated, and a similar reception awaited him. But, in Sydney, such violent demonstrations were got up against the entry of the foreigners that the government refused to permit any of the *Afghan's* company to disembark. Premier Parkes introduced a Chinese Restriction Bill that the Legislative Assembly passed through all stages at one sitting: but the Legislative Council declined to be hurried.[3]

Without the interposition of such a special Act, the existing statutes made it lawful for Chinese immigrants, not being British subjects (who were exempt), to enter New South Wales on paying a poll tax. The legality of the government's acting to the contrary, by executive direction alone, was challenged in the Supreme Court by *habeas corpus* in a series of cases that went wholly against the government. Chief Justice Darley held, and his coadjutors concurred, that New South Wales was not a "sovereign State" so that the issues fell to be determined by domestic law which, having regard to the existing statutes, would give relief to the applicants.

> Every person, whether the subject of Her Majesty or an alien, who is within our jurisdiction, is entitled to the protection of the law. He is amenable to the law. If he commits a crime he can be punished … Being thus amenable to the law, he is also under the protection of the law.[4]

It was an eminently sensible conclusion that the Parkes Government, driven by public mass hysteria quite out of proportion to the number of prospective immigrants, blatantly resisted, causing an extraordinary test of wills between the government and the Supreme Court. Eventually the government yielded with a bad grace, and the new harsh and exclusive legislation (with an "Act of Indemnity" provision) was acceded to by the Legislative Council. It had been an unedifying contest.

In Victoria, the passengers no longer being within the jurisdiction, Toy's test case was brought in damages against the Collector of Customs. With that wonderful sense of insularity that then saw New South Wales as remote, in legal relations, from Victoria as, say, Waziristan, not one of the New South Wales court decisions was even referred to in *Toy* v. *Musgrove*.[5]

"Construing Our Law as a Lawyer"

For presently material purposes the Victorian case raised two questions – was the action of the defendant an "act of State"; and could the government, without altering the statute law, act in defiance of existing legislation. The whole court agreed that power to do an act of State was not vested in the Governor and such an act could not be done by him with or without ministerial advice – it would require Imperial sanction: still less could it be done by Ministers acting independently. The other question was not answered so easily.

With a Full Bench of six judges, the risk existed of an evenly balanced result, with the opinion of the Chief Justice prevailing. That result was avoided in this case through the unlikely influence of the "journeyman judge" Sir Henry Wrenfordsley, then acting in the absence of Webb on leave. The "old guard" of Williams, Holroyd and a'Beckett predictably found, albeit reluctantly, that the existing legislation entitled a Chinese immigrant, on payment of the requisite poll tax, to enter Victoria. Wrenfordsley concurred. Higinbotham and, on different grounds, Kerferd, dissented.

The views of the majority may be summarized thus. Williams, who held that Victoria was "not a sovereign power; as far as we are concerned, the Imperial Government alone occupies that position",[6] looked disdainfully on the discursive and factitious propositions advanced by Higinbotham. "All these questions", he rejoined, "are no doubt full of interest, and elaborate treatises might be written upon them. But I do not desire to decide more than is necessary".[7] He felt "forced as a lawyer, construing our law as a lawyer" to differ from the Chief Justice, and to conclude that no Victorian law enabled the Governor or any Minister of the Crown to exclude aliens from the Colony.[8]

Any such right of exclusion was rather one affecting Imperial than colonial interests, he said. Construing the *Constitution Act*, only one "isolated expression" could be taken to confer on the Colony "the same rights and powers in regard to all colonial or local affairs … as the British Government possesses in regard to the affairs of Great Britain".[9] To rely on it would be "the enunciation of a proposition which is not only startling but positively unintelligible to me". The express powers granted by the Act were not, he thought, to be read expansively. "As a lawyer", he declared, "I protest against abusing these grand and beneficial principles to call into existence a primary power, or to supplement or aid that which has no existence".[10] Reading into the Act a prerogative or executive power to exclude aliens would be such an abuse.

Holroyd, on reviewing English history, considered that "the right of excluding alien friends from the United Kingdom is now vested in the Parliament of the United Kingdom, and not in the Sovereign alone". The same principles applied in Victoria, and the contrary argument impressed him as being "very subtle, but unsound".[11] The *Constitution Act* contained no authority for the Governor or responsible Ministers, of their own motion, to exclude aliens. a'Beckett briefly concurred with Holroyd.[12] Wrenfordsley held that the status of Victoria was of a limited character so that there would be "great difficulty of a practical nature, if the Government of this Colony is to be held free to act in respect of the high prerogative power which is claimed; or to be at liberty as a delegate of the Imperial Government … to pledge the Imperial Government to obligations of an international character".[13]

The result, therefore, according to the majority was that, on payment of poll tax, the Chinese immigrants had been legally entitled to land in Victoria.

"Responsible Government"

Before coming to the two dissenting judgements, it is convenient to mention the attempts made by all the judges to grapple with the meaning and implications of "Responsible Government"; whether it was a concept of real substance; and to what extent it had been conferred by the *Constitution Act* 1855.

In many ways "Responsible Government" always has had phantasmical properties that have eluded precise definition. In the late 20th century it was put, in the High Court of Australia, that "it should not be assumed that the characteristics of a system of responsible government are fixed".[14] A fair modern definition was attempted by Professor J.M. Ward when he wrote:

> Responsible government now means government by parliamentary ministers who normally depend for office, not on the will of the sovereign (or governor) but on the support of a majority of the elected members of Parliament.[15]

During the 19th century, however, it was a novel and developing concept.

In *Toy* v. *Musgrove* there was criticism of the *Constitution Act* and of its principal draftsman W. F. Stawell, that made insufficient allowance for the challenges he undertook in trying to reduce to words the essence of the parent English constitution that was unwritten and much dependent on convention and history. He elected, wisely, not to commit to legislation more of the English inheritance than was necessary, lest traditional powers, rights or privileges be lost or inadvertently diminished. Higinbotham, who considered that it was to the *Constitution Act* alone that "we must look for the legislative grounds of the self-governing powers of this people", criticized the generality of its drafting.[16] To limit that generality he then looked to "the authorised and authentic report of the words of the distinguished author of the Bill [Stawell] during the discussion in the Legislative Council".[17] From it, Higinbotham deduced that the Legislature had intended "to provide a complete system of responsible government in and for Victoria". He felt that the Act had such ambiguities, "peculiarities", and "apparently disjointed clauses" that its objects could not be "surely ascertained or confidently determined".[18] But he understood why the draftsman

> adopted the curious and very hazardous expedient of attempting to enact in a written law, by means of allusions suggesting inferences rather than by express enacting words, the provisions not only unwritten but unrecognised by English law, which regulate and determine the formation and action and conditions of existence of government in England.[19]

Even though the establishment of Responsible Government was not recited in the Act's preamble, or the nature of such government formally described, Higinbotham was confident that extraneous evidence sufficiently revealed the Legislature's clear intention that "the principle of responsible government should be established by law".[20]

Kerferd did not think it could be denied "that we have here in Victoria responsible Government as fully as it obtains in the mother country".[21] Williams agreed with Higinbotham that the *Constitution Act* contained "phraseology ... so vague and obscure in parts as to create grave doubts as to its meaning, where no doubt need have existed". He therefore questioned whether the primary object could have been to create a system of Responsible Government if one were constrained "strictly within the four corners of the Act". But, given the "infinite varieties and infinite degrees of a responsible government", he concluded that a measure of it had been created in Victoria – though it was "merely an instalment of responsible government".[22]

Holroyd was satisfied that the Parliament at Westminster had granted to Victoria "the whole measure of self-government which it possesses", but he was reluctant to go much further.

> At the outset, we must not be misled by abstract terms. No such thing as responsible government has been bestowed upon the colony by name; and it could not be so bestowed. There is no cut-and-dried institution called responsible government, identical in all countries where it exists. Whatever measure of self-government has been imparted to the colony, we must search for it in the Statute law, and collect and consolidate it as best we may.[23]

Concurring, a'Beckett could find no ground for concluding that Responsible Government had "a definite comprehensive meaning".[24] Wrenfordsley's opinion was that

> there does exist in this colony a form of Government, consistent with a full grant of representative institutions, limited, no doubt, in the application of prerogative rights, but possessing ample power with respect to all internal administration.[25]

While the case has been well described as "almost unique in the law reports, so far as it provides an elaborate examination of the scope and nature of responsible government",[26] it also attests the evanescence of the subject – as bright and appealing as a rainbow yet just as intangible. In Australian constitutional law "Responsible Government" never attained a precise or concrete meaning, though *Toy's Case* illustrates some of its shades of meaning.

"The Sovereign Power of Every Civilised Society"

The two dissentients proceeded by different paths. Kerferd was unwilling to explore constitutional issues in detail, for the case, in his opinion, came down to the breach, by the master of the *Afghan*, of the legislation limiting the number of permitted immigrants by reference to the tonnage of the ship. In this case, the master should not have been permitted "to enter his ship as being in port", because he had acted in fraud of the *Chinese Act* 1881. As to the passengers, it was a principle of public policy that the court not assist a person "who founds his cause of action upon an immoral or an illegal act".[27] The plaintiff therefore had no *locus standi*.

For Higinbotham, on the other hand, the case afforded a fortuitous and unique opportunity to reiterate, from the Bench, views he had so long propounded about the significance of Responsible Government in, and the "sovereign" status of, Victoria.[28] He spoke at very great length, and did not dissemble "the misfortune, my sense of which I could not adequately express in words", he experienced in differing from the majority.[29]

In his judgement, the authority of the responsible Minister in Victoria was a sufficient warrant for the defendant to have refused entry to the plaintiff and fellow passengers, notwithstanding that they tendered the requisite poll tax. The principles came down to this –

> Her Majesty's Government for Victoria are responsible to the Parliament of Victoria for the acts of the representative of the Crown in Victoria ... [And] an act done by the responsible Ministers for Victoria in the ostensible discharge and within the apparent limits of their functions as Ministers must be considered for all purposes, so long as Ministers are allowed to hold their offices, as the act of the Crown in Victoria, and it is properly described as having been done by the command of Her Majesty.[30]

The plaintiff, he said, had failed to displace a line of judicial authority showing that it was an existing prerogative of "the Sovereign of England" to prevent the landing of aliens, or to remove them on landing, on British soil.[31] It was a right "necessarily inherent in the Sovereign power of every civilised society occupying a territory with defined limits". Such a right, and its corresponding powers, were vested in the Victorian Governor as "the local Sovereign of Victoria",[32] and were exercisable by him on the advice of his responsible Ministers in Victoria. Such exercise was not forbidden by any rule of international law.[33]

Higinbotham extracted from the case six constitutional principles, the main effects of which were that, as amended, the *Constitution Act* 1855 was "the only source and origin of the constitutional rights of self-government of the people of Victoria", and that –

> the Executive Government of Victoria possesses and exercises necessary functions under and by virtue of *"The Constitution Act"* similar to, and co-extensive, as regards the internal affairs of Victoria, with the functions possessed and exercised by the Imperial Government with regard to the internal affairs of Great Britain.[34]

It followed that, apart from some powers admittedly reserved for Imperial control, such as defence and international relations, Victoria was to all intents a "sovereign State" possessing "very large and ... almost plenary powers of internal self-government".[35]

However sound those principles might have been in the abstract, they were ill applied to the particular circumstances of *Toy's Case*, for, as the majority pointed out, the entry of Chinese passengers by sea was governed by Victorian statutes, and the actions of the defendant had violated those statutes.

Although daring at the time, Higinbotham's pronounce-ments, when seen with the benefit of hindsight and with allow-ance for constitutional evolution, would thus far have stood as one of the great pillars of 19th century Australian constitutional law. And the more so given the elegant yet vigorous language and syllogistic reasoning with which they were presented. But their eminence was diminished by the addition, as *obiter dicta*, of much extraneous matter that gratified Higinbotham's obsession about the Colony's relations with the Colonial Office.

Declaiming against "the constant and still-continuing claim of the Imperial Government to interfere, by means of instructions, with the independence of the Queen's representative [the Gover-nor]", he protested that –

> Dishonour is done to the Crown when it is advised to make grants of powers that are void and to issue instructions that are illegal. Grievous injustice is done to the representative of the Crown who comes to the seat of his government misinstructed in his duties and powers, and is required to undertake obligations which he ought not, and cannot, and does not fulfil.[36]

It was "the duty of a judge of this Court", he insisted, to declare such interference unwarranted by law, and that all instructions by the Queen or the Secretary of State to Victorian Governors, not authorized by the law of Victoria, were "outside the law of the Constitution, and cannot be appealed to to explain, or add to, or detract from that law, or to restrict its free operation".[37]

The artificiality of those *obiter* protests was revealed by Higinbotham himself when he conceded that there was very little mischief to be remedied. The appalling illegality and gratuitous interference he had represented to exist were, in fact, little more than a misty wraith:

> The Imperial Government has never, I believe, even in the boldest of its attempts to interfere illegally with the Victorian Constitution, suggested that the Governor ought to exercise any of his statutory powers without receiving the advice of Her Majesty's Government for Victoria.[38]

In all, it was unfortunate that the Chief Justice so abandoned objectivity as to obscure an intricate question with issues which, however important and engaging in theory, had little relevance to the resolution of the specific question – as Mr Justice Williams had not failed to observe. Higinbotham, in short, was using his judicial position to pursue his "continued vendetta against the Colonial Office" – a property ill becoming a judge.[39]

"Delicate and Difficult Constitutional Questions"

In the name of the Collector, the Victorian Government appealed successfully to the Privy Council.[40] In the way in which their Lordships arrived at that result no encouragement was given to Higinbotham's theories. On the contrary, the Board asserted that the matter transcended the domestic interests of Victoria. It had become a sensitive diplomatic issue between Britain and China. Those countries were signatories to various treaties which, so the Chinese Emperor complained, were being violated by the treatment of Chinese citizens in Australia. London's *Times*, for example, had pointed out that China regarded New South Wales and Victoria as having disregarded "international law and comity", as well as the specific treaties, and that:

> The anti-Chinese agitation in Australia … has created a state of circumstances of a most difficult and delicate character, with which Lord Salisbury [the Prime Minister] has now to deal as best he may.[41]

The dispute had cooled somewhat by the time the case came for argument before the Privy Council in November 1890, and even more when the Board's advice was published in March 1891. Wrixon, Q.C., appeared with Sir Horace Davey, Q.C., for the appellant, just over a week after Wrixon had ceased to be Attorney-General in the Gillies-Deakin Ministry. Despite their long deliberation, the Board despatched the appeal in a perfunctory way. They praised "the very able judgment" of Kerferd,[42] with its reliance on the fraud of the master as disentitling the plaintiff to relief, and they agreed that, under the scheme of the Victorian legislation, breach of the Acts could not assist a prospective immigrant's claim to entry.

> The object of this legislation is obvious. It was to prevent the introduction into the colony by means of one vessel of more than the limited number permitted, and not to license it on payment of a penalty. It is not because the unlawfulness of an act is visited by a pecuniary penalty that the payment of that penalty makes it lawful.[43]

Beyond that, which alone would have disposed the Board to find in the appellant's favour, there was a principle of the common law necessary to be restated, given the international sensitivities aroused by the case:

> Their Lordships cannot assent to the proposition that an alien refused permission to enter British territory can, in an action in a British Court, compel the decision of such matters as these, involving delicate and difficult constitutional questions affecting the respective rights of the Crown and Parliament, and the relations of this country to her self-governing colonies.[44]

As to the wider constitutional issues, contended for so strenuously by Higinbotham and canvassed by the other judges in the Supreme Court, the Privy Council condescendingly noticed their having been "elaborately discussed in the very learned judgments" in the court below, but dismissed them precipitately.[45] They involved "important considerations and points of nicety which could only be properly discussed when the several interests concerned were represented, and which may never become of practical importance".

The last sentence, a virtual snub to Higinbotham, accurately assessed the position. The Chief Justice had ridden a hobby horse that was, for all utilitarian purposes, of no immediate concern to Victoria. It is disappointing that Higinbotham's able career in his highest office has, in the past, been viewed so much through the distorting prism of *Toy* v. *Musgrove* which depicts him not, as he was in so many other cases, committed to the strict and matter-of-fact disposal of the issues for trial, but as a judge "in the clouds" who pursued abstractions at the expense of reality.

The problems between the Australian Colonies and Chinese immigrants had all but dissipated by the time the Privy Council declared the law. Stringent legislation had passed both Houses of Parliament in Victoria and in New South Wales. It imposed such prohibitive poll taxes that few Chinese immigrants could afford to pay them. Higinbotham, however, still rankled over the fact that the overlordship of the Colonial Office had not yet been crushed.

10

"Her Majesty's Chief Magistrate in Victoria"

"High Abstract Principles"

On 27 January 1887 Governor Sir Henry Loch wrote to the Chief Justice "intimating that the Secretary of State would have pleasure" in submitting his name to the Queen "before Her Majesty's Birthday for the honour of Knighthood".[1] One can imagine the mixed feelings of pleasure and annoyance with which Higinbotham received the news. Pleasure, in Higinbotham the royalist, to be recognized by the Queen: but rage, in Higinbotham the radical, because the proposed recognition was by grace of the Colonial Office, not of Her Majesty's advisers in Victoria. He replied to the Governor, requesting

> that you will be so good as to convey my thanks to [the Secretary of State] and the assurance of my regret that I am unable under existing circumstances to do myself the honour of accepting the title.[2]

Loch telegraphed the reply to Downing Street where the file was minuted: "Query is this declension based on high abstract principles or on the more troublesome ground that Mr H. would prefer K.C.M.G." – the latter honour having been proposed for Chief Justice Darley in New South Wales.[3] Sir Robert Herbert came closer to the mark in deducing that Higinbotham "probably means that he will accept nothing from H.M. Govt until his peculiar views as to the constitution of the Colony are accepted by them". Higinbotham thus remained the only Chief Justice in 19th century Australia not to be knighted.[4]

There was an element of inverted snobbery about Higinbotham, and his liking to be seen to be different has been remarked upon, as has his failure to accept the title of Queen's Counsel when Attorney-General. But it should not be assumed that, had the offer of knighthood originated from the Colony, he would have refused it, even though, in 1873, he had attacked knighthoods as a "base, contemptible distinction" that merely gave the recipient "a handle to his name".[5] He explained his position in a letter to Sir Henry Holland, Secretary of State, in 1887, when he strongly disapproved of hereditary titles in Australia as being "opposed to the spirit of our laws and to the principle of equality which is the foundation of the theory of our political system" (so he supposed). As to honours for life, their bestowal by exercise of the royal prerogative was, he contended, "regarded in Australia with only cold indulgence. It does not and cannot in any case express spontaneous national sentiment". He therefore urged that the relative prerogative power be transferred to the several Australian colonial Governors to be exercised on Executive Council advice after recommendation by both Houses of Parliament.[6]

Showing that he was far from averse to titular distinctions, if granted on those terms, he concluded that:

> if life titles of the highest rank could be awarded by the Crown in such a way as to express the public sense of honour for meritorious public services, while at the same time they should be effectually guarded against becoming the prize of personal or party intrigue, it is probable, I think, that they would be regarded in Australian communities with cordial welcome instead of with coldness, and that they might become important and most valuable factors in the formation of national character, while they would also be an object of the most legitimate individual ambition.[7]

Again the seer, he had, in effect, anticipated the Order of Australia by nearly a century!

In many ways Higinbotham was a great respecter of tradition and ceremony. The *Australasian* wrote of him:

> one who in politics was a quondam democrat and a leveller of public thought and sentiment … when elevated to the bench and surrounded by the insignia of office [became] one of the severest champions of the forms and ceremonials of the law ever seen on the Victorian bench.[8]

Accordingly he favoured advancing the prestige of the judiciary of which two instances may be cited despite their bearing little fruit. Soon after becoming Chief Justice he wrote to the Attorney-General urging that all Supreme Court Judges be appointed to the Executive Council by analogy to English practice:

> A large proportion of the Judges of the Higher Courts in the Mother Country are usually summoned to attend the Privy Council upon their appointment as Judges. My Brother Judges are of opinion that a similar mark of honour and of the confidence of the Crown may fairly be claimed for the Judges of the Supreme Court in Victoria.[9]

The matter was agitated for a year, but came to nothing and was "postponed indefinitely".

In 1888 Melbourne became the venue for a Centennial International Exhibition, the organizers of which were gratified, at first, that Chief Justice Higinbotham agreed to be President of the Exhibition Commission. The agreement was reluctant, he "not feeling attracted by [the Exhibition], nor specially suited for its work or its ceremonial", but the Gillies-Deakin Ministry persuaded him to accept on the curious ground, so Professor Morris claimed, that:

> The Government did not wish the President to be distinguished for wealth or landed estates, because this Centennial Exhibition was not to be simply a show of material products. The strong desire of its designers was to make it also intellectual, to use it as a means of education in the fine arts, to connect with it conferences on social questions.[10]

In the capacity of President, Higinbotham attended the Centennial Australia Day ceremony in Sydney in January 1888: he lunched on the *Nelson* with a distinguished party that included Lord Carnarvon, who wrote, "I had a long talk & an interesting one with Ch Justice Higinbotham – Victoria – he is a remarkable man".[11]

Not everyone applauded Higinbotham's Exhibition appointment – "wise men, who knew his excessive earnestness, and appreciated the duties of his post, shook their heads and prognosticated mischief. Their fears were not slow of realisation".[12] His fellow Commissioners, businessmen of eminence, had no time for his sense of decorum, his formal and dilatory manner of directing meetings, or his desire to involve himself in meticulous oversight of all Commission activities. His colleagues resented his doubts and reservations, manifest in his philosophy that so large a body "acting chiefly through committees, would probably outrun their powers and their finances unless supervision was concentrated in some centre".[13]

Those views were partly vindicated when the Commission, by majority, appointed Frederick Thomas Sargood to be Executive Vice-President, as a polite hint to Higinbotham to disengage himself from the Commission's daily routine. Under Sargood "the Exhibition was a success but expensive".[14] Recriminations had followed soon after Sargood's appointment and, amidst declarations of regret coupled with profound relief by the organizers, Higinbotham resigned. Had he not done so, one writer reckoned that "there would have been an administrative breakdown or a *coup d'état* in the form of a mutiny". Thus, for the moment, ended an "affair ... entitled to all the consideration of a dramatic incident".[15]

More excitement followed. The Commissioners invited Higinbotham to attend the official opening of the Exhibition and to lead a judicial party in a grand procession. With him would be the Chief Justices of New South Wales, South Australia and Tasmania; along with all Victorian Supreme Court Judges and other puisne judges from New South Wales and South Australia. In those days precedence at public ceremonies was a status symbol of immense importance and often fought over. Higinbotham was incensed to find the judicial party ranked below Presidents, Speakers and Clerks of the Parliaments of all participating colonies.[16]

He contended that the office of Chief Justice ought to rank next after the Governor. Given his supposed egalitarianism he might have been expected to pursue the matter diplomatically through informal discussion with the Governor and the Commissioners. Instead, he began an inflamed epistolary battle with them, which he lost. Accordingly, on that most public of occasions in Victorian contemporary history, he boycotted the opening ceremony, supposedly out of regard for the dignity of his office.[17] It seemed an absurd display of gall, given that the other judges attending did not object to their place in the order of precedence. But Higinbotham could be relied upon to be seen to be different.

Some said that his action reflected his resentment of the way the Commissioners had treated him when President. He insisted that he was moved only by the question of principle touching the office of Chief Justice. If that were so, he had done much to fracture the principle. His intransigent and unaccommodating insistence on holding his high office, subject to conditions he prescribed, had demeaned the office and severed the nexus between the positions of Lieutenant-Governor and Chief Justice, as noticed on later pages.[18]

The whole subject was, no doubt, reviewed light heartedly when, on 3 August 1888, he was host to an Australian judicial conference, including luncheon at the – to Higinbotham at least – unfamiliar environment of the Australian Club.[19] There was a further amusing sequel when, in October 1888, his curiosity got the better of him and he went to see the Exhibition for himself. The press reported that: "The Chief Justice, honest George Higinbotham ... passed through the Exhibition turnstile on Saturday afternoon, and planked down his shilling for admission. How characteristic of the man!".[20]

His eccentricity in the matter of money has already been noticed. It was mammon he could not serve: hence his penchant for rendering low fees at the Bar, and for distributing what he regarded as surplus cash (little thought being spared for his own family's needs) as largesse to "the poor, beggars galore" who cluttered the entrance to his professional chambers.[21]

As Chief Justice he received a stipend of £3500. It was £500 more than the salaries of the puisne judges. His disposal of that excess was unprecedented. Disclaiming personal interest in it, he frittered it away on lavish and idle entertainments. For a man so possessed by principles of thrift and accountability, his actions were out of character.

> In his opinion, a Chief Justice was merely *primus inter pares*. True, he acted as Chairman and official representative of the bench; yet he considered that his powers were to all intents co-extensive with those of his colleagues. So he took the extra £500 reluctantly – at all events with some qualms of conscience. Truly a quixotic Chief Justice![22]

Having disowned the £500, a princely sum in itself, he might have been expected to apply it in augmenting the collections of the Supreme Court Library, or endowing scholarships, or making donations to hospitals. But, with typical perversity, he disbursed the unwanted sum in a way that seemed contemptuous of the public purse.

> He gave four dinners at the beginning of the legal year in a leading Melbourne hotel, to one of which he invited all the judges, the leading Court officials, every member of the bar, and an equal number of solicitors. At these friendly functions, he was the most genial of hosts.[23]

That too was out of character as Higinbotham was anything but a clubbable man, and most observers, apart from a circle of intimates, regarded him as lacking any sense of humour.[24] Nor did the extravagance serve any material ends of his. He did not need to win favours, and would have been the last person to seek them. This facet of his Chief Justiceship suggests pure eccentricity. His descendants continued for generations to chafe at his prodigality at their expense.

> For that reason the family thought ill of him and considered him unloving and mean-spirited to them. His behaviour possibly reflected his egalitarianism. He saw no reason why his family should derive a benefit through the accident of his being Chief Justice.[25]

"A Question Asked by One Politician of Another Politician"

On 30 September 1886 Sir Henry Loch wrote to Edward Stanhope, then Secretary of State, advising him of Stawell's resignation as Chief Justice, and of the government's nomination of Higinbotham as successor. Loch also brought to Stanhope's attention Higinbotham's views on constitutional matters, but would have been displeased to know that, at Downing Street, Sir Robert Herbert minuted the file:

> personally I agree with them [Higinbotham and Wrixon] in thinking that the [Governor's] Instructions do not in all respects sufficiently recognise the responsibility of "Her Majesty's Ministers for Victoria", as they like to style themselves.[26]

He noted that the Australian Colonies had a common interest in securing more appropriate gubernatorial instructions, and he referred to changes already made to the Canadian instructions, as mentioned earlier.

Bramston was antagonistic to Higinbotham's initiatives – "we must … I fear face this crochet of his" – and proposed that the English Law Officers be consulted.[27] Herbert, however, remained conciliatory and recommended that Higinbotham and Wrixon elaborate their grounds of complaint.[28] Loch was so advised, his despatch having been "read with attention".[29] Stanhope meanwhile had relinquished office, and left to his successor Sir Henry Holland (later Lord Knutsford) a whirlpool of complexity generated by Higinbotham's reply to the invitation to give further particulars.

The Chief Justice addressed his reply directly to Holland, instead of to the Governor for transmission, affecting to approach him on equal terms.[30] That was a serious breach of protocol. Superficially he was deferential, self-depreciating, obsequious and almost apologetic for obtruding. Yet below the surface he developed his case pompously and with such exaggeration, pejoration and aggression as to frustrate Herbert's hopes of an amicable agreement. Higinbotham also wrote more discursively than was appropriate, given his admission that the subjects of his criticism were so abstruse that Victoria's community viewed them with indifference if they viewed them at all.

> no intelligent opinion of any kind whatever exists upon this subject in any section or class of the community. I should mislead you if I allowed you to believe that my individual opinions possess any claim whatever upon your attention founded upon their present popularity. I could not affirm that they are at this moment either intelligently approved or intelligently dissented from by a dozen persons out of the whole population of Victoria.[31]

He did not presume, wrote Higinbotham, to address Holland as Secretary of State, but rather "in your private capacity as an English politician interested in Colonial affairs". He disclaimed having "any ground for addressing you in your official character", and offered his views as an individual "for your information". That was not the basis on which he had been invited to express his opinions. He regurgitated the 20 year history of his crusade to rationalize the instructions to the Governor, along with details of his 1869 resolutions – "disregarded by the Government of the day and by all succeeding Governments". That disregard, he thought, was sinister and conspiratorial, especially as it was embraced by so inscrutable and unaccountable a department as the Colonial Office.[32]

It was wholly to serve the interests of that Office, he protested, that the vice-regal instructions had stood almost unchanged for 36 years, while the constitutional position of Victoria had been transformed.[33] He believed that preserving the *status quo* flowed

> from the natural but very censurable desire of irresponsible subordinate officers to retain for their department by stratagem a power which they know has been taken away from it by law.[34]

The Colonial Office bureaucrats accordingly "affect to ignore altogether the existence of Responsible Government" and, to suit themselves, left the royal instructions unaltered,

> solely for the purpose of asserting, and with the intention of enforcing whenever it is deemed possible and prudent to do so, the claim of this department of the Imperial Government to control the Representative of the Crown in the exercise of all his functions and authorities alike.[35]

Canvassing the particular clauses of the royal instructions to which he objected, mainly for being spent or inapplicable, he deplored particularly clause 11 (prerogative of mercy in capital cases), and he revived his opposition to judges being answerable to the Governor for the way in which capital sentences should be reviewed, damning the clause as "a glaring instance of a … flagrant illegality". That was too much for Loch who, though not a lawyer (despite becoming Baron Loch of Drylaw), valiantly but ineffectually tried to repel Higinbotham's attacks. Of the "flagrant illegality" proposition Loch observed that it would be "most dangerous in the public interests that the Instructions under this clause should be either altered or modified".[36]

Higinbotham thundered on with complaints about "systematic violation of public law by the Colonial Office", about its "sole apparent purpose in the past … at once to covertly advance its unlawful claim of right to interfere in the domestic affairs of these Colonies, and to conceal from the Colonies the fact as well as the extent and the grounds of its claim". Such interference, he believed, was achieved "by indirect coercion or control of the Representative of the Crown in the exercise of his powers" along with other "vacillating and imbecile conduct of the Colonial Office".[37]

Then, realizing perhaps that he had overstated his position, there came a frank admission that the constitutional enormities he had represented did not in fact amount to much, and the explanation that –

> I cannot allow you, sir, to suppose that I waste time and attention upon the obscure phraseology of documents which do not in fact possess most real influence and have not been and are not attended with important practical consequences.[38]

Holland might have been excused for thinking otherwise.

Attorney-General Wrixon supplied a more temperate opinion couched in professional language better adapted to persuading the Colonial Office to change its ways. He conceded that the royal instructions contained "seeds of trouble" but little more. Every form of government, he maintained, was concerned rather with its actual working than with written theory.[39] In Victoria that working was patent, and "Responsible Government in local affairs has been in actual practice fully conceded to us by the Home Government" for decades past. In most respects he thought Higinbotham right in principle but astray in reality –

> the Attorney-General does not attach the same practical importance to the question that the Chief Justice does, inasmuch as the really important matter is not what the powers of our Governor are on paper, but what they are in fact, and all must freely acknowledge the full scope of local self-government that we actually enjoy with the cordial co-operation of our Governors.[40]

The one area in which Wrixon wholly supported the Chief Justice was clause 11 relating to the prerogative of mercy.[41] Wrixon contended that such a clause reduced Victoria to the status of a Crown Colony under which "Responsible Government is in abeyance" and "the community have no one responsible to them for the administration of this supreme act of public justice".

In his submissions Higinbotham had not emerged in his best light. He had allowed reason to be controlled by enthusiasm – another case where "his passions dominated his intellect".[42] He had so forgotten his position as to boast that his letter to Holland was

> written by me as an Australian politician, a title which I have the pleasure to claim in addition to and not inconsistent with that which I have the honour to bear as Her Majesty's chief magistrate

in Victoria, although I do not understand or use the term "politician" in the lower and more common sense to which it has been degraded in practice by English political parties.[43]

After desultory exchanges between the two touching the question whether the principal correspondence was confidential, Higinbotham became heated over the refusal of Lord Knutsford (as Holland had become) to give a positive answer. He protested his

> feeling of displeased wonder that a simple and fair question asked by one politician of another politician ... should not have received during nearly 15 months a short, direct, and unambiguous answer.[44]

He was affronted that Knutsford had offered no "explanation" – as if a mere colonial judge was entitled to one! If he did not promptly receive such an explanation, he would "finally determine for myself the question whether I am or am not at liberty to use the correspondence according to my discretion".

He concluded that Knutsford probably considered the substance of the correspondence "quite insignificant". But he reiterated his abhorrence of the power exercised at Downing Street by "irresponsible and unknown officials", and his personal observation of "the sinister and clandestine policy which the office over which you preside has successfully pursued for the third part of a century", which policy aimed at maintaining a state of colonial ignorance of "the true legal relations at present existing between the Governments of Great Britain and of these colonies".[45]

The Colonial Office were old hands at dealing with people like Higinbotham, but first they indulged in some recrimination, leaving pages of minutes dripping with vitriol. Herbert, in particular, took umbrage at Higinbotham's course, and observed that:

> There runs throughout the remarks of the Chief Justice such a bad, almost offensive, tone that I should be glad to leave them unnoticed except by a simple acknowledgement.[46]

Herbert remained sympathetic to the idea of shortening and simplifying the instructions to Australian Governors, using the Canadian instructions as a model. But his sympathy was not won by Higinbotham's methods:

> The Chief Justice of Victoria is unfortunately very ignorant of the law (Constitutional) as well as of the practice in respect of these matters as to which he has been for more than 20 years in a fog,

which he has not desired to dispel by acquiring information on rudimentary points. He still dreams that a Satanic influence like that of "the Clerk Rogers" affects successive Secretaries of State, and that the latter always systematically neglect their duties.[47]

Eventually a brief reply closed the correspondence with a body blow administered by a velvet glove. Knutsford, with inverted deference, regretted showing any want of courtesy to the Chief Justice, as he regretted any misunderstanding between them. But he regretted more "the tone of some parts of your letter" and the use of such emotive expressions as "clandestine" and "sinister". Where or how, he asked rhetorically, had he considered the principal subject to be "insignificant".

> So very much the reverse is the case that after consulting the law officers [in England] I have redrafted "instructions", with a view to meeting many of the points which you brought under my notice, and of bringing them more into conformity with the existing state of things.[48]

Publication "in any form" of their confidential exchanges was prohibited

Higinbotham was not to know the fact, because the Governor and the Ministry concealed it from him, that Knutsford had sent draft revised instructions to Victoria some weeks previously, but they were passed over for reasons to be considered presently.[49] The concessions thus made by the Colonial Office magnified the appalling and insulting way in which Higinbotham had sought to make his case. Being brought partly to his senses, he tendered to Knutsford a humiliating apology.[50]

The correspondence had extended over 18 months by which time Higinbotham's intransigence had led to his being passed over as Administrator of the Colony. Throwing restraint, protocol and diplomacy to the winds, he then submitted to the *Argus* and the *Age* almost all of his correspondence with Knutsford and with Loch, which those newspapers obligingly published.

The *Argus* editorially criticized Higinbotham's stance in which the letters grew "warmer and warmer on the part of the Chief Justice, so that at the close his Honour is found to be lecturing Lord KNUTSFORD handsomely". It deplored Higinbotham's disposition to "let off steam" – "If the existence of so much mental blindness and political obstinacy makes the Chief Justice wrath, who is to wonder at that? And yet must not the idea occur to his Honour that, with all this practical opinion against him, it is possible he may not be right". It also deplored his methods –

> There is all the old style about his Honour's letters, the old forcible way of stating a case, with the old fault of vehemence of expression; the old striking form, and the old erroneous substance. For two years, it seems, has the Secretary of State been using courteous endeavours to ameliorate the Chief Justice – with what success is easily imagined. No doubt his Honour after taking sides is perfectly open to conviction, but the able and lucky man has not yet been found who could convince him. Where others have signally failed Lord KNUTSFORD has not succeeded.[51]

In the opinion of the *Ballarat Courier*, when the controversy was viewed with "broad common sense", sympathy could not lie with Higinbotham. It lamented the result as lowering his standing in Victoria:

> The whole thing is clearly a mistake, that is, the raking up of old grievances, and the insisting upon obsolete demands, and more than a mistake, because it has prevented Mr HIGINBOTHAM from occupying a position [as Administrator] which all Victorians would like to see him fill.[52]

The *Age*, however, supported Higinbotham and thought he had "rendered an important service to the public" through his remarks. While Responsible Government had worked smoothly because successive Governors had chosen to ignore the strict letter of their instructions and to be guided instead by their colonial advisers, the *Age* reckoned that a headstrong Governor could quickly create a crisis.[53]

Loch anxiously telegraphed the Colonial Office that Higinbotham had broken the confidentiality of the letters in question, but the news was received with derision. "He [Higinbotham] has succeeded in making himself ridiculous except in the eyes of the *Age*", so the minutes recorded; while Bramston wrote:

> Mr Higinbotham has all along been bursting with the desire to give his letter of 28 Feb. 87 to the world and he evidently can contain himself no longer: he must be disappointed at the newspapers.[54]

The Colonial Office's death sentence was delivered by Herbert with the words "Put by. He *is* a 'crank'".[55] Accordingly, reformed royal instructions to the Governor, which Herbert had been all but ready to concede, were further deferred thanks to Higin-botham's uncompromising and provocative style.

"Responsibility Cannot be Severed From Power"

The Chief Justice contrived another confrontation, in September 1887, when Bridget Mepham was tried before him and a jury at Beechworth for the murder of her sister, was convicted, and was sentenced to death.[56] Attorney-General Wrixon advised Higin-botham that the Governor had appointed an Executive Council meeting to review the case, and invited him to attend and give his report. Higinbotham declined: Wrixon rejoined expressing regret.[57]

In a furious response, occupying 17 manuscript foolscap pages, Higinbotham told Wrixon of the "considerable surprise and also pain" he had experienced in discerning implicit disap-proval of his decision.

> I find it difficult to conjecture upon what grounds you could have reasonably expected for your request a different reply … On December 21st 1885 I addressed an official letter to your pre-decessor in which I definitively stated my intention, under the circumstances then existing and which have since undergone no change, to take that course.[58]

He repeated the conditions on which he had agreed to become puisne judge and eventually Chief Justice. He would not budge from them, and he enlarged upon his views:

> This is a matter which in fact is not permitted to come and does not in fact come within the operation of responsible Government at all. When you deal with it or any other matter of the same kind you do not in fact deal with it as a responsible Minister. Responsibility cannot be severed from power. Where there is no power there is no responsibility. You cannot be responsible to Parliament for the advice you tender because you have no power to give effect to your advice by the ordinary constitutional means.[59]

The Attorney-General, he said, was not advising the Crown as to the exercise of the prerogative of mercy in capital cases, but he was advising "an officer of the Imperial Government". That could not be "responsible advice" because it might be rejected with no recourse if it were. So, "when you enter the Council Chamber to

214

advise the officer of the Imperial Government you leave your character of responsible adviser behind you at the door".[60]

The 1869 resolutions were then rehearsed, along with the claimed negligence of the colonial government in doing nothing to resist Imperial interference, but in continuing to sanction the Governor's "illegal instructions". Thus had the law "fallen into disesteem". Although the Chief Justice recognized his obligation to give all possible assistance to a "responsible Minister" concerning capital cases, he could not regard Wrixon as such a Minister.[61] The argument was excessively precious. Wrixon declined to be hectored and replied that, while he would willingly discuss the issues unofficially, he would not further notice them officially: and he would not "concede your right on this occasion to question my constitutional position".[62]

Governor Loch looked with dismay on the latest eruption of the war of attrition. In a memorandum, he indicated that, in exercising the prerogative of mercy under the royal instructions, he was entitled to have the best information he could obtain, which necessarily included "a Report from the Judge and the Judge's notes, or any other information personal or otherwise that the Judge who tried the case can supply".

With yet another reminder of Higinbotham's depiction of judges as "officers in his department" when he was Attorney-General, Loch showed that his patience was flagging. It was the settled practice, established by Higinbotham himself, for the Attorney-General to be the medium of communication with the judges concerning capital cases.

> any disregard therefore by a subordinate, however highly placed, to a requirement made by the Head of a Department, is a matter for the consideration of the Governor's responsible Ministers.[63]

Yet, despite the protraction of the war, Loch seemed still oblivious to the claim Higinbotham had so consistently pressed of illegality in clause 11 of the instructions concerning exercise of the prerogative of mercy. Loch noted that "there can be no doubt as to [the Governor's] Constitutional Right to decline to accept the advice of His Ministers upon this as upon any other subject upon which advice may be tendered to the Governor by his Ministers".[64] That was, of course, the very matter open to doubt and the essence of Higinbotham's objections to clause 11. If there were true Responsible Government in Victoria, the Governor was bound to accept the advice of his Victorian Ministers.

In that lay a paradox. The Colonial Office, while maintaining that the Governor was not a "sovereign" but only a representative of the Crown, long insisted that the representative had complete discretion, subject only to accountability to Downing Street, in exercising the prerogative of mercy. Higinbotham, who maintained that the Governor was a "sovereign", would have reduced that prerogative power to nothing but a reiteration of the advice tendered to the Governor by his Ministers.

Wrixon tried awkwardly to negotiate a middle course. On the one hand, he put it that, as Departmental Head, the Attorney-General, in communicating with the judges concerning capital cases, was following not merely a practice but the prescription of an Order-in-Council of 5 September 1864.[65] But, on the other hand, he contended that responsibility for obtaining information about capital cases rested solely with the Governor's advisers; that in Mepham's case sufficient information could be obtained from the Chief Justice's notes; and that the personal attendance and report of the judge were neither necessary nor compellable.[66]

Higinbotham's posturings against putative miscarriages of justice through misuse or misunderstanding by Governors of discretionary and prerogative powers were not, however, the true catalyst of change to the Governor's instructions. The Chief Justice had engaged in a theatrical war – a war "with the forces of evil" that had yet to manifest themselves and dwelt only in the realms of hypothesis.[67] But the Colonial Office was made aware forcefully that his ideas had substance when, in 1888, an unlikely case in Queensland captured its attention. Benjamin Kitt was convicted before the District Court at Townsville of stealing two pairs of boots, and sentenced to three years' imprisonment. Premier Sir Thomas McIlwraith resisted the decision of the Governor, Sir Anthony Musgrave, to reject two Ministerial recommendations that Kitt be released.[68] McIlwraith protested that "this refusal to accept the advice of your Ministers is a grave departure from the principles of responsible government". Allowing for Kitt's previous good character and the relatively minor nature of the offence, the Ministry adhered to their decision that the sentence was "unjust and unnecessarily severe".[69] They regarded

Musgrave's contrary decision as indicating a want of confidence in them. He remained obdurate: they resigned.

Huge files were generated at the Colonial Office concerning the case, the result being that Kitt's release was ordered by the Secretary of State. Musgrave, however, received a capital sentence from a higher power. His clash with the government, and the failure of the Colonial Office to support him, were too much for the Governor who succumbed to a heart condition and died on 9 October 1888.[70]

Of present interest is the dawning recognition by the Colonial Office that Higinbotham's fears, although not borne out in Victoria, had substance. A Governor in a colony enjoying Responsible Government had rejected the advice of his responsible Ministers. Sober notations appeared in Colonial Office minutes:

> Sir A. Musgrave [was] technically right that he has this power – but this is not the real point which he has to meet: the question is whether he was right in insisting upon the exercise of the power … The longer responsible Govt. exists, the less possible it becomes to exercise the personal powers vested in the Governor at the commencement of the Constitution.[71]

That was precisely the point Higinbotham had been adumbrating for 20 years, though with more heat than Victoria's circumstances warranted.

The detailed Colonial Office minutes must be passed over here, except to note Sir Robert Herbert's conclusion that "very few Crown Colony Governors [as Musgrave had been] are able to learn, late in life, the art of governing under Responsible Government", and that it had been "extremely unwise" of Musgrave to press his personal opinion, and to exercise his discretionary power "in the matter of two pairs of boots".[72]

Ultimately a much stronger impetus for reform came from New Zealand where the commutation of a death sentence raised afresh the method of exercise by a Governor of the prerogative of mercy.[73] The Colonial Office, at first, regretted that the question had "not been aired at a very opportune moment" given that thoughts of an Australasian Federation were being mooted at Convention meetings.[74] In the event of such a Federation the royal instructions would probably be changed along the lines of the precedent established for Canada in the 1870s through the initiative of

Edward Blake, Q.C., as Minister of Justice.[75] Blake's achievements have been noticed in Chapter 6, and it was further said of him that:

> He brought about a considerable diminution in the powers and prerogatives of the Governor-General, in regard especially to the pardoning power and the reservation of Bills for the signification of the royal pleasure. In this respect he may be said to have put the coping-stone on the edifice of self-government in the Dominions.[76]

Higinbotham seems to have been unaware of Blake's success. Properly advised, the Chief Justice might privately have put it to the Victorian Ministry that the Colonial Office be requested to extend the same concessions to Victoria. Instead, he proceeded with the acrimonious and unsuccessful frolic of his own. Herbert, in considering the matters raised from New Zealand in 1891, took the view that, in preparing vice-regal instructions for Australia, no real difference would exist between a colony under Responsible Government and a Federation with such government. He believed that all "the Australasian Colonies" should have the Governor's instructions brought into conformity with the Canadian model.[77]

Lord Knutsford was doubtful. He noted that, at a Colonial Conference in 1887,[78] New South Wales, South Australia and Tasmania wished the instructions to remain unchanged. He thought the Canadian precedent "badly worded", and was in two minds whether to concede a uniform change to all the Australian vice-regal instructions "or whether in view of the 'Commonwealth' we should leave things as they are at present".[79] So he did nothing until, just before relinquishing the seals, he relented and, in July 1892, caused common instructions to be issued for all the Australian Colonies.[80] Western Australia had attained Responsible Government in 1890 and thus shared equal constitutional standing with the others. The new instructions for Victoria were gazetted on 2 September 1892, four months before Higinbotham's death. They owed very little to him.

His role in these matters of high constitutional moment has at times been misunderstood. There are such common fallacies as that "he stopped the Colonial Office from interfering in Australian domestic matters", and that he "was a political adult living in a society that was largely adolescent [and] did not realize the nature of self-government".[81] The otherwise authoritative

Australian Dictionary of Biography article on Higinbotham states that "he successfully convinced [the Secretary of State] in 1892 that the Governor's instructions should be redrafted to meet his objections".[82] Which overlooks the fact that the Colonial Office had long since closed its file on Higinbotham's representations and, although Deakin supported them at the 1887 Colonial Conference, the Munro Ministry, in 1891, "deprecated" any change to the instructions.[83] So far from bringing an "adult" perspective to the debate, Higinbotham's methods were immature to the point of puerility, lacking any of the acumen that might have been expected of a self-styled "politician". His belligerent, discourteous approaches to the Secretary of State set back the reforms he championed by many years. When those reforms at length were won, they were won by others, not by him.

He lived in a microcosm where he entertained exalted notions of his own importance. Apart from his initial voyage out from England, Victoria had become his whole world. He traversed it on circuit. Otherwise, he went to New South Wales perhaps no more than twice and to Tasmania once.[84] His outlook was narrowed by his environment. The Colonial Office, accustomed to dealing with community leaders from around the world, perceived him to be a provincial curiosity and a nuisance.

His approach to that Office rested on a false premise – that it deliberately sought to extend its power over Victoria. At the material time, the Empire-building aspirations of British foreign policy, with the acquisition of new possessions particularly in Africa and the creation of many new protectorates, left the Colonial Office too stretched to be interested in any empire-building of its own powers over older colonies.[85] When, for example, a British resident of some influence solicited the Colonial Office in 1879 to alter the Victorian Governor's instructions to clarify the extra-territorial administration of a Victorian intestate estate, Sir Robert Herbert replied:

> it would not be in accordance with constitutional usage for the Secretary of State to give any instructions to the Governor of Victoria on this subject, which is within the jurisdiction of the local government.[86]

It was regrettable that Higinbotham sought to convert his position of Chief Justice into that of a "politician" (however he defined the word), and to pursue his contentions, however meritorious in principle, with the Secretary of State with such temper and want of tact. The impression is irresistible that he pursued those contentions so fanatically and with such pettiness as to show that he was indeed pursuing a vendetta to which diplomatic and reasoned discourse was subordinated.

"A Decent Way of Getting Rid of the Present Chief Justice"

There remained the matter of administering the Colony in default of a Governor. On Higinbotham's accession to the Chief Justiceship, Loch worried about the prospect of his succeeding also to the office of Administrator under the dormant commission. Loch feared that, because Higinbotham had agreed to serve only under the conditions prescribed by himself, "he would be at liberty to conform only to such portions of his instructions as he might personally consider to be in accordance with law".[87] Loch circumvented that by appointing Stawell to be Lieutenant-Governor "in recognition of his long and distinguished services". It was an ingenious solution, given that the office of Lieutenant-Governor had been in abeyance for some years. Higinbotham, caught unawares, could do nothing but profess "gratification" at the news.[88]

The Colonial Office thought the outcome admirable for the moment, but questioned Higinbotham's future position under the dormant commission in which he continued to be named:

> it may be somewhat inexpedient to have an Administrator who has expressed himself strongly, and with unconcealed animus, on a subject affecting the relations between this Dept. and the Governor.[89]

Stawell's health was failing and he would never be called again to administer the Colony. Loch, who had served as Governor since July 1884, and was contemplating leave of absence, decided to take other initiatives. Early in 1887 he sought advice from Attorney-General Wrixon, from Sir Alfred Stephen (recently retired Chief Justice of New South Wales), and from Sir Samuel Way (Chief Justice of South Australia). Wrixon was asked to what extent the Governor might delegate his powers, and replied that there might be delegation in limited cases and that the Secretary of

State should be invited to enumerate them. He gave "no positive opinion" in response to further questions whether the Governor might, during a temporary absence, sign official documents. But the Attorney-General pointed out that no act requiring sanction by the Executive Council could be effected in the absence of the Governor or the Administrator.[90]

On the question whether the Governor could authorize a deputy to assent to Bills, Wrixon doubted that the deputy could come within the definition of "the person lawfully administering the Government". Chief Justice Way considered that the deputy would represent the Queen "as much as the Governor himself does".[91]

Chief Justice Stephen, on the other hand, considered that there could be no informal deputy: that a Lieutenant-Governor should act in default of the Governor: and that, until entering upon his duties, a Lieutenant-Governor ought not to be sworn in. Where a dormant commission was in force, the individual named in it had "no personality (so to speak) or existence" unless the commission was enlivened. Until formally assuming office in either of those ways, no powers or duties attached to the individual in question. Were it otherwise, the oath of office would have no meaning. Where such a person acted by deputation from the Governor during a temporary absence he would "not represent the Crown but the Governor only – and his powers will be limited by the terms of the deputation".[92]

Confused, no doubt, by such conflicting and tentative advice, Loch deferred action until deciding, later in the year, to confront Higinbotham personally. At an interview, he sought to establish the position the Chief Justice would take if called upon to administer the Colony. "You told me", Loch recalled as a matter of record,

> you would be unable on conscientious grounds, to communicate with the Secretary of State, either directly or indirectly, on any matters connected with the government of the colony, … and further that you would decline to be bound by certain clauses in the Royal instructions.[93]

He asked that his understanding of the discussion be confirmed so that he might report it to the Secretary of State. Higinbotham replied at great length, confessing that he would "feel very deep pain and regret" were his name omitted from the dormant commission.[94] Despite fully understanding the conventions attached to the Administratorship, he maintained that it was an office incident to that of Chief Justice and that his "supposed personal inclinations" ought not to disqualify him and thus be seen to diminish the stature of the Bench.

Meanwhile the Colonial Office had sent to all Governors of the Australasian Colonies a draft of a new commission and instructions proposed for future Governors. The draft was not well received in Victoria.[95] The Ministry, which considered that "however defective the existing instructions may be, they are well known and no practical difficulty or inconvenience results from them", recommended that the draft not be disclosed to Higinbotham. Loch concurred, reckoning that it would be unlikely to answer his objections.[96] Accordingly, Loch proposed to the Secretary of State that the new instruments be considered only when the next Governor was to be appointed, their terms first being settled by the English Crown Law Officers. Higinbotham was thus unaware that he had been excluded deliberately from considering the new instructions; while the Ministry's abandoning and stultifying him confirmed that his position was regarded as an embarrassment to the Victorian Government.

In July 1888 the Secretary of State advised Loch that the Crown Law Officers in England confirmed the constitutional legality and propriety of the system of correspondence and reporting between colonial Governors and the Imperial authorities,[97] and that the Colonial Office would therefore insist upon

> full and frank communication between the Governors of a colony and Her Majesty and her Government at home, through the constitutional medium of the Secretary of State for the Colonies, [as being] manifestly to the interest of the empire.[98]

It was suggested that Higinbotham be shown the confidential despatch to which the proposed new instructions were appended, but the Ministry decided otherwise.[99]

By November, Higinbotham reverted to vituperation. It was plain to him that Knutsford "has not yet been able to give adequate and serious attention to the subject ... [for he] has been engaged in making numerous and minute inquiries into a small and comparatively unimportant part of [it]". The appointment of an Administrator ought, in any event, to be a matter for "Her Majesty's Ministers for Victoria".[100]

Downing Street's decision was conveyed to Loch in December. A "gentleman outside the colony" (Sir William Robinson) would administer Victoria while Loch took six months' leave. If the Chief Justice persisted in his opinions, the Secretary of State, on a future absence of the Governor, would then consider what alternative arrangements should be made for the Colony's administration.[101]

The protracted correspondence between Governor and Chief Justice continued at a level of cold formality – "My Dear Chief Justice" and "My Dear Sir Henry Loch" being replaced by an introductory "Sir" on both sides. On 15 December, Higinbotham protested at the taking of a course he found unprecedented and unexplained – as if the explanation were not obvious. Knutsford's decision was "inconsistent with and opposed to the public law of Victoria".

> I decline to give my sanction or recognition to this illegal practice of the Colonial Office, on the ground that such practice is deemed by that department of the English Government essential to its policy. Lord Knutsford will consider and adopt whatever course he may, in any contingent event, think proper. But I have to desire that he will not, under any circumstances, presume to advise the Crown to impose upon the Chief Justice of Victoria, in the event of that person being honoured by Her Majesty's command to administer the government of Victoria, conditions or obligations inconsistent with the public law of this part of Her Majesty's dominions.[102]

There were, in this, shades of the troublesome Mr Justice Benjamin Boothby late of South Australia.[103]

There followed further truculent letters in which Higinbotham complained about the "quite unmerited indignity offered" to him. But had he anyone but himself to blame?[104] He then resorted to his supposedly ultimate weapon of having all the correspondence published in the press, expecting that it would evoke floods of sympathy for him.[105] It did not. Sir William Robinson, recently Governor of South Australia, assumed the government between March and November 1889. The Earl of Hopetoun then became Governor, Loch having been appointed High Commissioner for South Africa and Governor of Cape Colony – a practical testimonial of the Colonial Office's approval of the way in which he had managed difficulties in Victoria, many of them generated by the Chief Justice.

Lord Knutsford had the last word. In preparation for the accession of Lord Hopetoun, new letters patent and instructions were issued, and it was proposed that a new dormant commission name the President of the Legislative Council as Administrator should the need arise. Knutsford closed the file, "I agree. It is a decent way of getting rid of the present Chief Justice".[106]

In an informed contemporary paper, written under the pseudonym "Constitutionalist" (possibly by Sir Henry Parkes) and published in Sydney,[107] Higinbotham was taken to task personally and for the substance of what he had propounded. The "rudeness and offensiveness for which there was neither cause nor justification", displayed in his letters to Knutsford, were deprecated, and his understanding of constitutional law and conventions was challenged. Despite Higinbotham's protest at the little alteration made to the Governor's instructions over decades,

> did it never occur to him that there may have been good reasons why no greater changes have been made? That it may have been, not because the subject had been overlooked, or because some evil-minded official was bent upon keeping his hold over the Governors, but because no more important alterations were necessary.[108]

The critic attacked Higinbotham's premise that put the Governor in the position of a mere figure-head, a virtual puppet whose strings were to be pulled by his Ministers so that he must do exactly as they pleased. There remained many areas, at that stage of colonial development, in which the Governor needed to make up his own mind and exercise for himself discretions reposed in him.

Those criticisms were shared by Sir Archibald Michie, Q.C., who wrote to the *Argus* that he accepted the need to replace obsolete royal instructions to Governors, but he rejected Higinbotham's way of going about it. In a style alternately whimsical, satirical and pertinent, Michie feared the he might be committed for contempt in criticizing the Chief Justice, the self-avowed "officer of the Attorney-General's Department". But he and Higinbotham had been colleagues together in McCulloch's first Ministry when Higinbotham, as Attorney-General, had done nothing to rectify the alleged defects he exposed so relentlessly as judge or Chief Justice. Michie asked rhetorically:

What was Mr Attorney about during that five years' tenure of office ...? Did he at any time do anything to vindicate what he calls "public law"? Did he ever call upon Sir Charles Darling or Lord Canterbury to protest against the indignity of illegal invasion of their office [as Governor] by "the sinister and clandestine" machinations of Her Majesty's Ministers?[109]

Michie deplored the way in which Higinbotham had "exceeded his duty" by a "piece of ludicrous impertinence" that overlooked a colonial Governor's being invested with two duties – one to the colony, the other to "the parent state". In performing the latter duty there would be many circumstances that warranted or demanded the Governor's making private reports to Downing Street and otherwise exercising discretions without derogating from his duty to the colony. Higinbotham had sought to intrude upon "the unique and exclusive functions of his Royal mistress ... [and] the servant cannot be admitted to dictate to his mistress; but this ... is exactly what the Chief Justice is claiming to do".[110]

Nearly half a century later, Mr Justice H.V. Evatt, of the High Court of Australia, considered Higinbotham right in calling attention to the "extraordinarily autocratic" and partly spent nature of the Governor's instructions, but wrong "in asserting the illegality of the Instructions".

> neither the Imperial nor the Victorian Statutes attempted to define and describe the general discretionary authority of the Governor in relation to his Ministers ... [The] provisions of the [*Constitution Act*] did not, of themselves, direct or require the Governor for the time being to act only upon the advice, and always on the advice, of Ministers possessing the confidence of the popular Assembly.[111]

And that recalled the intangible elements of discretion and trust that necessarily existed between a Governor and the Crown, and the impracticability of attempting to specify them. As the English Crown Law Officers had put it, in 1888:

> We think it impossible to define the limits within which suggestions or advice relating to Colonial affairs can properly be given to the Governor by the Secretary of State, and instructions as to such affairs can seldom be in question.[112]

While it may be that, in some of these matters, Higinbotham "had the future with him"[113] or, as to domestic self-government, "had history on his side",[114] those are conclusions dependent on hindsight. For his own day, he had set back attaining the very principles for which he had struggled. As the Colonial Office summed up the result –

> Although the Letters Patent and Royal Instructions were amended as a result of these representations, it does not follow that Sir [*sic*] G. Higinbotham's or Sir H. Wrixon's views were adopted, and the opinion of the [Law Officers] shows that ... much of their representations was considered to be misconceived.[115]

Higinbotham had moved so far beyond his province of Chief Justice as to raise doubts whether his judicial objectivity had not become compromised. If he had wished to pursue his constitutional notions as a "politician" his better course would have been to resign his commission and return to the Legislature. His vehemence and intractability in pursuing his cause suggest that he had lost sight of his true public position. He all but conceded the fact when, in 1892, the last year of his life, he wrote privately to Christopher Crisp, editor of the *Bacchus Marsh Express*,

> The state of my health and the condition of the public mind at present alike forbid me to take an occasional part in politics and confine me to *my proper duties*.[116]

Chief Justice Higinbotham in 1886

11

"Perplexed by Paradox, Stunned by Contradictions"

"The Father of Consolidation" of Statutes

George Higinbotham's greatest legal monument was his consolidation of Victoria's statute law, undertaken from 1863 to 1865 when he was Attorney-General, and again from 1888 to 1890 when he was Chief Justice. Statutory consolidation has been described as

> the process of modernizing statute law which it is desired to retain in force … it is the process whereby the provisions of many statutes, dealing with one branch of the law, are reduced into the compass of one modern statutory statement of the law.[1]

Keeping abreast of the statute book was a problem, even for lawyers, in 19th century Australia. In New South Wales, Thomas Callaghan's *Acts and Ordinances of the Governor and Council of New South Wales*, published in two volumes in 1844 and 1845 with supplements to 1852, provided a methodical arrangement of the statutes, and was consolidated less effectively by Henry Cary in 1861. Some Victorian lawyers believed that a similar but improved course should be adopted there. Dr George Mackay, for instance, proposed in 1864 that copies of the New South Wales statutes should be purchased for official use in Victoria, to be augmented by "the whole of the Victorian statutes printed in two more volumes …, with a carefully compiled index".[2]

Despite the efforts of Travers Adamson, who produced three volumes of *Acts and Ordinances in Force in Victoria* between 1855 and 1857, questions constantly arose in the Colony whether English domestic or Imperial law, pre-Separation New South

Wales law, or purely local law was applicable to particular circumstances.[3] And in days when, for example, individual crimes were dealt with by individual enactments, ascertaining the applicable Act and verifying its currency, with or without intervening amendment, could be difficult and time consuming. Ten years after Separation, G.F. Verdon appears to have been the first to propose consolidating the statutes. Ireland, as Attorney-General, then set out to consolidate the law as to indictable offences, and planned a new edition of the statutes: but he left office before he could accomplish either.[4]

In England, statutory consolidation had been entrusted to Commissions with significant resources. Victorian governments were disinclined to incur such expense, so the matter languished until, from his appointment as Attorney-General in 1863, Higinbotham determined to manage the task himself. Not that he undertook all the drafting,[5] but he devised a system which he described as expedient – "merely a rough classification" – rather than as especially ordered or scientific.[6] He parcelled out groups of statutes to members of the Bar for reshaping as consolidated Bills. He acknowledged the draftsmen's careful attention and research, and the assistance of senior public servants in commenting on Bills affecting their Departments.[7] In the opinion of Sir Leo Cussen, who carried out similar work in the early 20th century, Higinbotham, who had personally reviewed all the draft Bills, achieved "wonderful accuracy".[8] Inevitable slips occurred, as when a section of an earlier Act was inadvertently repealed by the consolidation. But they were few and minor.[9] Added to the Attorney-General's ordinary burdens of office, the creation of a system and seeing it through to the submission of Bills to Parliament devoured much of Higinbotham's private time. Between 500 and 600 enactments were examined in the consolidation process, with the aim of reducing them to 50 or 60 measures.

There remained the task of cajoling an uninterested Assembly, and an often hostile Council, into entertaining the consolidation Bills. Debate, at one stage, bogged down in dispute over payment of about £500 to Professor W. E. Hearn (later the author of an unsuccessful codification of Victorian law) for drafting assistance. To Higinbotham's explanation that he selected helpers "best qualified by possession of leisure, ability, and learning" to do the work, a Member rejoined that, if the Professor had so much leisure, the House "would do well to remember the circumstance when the Estimates came on",[10] Hearn being paid by the government.

Higinbotham could only bear with such diversions and crave the indulgence of the chamber:

> He had felt considerable difficulty … in addressing the House on the subject, and he still felt that it was almost impossible to explain the advantages to be derived from the adoption of the course which he proposed … He felt that it was impossible to lay any proposition of this nature before the House which did not involve the necessity of asking from Parliament a very large amount of indulgence and confidence.[11]

Not the least indulgence was the request, not always conceded, that the House take the Bills on trust and not debate them as if entirely new legislation which might occupy them "for an entire session".[12]

Demonstrating financial, rather than legal, benefits flowing from consolidation assured him of support. He showed that drafting fees and printing costs had increased alarmingly. Whereas the *Local Government Act* had cost £150 to draft and print, its repeated amendments had required £694 more. A *Land Act Amendment Act* costing £11 had been amended at a cost of £394, while the *Municipalities Act* cost £36 to print and £518 to amend.[13] Many other instances confirmed how economical statutory consolidation would be. Less practical was the suggestion that Acts be kept by the Government Printer in standing type not requiring complete resetting should changes be made.

Higinbotham hoped that the recent appointment of a Parliamentary Draftsman would enable the consolidation process to be continuous – a false hope as it transpired;[14] and he planned for a "compendious index of statutes" to be published.

This was Higinbotham at his best and most productive – an indication of what he might have achieved as Attorney-General had his approach to greater public issues been as positive and as conciliatory. The Houses generally warmed to his consolidation proposals, and the passage of many consolidating Bills over the ensuing two years produced a sense of parliamentary achievement absent from the constant disagreements over more contentious legislative programmes.

There were a few snags along the way. The wrath of the Supreme Court Judges, at Higinbotham's attempt to control their tenure by provisions of a consolidating Act, has been noticed already.[15] Their protestations caused the Legislative Council to omit the offending clauses. The Council also insisted on amending the Public Moneys and Audit Law Consolidation Bill in 1865, leading to an acrimonious clash with Higinbotham.[16] But, in consolidation measures generally, such disagreements were rare.

In 1890, Wrixon, then Attorney-General, recalled that Higinbotham was entitled to be called "the father of consolidation in Victoria". His had been a "gigantic work" in which he had

> to construct the consolidation of the law out of materials which had to be found in divers quarters. Ordinary consolidation was to a great extent the laying of bricks together, but … when [Higinbotham] undertook the work, he had not only to lay the bricks together, but to find them and make them.[17]

Higinbotham thought, on completing the work in the 1860s, that it would "form the basis of a more scientific classification, which he hoped to see at some future time".[18] But, until he became Chief Justice, those hopes stood unfulfilled and the statute book had returned to its cluttered and fragmented state. Again he undertook to manage the task of consolidation, a formidable one for a man so burdened with judicial duties, and completed only at a high cost to his health.[19]

He took ultimate responsibility for the work, personally planned its course, and supervised and checked its completion. Donald Mackinnon[20] and Francis Hugh Mackay were engaged as draftsmen and, this time, the project enjoyed great advantages over its predecessor. It was undertaken with the government's blessing, and it received complete parliamentary support. The result was publication of five volumes of consolidated public Acts, a sixth volume of private and local Acts, and a final volume containing Imperial Acts "received" in New South Wales in 1828 and still deemed operative in Victoria, "enactments" of the Federal Council of Australasia, and other useful sources. The first volume described the methodology employed, which was a vast improvement on the "rough classification" Higinbotham had devised in 1864. The seven volumes were published, as the official text of current Victorian legislation, in 1890: all pre-existing statute law was repealed. Thus some 1200 Acts were reduced to a little over 100 in consolidated form, yet printing even those obliged the Government Printer to import a large quantity of type from England.[21]

In June 1890 the Legislature approved an appropriation for the purposes of the publication. Sir Bryan O'Loghlen, in response to doubts whether the Assembly could be satisfied with the accuracy of so many consolidated measures, fairly observed:

> it would be utterly impossible for any individual member to undertake the labour which had been performed gratuitously by the Chief Justice … [and he] having made himself responsible for it, the House was justified in taking the bills from him upon trust.[22]

In October 1890 Premier Gillies proposed that the Assembly record "its high sense and appreciation of the valuable services" of the Chief Justice in completing the consolidation. "It was scarcely possible", he said, "for any man, or any body of men, to have done the work in a better or grander manner than he had done".[23] Moreover, Higinbotham had "worked with a noble object, and employed every hour of his leisure time to accomplish a work that was bound ultimately to do a large amount of good".[24] As Mackinnon recorded of the labour involved:

> From the 1st of March to the 1st November, 1889, he [Higinbotham] worked upon those bills daily from four o'clock, when the Court rose, until eight and often till ten at night, at which hour he went home to dinner. All Saturday, not being a Court day, and every day during the fortnight vacation in winter, was occupied in the same way.[25]

On 16 December 1890, at an event that must be unique in Australian judicial and parliamentary history, the Chief Justice, in his ceremonial robes, attended by invitation at Parliament House to receive the thanks of the Houses, which was, as the Speaker said, "the highest honour we can bestow".[26] It was the zenith of Higinbotham's career. In a gracious acknowledgement, he insisted that the task was incomplete, and that more must be done to keep the statute book in order in the future. Although Professor Hearn's proposals of 1887 to codify Victorian law had come to nothing, Higinbotham had supported the concept then,[27] and presented it, in 1890, as a new challenge:

The Consolidation Acts which the Victorian Legislature has just enacted are themselves but a confused and unarranged medley of enactments constituting a small part only of our law, wanting in uniformity in the use of terms, and containing provisions not always easy to be reconciled with one another. The laws which are intended to govern the actions of a free people ought not to be open to cavil or overthrow and defeat, as now they often are, upon grounds like these. Until the law is codified, it cannot be understood by the general body of the people.[28]

"No Federation For the Present"

That Higinbotham lacked any sense of national statesmanship was manifested in his negative attitude to Australian Federation, despite its rapid acceptance throughout the country in his closing years on the Bench. To him "the nation" and "the country" were defined as that part of Australia lying south of the River Murray. He wanted it to stay that way. The English visitor Stanley Leighton, meeting him in 1868, asked what he thought of federalism. Higinbotham replied that "he did not see his way yet to a Federation of the Colonies, and he thought there was no chance of it for many years to come".[29]

In 1871, when he repelled his constituents by an electoral address which so disdained local issues that he lost the seat of Brighton, he had no good word to say for Federation. Nothing could be attained, he said, by federating the Australian Colonies, that could not be attained by preserving the *status quo*. "I fear", he told them,

a merely artificial and formal union between these colonies may prove the occasion, not of increased good-will, but of jealousy and strife. I am sure that an immediate and certain result of the federation of these colonies would be to cripple and restrict the self governing legislative powers of each of these colonies, and I own it to you that I for one should be unwilling to see the legislative powers of any of these colonies diminished at a period when we have not as yet learned either the full value of these liberties or the art of using them wisely.[30]

An Australian Federation would be "more distasteful" to his mind because the union of the Australian Colonies would force them, so he claimed, to "be separated from our mother country".

By 1885 Higinbotham had become puzzled by the very concept of Federation and then understood it to be something inspired in London to enable the Australian Colonies to be represented together on a body "created to deal with Imperial questions". He looked upon such a scheme with deep suspicion as being yet another device to hide the "illegal assumption by the Secretary of State of a right to interference in our local affairs". Such a Federation, he believed, would have insuperable difficulties in its way.[31] That was not, of course, the path that the proposed Federation was taking, but he had come already to close his mind to the notion, however it might emerge.

When it became clear that Federation was a purely Australian concept that could not be stopped, Higinbotham became duplicitous. Although he regarded the momentous speeches of such men as Griffith, Parkes and Deakin at the Federation Conference held in Melbourne in 1890, and at the ensuing National Convention in Sydney in 1891, as all but a betrayal, he led his "disciple" A.I. Clark of Tasmania to believe otherwise. Clark reckoned that Higinbotham "watched the sittings of that Convention with great interest and he was deeply desirous of seeing the federation of Australasia accomplished".[32] That was wishful thinking.

Although Higinbotham wrote to Clark, assuring him that he and his Convention colleagues had "my warm sympathy and my best wishes for your success in the noble and very difficult work on which you are engaged",[33] his hopes were otherwise. He warned Clark that he could have little confidence in the outcome, being particularly troubled by the proposed federal bicameral Legislature. To avoid conflict he thought that the powers of the respective chambers, and their relations *inter se* and with the English Government, ought to be specified with great particularity. Harking back to the Victorian experience, as he saw it, he feared a "very dangerous interference by the Imperial Government with our legislation" at the federal level if any latitude were permitted to Downing Street. He revived memories of old wars, visiting his evergreen censure upon Edward Cardwell for actions that were "illegal and unconstitutional … but had a powerful effect at the time".

His lack of enthusiasm was at its plainest when he wrote:

> It would be better, in my opinion, that there should be no
> federation for the present than that we should institute a Federal
> Constitution that would create new doubts and lead to new and
> bitter and endless controversy.[34]

Unless the Convention settled for all time the respective rights
and powers of the federating states and the residual imperial superintendence, he would "hazard the prediction that the Federal
Convention will result in a grievous and lasting failure".[35] His
powers of prophecy deserted him on that occasion.

He also berated his most devoted "disciple" Alfred Deakin,
for not taking a stronger stand against critics of the ties between
Britain and the Australian Colonies. In a flash of old rhetoric, he
thought it inappropriate that powers over such matters as trade
and commerce and foreign affairs, ordinarily the preserve of
"sovereign states", were being sought for the new federal government simply because "the Imperial Government may be imbecile
enough and regardless of its duties to grant them". He thought
the draft Constitution Bill undeserving of adoption by Victoria
and, unless radical alterations were made, he would prefer to see
Victoria "postpone Australian Federation to the date of the Greek
Kalends", in other words, indefinitely.[36]

Higinbotham's acerbity was, perhaps, no more than a
product of becoming old – "your old men shall dream dreams,
your young men shall see visions".[37] He had ceased to see visions.
Although, after 1871, he made no public pronouncements about
Federation, his private views were all too plain. Deakin was
trifling with the truth when he wrote of Higinbotham:

> Federalist at heart and soul (though his position as Chief Justice
> sealed his lips upon the question), it was he who imported to the
> Federal Cause in Victoria a special note of undeviating loyalty to
> the Empire.[38]

Deakin knew, more than did most public figures, how anti-
pathetic to the federal cause Higinbotham really was. And he can
have been left in no doubt when, in 1893, Crisp published in the
Bacchus Marsh Express a private letter Higinbotham had written to
him a year previously, remarking that, "the Sydney scheme of
Australasian Federation is, happily in my opinion, dead for a
time, though it has not been condemned for its real demerits".[39]

Professor Morris attributed to an unidentified visitor the recounting of Higinbotham's assertion that there was no urgency about Federation and that he

> would consent to any postponement rather than see Responsible Government in the British sense weakened in the least by its adoption. On this point [the visitor] found him as Conservative as the most true-blue Constitutionalist could desire.[40]

Of course, Higinbotham had no wish to bring a "Conservative" mind to the question. He believed that Victoria stood on its own feet, was the dominant "nation" in Australia, and ought not to be subordinated to some new and untested central government.

"Peculiar Views on the Question of Education"

Another of his great undertakings was Higinbotham's chairmanship of a Royal Commission on education, established in 1866 with the object of framing a Public Instruction Bill. This work, though conscientiously pursued, ended in failure. The subject has been covered so authoritatively by Gwyneth M. Dow, in *George Higinbotham: Church and State*, that it is unprofitable to offer more than a sketch here for the sake of completeness.

In 1862 Richard Heales sponsored the *Common Schools Act*, a measure intended to bring rationality to the development of schools and to create a unifying Board of Education. It aimed for a largely secular system of education that would stop religious denominations competing in the establishment of schools, thereby creating too many schools in some places, while leaving others neglected. Under the Act the property of public schools was vested in the Board, and it was intended, but not realized, that church schools would follow that lead. Schools under the Board's control were obliged to give four hours of secular instruction daily, to which religious instruction could be added. The Board was constituted by members representing different religious denominations. Its power lay in controlling funds appropriated by Parliament, and distributing them to schools that met its requirements.

As the experiment was less than successful, the 1866 Commission was set up to recommend a better way forward. Higinbotham did not come to the task with an entirely open mind. Some time before his appointment he had stated in the Assembly:

> The Roman Catholic clergy entertained peculiar views on the question of education; they would perfectly isolate the body they belonged to from the rest of the community. He had reason to believe, however, that these views were not universally held, especially among the more educated portion of the denomination.[41]

Sentiments like those weighed against concord in the Commission even before it commenced. It followed that when the Commission was formally constituted, in September 1866, Catholic invitees declined to become Commissioners, and Bishop Goold declined even to participate as a witness before the Commission. The other Commissioners, aside from Higinbotham, represented various denominations or sects.

With typical industry and energy Higinbotham threw himself wholeheartedly into the Commission's work. David Blair, secretary to the Commission, recorded that:

> The Commission sat for five months, and in that time held fifty-two meetings, some of them from six to eight hours of unbroken length. This was an amount of work two or three times greater ... than [was] usually performed by Royal Commissions. The unremitting zeal of their Chairman acted like a charm on the Commissioners.[42]

The Commission also examined 37 witnesses, "questions being put only by or through the Chairman".[43] One sees in this Higinbotham's style of trusting no-one but himself, delegating nothing, and being the focal point of the enterprise. How then, it may very well be wondered, did he manage also the concurrent duties of Attorney-General, a full-time commitment in themselves.

The result was a report published in 1867, to which a Public Instruction Bill, no doubt of Higinbotham's principal drafting, was appended. It provided for the appointment of a Minister of Public Instruction having superintendence over a Department of Public Instruction, with authority to administer all money appropriated by Parliament for its purposes, to establish and maintain public schools, and to distribute aid to registered schools. The Board of Education was to be dissolved and its assets vested in the Minister.[44]

It was to be obligatory for parents to send to school their children aged between 7 and 14 years. No child was to be refused admission "on account of the religious persuasion of such child", and no child was to be required to participate in "any religious or sectarian teaching, exercise, or formulary", to which the parents might object. Moreover, the Minister was to be under a duty to prohibit, in school hours, "instruction in creeds catechisms and formularies, and all other sectarian teaching and practices in all public schools".[45]

Catholic interests vehemently opposed the secularizing tendencies of the Bill, and, because of such antipathy, which included that of clergy of other denominations, the Commission "achieved little more than to expose the nature of the dilemma".[46] It followed that when Higinbotham introduced the Commission's Bill in Parliament in 1867 a "wave of anger" broke over him.[47] Premier McCulloch disowned the Bill: it received so little encouragement in the Assembly that Higinbotham, in humiliation, had to withdraw it before it could be discussed in detail. He would not brook the thought of accepting amendments "of an important character" to a measure on which he had worked so hard.[48] He was dismayed by the intransigence of the churches, who were even more uncompromising than he, and he reflected bitterly that "[no] more melancholy spectacle can be presented than that which is presented by these religious bodies, when viewed merely as competing companies or corporations".[49]

Seeing the draft Bill translated into legislation was a task few individuals could have accomplished: and certainly not without reasonably common cause among the religious groups. Higinbotham was not the right man for the job. He lived too much in a theoretical world, and was swayed too much by his own unconventional religious views, that will be considered presently. While he dominated and charmed the Commissioners and attracted them to his own position by the force of his magnetic personality, persuasive address and exemplary commitment to work (most of which he did unaided), he was leading his colleagues nowhere. The result was a reflection, in miniature, of the way in which, at the same time, he was leading his colleagues in government nowhere.

He remained despondent about the course of educational policy and complained publicly, in 1871, that education was "not the mere stuffing of the intellect of the child with the materials of knowledge, but the training of his character". The community was entitled to feel the "deepest anxiety" that such training had miscarried, and that children were being denied instruction "not only [in] the principles but the habits of truth and sincerity, and goodwill and honesty, which indeed are the qualities upon which society among adults exists and depends".[50]

It fell, incidentally, to J.W. Stephen, as Attorney-General in the Francis Ministry, to introduce and see through Parliament an Education Bill that was enacted in 1872. It made Victorian education free, compulsory and secular. Stephen, until his appointment to the Supreme Court Bench in 1874, served as Victoria's first Minister of Public Instruction. An essentially more practical and conciliatory man than was Higinbotham, Stephen had found the *via media* to reform.

"Like a Polar Bear Afloat in Mid-Ocean"

Allied to Higinbotham's views on education were his views on religion and morality. His religious convictions were as puzzling and as changeable as were so many other aspects of his character. As noticed at the outset, he turned against many of the principles in which he had been nurtured in childhood under the Irish Protestant Ascendancy. Outwardly, in mature life, he followed the tenets of the Church of England and, with his wife, was a regular parishioner at St Andrew's Church, Middle Brighton. But, unlike his judicial predecessor Sir William Stawell, he took no part in church governance and found himself often at odds with the Anglican Bishop, Charles Perry.[51]

According to Professor Morris, the character of Higinbotham's "creed" could be embraced fully in the words "I believe in God the Father Almighty": for the rest of the Trinity he had less belief.[52] Judicial office seems to have inspired him to speak his mind on such personal issues. Invited to discuss education at the 1882 Church of England Congress, he volunteered in his speech that he did not "share the self-mutilating creed of the agnostic".[53]

Next year, at Scots Church, Melbourne, Higinbotham, at the invitation of the controversial Presbyterian cleric Charles Strong,[54] delivered a lecture "Science and Religion or the Relations of Modern Science with the Christian Churches".[55] Higinbotham forecast the storms ahead when he admitted, "what I shall say will, I fear, be in part unwelcome and probably displeasing to some of you". He disclaimed any intention of giving offence, stating that he was "not responsible" for the subject of the lecture or the manner of treating it, as if he were merely reciting the words and thoughts of another.[56]

But it was all too clear that his provocative address was his own work. His theme was "the growing division between the minds of the clergy and of the educated thinking laity in the Christian churches", with the conclusion that the intellects of the majority of the latter lay "wholly outside the influence of the intellectual teaching" of the former.[57] There was, he asserted, by reference to overseas communities, a profound distrust, on the part of intelligent laymen, of "all church systems of religious and moral belief".

Too much, the churches had failed in their fundamental mission to teach: and, when they did teach, their students all too often were not men of the world, but women and children. Men, he maintained, were failing, for want of religious instruction, in their duty to apply "the science and the art of educating and training the undeveloped mind of the child and the receptive and dependent mind of the woman".

Scientific discoveries had evoked new thoughts about creation. Man was no longer to be seen as the centre of everything, but as "one of the smallest of the works of God". It followed that "anthropomorphism, or the representation of God in the likeness of man", was no longer acceptable.[58] Science had gained confidence and courage as "ecclesiasticism" had become less violent and aggressive, so that there was a diminishing tension between the two.[59]

But the churches suffered from discord and, so he insisted, "not one of the Christian churches can successfully set up so much as a shadow of a rational claim to regard itself, or to be regarded by others, as being itself the sole Church of Christ".[60] There needed to be unity in the object of worship and in the principles of belief of all Christian Churches. That unity should be found in a return to Christ's "primitive simple doctrines", discarding all glosses, additions and dogmas contributed over the intervening centuries – some of which were "revolting and odious to the natural conscience and to the understanding of man", and had been exposed as such by scientific discoveries.[61] He particularly reprobated the concept of Adam's fall from a perfect state, and he relied on geological science to support his conclusion,

That man at the first did not fall from a higher state of existence, but that he rose from a lower; and that what we call death, or the change and dissolution of the organic form in which life temporarily resides, existed on this planet from the time that life first appeared upon it.[62]

He considered that clergy, generally, were trained from the outset to maintain the particular tenets of their respective denominations with inappropriate inflexibility, and that "the creeds of the Christian churches … have … been the most dangerous and insidious enemies of the religion of Christ". Therefore the opposition of the clergy to reform had to be overcome, and:

The salvation of the mind of Christendom at present appears to depend … upon union amongst laymen of all churches, who still retain an intelligent hold upon the ultimate object of faith, and who will combine to cast out from their own minds and from the Christian churches the spectres of old and now discredited fallacies.[63]

All of which was completely in character with a man who was so self-assured that he presumed to lecture Secretaries of State, Governors, judges and prelates alike as to their proper conduct.

Higinbotham's address was disastrous for Strong who, on being threatened with charges of heresy for not condemning the speaker's assertions, resigned from Scots Church. Nevertheless, the thesis that too many clergy were out of touch with laymen, and had lost their proper sphere of influence, was pursued by several writers, notably by Andrew Garran in articles published in the *Sydney Mail*.[64]

In 1887, Higinbotham spoke at the opening of a new Unitarian Church building – the church much supported by Sir William a'Beckett when first Chief Justice of Victoria. Although Higinbotham frankly stated that new church buildings were scarcely required in a city replete with such edifices, he praised the doctrine of the Unitarian Church especially *vis-à-vis* other denominations. It alone, he said, preserved the idea of the unity of God – "it alone carries the lighted torch by which, according to its belief, the dark steps of humanity require to be guided". He found the faith reassuring in which "God is the first and the supreme mind, by whose personal will all matter and all derived minds have been called into being".[65]

He deplored the wrong and injustice long suffered by the Unitarian Church which, he thought, had become "an outcast" –

hated, and also feared, by all the other Christian churches; and it is so hated and feared because it alone has clung with unwavering fidelity to the great truths of the unity of God and of the relation of man's mind to the Supreme mind – the truth that was declared by the Founder of Christianity to be the first of the great principles of sound philosophy, and of action regulated by law.[66]

That produced a spirited response from the Revd Alexander Gosman, lately Chairman of the Congregational Union of Victoria, who expressed "true pity for those whose religious outlook is as dark and gloomy as that of Mr Justice Higinbotham".[67] The judge, who was on the very threshold of becoming Chief Justice, might have been expected to eschew public and religious controversy. But Gosman did not respond in anger: he felt sorry for the state of mind that induced Higinbotham to speak as he did and to propound "the notion that God will have to go into retirement for a time". He likened the judge to a man who had elevated doubt into a religion and who was

> propelled by his cold and unsympathetic nature, towards the ice-bound regions of the sphere of thought, [and] may find himself some day like a polar bear afloat in mid-ocean on an iceberg, with all that he has to stand upon melting away from under him, and nothing in sight to inspire the hope of deliverance.[68]

As has been put repeatedly in these pages, Higinbotham liked to be seen to be different, and, in matters religious, he paraded most conspicuously his unconventional attitudes to faith and belief. They helped to advance another myth of saintliness that developed about him. As the English journal *The Inquirer* put it, in an obituary notice prompted by "a relative who shares the same great and glorious faith" (no doubt, Professor Morris),[69] Higinbotham,

> was a true servant of God. Everything he did was done in the love and fear of God. He gave himself for his fellow man; he spent himself and his substance in their service, never thinking of himself for one moment.[70]

"Wiser Than the Laws"

A puritanical air accompanied that supposed saintliness. Higinbotham despised all forms of intemperance and immorality. He condemned those who consumed alcohol to excess as he opposed

241

all gambling.[71] But, when Attorney-General, that opposition yielded before a stronger and astounding desire to resist a Supreme Court decision he thought to be wrong. Higinbotham's affected purity was widely ridiculed when he publicly denounced raffles conducted at ladies' bazaars. One such case, in 1866, drove him to an irrational fury. In *Bergin* v. *Cohen*,[72] the complainant appealed to the Full Supreme Court from the decision of magistrates that Cohen was not "beneficially interested" as promoter of a lottery for disposal of fancy goods in aid of Melbourne Hospital. The case turned on the tricky wording of s. 31 of the *Police Offences Act* 1865, consolidated by Higinbotham.

The section rendered it an offence to "establish", "commence", "be a partner in", and "be otherwise interested in" a lottery. The complainant argued, in effect, that those words were to be read disjunctively so that proof of any one founded a prosecution. The Full Court rejected that submission. Stawell, C.J., pointed out that the court was not required to consider whether alternative ways were open for suppressing lotteries, but simply to construe the section. Barry, J., with perhaps a tilt at Higinbotham, deprecated "the singular mode in which the Act is drawn". So far as Stawell was concerned, under the section "a partner in a lottery is not answerable unless he is beneficially interested": nothing showed that Cohen was so interested, and the magistrates had been right. Barry and Williams concurred.[73]

Higinbotham did not forget what he regarded as an unjust and excessively technical piece of statutory construction by the court. In 1868 the opportunity arose for him to assert his position and reveal the "error" of the judges. In April, Hugh Peck, a large landowner, applied to him for permission to proceed with the sale of his land by the medium of shares in an art union. Despite Higinbotham's abhorrence of gambling, and the obvious fact that Peck was beneficially interested in the sale of shares in a chance, Higinbotham appeared to agree.

Unfortunately for Peck, Higinbotham lost office in the month following, being effectively succeeded by G.P. Smith who "determined to disallow lotteries, even those commenced prior to his coming into office".[74] In a Police Court prosecution, it was alleged and accepted that Peck had obtained Higinbotham's permission by fraud and deceit. Peck, on losing the case, applied to

Higinbotham for confirmation that his application had not been fraudulent.

Higinbotham replied that he had not been misled by the April application nor did he think it calculated to mislead. Although his private inclinations were so strongly against lotteries, Higinbotham was prepared to subordinate them to teaching the Supreme Court a lesson, or so he thought. He wrote to Peck that "believing the law relating to lotteries, as it was decided by the Supreme Court, to be an unequal and therefore an unjust law, I would not enforce it in any case whatever".[75] Only on that footing had Peck received his permission.

That was a remarkable, and almost petulant, position to take. It exposed Higinbotham to press censure that he had indulged in "lawless tantrums", and,

> There is a sort of sublimity in Mr HIGINBOTHAM'S mode of setting aside the law. In his view an Attorney-General is appointed, not to administer the law, but to correct its defects. In the exercise of this authority he is free from all restraint and is above all advice. Nothing but his own sense of right and of public convenience restrains him … He thus repeats his determination to be wiser than the laws.[76]

While his methods were much at odds with his professed hatred of gambling, he acted as he did partly out of annoyance and partly, it may be supposed, to prompt Parliament to amend the law. Until he did so, his clear duty, as Attorney-General, was to apply, not to arbitrate upon, the law declared by the Supreme Court.

"Still Calling Myself a Victorian Politician"

As has been seen, Higinbotham, as judge and Chief Justice, perceived himself still to be a politician. He qualified that by claiming to be no more than a person interested in political science. But his actions suggested otherwise, and his participation in sensitive political issues seemed to attract the judicial office in support of his controversial views – a course that was as imprudent as it was unconventional.[77]

The first such issue was his concern about British Imperial policy in the Pacific, which led him into another unbecoming clash with the Secretary of State. From the early 1850s France had caused alarm in Australia by its annexation of New Caledonia and its determination to establish there a penal colony for recidivists. Twenty years later it had designs on that part of New Guinea not controlled by the Dutch, to set up a new "Empire" in the southern hemisphere. In something of a chess game, Britain unenthusiastically accepted the cession of the Kingdom of Fiji in 1874, while Germany annexed, but then released, New Britain, while being goaded by German traders to occupy and colonize New Guinea.

In 1883, the British Government having shown no interest, the Queensland Government of Sir Thomas McIlwraith purported to take "possession" of New Guinea at Port Moresby. After 12 months of agitation, of no present relevance, Britain reluctantly agreed to establish a Protectorate there.

Higinbotham had concerned himself in such questions since his *Argus* days. In one of his final editorials he complained that Australians were so preoccupied with domestic matters

> that they have practically in a great degree overlooked the existence of communities situated in their neighbourhood which are considered of no small importance by foreign nations ... It is high time that this community should take a more active interest in the affairs of Polynesia.[78]

The *Argus*, however, dropped the subject after his resignation.

Queensland's 1883 actions evoked strong condemnation by other colonies. In July, about 2000 citizens at Melbourne's Town Hall said as much, though, as Higinbotham explained it, they "endeavoured to excuse that clearly illegal act, and to induce the Imperial Government to ratify it" so as to control "the slave traffic and slavery" (then commonly known as "blackbirding"). Privately he thought that there could be no excuse, because "in this work of annexation all civilized nations alike are robbers".[79] Undeterred by the constraints of judicial office, he attended and spoke at the meeting, urging that Britain use its international power to clarify the position, but receiving "the loudest cheer from the enthusiastic audience when he called for united Australian action to prevent more French convicts reaching their shores".[80]

His personal convictions deplored the course taken by the English Government and the Colonial Office. The latter, he wrote to a friend, ought to have acceded promptly to Australian wishes and, though it might have been "robbery", to have annexed eastern New Guinea so as to forestall rival European powers; or, in the alternative, it ought to have said frankly that such a course could not be adopted:

> we could not be permitted to advance claims and to commit unauthorised acts for which England might be held responsible by other Powers, and that if we insisted upon acting independently in extra-territorial questions without the sanction of the Imperial Government, we must accept the responsibilities of complete independence and submit to be dis-annexed from the parent state.[81]

He reckoned that Queensland's "ill-advised and reckless acts" had been encouraged, rather than corrected, "by the vacillation and panic fears of the English Colonial and Foreign Offices".

The subject simmered until, in February 1887, he wrote his remarkably hostile letter to Sir Henry Holland, then Secretary of State, in which he incorporated the New Guinea episode as illustrating "the systematic violation of the public law by the Colonial Office". He depicted that office as having engaged in "vacillating and imbecile conduct" on the question, leading it to produce only "feeble and timid modes of action". Its duty of openness and decisiveness had not been fulfilled, so he said, and it was "quite manifest" to him, that the office was "at present unequal to the discharge of this or of any other great duty".[82]

A politician might, perhaps, have ventured upon such excessive and provocative comments. But it was not, and is not, apparent how they formed a legitimate part of the functions of a Chief Justice or contributed to the sense of detachment becoming such a position. Higinbotham continued, unconvincingly, to explain away the irreconcilable – "I claim the right of still calling myself a Victorian politician, though I have retired from active service".[83]

From there it was a short step to enter upon the truly contentious politics of industrial turmoil that reached a climax in Victoria in the closing years of Higinbotham's life. He had interested himself in labour issues since *Argus* editorials that advocated high wages "and we regard the prosperity of the great mass of the people as more important than almost any other consideration". Yet he did not condone the "loud drones" who incited industrial strife, discouraged others from honest work, and lived "on the wages of agitation".[84]

He was not then an unqualified apologist for organized labour and, even when he became a judge, his sympathy for "the worker" in cases arising out of industrial accidents, was tenuous, as has been seen. He was not committed to any developed concept of a safe system of work, and dealt severely with injured workers whom he found guilty of contributory negligence.[85] His position was typically eccentric. He was not so much for employees, as he was against employers who might abuse their unequal bargaining power.[86]

Late in life he recalled a sentimental affinity between his earlier career and the aims of the labour movement. In 1891, he wrote to J.T. Ross, General Secretary of the Locomotive Engine Drivers' Association, describing himself as "one who long ago and for many years was a fellow servant of the members of your Association in the Public Service of Victoria", and describing the memory as "one of the dearest and most intimate and also the most venerated of my personal memories".[87] It was unsurprising then that Higinbotham was a principal guest and speaker at the opening of a new Council Chamber at Melbourne's Trades Hall in 1884. Immensely moved by the presence of the visitor, Deakin described him as "cherubic", but seemed less moved by Higinbotham's address on the subject of principled politics, including the assertion that "almost all compromises, almost all concessions … are so many abandonments of principle".[88] That was the epitome of Higinbotham's own failure in politics: his inability to see that compromise could be equally principled and constructive.

In 1882, when already a judge, Higinbotham had been ambivalent about the founding of a new Working Men's College in Melbourne, proposed by the grazier Francis Ormond who contributed £20,500 to the project. Higinbotham applauded the generosity, but, seeing a "squatter" as if a Greek bearing gifts, he raised difficulties that created delay. He maintained that such a college must enjoy "self government" and not be open to exploitation by such "foreign bodies" as the University, the Public Library, "or even casual subscribers". He proposed "absolute freedom in the selection of subjects of voluntary study in the College curriculum". Politics and "unsectarian theology" ought, he said, to hold "honored places" in such a curriculum – "otherwise this College will be only a new Mechanics' Institute".[89] Instead of seeking a middle ground by negotiation, Higinbotham, sensing that his conditions were not going to be met, withdrew his support and declined to speak at a launching ceremony. The new College did not materialize until 1887.[90]

As Australia drifted into a debilitating financial depression in 1890, Victoria, although in a relatively strong economic position, suffered from a maritime strike precipitated by the wish of merchant navy officers to become affiliated with other maritime unions. The employers' resistance was met with violent flexing of union muscles. A prolonged waterfront strike attracted sympathy strikes in other industries including the attempt by workers to paralyse Melbourne by cutting off gas supplies.

Although opposed to strikes, the influential union leader Benjamin Douglass organized a fund from which to support strikers and their families. At his suggestion, Higinbotham, one of his closest friends, agreed to contribute.[91] Thus emerged one of the strangest letters ever written from judicial chambers in Australia. It began, "The Chief Justice presents his compliments to the president of the Trades-hall Council". It enclosed a cheque for £50 towards the fund and a promise of £10 weekly "while the united trades are awaiting compliance with their reasonable request for a conference with the employers".[92] True to the promise, he contributed about £150 in all. There was a sarcastic suggestion that, in protest, "the Victorian legal profession" had vowed "to contribute an equal amount to the Employers' Union".[93]

The strike collapsed, no conference having been convened, yet Higinbotham continued his weekly donation for some time, as "a test of the honesty of the Trades-hall Council – to find out how much principle, if any, lives in that body", so the *Australasian* maintained.[94] There was fury in the city at the Chief Justice's action, one capitalist was said to threaten that "if he had his will a company of the Permanent Artillery should haul the Judge from the Bench, put him against a wall and shoot him".[95]

The *Argus* regretted that the Chief Justice, by his "impulsive and foolish action", had "descended into abetting faction and supporting a class tyranny".[96] More relevantly, it pointed out the embarrassment that could arise should any aspects of the proceedings come formally before the Supreme Court. It was irresponsible for the Sydney *Bulletin* to rejoin that whether the Chief Justice disqualified himself from presiding judicially was "entirely his own affair" because the Chief Justice "merely represents the law, and the law represents nothing in particular except the lawyers".[97]

What Chief Justice Higinbotham chose to do privately to support a strike fund was indeed his own affair. But to implicate his office in the gesture was a most serious error of judgement. The socialist journal *Tocsin*, which regarded "Democrat" Higinbotham as a hero, published over several months a series of his "public utterances", as if so many liturgical collects, epistles and gospels for the day.[98] All too often they demonstrated that he did not practise what he preached. One of them recalled Higinbotham's reflections on Williams, J., with the suggestion that a Supreme Court Judge who canvassed political questions ought to quit the Bench.[99] But Higinbotham saw himself in a different light and under a special dispensation:

> It is a common belief (and it seems to me to be a belief as false in theory as it is unfounded in practice) … that a man who has been a politician all his life when he desires to enter the kingdom of judicial heaven is bound to become a political eunuch, and is not at liberty for the rest of his natural existence to enjoy the lawful pleasures of political life … I do not believe that theory is sound. I am sure it is not a fact.[100]

Fortunately for the impartial administration of justice that view has generally not commended itself to Australian superior court judges.

Nevertheless, Higinbotham remained revered by the Union movement. For instance, a "large photographic picture" of him was installed, soon after his death, at Ballarat Trades Hall, with the inscription "a friend and sympathiser of the worker, an advocate of justice for the unionists".[101] Shortly afterwards, the Bendigo branch of the Amalgamated Miners' Association presented Professor Morris with an illuminated address in memory of the Chief Justice.[102] Transcending all, but long delayed in its achievement, was Paul Montford's statue of Higinbotham in judicial robes, unveiled in 1937 shortly before the sculptor's own death. Sited north of Melbourne's Treasury Building, the memorial is unusual, not only because Chief Justices are rarely so honoured, but also because it became a symbol, not so much of judicial achievements, but of the place accorded to Higinbotham in the history of organized labour in Victoria.[103]

"Duty Was Life"

The burdens of the Bench, and concern for his health, decided Higinbotham to quit Brighton in 1887 and to move to 17 Murphy Street, South Yarra, so as to be closer to the court house. Nevertheless, the arduousness of his duties, especially after he became Chief Justice, began to take its toll. In keeping with his precept that he should receive nothing from the public that he did not earn – a precept that had caused him to decline a parliamentary rail pass even though entitled to one, and to propose that parliamentarians, if paid at all, be paid only by their constituents[104] – he refused to apply for any leave when a judge.[105] Most court vacations and public holidays he applied to his work.

It followed that, with the added strain of statutory consolidation, he succumbed to heart disease, and suffered from angina for several years before he died in 1892. His health had been further impaired by his addiction to cigarette smoking.[106] In those years he forced himself to attend to court business every day, without once being absent through illness. The price was high, for "as soon as the vacation came he suffered a relapse each year".[107] He saw through all the 1892 court commitments and seemed in fair health and spirits on Christmas Day. But he died suddenly, on New Year's Eve, after a severe angina attack. As the *Ballarat Courier* observed, "to the late Chief Justice ... duty was life, and his dearest wish, which has been gratified, was that he might die in harness".[108]

At a time when great public funerals were expected for great public figures, Higinbotham chose, as usual, to be different. He directed that his remains should be farewelled in strict privacy: neither the place nor the time was to be announced.[109] At St Andrew's Church of England, Middle Brighton, on 2 January 1893, no grand cortege or procession attended, no dignitaries were present, nor were any leading clergy or any lawyers there save for Gerald Piggott, the Chief Justice's former Associate. The widow, as was then common, was absent. Three daughters, one son and Professor Morris the son-in-law, formed the congregation with Higinbotham's medical adviser Dr Dunbar Hooper.[110]

The Revd J.F. Stretch read the funeral service "in a solemn and impressive tone" and offered some formal expressions of condolence. The Chief Justice's body was then interred at

Brighton cemetery "in the Episcopalian compartment", not, as he had wished, next to his brother's grave in the burying ground of St Andrew's Church, where recent health regulations precluded further interments.[111]

Higinbotham left no real estate; his personalty was sworn at £17,500. His will, of 4 May 1890, appointed his wife executor and bequeathed to her all residuary estate after payment of a bequest of £3000 to his sister Jane.[112] Margaret Higinbotham, "who intends living at home altogether",[113] sailed for England in the *Britannia* as soon as arrangements could be made, and lived out the rest of her days, until her death in December 1910, in the household of another son-in-law Commander Lyon of the Royal Naval Reserve.[114] Hers had been a life set in the minor key.

"Patriots and Revolutionaries"

What was lost in public celebration of so remarkable a life was compensated for by instantaneous eulogies in Victoria's newspapers. City prints contained elaborate notices, and provincial editors often had original things to say. Even in smaller communities columns were copied from more extensive obituaries.[115]

The *Argus* published a combined valediction and biography – "Death of Chief Justice Higinbotham: Close of a Memorable Career" – of considerable length, accuracy and balance.[116] It described him as having "occupied a unique place in the public mind" and was frank, but not judgemental, in reviewing his achievements. Editorially it went further, insisting that "no man in his time played a more conspicuous and more important part in the making of the colony" – a view that appeared to have forgotten the efforts of Foster, Stawell and others – and whose leadership in journalism and in law was overshadowed by his leadership in politics:

> his powerful personality … conquered the country as a whole for a time, and … he had an almost absolute sway, the like of which had not been known in the past, is not known at present, and is not likely to re-occur in the future.[117]

Yet the political paradox had to be recognized. The controversies that he pursued with such passion turned out to be "barren, [and] they served no good end", while "His intensity rendered him impossible. It deprived him of that 'sweet

reasonableness' without which no public career can be a permanent success". In particular, it regretted his campaign against the
Colonial Office which had been "preached in vain" when there
was "no real grievance" and the supposed wrongs were "either
matters of form or were purely imaginary". It concluded that:

> The faults that marred the political career of GEORGE HIGINBOTHAM
> were of the head, and not of the heart. His public life was a broken
> column. But if the marble was not without deep flaws it was with-
> out a dishonouring stain.[118]

The *Age* took a more egalitarian stance, noting that, throughout his career, Higinbotham had "sought to act up to the demands
of a somewhat exigeant conscience", but that the community
would respect his memory for different reasons –

> To the mass of people among whom he lived his crowning merit
> will be that he remained to the end plain George Higinbotham, the
> sole Chief Justice in the colonies without a handle to his name. Like
> the best of old Romans he lived and died in the belief that the only
> compliments worthy of manly estimation are those which spring
> from the heart of a gratified people.[119]

Melbourne's *Herald* drew attention to the eccentricities of the
man. In politics his career had "something of the erratic course as
well as the brilliancy of a great comet", while, judicially, he had
"if not the sure and luminous intellect of a great lawyer, yet the
knowledge of a scholar, the integrity of a saint, and the courtesy
of a high-minded gentleman".[120]

The *Leader* associated Higinbotham with "the promotion of
Liberal opinions at a time when a new State was being generated",
and it credited him with giving "that high tone to politics which
long distinguished Victoria from the other colonies", in the
context of raising "the public estimation of politics from the municipal to the national level" and stimulating a popular enthusiasm
for broad political principles. It praised his unceasing resistance to
"a band of monopolists who had acquired possession of the bulk
of the public territory, and an undue share of political power".[121]

The *Australasian* published three memorial pieces. It described him as having been a "landmark" in the Colony for 40
years, and, as such, "he had views to announce, he had a doctrine
to preach, a religion to impose on the people, and he seized the
occasion the instant it offered". But it noticed that his values, in

their abstraction, often differed from those of the community at large. He had never been

> in close, familiar, and if you like, vulgar touch with the everyday facts of life. He was a politician of the study and the imagination. He never knew men as the man of the world knows them; he only saw one side of women – the perfect side.[122]

For such reasons, and because of his retiring way of life, the *Australasian* reckoned that, by 1893, "the present generation [were] almost unaware of his presence and certainly totally unaware of his great moral and political force" – a sobering reality that his "disciples" soon set out to remedy.

The *Illustrated Australian News* (Melbourne), on the other hand, asserted that:

> No man stood higher in the estimation of the whole community than the late Chief Justice. His political services in past times have not been forgotten, and his abilities as a lawyer and painstaking judge have always been fully recognised.[123]

A more cutting "Character Sketch" by "Timotheus", in the *Australasian*, reckoned that Higinbotham "seldom had even a momentary victory to lighten up his fighting career as a politician", and that "his big efforts were all failures", because his object (to assert the supremacy of the Legislative Assembly over all other powers) "was wrong" and because his method "was bad". But "Timotheus" balanced his condemnation of Higinbotham's political extremes by acknowledging, as his greatest qualities, "rectitude, courtesy, and a noble sense of duty".[124]

Melbourne's *Weekly Times* introduced some superlatives, farewelling "Victoria's noblest citizen", one of "the few great men" of Australia, who, as a politician had "wielded for a decade the most powerful influence in Victorian affairs". Yet it had to concede that, politically, Higinbotham's career "was remarkable for its oratorical brilliance rather than for its administrative success. A master of political theory Mr Higinbotham was by temperament impractical as a politician". So there was "failure as well as success, disappointment as well as gratification".[125]

There were superlatives too from Melbourne's short-lived *Evening Standard* which maintained that "few judges have so thoroughly enjoyed the implicit confidence of the people as did" Higinbotham – a journalistic frolic unsupported by history or

even by objective contemporary evidence. Yet the writer continued that Higinbotham's character was without peer:

> It shines out in a splendour of manly rectitude and unswerving
> fidelity to justice and right which is uneclipsed by the records of
> any of the greatest Australian men of mark.[126]

Outside Melbourne, Higinbotham received unqualified
praise from Christopher Crisp of the *Bacchus Marsh Express* who
regarded him as "the George Washington of the community
whom he served". With much editorial licence, Crisp described
his hero as having "emancipated these colonies from Crown
colony treatment" and as having created "a House of Commons in
this colony as the central and paramount but not absolute deposi-
tory of political power". On safer ground, Crisp wrote:

> His sense of duty so entirely subordinated his personal entity to an
> abstraction in his own estimation that he really did not do justice to
> his intellect and to the unique position he had gained in the minds
> and hearts of Victorians.[127]

The praise of the *Ballarat Star* was as boundless, though it
concluded that, despite claimed political successes, Higinbotham
had "paid the penalty that martyrs pay". He was, it contended,
Victoria's "one public man whom all men held in reverence".

> That a man who knew no compromise and admitted none, should,
> in spite of his unbending rigidity of principle, become the idol of
> the people and a trusted leader in journalism, in politics and in law,
> successively, shows that the great popular heart might be trusted
> more often than it is.[128]

The *Gippsland Times*, at Sale, in an effusion of hyperbole,
described Higinbotham as "a friend of the humblest of his fellow
men", and, unusually among the provincial prints, commended
rather the judicial than the political standing of its subject. He had
been, so it asserted, "the one man who above all others had the
entire confidence of the people", and by whom he was "loved".

> The supreme court bench has been the pride of Victorians for many
> years, and the late chief was admittedly the foremost of an able and
> conscientious bench of justices … and we are safe in asserting that
> if the people of a federated Australia had been free to make choice
> of a leader, the late Chief Justice would have been chosen by an
> overwhelming majority.[129]

The news seems not to have reached Sale that Higinbotham stoutly resisted the very concept of Federation.

The *Gippsland Mercury* more accurately recorded that the Chief Justice had left "thousands of sorrowing friends" by whom his memory would be cherished. It thought that "he was too impracticably honest to ever become a failed diplomatist, and the very qualities which debarred him from fame as a statesman were precisely those which best fitted him for the higher and nobler office of judge".[130]

The *Bendigo Advertiser* concurred that Higinbotham had been "revered and loved and honored as few public men have been". It praised his oratory before which "his audience listened spell-bound to the sweet music of the words which carried conviction to their minds". And it spoke for his popularity:

> Few men have ever held such power over the masses in Victoria. They trusted him implicitly – not alone for his democratic tendencies, but for his calm wisdom, the integrity and nobility of character.[131]

There were some notices in other colonies. The most prominent was that of Adelaide's *Register* which depicted Higinbotham as "one of the greatest men in Australia" who had enjoyed "a foremost place in that special galaxy of Australasian statesmen". It rightly acknowledged his commitment to independence – in which he would be "neither a local member in his district nor an indiscriminating party man in the House" – and to principle. But it regretted that his policies had stimulated "the anti-federal protectionism which has since so retarded Australian commercial progress". It concluded that:

> He was a man of the highest honour and honesty and he had the stuff out of which patriots and revolutionaries are made, but he was withal extreme in his opinions, impracticable, and sometimes so wanting in diplomacy as to be very indiscreet.[132]

In New South Wales, the *Sydney Mail* published a biographical column, noting only that, in the political contests of his day, Higinbotham had been "looked upon as the people's champion".[133] The *Sydney Morning Herald* was less flattering, depicting him as "the moving spirit and central figure in the most belligerent period of Victorian history".[134] But it acknowledged that, in constitutional and legal matters, he was "the inspiring genius in some of the greatest struggles in the most stirring portion of Australian history". Sydney's *Daily Telegraph* reiterated biographical details published in the *Sunday Sun* (London).[135] An austere column appeared in the London *Times*.[136]

There were ceremonious addresses in the Supreme Court and in Parliament. Mr Justice Williams was reported to be in tears when he announced in court that "the hand of death has parted us from a loved and lovable and honest, good and sincere friend". The tears might have been inspired more by the immediate accession to the Bench after the ceremony of Dr John Madden, as fourth Chief Justice of Victoria, a station to which Williams considered himself entitled by seniority.[137] Isaac Isaacs, then Solicitor-General, was left to reflect eloquently on the late Chief Justice:

> The name of George Higinbotham is indelibly carved in the hearts of the people of Victoria. In every situation in which he was found, whether in the senate, at the bar or on the bench, he was animated by one desire – the welfare of his country.[138]

Mr Justice Hodges, on another occasion, delivered a separate eulogy, with the peroration that "Britain may have greater statesmen, Britain may have craftier politicians: but Britain has no son with a stronger, gentler, firmer, kinder, or nobler nature than the man who lately presided in this court".[139]

There were similar encomiums in the Legislative Council where Service spoke of Higinbotham as one of his oldest friends, "a self-contained man". He perceived a unanimous community feeling of admiration for Higinbotham, no matter where political allegiances lay, for he was the man who, if anyone could have accomplished it, might have brought about "that millennium, which the race has been looking forward to for so long a time". While not everyone could agree with his methods, "we could not help admiring the way in which he endeavoured to give effect to his views".[140]

In the Assembly, Shiels described his mentor as "Victoria's foremost citizen", and continued:

> It was here he put forth all the powers of his splendid mind and his great culture … I can see him again rising in this House and coming to the corner of the table. At first his sentences were halting, hesitating, but measured and clear in tone. Then, when the

nervous hesitancy had been shaken off and his ideas assumed a concrete form, I can still hear him pouring out "thoughts that breathe and words that burn".[141]

In Hobart, Andrew Inglis Clark, that other devotee of Higinbotham's principles, moved that the Tasmanian Parliament record its sense of loss at Higinbotham's passing, because "the name of ... the late Chief Justice of Victoria occupied a unique and prominent position in the affections of the people of Australia". His noble life ought, in Clark's view, to be treated as "the common property" of all Australians and venerated accordingly.[142]

Clark recalled the few occasions when he had heard Higinbotham speak, either in court or in the Victorian Parliament, as "among the most inspiring recollections of my life". The parliamentary speeches he did not hear, Clark "eagerly perused" in printed form. Whatever future Australian generations might bring forth in the way of public figures, "I feel I am not guilty of any exaggeration", declared Clark,

> when I say that it will be impossible for any of them to enrich its history with a more stainless record that that which George Higinbotham has bequeathed to us.[143]

All of these testimonials have been permitted to flow at some length and in their own words, partly because there were so many of them, partly because most were spontaneous, and partly because most of them rose above the level of empty panegyrics – so unhelpful to the biographer – to assess Higinbotham in such a variety of ways. Yet they had common strands, attesting his individuality, resourcefulness, courage and integrity that vouched for his extraordinarily high standing.

"Various Estimates of His Character"

The career of George Higinbotham may fairly be described as unique in Australia. But it may not fairly be described by the superlatives his "disciples" assigned to him. He was not the most outstanding politician of his age, nor was he its greatest statesman, if statesman at all. And he certainly was not the greatest Australian lawyer of the 19th century. Enigmatic, incongruous and puzzling, he was a man whose greatness was transient, and much dependent on a mesmerizing personality accompanied by rhetorical powers of an unusual order. It is unhelpful to depict him as the greatest orator of his day. The 19th century produced many brilliant orators throughout Australia: attempting to rank them in order of excellence is superfluous. But there can be no doubt that Higinbotham's command of the spoken word propelled him to the prominence he enjoyed.

He was neither a Victorian George Washington, as Christopher Crisp averred, nor was he greater than William Charles Wentworth, as Astley proclaimed. However much Morris, Deakin, Vance Palmer and others tried to weave together the Higinbotham myths to create the legend of Higinbotham as a figure of perfection, the fact remained that, in the area of politics which he esteemed above all others, Higinbotham achieved very little for the "nation" he strove so enthusiastically to serve. What he did achieve was the promotion of a new sense of self-confidence within the Colony in which Victorians saw themselves as members of a well developed and powerful state, being neither a mere offshoot of New South Wales nor a minor imperial outpost.

A caveat needs to be placed on some of the editorial licence overflowing in the newspaper obituaries noticed above. In particular, it was misleading to suggest, as so many editors did, that they spoke for the "community", unless they referred only to the ideal and sententious community of their habitual readership. As to the broader community, many, then as now, would neither know nor care who was the incumbent Chief Justice, except that, in Higinbotham's case, many would have recognized him, not for his judicial contribution so much as for his contribution to the Trades Hall Council during the maritime strike. By the time of his death, his political contribution had been largely forgotten, and there was little left to show for it.

Taking his term as Attorney-General as the summit of his political career, it is a wholesome balance to the superlatives of praise to examine some of the satire directed against him at that time by *Melbourne Punch*. Making allowance for its excesses, just as allowance should be made for the exaggerations of his supporters, that journal took points that illustrate well Higinbotham's want of political nous and acumen. To a cartoon, reproduced in this book, is subjoined a text in which Higinbotham says to himself:

> Let me see now: I've ruined a Governor, I've harried the Judges, I've confused the Statute Book, I've set everybody by the ears, I've

abused the Sects, I've tendered illegal advice to everyone who would take it, I've bungled three or four Tariff Bills – what the D-v-l shall I be up to next?[144]

In another cartoon, it depicted Higinbotham as a jack-in-the-box, wearing a cap marked "discord", springing out of a box marked "Appropriation Act", and accompanied by verse, reading in part:

I'm a terror to friend and a horror to foe;
Breed nervousness round me wherever I go;
Discord's my hobby, confusion my aim,
And the dodge – "conscientious" – is *my* little game.
I've had a good time here my spring's never bent,
I've bragged and I've bullied to my heart's full content;
I've popped up at "church", affrighted the "law",
And touched up the "bench" pretty smart on the raw.[145]

A favourite *Punch* line was to depict its subject as King "Higinbotham the First", robed, crowned, and proclaiming "*L'état c'est moi*". Another depiction of him was as "St Georgey" slaying dragons.[146]

The satire is droll and overdone, yet it exemplifies the greatest paradox of all. Higinbotham was described often as the unquestioned "leader" of his political colleagues who were almost literally enthralled by his dynamic speeches, bold plans, and violent attacks on objects of common hostility. Yet, when the storm had passed, with its vivid lightning of threats and earth-trembling thunder of oratory, the tempest had left damage and destruction, but none of the great things the "leader" had intended.

Only when his colleagues came to their senses and realized that he was leading them into a political desert, was his power curtailed, and Higinbotham himself left abandoned and disillusioned. The paradox in this was that all the fire and fury had been spent, not to achieve anything for Higinbotham personally, but ostensibly to serve the "nation". The results, however, were precisely the opposite of the intentions.

For the purposes of this book, Higinbotham may be recalled as a competent Chief Justice who did not spare himself in his devotion to duty. He had not been so praiseworthy as a puisne judge, being obstructive and unpractical in many of his views. The responsibility of the Chief Justiceship made him change his ways, and he presided with great success. He cannot be described as a jurist: very few of his judicial opinions retain currency as authoritative precedents. In the present assessment, his decision in *Toy* v. *Musgrove* was a judicial aberration. It stands as a reminder that Chief Justices, indeed judges generally, ought never to be permitted to stipulate terms and conditions on which they will accept office, and ought never to indulge in public political controversy while in office.

It cannot be conceded that Higinbotham was "the outstanding legal figure of colonial Australia", no matter how one defines "outstanding".[147] The pioneering work of Stawell eclipsed him in Victoria. Nor was Higinbotham as significant a legal figure as were Sir Francis Forbes and Sir Alfred Stephen in New South Wales. As a Chief Justice, Higinbotham ranked with, but did not outshine, Sir James Martin of New South Wales, Sir Charles Lilley of Queensland, and Sir Richard Hanson of South Australia. All were overshadowed by Queensland's Sir Samuel Griffith.

The most mistaken of the superlatives applied to Higinbotham must surely be that he was the greatest figure in the development of Responsible Government in Victoria. His contribution achieved the antithesis of Responsible Government, creating an absurd and prolonged brawl between the two parliamentary Houses. For a man so committed to Victoria's *Constitution Act* as the source of all constitutional power, it was bizarre that Higinbotham should have refused to accept the Legislative Council (whether he liked its composition or not) as an integral part of the constitutional machinery of Victorian government. The only way in which the bicameral system could function was through compromise, something he would never do. Rather than advance the cause of Responsible Government, he retarded it.

In an unrelated context Higinbotham himself spoke of a problem as being "perplexed by paradox, stunned by contradictions".[148] The phrase epitomized much of his own life and career. He was a monumental individual who wished well for Victoria, yet failed so often to achieve what he had promised. William Shiels, recognizing the paradox as to Higinbotham, summed it up thus:

> They talk of failure, and there are various estimates of his character. If it was a failure it was a failure which remains triumphant, for his influence remains.[149]

Abbreviations

(Used in the following notes)
(Conventional abbreviations are given to Law Reports)

A.D.B.	*Australian Dictionary of Biography* (Melbourne from 1966).
B.L.	British Library, London, England.
Bailey	K.H. Bailey, "Self-Government in Australia, 1860-1900", in Rose, Newton & Benians (Genl Eds), *The Cambridge History of the British Empire*, Vol. VII, Pt I Australia (Cambridge 1933), from p. 395.
C.O.	Colonial Office, with particular reference to papers of that office in the National Archives, Kew, Richmond, England, citing class, piece and folio (or page) numbers.
Carnarvon's Diary	The manuscript unofficial diaries of the fourth Earl of Carnarvon (held by the British Library).
Dean	Sir Arthur Dean, *A Multitude of Counsellors* (Melbourne 1968).
Dow	Gwyneth M. Dow, *George Higinbotham: Church and State* (Melbourne 1964).
Higinbotham Interview (1975)	Information obtained at an interview in London (1975) with Richard Nixon Higinbotham (son of Edward and grandson of George).
Higinbotham Papers	Scrapbook and other documents concerning George Higinbotham, held (1975) by Mr R.N. Higinbotham of London.
I.U.P.	Irish University Press Series, *British Parliamentary Papers* (Colonies – Australia) (Shannon 1969).
Leighton Journal	Stanley Leighton, Extracts from a Journal (1868), Vol. 2 (N.L. MS 360).
M.L.	Mitchell Library of the State Library of New South Wales.
McCaughey	Davis McCaughey, Naomi Perkins, Angus Trumble, *Victoria's Colonial Governors 1839-1900* (Melbourne 1993).
Morris	Edward E. Morris, *A Memoir of George Higinbotham* (London 1895).
N.L.	National Library of Australia, Canberra, A.C.T.
P.R.O.	Public Record Office of Victoria.
Turner	Henry Gyles Turner, *A History of the Colony of Victoria* (London 1904), Vol. II unless otherwise indicated.
V. & P.(L.A.)	*Votes and Proceedings (Legislative Assembly)*, Victoria.
V.H.	*Victorian Hansard* (to 1865).
V.P.D.	*Victorian Parliamentary Debates* (from 1866).

Notes

Chapter 1

1. Paul de Serville, *Pounds and Pedigrees* (Oxford 1991), 2.
2. Higinbotham Papers.
3. *Ibid.* Genealogical Office, Dublin Castle, Ireland, Registered Pedigrees, Vol. 27, 304. The same Thomas, probably in error, is registered as "Higginbotham", Dublin Castle, Wills, New Series, Vol. 13, "H", 230.
4. Morris, 4.
5. Registered Pedigrees, *loc. cit.* n. 3.
6. *The Story of the Bar of Victoria* (Melbourne n.d.), 178.
7. Morris, 5.
8. For example, the *Argus*, 20 April 1895, 4, wrote: "Firmness is the typical quality of the dyke-building Dutchmen, and emotion that of the Celt; and great resolution, coupled with an overpowering rush of emotion were the great characteristics of Mr Higinbotham in public life".
9. Morris, 7. As to Thomas Higinbotham, (1972) 4 *A.D.B.* 397.
10. Darley to Morris, n.d., Morris, 9-10.
11. *The Sydney Quarterly Magazine*, September 1887, 195.
12. *My Reminiscences* (London 1917), 289.
13. *Op. cit.* n. 10.
14. Quoted, Morris, 10.
15. Letter of Henry Brougham, 22 March 1893, quoted *ibid.*, 14.
16. Higinbotham Papers.
17. *My Life in Two Hemispheres* (Vol. II London 1898), 292.
18. Morris, 12.
19. *Op. et loc. cit. n.* 15.
20. *Argus*, 2 January 1893, 5.
21. She was the daughter of Sir John Macartney (first Baronet). She married, in 1826, the Revd Henry Brougham, Rector of Tallow, County Waterford. She was widowed in 1831.
22. *Review of Reviews*, 20 May 1895, 509.
23. Vance Palmer, *National Portraits* (3rd edn Melbourne 1960), 83.
24. Higinbotham to Henry Brougham, jr, 17 July 1892, quoted Morris, 15.
25. *See* Ch. 3, text following n. 3.
26. D.H. Rankin, "George Higinbotham" (1956) 27 *Victorian Historical Magazine*, 41 at 43-44; Morris, 37.
27. Unidentified newspaper cutting, Higinbotham Papers.
28. Professor Stuart Macintyre, *A Colonial Liberalism* (Oxford 1991), 21, gives as a reason the suggested failure of Henry Higinbotham's business in the Irish potato famine of the 1840s. It is not, however, transparently clear why a prosperous merchant with an affluent Dublin clientele would not have had custom and savings enough to weather the storm. Morris, 17, went no further than to remark that, for bright young Dublin men, going to London "was a natural thing to do".
29. (Mary Frances Elizabeth) Lady Stawell, *My Recollections* (London 1911), 215, n. 1. Higinbotham himself recalled, "I had constant and daily opportunities of observing our most distinguished statesmen in the mother country" (1869) VII *V.P.D.* 782.

30. G.D. Burtchaell & T.U. Sadleir, *Alumni Dublinenses* (London 1924), 396, entry "Higginbotham, George", who is listed as a fee-paying student ("pensioner") without reference to his scholarship.
31. Joseph Foster, *Men at the Bar* (London 1885), 218.
32. W.C. Richardson, *A History of the Inns of Court* (Baton Rouge 1975), 323, 326-328.
33. *Op. et loc. cit.* n. 22.
34. *Argus*, 11 March 1854, 4; *Melbourne Morning Herald*, 11 March 1854, 4.
35. *Age*, 29 January 1866, 6.
36. Morris, 34.
37. *Id.*, ix-x.
38. Dow, v; Macintyre, *op. cit.* n. 28, 20-21.
39. Higinbotham Interview (1975).
40. n.d. Higinbotham Papers; *Argus*, 20 April 1895, 4. John Reid in the *Melbourne Herald*, 22 April 1895, 4, was similarly complimentary – "We have nothing but praise for the book".
41. 20 April 1895, 11; copied in the *Leader* (Melbourne), 27 April 1895, 5. Charles Bright, in *Cosmos Magazine*, 31 May 1895, 461, accepted this as "trenchant criticism", but thought it "not merited". The *Tatler* (Melbourne) (Vol. 1, No. 17, 11 December 1897, 7) agreed that the book was "written in the best taste and judgment" while applauding the reduction in its price to three shillings and six pence, thus becoming "available to the most modest means".
42. 4 May 1895, 856. Professor A.C. Castles, *Annotated Bibliography of Printed Materials on Australian Law* (Sydney 1994), 221, described the book as "generally a dull, unimaginative study of one of the most significant figures in law and politics in Australia in the second half of the nineteenth century".

Chapter 2

1. *The New Colony of Victoria* (London 1851), 63.
2. Colin Roderick & Hugh Anderson (eds), Miska Hauser's *Letters From Australia* (Maryborough, Vic. 1988), 50 (Melbourne, 6 July 1855).
3. *Argus*, 11 March 1854, 4.
4. *Readings in Melbourne* (London 1879), 4.
5. Morris, 36; An Old Colonist [*scil.* Edmund Finn], *The "Garryowen" Sketches: Historical, Local and Personal* (Melbourne 1880), 74.
6. *The Golden Age* (Melbourne 1963, reprint 1968), 68, 69; Richard Broome, *The Victorians – Arriving* (Melbourne 1984), 75.
7. *Argus*, 5 April 1854, 5. The chronology is correctly noticed in Turner, Vol. I, 368 – "Mr James Service, whose entry into public life as mayor of Emerald Hill, … obtained the first knowledge of the district he was called upon to administer when canvas gave way to brick, and Mr George Higinbotham was his near neighbour". As to the change of name from Canvas Town to Emerald Hill, Professor Blainey has pointed out that, when in flood, the Yarra converted a small eminence into an island that supported prolific greenery when the waters subsided. It has been suggested (Michael Cannon, *Old Melbourne Town* (Main Ridge 1991), 184-185) that Edmund Finn ("Garryowen") was responsible for the name Emerald Hill.
8. In confirmation of which – Ruth Campbell, *A History of the Melbourne Law School* (Melbourne 1977), 1-2.

9. As with many other entries of the time, Higinbotham's admission was written on the roll in pencil by a clerk. It is the opinion of Mr James M. Butler, Supreme Court Librarian, that the roll was intended later to be signed in ink by those admitted, but the practice was not then enforced. In due course it was – *In re Charles Gavan Duffy* (1881) 7 V.L.R.(L.) 133. Higinbotham's admission date is independently corroborated in *Catalogue of the Library of the Supreme Court of Victoria* (Melbourne 1861), unpaged.

10. *Argus*, 8 May 1854, 5. Two years later, as editor of the *Argus*, Higinbotham condescendingly depicted Pohlman as "a calm, good-natured, conscientious man, a little slow, perhaps, upon any subject in which he is not keenly interested; but withal a very amiable and worthy gentleman", *id.*, 9 August 1856, 4.

11. Higinbotham Papers.

12. *Argus* (editorial), 4 February 1858, 4.

13. *Id.*, 22 December 1910, 7; Morris, 36; Higinbotham Papers.

14. Paul de Serville, *Pounds and Pedigrees* (Melbourne 1991), 32. A contemporary observation is that of Stanley Leighton, who visited Melbourne in 1868, and wrote (Leighton Journal, 5) that Higinbotham "had married a woman beneath him in rank, who was not received in society … He was not to be met with at the [Melbourne] Club nor was he to be seen in general society, *for he declined to go where his wife was not admitted*" (italics added). The italicized words mistake the position. Higinbotham, because of his independent isolation, had no intention of going "into society" – his wife's wishes, or how she might be received by others, were irrelevant issues to him. Similarly the assertion of Professor Morris, 49, that Higinbotham avoided society on the advice of Edward Wilson, proprietor of the *Argus*, is unpersuasive. Higinbotham needed no advice from anyone as to his independent course.

15. (1972) 4 *A.D.B.* 397. For the Brighton residence, *see* Ch. 3, text to n. 1.

16. *Age*, 20 April 1895, 11.

17. Stuart Macintyre, *A Colonial Liberalism* (Oxford 1991), 23.

18. Morris, 25; and *note* Macintyre, *op. cit.* n. 17, 24.

19. Quoted, Morris, 56, from an incorrectly identified source.

20. Dean, 76.

21. *Australasian*, 14 January 1893, 87; *Register* (Adelaide), 2 January 1893, 6. That view must, however, be regarded with caution for reasons advanced in the next chapter – *see* Ch. 3, text following n. 14.

22. Unidentified press cutting, Higinbotham Papers.

23. *Register* (Adelaide), 2 January 1893, 6.

24. *Argus*, 15 November 1856, 5.

25. *Id.*, 18 November 1856, 5.

26. *Ibid.*

27. *Victoria Law Times* (reprint pages), 409 at 410.

28. *Id.*, 21 at 22.

29. *Id.*, 116 at 118.

30. *Id.*, at 122.

31. All extant reports are imperfect in material respects, even in some instances as to the representation of the parties. The proceedings were reported as *Staughton* v. *Tulloh* in the *Argus*, 9 September 1856, 5, and in the *Herald*, 9 September 1856, 6. The longest, but also an unsatisfactory, report is in *Victoria Law Times* (reprint page), 281.

32. *Victoria Law Times*, at 164.
33. *Id.*, at 281, 282.
34. *Id.*, at 465-466.
35. *Id.*, at 90.
36. Generally, (1976) 6 *A.D.B.* 412.
37. *Fifty Years in the Making of Australian History* (London 1892), 93. William Westgarth, *Personal Recollections of Melbourne & Victoria* (Melbourne 1888), 101, considered that the stature of the *Argus* was enhanced when Wilson "retired in favour of more temperate editorship".
38. James Smith, quoted Morris, 50.
39. *Review of Reviews* (Australasian edn), 20 May 1895, 509. *Melbourne Punch*, 13 July 1865, 17, sarcastically recalled that "Mr HIGINBOTHAM'S articles became immediately known by their raciness of humour and luxuriant variety of anecdotic illustration. And yet, with all his many excellent qualifications as a journalist, he failed utterly in provoking an action at law against the paper, and thus enabling his proprietors to vindicate at magnificent cost the right of an editor to say anything he thought proper".
40. *Op. et loc. cit.* n. 38.
41. Charles Bright, "George Higinbotham", *Cosmos Magazine*, 31 May 1895, 461 at 463; Smith, *op. cit.* n. 38, 49.
42. *Review of Reviews*, cited n. 39, 510.
43. Smith (*op. et loc. cit.* n. 38), who claimed that Higinbotham addressed "an ideal public" giving it credit for "an amount of intellectual capacity, a moral elevation of purpose, a purity of motive, and a nobility of patriotism, which it certainly did not possess".
44. (London 1858), 83. As to Puseley – John Alexander Ferguson, *Bibliography of Australia* (Vol. VI Canberra 1977), 1134-1135.
45. (1969) 3 *A.D.B.* 56.
46. (1972) 4 *A.D.B.* 287.
47. William Astley Papers, Dixson Library of the State Library of New South Wales (MS Q513), "A Forgotten Democrat", 30 January 1893, 169.
48. *The Rush to be Rich* (Melbourne 1974 edn), 32.
49. Respectively, *Argus*, 6 September 1856, 4; 21 November 1856, 4; 5 November 1856, 4.
50. *Op. et loc. cit.* n. 39.
51. 6 September 1856, 4.
52. 21 October 1856, 4.
53. 22 October 1856, 4.
54. 23 October 1856, 4.
55. 13 November 1856, 4.
56. 14 November 1856, 4.
57. 1 and 15 December 1856, 4.
58. Denison to Henry Labouchere (private), 12 June 1856, in Sir William Denison, *Varieties of Vice-Regal Life* (Vol. I London 1870), 351.
59. *Argus*, 5 November 1856, 4; *cf id.*, 4 October 1856, 4.
60. 5 November 1856, 4.
61. 2 September 1856, 4.
62. 20 August 1856, 4.
63. 13 August 1856, 4.
64. *Op. cit.* n. 17, 25; but contrast "Public Opinion in Victoria", *Argus*, 4 September 1856, 4.

65. 12 November 1856, 4.
66. 22, 27 November 1856, 4.
67. 25 November 1856, 4. The practice of wearing top hats in the chamber endured well into the 19th century – Serle, *op. cit.* n. 48, illustration facing p. 37.
68. 24 January 1857, 4.
69. 9 March 1857, 4.
70. *Ibid.*
71. (1969) 3 *A.D.B.* 380. Higinbotham, however, thought well enough of Chapman's abilities as to retain him as an editorial contributor to the *Argus*.
72. *Argus*, 10 March 1857, 4.
73. *Ibid.*
74. 26 March 1857, 4.
75. (1966) 1 *A.D.B.* at 484.
76. *Argus*, 22 June 1858, 4.
77. 23 June 1858, 4.
78. 24 June 1858, 4.
79. 14 April 1859, 4.
80. Wilson to Parkes, 4 July 1856, Parkes Correspondence, Vol. 60 (M.L. A930), 728 at 729.
81. *Argus*, 29 December 1856, 4.
82. *Id.*, 5.
83. 31 December 1856, 4.
84. 14 May 1857, 5 (italics added).
85. *Argus*, 22 May 1857, 5.
86. 18 May 1857, 5.
87. Turner, 78, thought Higinbotham's responses to have lacked "convincing logic", a conclusion not supported by a well considered reading of the exchanges.
88. *Argus*, 6 April 1858, 4.
89. 7 April 1858, 4.
90. 8 April 1858, 5.
91. 8 April 1858, 4, 5.
92. 12 April 1858, Parkes Correspondence, *op. cit.* n. 80, 754 at 756.
93. *Op. cit.* n. 39, 510.
94. Vance Palmer, *National Portraits* (3rd edn Melbourne 1960), 84.
95. Higinbotham to James Smith, 19 July 1859, Smith Papers (M.L. MSS 212/1), 83 at 84, 85.

Chapter 3

1. From a description in the *Australasian*, 5 February 1876, 184.
2. 24 February 1882, 3.
3. Weston Bate, *A History of Brighton* (2nd edn Melbourne 1983), 348.
4. Higinbotham Interview (1975). A quite different perspective is given in Stuart Macintyre, *A Colonial Liberalism* (Oxford 1991), 24.
5. *Australasian*, 3 January 1874, 20.
6. Sands and Kenny, *Melbourne Directory* (1858), 89, and for several succeeding years. Higinbotham's was said to be "an attic apartment", *Melbourne Punch*, 13 July 1865, 17
7. William Kelly, *Life in Victoria* (Vol. I London 1859), 93.

8. F. Maxwell Bradshaw, "The Homes of the Bar", in Dean, 296 at 297.

9. *Ibid*. Sands and McDougall, *Melbourne Directory* (1866), 307. By contrast, Sir James Martin, in New South Wales at a similar period, continued to accept private practice when in office as Premier and Attorney-General – J.M. Bennett, *Lives of the Australian Chief Justices – Sir James Martin* (Sydney 2005), Ch. 10.

10. Theodore Fink Papers, Melbourne University Archives, Box 7, file 1, item 2, "Law Notes for Memoirs" (97/127), unpaged.

11. *Argus*, 5 January 1893, 6.

12. *Law in Victoria* (Melbourne 1859), 6-9, 11, 12. A colourful description of Parsons is in the *Australian Jurist*, 6 June 1870, iii.

13. *Op. cit*. n. 10.

14. *Ibid*.

15. For example, the *South Australian Register* (Adelaide), 2 January 1893, 6, wrote in this context, "As a lawyer [Higinbotham] was not only a powerful but a closely argumentative speaker, and yet copious in felicitous illustration. He always mastered his brief before he spoke upon it, possessed his mind of the first principles of his case, and never relapsed his grip of them ... He did not adopt the worldly-wise maxim of Serjeant Ballantyne, that it was the duty of a lawyer to see that his side won, except with this reservation – that it was the first duty of an advocate to be certain that he was pleading for the right as well as for his client".

16. *Australian Jurist*, 6 June 1870, iii.

17. 1 W. & W. (L.), 302.

18. (1862) 1 W. & W. (I.E. & M.), 57.

19. *See* generally, Dean, 249-253. It was an open secret that Mrs Molesworth had committed adultery with R.D. Ireland of the Bar.

20. *Op. cit*. n. 18, at 61.

21. There was some evidence that he might, as in his persistent and hostile questioning of Higinbotham in *Levi* v. *Learmonth* (1862) 1 W. & W. (L.), 283 at 286-287.

22. Dean, 253; *Age*, 14 December 1864, 5.

23. (1863) 2 W. & W. (L.), 104.

24. P.A. Jacobs, *Famous Australian Trials* (2nd edn Melbourne 1943), 127, confirmed that Higinbotham's fees were "absurdly modest", to the chagrin, no doubt, of his clerk who took a proportion of the fee charged. As Attorney-General, he was said to allow defence counsel five pounds, not five guineas, leaving such counsel to pay their clerks personally, *Melbourne Punch*, 21 July 1864, 31.

25. *Op. cit*. n. 10.

26. Leighton Journal, 4.

27. *See* Ch. 10, text following n. 20. Higinbotham was not alone in this. T.H. Fellows was said to have handed out money every day to poor people waiting outside his chambers, and no doubt others followed these examples, J.L. Forde, *The Story of the Bar of Victoria* (Melbourne n.d.), 158-159.

28. 7 January 1893, 22.

29. Report of Bar Meeting of 1 September 1864, Higinbotham Papers.

30. *Ibid*.

31. *R*. v. *Supple* (1870) 1 V.R. (L.), 151.

32. At 152, 153.

33. (1976) 6 *A.D.B.* 221.
34. For example, Alfred Deakin (ed. Herbert Brookes), *The Federal Story* (Melbourne 1944), 36; (1976) 6 *A.D.B.* 445 describing Henry John Wrixon as "a disciple of George Higinbotham"; Nettie Palmer, *Henry Bournes Higgins* (London 1931), 75; Walter Murdoch, *Alfred Deakin: A Sketch* (London 1923), 58.
35. Deakin, *ibid.*, 36-37.
36. *Democracy in Australia* (Melbourne 1868), 3-4.
37. (1988) 11 *A.D.B.* 595 at 596. As to Shiels' Divorce Bill, *note* Higinbotham to Shiels, 16 December 1889, William Shiels Papers, La Trobe Library, Melbourne, MS 8730, Box 945/26.
38. Palmer, *op. et loc. cit.* n. 34.
39. Geoffrey Bolton, *Edmund Barton* (St Leonards 2000), 140; Eddy Neumann, *The High Court of Australia* (2nd edn Sydney 1973), 56; Deakin (ed. Brookes), *op. cit.* n. 34, 68, 88.
40. (1981) 8 *A.D.B.* at 249.
41. Deakin, *op. cit.* n. 34, 7-8.
42. *Id.*, at 36.
43. *Argus*, 15 August 1856, 5; (1972) 4 *A.D.B.* at 161.
44. *Argus*, 16 August 1856, 4.
45. *Id.*, 27 August 1856, 4.
46. A. Patchett Martin, *Australia and the Empire* (Edinburgh 1889), 89.
47. *Argus*, 13 May 1861, 5.
48. *Ibid.*, 4. W. A. Brodribb (who took the seat in 1861) had been urged to stand, but declined because he thought Higinbotham's opinions "so nearly in accordance with his own", *Examiner* (Melbourne), 18 May 1861, 1; to similar effect, *Argus*, 14 May 1861, 5.
49. 5 August 1861, 4.
50. *Examiner* (Melbourne), 3 August 1861, 5.
51. Dow, 4; *Illustrated Australian News* (Melbourne), 1 February 1893, 10; *Melbourne Punch*, 13 July 1865, 17, described him as "being supplied by the Government with an uniform of grey serge and a suitable firearm; Bate, *op. cit* n. 3, 279.
52. "Brighton Free Library – The Late Chief Justice" and "The Founders of the Free Brighton Library – September 1894", unidentified press cuttings, Higinbotham Papers.
53. *Argus*, 8 April 1862, 5.
54. *Ibid.*
55. (1862) VII *V.H.* 942.
56. "Timotheus", *Australasian*, 14 January 1893, 87.
57. (1862) VII *V.H.*, 217.
58. *Ibid.*
59. (1863) IX *V.H.* 588.
60. At 591-592.
61. (1861) VII *V.H.* 1006.
62. At 1009.
63. *Ibid.*
64. (1863) IX *V.H.* 850.
65. At 851.
66. At 853-854.
67. (1861) VII *V.H.* 1146, 1147, 1148.
68. (1863) IX *V.H.* 537, 538. *Note* also his views at Ch. 2, text following n. 82.

69. *See* further, Geoffrey Serle, *The Golden Age* (Melbourne 1968), 304; McCaughey, 78.
70. (1861) VII *V.H.* 1281
71. *Id.*, at 1183, 1184; and *note* Higinbotham's relevant observations in debate on the Appropriation Bill, *id.*, at 1280-1281.
72. (1863) IX *V.H.*, 356.
73. *See* further Ch. 10.
74. (1862) IX *V.H.* 64.
75. *Id.*, 8
76. *Id.*, 9.
77. *Id.*, 66.
78. *Age*, 24 October 1864, 5.
79. (1863) IX *V.H.* 328.
80. *Id.*, 584, 585.
81. *Id.*, 896.
82. (1862) IX *V.H.* 105.
83. (1862) VIII *V.H.* 1027.
84. (1862) IX *V.H.* 56, 188.
85. *Id.*, 189.
86. *Id.*, 228-229, 281.
87. *Id.*, 291.
88. *Id.*, 380.

Chapter 4

1. 29 June 1868 (1868) VI *V.P.D.* 464.
2. (Mary Frances Elizabeth) Lady Stawell, *My Recollections* (London 1911), 215 (note).
3. *Life's Panorama* (Melbourne 1930), 267.
4. Turner, 137.
5. Some examples are at (1864) X *V.H.* 208, 401; (1864) XI *V.H.* 22; (1865) XI *V.H.* 424-425; (1866) II *V.P.D.* 157, 322, 417; (1868) VI *V.P.D.* 405.
6. (1865) XI *V.H.* 416.
7. *Id.*, 1075.
8. (1866) II *V.P.D.* 108.
9. *Id.*, 123.
10. *Id.*, 131.
11. *Id.*, 75. Progress was lamentably slow – Supreme Court Library Committee, *The Supreme Court of Victoria* (Melbourne 1969), 8. The Exhibition Building "at the west end of the town" was a precursor to the grander Exhibition Building that still stands in Carlton Gardens.
12. (1865) XI *V.H.* 345, 860.
13. *Id.*, 237, 635; (1864) X *V.H.* 424.
14. (1866) II *V.P.D.* 512, 518.
15. The episode is considered at greater length in J. M. Bennett, *Lives of the Australian Chief Justices – Sir William Stawell* (Sydney 2004), 101-108.
16. 14 December 1864, 5.
17. Higinbotham to the Governor, 16 April 1864 and minute of February 1864, (1864) 3 *V. & P. (L.A.)* (paper C2), 32, 36-37. In Parliament ((1865) XI *V.H.* 779) Higinbotham offered an ungracious retraction as to "officers in his Department" – "He regretted it, not because he did not believe it to be a strictly accurate expression, and one easily to be

defended as appropriate, but because he believed the use of it had tended to strengthen the impression or prejudice that there was some covert design on the part of the Executive … to interfere with the independence of the judges".

18. *V. & P., ibid.*, 42-43.
19. (1865) XI *V.H.* 534.
20. At 540.
21. Quoted, *Urquhart* v. *Wilson* (1865) 2 W.W. & a'B. (L.) 28 at 29. On 9 August 1864, 4-5, the *Argus* had already criticized Higinbotham's handling of the matter, declaring, quite properly, "the Attorney-General is not … a judicial tribunal, nor is his office a court of appeal from the justices".
22. *The Urquhart Scab Case*, pamphlet (Melbourne 1865): the proceedings at (1865) 2 W.W. & a'B. (L.) 28 were a virtual appeal to the Full Court that did not succeed.
23. Quoted (1865) XI *V.H.* at 537, 534 respectively.
24. *Id.*, 534.
25. *Id.*, 537-538.
26. *Id.*, 538. For another instance of his setting himself in opposition to the judges – Ch. 11, text following n. 72.
27. *Argus*, 24 March 1865, 4.
28. *Id.*, 25 March 1865, 4-5.
29. *The Story of the Bar of Victoria* (Melbourne n.d.), 180. The proposition seems out of character with Higinbotham's stubbornness. Perhaps Forde's recollection was of the obscure events mentioned by Morris, vi – "On one occasion when a difficulty had arisen with the Maoris, at my suggestion he was invited by the Government to come to New Zealand to act as arbitrator, and at great inconvenience to himself he had agreed to come. Political changes unfortunately put an end to the proposal".
30. (1863) IX *V.H.* 1054, 1080.
31. (1866) II *V.P.D.* 537.
32. *Ibid.*
33. For example, (1865) XI *V.H.* 480; (1866) II *V.P.D.* 446-447.
34. (1866) I *V.P.D.* 112.
35. *See* generally, Bennett, *op. cit.* n. 15, 112-116.
36. (1866) I *V.P.D.* 284.
37. As to which the government was demonstrably duplicitous, *id.*, 298-301.
38. *Id.*, 286
39. *Id.*, 349, 350.
40. *Id.*, 363.
41. *Ibid.*
42. *Id.*, 351.
43. (1866) II *V.P.D.* 385
44. *Id.*, at 414, 415, 416-417.
45. *History of Australia* (Vol. III London 1883), 332.
46. (1866) I *V.P.D.* 349.
47. Member for East Melbourne.
48. (1866) I *V.P.D.* 298, 299.
49. *Id.*, 301.
50. *Ibid.*
51. *See* generally, Cyril Pearl, *Rebel Down Under* (Melbourne 1970); Morris, Ch. X; Sir Ninian Stephen, "George Higinbotham", Daniel Mannix

Memorial Lecture, University of Melbourne, 13 September 1983, N.L. MS7738, 21-23; Stuart Macintyre, *A Colonial Liberalism* (Oxford 1991), 49; Charles Parkinson, "George Higinbotham and Responsible Government in Victoria" (2001) 25 *Melbourne University Law Review*, 207-208.

52. 27 January 1865, C.O. 309/71, f. 244 at f. 244a.
53. *Ibid.*
54. 30 January 1865, *id.*, at f. 273.
55. 15 February 1865, *id.*, f. 253 at f. 253a.
56. *Ibid.*
57. 16 February 1865, *ibid.* Higinbotham had also given a long opinion on 14 February (after the vessel's departure), *id.*, at f. 345, that the commander of the *Shenandoah* could not resist the execution on board ship of a warrant pursuant to the *Foreign Enlistment Act.*
58. Bailey, 409.
59. Payable in gold within 12 months.
60. (1873) XVI *V.P.D.* 236-237.
61. *Op. et loc. cit.* n. 58.
62. McCaughey, 107.
63. Cardwell's assurance, 26 April 1865, C.O. 411/8 p. 312 at 313, that Darling had "acted with propriety and discretion", was decidedly premature.
64. George H.F. Webb, *New Constitution Bill* (Melbourne 1854), 70-71.
65. Often precariously, given the frequent tendering of his Ministry's resignation. As to Higinbotham's part, Dow, 23, 24.
66. *Op. cit. n.* 45, 296.
67. Rusden gave the title "Higinbotha-mania – pseudo liberals etc." to a volume of press cuttings that included material on Higinbotham – Rusden Papers, Vol. 14, item XI, Leeper Library, Trinity College, University of Melbourne.
68. (1863) IX *V.H.* 1038.
69. *Id.*, 1039.
70. *Id.*, 1243, 1269.
71. (1863) IX *V.H.* 1116.
72. *Id.*, 1133, 1209-1211, respectively.
73. Turner, 113.
74. (1864) X *V.H.* 107.
75. *Id.*, 110.
76. *Id.*, 336.
77. *Age*, 24 October 1864, 5; *Argus*, 24 October 1864, 5; *Australasian*, 29 October 1864, 7.
78. *Ibid.*
79. *Age*, 24 October 1864, 6.
80. *Ibid.*
81. *Ibid.*: "wealthy lower orders" was there rendered "wealthy lower order".
82. 24 October 1864, 4.
83. *Ibid.*; and *Australasian*, 29 October 1864, 3.

Chapter 5

1. (1864) XI *V.H.* 74; and *note* (1866) II *V.P.D.* 11.
2. G.W. Rusden, *History of Australia* (Vol. III London 1883), 298.

3. (1864) XI *V.H.* 72.
4. *Id.*, 162.
5. Turner, 119.
6. (1865) XI *V.H.* 237.
7. Turner, *op. cit.* n. 5, 121, observed, "however unpalatable the adoption of such views [on Protection] may have been at the outset to the Attorney-General, when they had once involved him in the dispute with the Council, every consideration gave way before the one dominant desire for victory": and *note* (1862) IX *V.H.* 72; (1865) XI *V.H.* 273, 274.
8. Governor Darling (to Cardwell, 21 November 1864, 25 I.U.P. 39) conceded that "the popular opinion has been decidedly in favour of those views".
9. Turner, 114-115; Stuart Macintyre, *A Colonial Liberalism* (Oxford 1991), 42.
10. 25 I.U.P. 45; for a criticism, Turner, 122.
11. To Cardwell, 25 August 1865 (25 I.U.P. 42 at 43).
12. Rusden, *op. cit.* n. 2, 299.
13. That interpretation was robustly criticized by Higinbotham, (1865) XI *V.H.*1187-1193, substantially because "the absence of any rule expressly forbidding a particular course furnished no argument at all against it". His reference to 17th century English precedents received "ironical cheers" from the Opposition (at 1188).
14. *Id.*, 1193.
15. *Id.*, 472.
16. Higinbotham later remarked ((1866) I *V.P.D.* 202) that "It had been admitted by the ablest authorities that this was no tack".
17. 25 I.U.P. 45.
18. To Cardwell, 25 August 1865, 25 I.U.P. 42 at 43.
19. 25 I.U.P. 41 at 42. There had been successful conferences between the Houses over the Land Act Amendment Bill and a current Water Works Bill. Higinbotham blamed the difficulties on party politics – "This House was for the most part torn by faction. It was seldom they agreed for any length of time on a consistent course of policy on any question, and when they did happen to agree, they were met by the representatives of the people in another place" (1865) XI *V.H.* 779.
20. *Op. cit.* n. 2, 207.
21. The Council specifically indicated that it would not so resist. Rusden, *id.*, 309; Darling to Cardwell, 20 October 1865, 25 I.U.P. 71 at 72 (para. 9).
22. Darling to Cardwell, *ibid.*, at 77 (para. 59).
23. A summary is in Darling to Cardwell, 18 September 1865, 25 I.U.P. 48 (and *note*, 78-79); Dorothy P. Clarke, "The Colonial Office and the Constitutional Crisis in Victoria, 1865-68" (1952) 5 *Historical Studies*, 160.
24. Darling to Cardwell, 22 September 1865, 25 I.U.P. 62.
25. *Ibid.*
26. Legislative Council petition to the Queen, *id.*, 78 at 80, paras 17-21; Turner, 126; Charles Parkinson, "George Higinbotham and Responsible Government in Colonial Victoria" (2001) 25 *Melbourne University Law Review*, 181 at 201.
27. Undated, *P.S.* to Darling to Cardwell, 22 September 1865, 25 I.U.P. 62 at 66. Sir Arthur Dean (Dean, 51) thought it "astonishing that Higin-

botham can have accepted this plan". For a vigorous condemnation of Higinbotham's course, claiming that he had become "somewhat of a cats-paw", *note* an article attributed to Archibald Michie, *Melbourne Punch*, 28 September 1865, 105.

28. A much longer joint opinion, by Higinbotham and Michie, was given on 22 September 1865 (25 I.U.P. 82 at 83). It suggested that "a thousand accidents may prevent the passing of an Appropriation Act. Wherefore, the expenses of preserving the State by the functions of Government seem to be at the disposal of the Government for the time being, subject to being reviewed and audited".

29. 25 I.U.P. 78 at 81.

30. *Id.*, at 80. The Secretary of State agreed, writing to Darling (26 January 1866, C.O. 309/74, f. 404) that the Queen had received the Council's petition "very graciously", had been advised "that the proceedings which gave rise to it were contrary to Law, and had given instructions intended to prevent their recurrence". Under-Secretary Rogers thought that Darling ought to "have said plainly" that he would refuse to adopt the contrivance of obtaining bank advances "which, though it appeared to him questionable, was alleged to be legal by the lawyer [Higinbotham] whose advice he was bound to receive & *prima facie* to defer [to] in such matter" (minute at C.O. 309/74, f. 385a).

31. Darling to Cardwell, 20 October 1865, 25 I.U.P. 71.

32. *Id.*, at 72-73.

33. *Id.*, at 73 (para. 17).

34. *Id.*, at 75 (para. 41).

35. *Id.*, at 76 (para. 44).

36. Darling to Cardwell, 24 November 1865, 25 I.U.P. 103 at 104; and 25 November 1865, *id.*, 106.

37. *Id.*, 112, 113.

38. Cardwell to Darling, 27 November 1865, 25 I.U.P. 139 at 141.

39. Cardwell to Darling, 26 January 1866, *id.*, 142; draft at C.O. 309/74, f. 387.

40. They may be identified collectively as *Stevenson* v. *The Queen* (1865) 2 W.W. & a'B. (L.) 143.

41. At 159.

42. *Op. et loc. cit.* n. 29.

43. Opinion of "October 1865", 25 I.U.P. 85-86.

44. Minute at C.O. 309/77, f. 49 at f. 52.

45. Minute at C.O. 309/74, f. 386. Nor was the conclusion in Dean, 53, that Higinbotham had "openly flouted the Supreme Court" strictly true. Higinbotham did not condescend to notice similar criticism in his own day beyond insisting that those who made it did not "entertain a scintilla of belief in their own minds of its truth" – *Argus*, 29 January 1866, 6.

46. An extravagant assertion quoted by Rusden, *op. cit.* n. 2, 344.

47. *Stevenson* v. *The Queen [No. 2]* (1865) 2 W.W. & a'B. (L.) 176 at 178.

48. *Age*, 29 January 1866, 6.

49. He deluded himself in suggesting that "my constituents were comparatively indifferent to the merits or the demerits of the Tariff", (1866) I *V.P.D.* 107.

50. Darling to Cardwell, 24 March 1866, 25 I.U.P. 206. Turner, 130, described Higinbotham's preamble as "aggressive".

51. (1866) I *V.P.D.* 109; *note* also, 203-204.
52. *Id.*, 112.
53. *Id.*, 112-113.
54. *Id.*, 107.
55. Darling to Fellows, 26 March 1866; Darling to McCulloch (undated), 25 I.U.P. 234-235.
56. Minute (undated), *id.*, 235, 239.
57. Responding to criticism of this, Higinbotham asserted that, in so acting on advice, the Governor "merely discharges a duty for which he is not personally responsible, and in respect of which, therefore, his conduct should not be called in question", (1866) II *V.P.D.* 8.
58. The present assessment subscribes to the view of Professor F.K. Crowley ((1972) 4 *A.D.B.* at 21) that "Darling had been a failure. He had been neither prudent nor cautious and had allowed his partisan sympathy to undermine the functioning of the parliament and the rule of law. He had become a mouthpiece of McCulloch and his ministers, especially of the Attorney-General, George Higinbotham". According-ly, the present assessment does not share the opinion expressed in McCaughey (at 124) that Crowley's judgement "may be too harsh". Turner, 112, wrote that Darling had been "as wax in the hands of such dominant men as James McCulloch and George Higinbotham, and they became the virtual rulers of the colony". The anonymous author of "Democratic Government in Victoria" in the *Westminster Review (New Series)*, No. LXVI, April 1868, 480 at 520, described the Governor as "a mere puppet in the hands of his Ministers".
59. "Address from Persons who have been Members of the Executive Council", 25 I.U.P. 124. Higinbotham was incensed by their action – "How are we to explain … that twenty-two gentlemen occupying the highest position in this country … can be found so far forgetful of their duties to responsible government here as to seek to create an appellate jurisdiction in the mother country", (1866) II *V.P.D.* 240.
60. Darling to Cardwell, 23 December 1865, 25 I.U.P. 115 at 123.
61. Cardwell to Darling, 26 February 1866, *id.*, 146 at 147, 148.
62. Darling to Cardwell, 18 April 1866, *id.*, 240 at 242.
63. Morris, 110; Dow, 34 n. 39, 35.
64. More will be said about such portrayals in the final chapter.
65. McCaughey, 115; *cf* Clarke, *op. cit.* n. 23, 164; Rusden, *op. cit.* n. 2, 399, characterized Darling as "infested with the obstinacy of his advisers".
66. (1866) II *V.P.D.* 235.
67. (1866) I *V.P.D.* 111.
68. (1866) II *V.P.D.* 236.
69. 23 May 1866, quoted in *Australasian*, 26 May 1866, 237.
70. The petition and the petitioners were energetically attacked by Rusden, *op. cit.* n. 2, 341.
71. The correspondence is at 25 I.U.P. 383-418.
72. Rogers to Darling, 11 December 1866, *id.*, 391.
73. Adderley to Darling, 31 January 1867, *id.*, 409.
74. *See* McCaughey, 126-139.
75. *See* further, Clarke, *op. cit.* n. 23, 166.
76. Minute of 17 July 1867, 25 I.U.P. 537; response of Darling, 18 July 1867, *ibid.*; confidential despatch of Darling, 26 July 1867, quoted McCaughey, 130.

77. (1867) IV *V.P.D.* 1676. Ireland protested: Higinbotham lost his temper, and continued – "The constitutional party was the most pretentious party which ever existed in this country. It included, according to its own account, all the self-styled respectability, the wealth, and the intelligence of the country. Wealth it certainly had, and it grossly abused that wealth; respectability – why its respectability was the mere unfounded insolent pretence of a class; intelligence – well, sir, its intelligence I suppose, is fitly represented by honorable members I see opposite". B.C. Aspinall (at 1677) rejoined, in amazement, at Higinbotham's adopting "a tone with reference to the morality of his own colleagues and supporters, and the entire House, which assumes that there is not a human being here, or anywhere else, who has the slightest claim to the moral altitude which he appears to have reached".
78. Rusden, *op. cit.* n. 2, 352.
79. Opinion of 21 August 1867, 25 I.U.P. 540. Higinbotham hedged this, to protect his own position, by instructing the Crown Solicitor not to permit judgement to be signed against the government, unless for payment of public service salaries, without specific approval of the Crown Law Officers – memorandum of 11 November 1867, *id.*, 574.
80. Minute of McCulloch, 22 August 1867, *id.*, 541 at 542.
81. Memorandum, 23 August 1867, *id.*, 544.
82. Response of Fellows, 24 August 1867, *ibid.*
83. Darling to Buckingham, 27 September 1867, *id.*, 558 at 559. London's *Standard*, 16 October 1867 (republished in the *Argus*, 19 December 1867, 7), was outraged by the Assembly's behaviour, and wrote, "They would have crammed the grant to Lady Darling down the throats of the Council, just as they sought to cram the tariff – the original cause of all the trouble. They have deliberately made their policy as offensive as possible to the Upper House, as it would seem almost with a foregone determination and hope that there should be another crisis … In a speech boiling over with anger and malice, which deserves to be studied as a sample of the temper of the Victorian democracy, Mr Higinbotham, the Attorney-General, without any provocation whatever from the other side, declared that the Government had purposely made their measure as disagreeable as possible to the Legislative Council".
84. Buckingham to Darling, 1 January 1868, *id.*, 583. For years Higinbotham persisted in portraying this despatch as "an act of violent and illegal affront", *Australasian,* 11 March 1871, 308. Rusden, *op. cit.*, n. 2, 364, reduced Higinbotham's position to this – "Till the crack of doom the House should not give way. Sufferings of others in the community were but dust in the balance compared with the importance of securing the absolute supremacy of the Assembly". He also pointed out that, at this point, what he had earlier (at 336) described as Higinbotham's "knotty consistency" was beginning to desert him.
85. Buckingham to Manners-Sutton, 1 February 1868, *id.*, 584 at 585.
86. Manners-Sutton to Buckingham, 3 March 1868, *id.*, 597. The *Argus*, 31 December 1867, 4, declared of Manners-Sutton that "in dissolving the Lower House without even attempting to bring the country's affairs within the scope of the law, he is sacrificing himself on the altar of Mr HIGINBOTHAM'S infallibility and Mr McCULLOCH'S obstinacy".

87. *The Crisis in Victorian Politics, 1879-1881* (ed. J. A. La Nauze and R. M. Crawford, Melbourne 1957), 22.
88. Turner, 144.
89. Dean, 310.
90. (1867) 4 W.W. & a'B. (L.) 285; *Argus*, 25 December 1867, 4.
91. *Argus*, 7 December 1867, 6. The *Age*, 9 December 1867, 4, responded that the course of the solicitors "in offering a brief to the Attorney-General was either a very silly or a very improper one, for it was virtually asking him to come into court to have his conduct called in question, without affording him the position of a party in the case – to resign himself, in short, into the hands of his enemies"; and it published acidic editorials on the subject (26 and 27 December 1867, 4).
92. 4 W.W. & a'B. (L.) at 308.
93. *Ibid.*
94. *Id.*, at 310, 313.
95. At 321. The *Age Supplement*, 27 December 1867, 1, thought it "charitable" to suppose that "the Chief Justice is in his dotage". The *Argus Supplement*, 27 December 1867, 1, retorted that "Without supplies the Government cannot be carried on, and it is improbable that the genius of the Attorney-General will find any other gate of illegality to open for the escape of his party"; and *see Argus*, 5 December 1867, 4.
96. (1868) VI *V.P.D.* 410.
97. Buckingham to Manners-Sutton, 1 February 1868, 25 I.U.P. 584.
98. Manners-Sutton to Buckingham, 28 March 1868, *id.*, 601; minute of 10 March 1868, *id.*, 602 at 603.
99. (1873) XVII *V.P.D.* 1442; for a commentary, Rusden, *op. cit.* n. 2, 364, and Clarke, *op. cit.* n. 23, 168.
100. Described as a "stop-gap ministry from conservatives in both Houses" (1976) 6 *A.D.B.* 133.
101. The details appear in 25 I.U.P. 606-609.
102. (1868) VI *V.P.D.* 71-72, 73.
103. *Id.*, at 72.
104. *Id.*, 466-467.
105. *Id.*, 77.
106. J. M. Bennett, *Lives of the Australian Chief Justices – Sir William Stawell* (Sydney 2004), 121-125.
107. For example, (1863) IX *V.H.* 1058.
108. *In re Glass* (1869) 6 W.W. & a'B. (L.) 45 at 57-58.
109. (1869) VII *V.P.D.* 781.
110. At 780. For a contrary view, *Ballarat Star*, 4 May 1869, 2.
111. VII *V.P.D.* at 781, 782. Opinions have varied over the years whether courts should construe legislation with or without the aid of its history. Higinbotham was committed to treating such history as essential to statutory interpretation – *see* also Ch. 7 text to and following n. 63, and Ch. 9 text following n. 15.
112. Higinbotham remembered, on first arriving in Melbourne, perceiving Stawell to be "fitted to be the peer of the best English statesmen", a man who "when the very foundations of society were in the course of formation, himself undertook, almost single-handed, the work of laying them – who, surrounded by dwarfs, as he was, bore almost solely upon his own shoulders the whole burthen of administration and legislation" (VII *V.P.D.* 782).

113. *Ibid.* The phrase was long remembered. Of Higinbotham's elevation to the judicial Bench, Frank Gavan Duffy's poem "A Dream of Fair Judges" rejoined, "Alas, what is the end of hopes and fears – Splendid obscurity!" (quoted Dean, 310).

114. VII *V.P.D.* 786. He did not think it would be "a shocking thing" if there were a collision between the Assembly and the court, because only the Assembly could win – "the House may call forth all the police force in the colony, if it pleases to support its own orders, and to retain in custody its own prisoners" (*ibid.*). The remark was much misunderstood by the public, a common misconception being that Higinbotham "grandly proposed that the Executive should order the police to take the judges into custody and thereby assert the authority of their House" – Leighton Journal, 107.

115. 29 April 1869, 4. For excerpts from other prints – *Herald* (Melbourne), 30 April 1869, 2.

116. Margaret Kiddle, *Men of Yesterday* (Melbourne 1967 edn), 259.

117. (1871) 2 A.J.R. 41 (at 59, reprint page).

118. (1869) VIII *V.P.D.* 985-986.

119. 27 August 1870, 276.

120. *Australasian*, 5 March 1871, 304.

121. *Id.*, 11 March 1871, 308. He continued "desponding" and was convinced, by 1875, that the "liberal party" had "no existence at the present moment in Victoria" or, if it did, it was "without union and without settled object", *Age*, 5 November 1875, 2, and *id.*, 10 November 1875, 2.

122. He had meanwhile suffered from a very adverse press. For example, *Melbourne Punch*, 12 May 1870, 151, published a doggerel piece "A Congratulatory Effusion" on his being out of power, and irreverently reviewed his parliamentary career:

> But very soon he showed his hand,
>   Though we saw his "game" too late;
> And all were made to understand
>   A "dead-lock" in the State.
>
> Nor yet content, with every scheme
>   He has himself allied
> To gratify his self-esteem
>   And puff his boundless pride.
>
> From "woman's rights" to insurrection
>   Upholding each in turn
> (To gratify his self-affection,
>   What *would* he *not* have done?).

123. *Australasian*, 25 March 1871, 368.

124. (1873) XVII *V.P.D.* 1271. The *Age*, 16 May 1873, 2, retorted that "An interesting volume might be written on the eccentricities of statesmen. If justice were done to him, Mr HIGINBOTHAM would have a long chapter to himself".

125. *See* generally, Bennett, *op. cit.* n. 106, 168-171.

126. Quoted, *ibid.*, at 169.

127. Turner, 185.

128. Quoted, *Argus*, 2 January 1893, 6. For a thoughtful commentary on Higinbotham's position, *Sydney Morning Herald*, 9 February 1876, 6.

129. *Australasian Supplement*, 5 February 1876, 1; he nevertheless reiterated his aversion to party government.
130. *Ibid.*
131. *Ibid.*

Chapter 6

1. Chapter 10, text following n. 26.
2. (1869) VII *V.P.D.* 2138.
3. Anonymous, *Westminster Review (New Series)*, No. LXVI, April 1868, 480 at 520, 523.
4. *Hansard's Parliamentary Debates*, 3rd series, Vol. 191, (1868), cols 1963-2001.
5. *On the Position of a Constitutional Governor Under Responsible Government* (Ottawa 1878), 19.
6. *Op. cit.* n. 2, at 2131.
7. Quoted, Bruce Knox, "Imperial Consequences of Constitutional Problems in New South Wales and Victoria 1865-1870", (1985) 21 *Historical Studies*, 515 at 517 – which *see* for a review of the consequences of the debate.
8. *Op. cit.* n. 2, at 2132.
9. Carnarvon's Diary for 1887 (B.L. Add MSS60929), 5 November 1887, p. 64.
10. 2 November 1869. For details of the protest, Stuart Macintyre, *A Colonial Liberalism* (Oxford 1991), 56-57.
11. (1869) VII *V.P.D.* 2132. This was resolution 3 of the original five.
12. *Ibid.* This was resolution 4 of the original five.
13. *Ibid.* This was resolution 5 of the original five.
14. *Ibid.* This formed part of resolution 2 of the original five. For further consideration of Higinbotham's approach, *see* below, text following n. 23.
15. (1869) VII *V.P.D.* at 2136.
16. *Id.*, at 2136-2137.
17. *Id.*, at 2137.
18. *Op. cit.* n. 7, 532.
19. To the Revd R.W. Church, 15 September 1854, in G.E. Marindin (ed.), *Letters of Frederic Lord Blachford* (London 1896), 157. *Cf* C.H. Currey, *British Colonial Policy 1783-1915* (Oxford 1916), 164, "As [the dependencies] grew in stature and demanded enlarged privileges and assumed greater responsibilities, it seemed as if their goal was independence. If that were so, the mother country could only be thankful that she had parted with her grown-up children on good terms".
20. Marindin (ed.), *ibid.*, 299-300.
21. Text to and following n. 54.
22. (1869) VII *V.P.D.* 2137. For an echo of this in another context, *see* Ch. 10, text to and following n. 108.
23. As Professor Macintyre has put it, (*op. cit.* n. 10, 58), "Rather than sever the imperial connection, he wished to adjust it so that a real and lasting union would be freely conceded on both sides".
24. G.W. Rusden, *History of Australia* (Vol. III London 1883), 396.
25. Higinbotham to Sir Henry Holland, 28 February 1887, C.O. 309/134, at f. 143; *Argus*, 16 February 1889, 5.

26. (1869) VII *V.P.D.* 2139.

27. *See* also, Henry L. Hall, *Australia and England* (London 1934), 186-187.

28. *Oxford History of Australia*, Vol. 3, *1860-1900*, Beverley Kingston (Melbourne 1988), 105. Higinbotham to Crisp, 12 January 1892, Cristopher Crisp Papers (N.L. MS 743) item 354. That effectively negatived the opinions of *Melbourne Punch*, 7 December 1865, 185, that "you [Higinbotham] have set about your great work as socialist, communist, and permanent Attorney-General"; of Melbourne's *Herald*, 3 January 1893, 2, that Higinbotham "had grown to 'despair of the republic'" – he had never supported one; and of the *Town and Country Journal*, 9 October 1886, 747, that Higinbotham revealed a "healthy, true republicanism and democratism". A sound interpretation is that of Bruce A. Knox, "Province and Metropolis: 'A Person Named Rogers' and Others" (paper, unpublished, read at the George Higinbotham Centenary Conference, Melbourne, 27 November 1992), p. 1 – "To call [Higinbotham] a Whiggish devotee of constitutional monarchy would not be too much: hence his unreserved and enthusiastic admiration for Queen Victoria as a constitutional sovereign". In confirmation of the last proposition, Higinbotham wrote to Henry Parkes, 27 April 1872 (Parkes Correspondence M.L. A988, 293 at 295), "Queen Victoria is the wisest and best Constitutional Sovereign that has ever sat on the throne of England".

29. (1869) VII *V.P.D.* 2138-2139.

30. *Id.*, at 2139. His views on public fiscal policy remained eccentric throughout his life. He was, for example, reported (*Armidale Express* (N.S.W.), 17 April 1891, 4) to have published an article in England claiming that "the investment of British capital in the colonies has already attracted greater attention and confidence than is consistent with the future welfare of the colonies".

31. (1869) VII *V.P.D.*, at 2140.

32. Knox, *op. cit.* n. 7, 519.

33. Manners-Sutton (Canterbury) to Granville (confidential), 6 December 1869, C.O. 309/91, f. 364, reporting, at f. 366, that the Legislative Assembly "would regard as a great relief an opportunity of escape from the necessity of expressing an opinion on [Higinbotham's] regulations". Also Canterbury to Granville, 30 December 1869, C.O. 309/191, f. 383. *See* further n. 59 below. For a range of newspaper reactions, Hall, *op. cit.* n. 27, 189-190.

34. *Toy* v. *Musgrove* (1888) 14 V.L.R. at 381 (*per* Higinbotham, C.J.). And *note* Bailey, 396; Hall, *op. cit.* n. 27, 188. As to colonies claiming to be "sovereign States" – J.M. Bennett, *Colonial Law Lords* (Sydney 2006), 32-33.

35. (4th edn London 1913), 25; citing *Musgrave* v. *Pulido* (1879) L.R. 5 App.Cas. 102 at 111. For the modern Victorian position, *see* Greg Taylor, *The Constitution of Victoria* (Sydney 2006), 74-77 and sources there cited.

36. (1835) 3 Knapp 332 at 343; 12 E.R. 678.

37. (1841) 3 Moore P.C. 465 at 476; 13 E.R. 189. And *note* Joseph Chitty, jnr, *A Treatise on the Law of the Prerogatives of the Crown* (London 1820), 34, "The *governors* of colonies are in general invested with royal authority; they may call, prorogue, (adjourn) and dissolve the colonies assemblies, and exercise other kingly functions: but still they are but servants or representatives of the King".

38.	(1869) VII *V.P.D.* 2134-2135. That the proposition was legally unsound was confirmed in K. C. Wheare, *The Statute of Westminster and Dominion Status* (2nd edn Oxford 1942), 49.

39.	Chitty, *op. cit.* n. 37, 6, "The pardoning offenders and issuing proclamations, are also ranked among the prerogatives of the Crown". For a commentary on various views on the subject, including those of Higinbotham, H. V. Evatt, *The Royal Prerogative* (Sydney 1987), 117-119.

40.	A. B. Keith, *Responsible Government in the Dominions*, Vol. 1 (2nd edn Oxford 1928), 209; T. P. Webb, *A Compendium of the Imperial Law and Statutes in Force in the Colony of Victoria* (Melbourne 1892), 162. Carnarvon's circular despatch, of 20 October 1875, is at C.O. 854/16, f. 232.

41.	*Bonanza Creek Gold Mining Co. Ltd* v. *The King* [1916] 1 A.C. 566 at 585-586.

42.	*Op. cit.* n. 39, 94 at 109. It followed that Evatt claimed (at 26) that, in 1924, "the Governor of a self-governing State … is not only a local constitutional Monarch to a greater or lesser extent, but he is also an Imperial officer", a position Higinbotham would have embraced but could not as the law stood in his day.

43.	*Parliamentary Government in the British Colonies* (2nd edn London 1894), 118.

44.	(1869) VII *V.P.D.* 2135.

45.	To some extent the Colonial Office adhered to the precept of the all-powerful Sir James Stephen, when Under-Secretary, that such documents mattered less than that the Governor understood what was expected of him – "What is really thought important enough to be said at all, had best be said in the common language of our social intercourse; not in the dark phraseology of legal instruments", memorandum of 1 July 1847, C.O. 144/2 (East India & China Association).

46.	(1869) VII *V.P.D.* 2135.

47.	*Ibid.*

48.	Higinbotham to Henry Parkes, 27 April 1872, Parkes Correspondence, Autograph Letters (M.L. A988), 293 at 297a.

49.	Henry L. Hall, *The Colonial Office: A History* (London 1937), 95-96.

50.	Bailey, 396.

51.	Section xliii of the originally submitted draft.

52.	Bailey, 397.

53.	*Op. et loc. cit.* n. 40. *Note* also A. Wood Renton (ed.), *Encyclopaedia of the Laws of England*, (Vol. III London 1897), *s.v.* "Colonial Governors" at 112.

54.	Minute at C.O. 309/91, ff. 288-289.

55.	Minute at C.O. 309/90, f. 443.

56.	Minutes at C.O. 309/93, ff. 186 and 187; and C.O. 309/91, ff. 385-386a. Rogers had earlier depicted Higinbotham as "the vehement leader of the anti-Downing Street – anti-squatting – anti-Legislative Council policy" – minute at C.O. 309/91, f. 288a.

57.	Minute at C.O. 309/93, f. 186 at f. 187.

58.	Knox, *op. cit.* n. 28, 6. As to Rogers' counter-attack, Knox, *op. cit.* n. 7, 527-528, 530-531. For Rogers' "Rough Notes on Colonial Relations", *see* D. P. O'Connell and Ann Riordan, *Opinions on Imperial Constitutional Law* (Sydney 1971), 5-9.

59.	Minutes by Rogers, C.O. 309/91, f. 385 at f. 386, and C.O. 309/93, f. 42.

60. Carnarvon's Diary for 1867 (B.L. Add MSS 60899), 17 December 1867, p. 182. He then feared that the "revolution" could sweep away "the very foundations of the Constitution". And *note*, Bruce A. Knox, "Conservative Imperialism 1858-1874" (1984) 6 *International History Review*, 333 at 344.

61. Sir Robert Herbert (ed.), Henry Howard Molyneux, Fourth Earl of Carnarvon, *Essays, Addresses and Translations* (Vol. III London 1896), 9.

62. Bruce A. Knox, "Colonial Influence on Imperial Policy, 1858-1866" (1963) 11 *Historical Studies*, 61 at 78.

63. *See* generally, Knox, *op. cit.* n. 60; Macintyre, *op. cit.* n. 10, 56.

64. For a confirmatory comment and an incongruous sequel – H.E. Egerton, *A Short History of British Colonial Policy* (4th edn London 1913), 382. The failure of governments to support his resolutions was seen by Higinbotham as "the cruellest blow and he blamed the pusillanimity of his former ministerial colleagues for the apparent indifference of the colonists to the restrictions on their autonomy", Macintyre, *op. cit* n. 10, 58. When Higinbotham tried to reactivate the matter in the House in June 1875 he received almost no support, George Paton Smith moving the adjournment to silence him, while protesting that Higinbotham "should perpetually bring to bear his great influence not only in this House but in the country, and his great knowledge of political life and procedure, upon matters which are really unworthy his attention" (1875) XXI *V.P.D.* 510.

65. Quoted, Knox, *op. cit.* n. 60, 355.

66. *Bulletin* (Sydney), 7 January 1893, 9. Astley wrote under the *nom de plume* "Price Warung". *Cf Melbourne Bulletin*, 24 February 1882, 3 – "You [Higinbotham] dwell in thousands of memories, as, next to Wentworth, 'The Australian Patriot'".

67. *See* generally, J.M. Bennett, *Lives of the Australian Chief Justices – Sir James Martin* (Sydney 2005), 51-54.

68. "Australia and the Empire, 1855-1921", in Rose, Newton & Benians (Genl Eds), *The Cambridge History of the British Empire*, Vol. VII, Pt I Australia, (Cambridge 1933), 521 at 522. Even the eulogistic William Astley conceded (Astley Papers, Dixson Library, State Library of New South Wales (MS Q513)) that Higinbotham was "Something too much of an idealist, his work has not lain chiefly in the domain of constructive statesmanship".

69. Bailey, 395.

70. But *see* generally, D.M. Farr, *The Colonial Office and Canada, 1867-1887* (Toronto 1955), particularly Ch. 4.

71. Egerton, *op. cit.* n. 64, 369. As to Edward Blake – W. Stewart Wallace, *The Dictionary of Canadian Biography* Vol. 1 (2nd edn Toronto 1945).

72. Todd, *op. cit* n. 43, 110.

73. *See* further, Knox, *op. cit.* n. 7, 522.

74. Granville to Belmore, 4 October 1869, 27 I.U.P. 210. For Higinbotham's comments in Parliament, (1875) XXI *V.P.D.* 510.

75. The material documents are set out in 27 I.U.P. 25 (C.1202) and 267 (C.1248). *Note* also, Todd, *op. cit.* n. 43, 354-355; (1976) 6 *A.D.B.* 48 at 49; Sir Henry Parkes, *Fifty Years in the Making of Australian History* (London 1892), 282-292; Farr, *op. cit.* n. 70, 122-123.

76. Bennett, *op. cit.* n. 67, Ch. 12.

77. But, *see* further, Todd, *op. cit.* n. 43, 348; Todd, *op. cit.* n. 5, 20.

78.   4 May 1875, 27 I.U.P. 267 (C.1248), 274 at 275. For Higinbotham's public comments on Carnarvon's views, (1875) XXI *V.P.D.* 506-508.
79.   Farr, *op. cit.* n. 70, 131 n. 50.
80.   Frank H. Underhill, "Edward Blake and Canadian Liberal Nationalism", in H. Flenley (ed.), *Essays in Canadian History* (Toronto 1939), 132.
81.   Farr, *op. cit* n. 70, 22.
82.   Joseph Schull, *Edward Blake – The Man of the Other Way* (Toronto 1975), 156-157.
83.   *Id.*, 160.
84.   Marindin (ed.), *op. cit.* n. 19, 263.
85.   Keith, *op. cit.* n. 40, 110-113.
86.   Underhill, *op. cit.* n. 79, 148; Todd, *op. cit.* n. 5, 26; A.B. Keith, *The Sovereignty of the British Dominions* (London 1929), 48-49.
87.   Todd, *op. cit.* n. 43, 114, 116.
88.   The text is reproduced in Webb, *op. cit.* n. 40, 229.
89.   Carnarvon's Diary, *loc. cit.* n. 9.
90.   "Higinbotham's theory was a house of cards without a solid foundation … [T]he strength of his theory … [was] that it presaged future constitutional development, and its weakness … [was] that its rigidity acted as a fetter to further constitutional evolution", Charles Parkinson, "George Higinbotham and Responsible Government in Colonial Victoria" (2001) 25 *Melbourne University Law Review*, 181 at 217.

Chapter 7

1.   Morris, 258.
2.   *Argus*, 2 January 1893, 6; *cf Australasian*, 7 January 1893, 29; *Ballarat Star*, 3 January 1893, 3.
3.   Barry died on 23 November 1880.
4.   *Argus*, 11 January 1893, 9.
5.   Higinbotham to Service, 16 July 1880, La Trobe Library, Melbourne, Australian Manuscripts Collection, MS10035, p. 8.
6.   *Id.*, p. 1.
7.   *Australasian*, 24 July 1880, 116.
8.   (1976) 6 *A.D.B.* at 108.
9.   *A History of the Colony of Victoria* (Vol. II London 1904), 212.
10.   *Op. cit.* n. 5, pp. 2, 3.
11.   "Cantab", *Upper Chambers and Constitutional Reform* (Melbourne 1878), 22; *Bendigo Evening News*, 22 May 1880; *Argus*, 22 May 1880, 7 (where Berry was very critical of Higinbotham), and editorial at 6. For a collection of numerous press opinions on Service's measure, C.O. 309/121, from f. 171.
12.   *Op. cit.* n. 5, p. 4. For his carrying the "duty" into effect, *see* Ch. 8, text following n. 4.
13.   *See* generally, David Solomon, *The Political Impact of the High Court* (North Sydney 1992); Graham Fricke, *Judges of the High Court* (Hawthorn 1986), 78-81; J.M. Bennett, *Keystone of the Federal Arch* (Canberra 1980), 33.
14.   *Op. cit.* n. 5, pp. 6, 7-8.
15.   *Id.*, pp. 10, 11.
16.   *Argus*, 21 July 1880, 5.
17.   *See* Ch. 8 text to n. 5.

18.   J. M. Bennett, *Lives of the Australian Chief Justices – Sir William Stawell* (Sydney 2004), 120-121.

19.   (London 1911), 215 (note).

20.   *Op. cit.* n. 18, 108.

21.   29 July 1880, quoted Morris, 259.

22.   *Age*, 20 July 1880, 2; *Argus*, 21 July 1880, 5; *Australasian*, 24 July 1880, 116.

23.   20 July 1880, 4.

24.   20 July 1880, 2. Professor Morris capped this (Morris 258) with the extravagant assertion that the appointment was seen to be "extremely popular with the people of the colony of every shade of opinion". There was no evidence from which such a wide generalization could be drawn.

25.   Kelly's criminal exploits at Glenrowan in June 1880 remained the talk of the Colony. He was convicted of murder and sentenced to death in October, and hanged on 11 November – (1974) 5 *A.D.B.* at 8.

26.   For a collection of them, *Herald* (Melbourne), 20 July 1880, 2.

27.   31 July 1880, 142.

28.   22 July 1880, 31.

29.   Normanby to Kimberley, 19 July 1880, C.O. 309/121 f. 342, and minute paper, *ibid.*, at f. 341a.

30.   (1974) 5 *A.D.B.* at 366; and *note Melbourne Punch*, 7 October 1886, 169.

31.   22 July 1880 (Summary for Europe), 1.

32.   *The Story of the Bar of Victoria* (Melbourne n.d.), 182.

33.   *Melbourne Bulletin*, 24 February 1882, 3. The aspiring English politician Stanley Leighton, who visited Melbourne in 1868 and waited upon Higinbotham, confirmed that he was "a small gentlemanly looking man with a pleasant and engaging manner", Leighton Journal, N.L. MS 360/2, 6.

34.   Alfred Deakin (ed. J. A. La Nauze and R. M. Crawford), *The Crisis in Victorian Politics, 1879-1881* (Melbourne 1957), 22.

35.   For example, *Taylor* v. *Plumpton* (1883) 9 V.L.R.(L.) 48 at 49; *Stewart* v. *Bank of Australasia* (1883) *id.*, 240 at 247

36.   For example, *Atkins* v. *Walsh* (1885) 11 V.L.R. 785; *Australian Mont de Piete Co.* v. *Ward* (1885) *id.*, 793; *Stewart* v. *McKinley* (1885) *id.*, 802; *Daly* v. *Ryan* (1886) 12 V.L.R. 81; *Hongkong & Macao Glass Manufacturing Co. Ltd* v. *Gritton* (1886) *id.*, 128.

37.   (Melbourne) 7 January 1893, 20; *cf Argus*, 2 January 1893, 5-6; *Australasian*, 2 October 1886, 650.

38.   Unidentified newspaper cutting, January 1893, Higinbotham Papers.

39.   Quoted, Dean, 310.

40.   *Ibid.*, at 326 (last n. 3).

41.   *Argus*, 11 January 1893, 9.

42.   Alfred Deakin (ed. Herbert Brookes), *The Federal Story* (Melbourne 1944), 7-8.

43.   *Id.*, 8.

44.   Chapter 11.

45.   Paul Finn, *Law and Government in Colonial Australia* (Melbourne 1987), 84, 108; and *see* Ch. 11, text to n. 147.

46.   Charles Parkinson, *Sir William Stawell and the Victorian Constitution* (Melbourne 2004), 103; Alastair Davidson, "The Judiciary and Politics in N.S.W. and Victoria 1856-1901", *Monash Occasional Papers in Politics*

No. 1 (Monash University n.d.), 49 – where it is put, erroneously in the present view (for the reasons given in the text following n. 47), that, at the material time, "The [Legislature] could not control the Courts by legislation, since the latter were not merely in such a system the interpreters of the law made in another place, but would decide whether the law was legal according to their criteria of legality. The [Courts] could control the Legislature by decision". That interpretation seeks to apply, anachronistically, to colonial Victoria, the circumstances of post-Federation Australia, regulated by a Constitution ultimately interpreted by the High Court.

47. In *Black* v. *Zevenboom* (1880) 6 V.L.R.(L.) 473, sometimes cited as demonstrating Stawell's claimed predisposition to subordinate the Legislature to the power of the court, the true position was quite the reverse. The *Instruments and Securities Act* 1864 rendered a bill of sale void as regards third parties if the Act's requirements were not complied with, but allowed it to remain valid as between the parties to it. An amending Act of 1876 rendered a bill of sale totally void unless within 12 months of its registration an affidavit were filed stating the amount owing under the bill, and other details. In this case, the affidavit incorrectly stated the details, and no correction was filed within time. The Full Court (Stawell, Stephen *and* Higinbotham) held that the bill of sale was therefore irretrievably void as against all parties. Stawell (at 477) acknowledged the superior authority of the Legislature, holding that "as the second Act uses much stronger language than the first, the Court is not at liberty to put the same construction upon both".

48. Text to n. 56.

49. A striking instance was *Scott* v. *Collingwood Corporation* (1881) 7 V.L.R.(L.) 280, where Higinbotham cited 20 precedent cases: and he would follow that practice even when concurring, as in *Shire of Gisborne* v. *Murphy* (1881) 7 V.L.R.(L.) 63 at 71

50. (1882) 8 V.L.R.(L.) 347. Joint judgements in the past had rarely extended beyond three or four pages at most.

51. (1880) 6 V.L.R.(L.) 493.

52. At 500, 501.

53. At 498, 499. The respective English authorities were *Parker* v. *Wallis* (1865) 5 E. & B. 21, and *Kibble* v. *Gough* (1878) 38 L.T. (N.S.) 204 at 205. George William Bramwell, former Baron of the Exchequer, was appointed a Lord Justice of the Court of Appeal, on its establishment in 1876 pursuant to the *Judicature Acts*.

54. (1880) 6 V.L.R.(L.) at 499.

55. Particularly *Howse* v. *Glowry* (1882) 8 V.L.R.(L.) 280; *McVea* v. *Pasquan* (1882) *id.*, 347; *Oakden* v. *Gibbs* (1882) *id.*, 380; *Harding* v. *Board of Land and Works* (1882) *id.*, 402. For the change in the court's conventional methods, *see* Parkinson, *op. cit.* n. 46, 102-103.

56. *R.* v. *Call; ex parte Murphy* (1881) 7 V.L.R.(L.) 113 at 123.

57. For a comment on the possible exercise of judicial power by Parliament, *see* Anne Twomey, *The Constitution of New South Wales* (Sydney 2004), 204.

58. Below, text following n. 64.

59. Of which a powerful modern exposition was given by Gibbs, C.J., in the High Court, in *Cooper Brookes (Wollongong) Pty Ltd* v. *Federal Commissioner of Taxation* (1981) 147 C.L.R. 297 at 305; *cf* the statements of

Griffith, C.J., in *Tindal* v. *Calman* (1905) 3 C.L.R. 150 at 154, and in *Colon Peaks Mining Co.* v. *Wollondilly Shire Council* (1911) 13 C.L.R. 438 at 445.

60. For instances of Higinbotham's following those precepts when Chief Justice, *see Albrecht* v. *Patterson* (1886) 12 V.L.R. 821 at 826 (unjust laws to be applied until altered by Parliament); and *R.* v. *Fitzgerald* (1889) 15 V.L.R. 40 at 46-47 (statute not to be construed to create absurdity).

61. *Per* Gibbs, C.J., *op. et loc. cit.* n. 59.

62. (1882) 8 V.L.R.(L.) 380 at 387. Yet he seemed to argue against that approach when, in *In re Gair* (1884) 10 V.L.R.(L.) 108, (a case in which the *Supreme Court Rules* were strictly enforced against an articled clerk), Higinbotham said (at 109) that the duty of all courts was "to interpret truly, and apply equally and with unvarying uniformity the provisions of the Statute law".

63. (1884) 10 V.L.R.(L.) 133 at 138. For similar Higinbotham dissents, based on intricate reviews of legislative history, *see R.* v. *McCormick; ex parte McMonigle* (1884) 10 V.L.R.(L.) 268 at 270; *In re Warne* (1885) 11 V.L.R. 320 at 325; *Davey* v. *Pein* (1885) *id.*, 446 at 462.

64. (1884) 10 V.L.R.(L.) at 139. Higinbotham, as Chief Justice, reiterated this principle strongly in *Toy* v. *Musgrove* (1888) 14 V.L.R. 349 at 386-387, when he said, "We are bound ... in trying to arrive at the meaning of [Acts], ... to consider the history and external circumstances which led to their enactment, and for that purpose to consult any authentic public or historical documents that may suggest a key to their true sense". Williams, J., (at 418) disagreed, indicating that one should look "merely at the Act itself (which in construing [any] Act of Parliament is the legitimate course), and not at despatches or speeches in ... Parliament (which for the purpose of giving a legal construction to legislation, are, in my opinion, clearly valueless". a'Beckett, J., (at 434) agreed that "this is a question of legal construction in which we cannot be assisted by the speeches or despatches of statesmen".

65. At 140, 141.

66. At 145. For Higinbotham's counter position as to conjectures, *see R.* v. *Nicolson; ex parte Minogue* (1884) 10 V.L.R.(L.) 255 at 260; *R.* v. *Alley; ex parte Davey* (1883) 9 V.L.R.(L.) 59 at 67.

67. (1881) 7 V.L.R.(L.) 47.

68. For Higinbotham's vigorous support of that principle – (1882) 8 V.L.R.(Eq.) 128 at 138.

69. (1881) 7 V.L.R.(L.) at 49, 50.

70. At 50, 51.

71. (1880) 6 V.L.R.(L.) 467.

72. At 469.

73. (1882) 8 V.L.R.(L.) 402.

74. At 411.

75. At 408, 409.

76. (1885) 11 V.L.R. 386 at 395.

77. John G. Fleming, *The Law of Torts* (5th edn Sydney 1977), 489.

78. (1885) 11 V.L.R. at 433.

79. At 436.

80. At 424, 425.

81. At 429.

82. (1885) 11 V.L.R. 410.

83. At 426.

84. At 429, 430.
85. (1886) 12 V.L.R. 384 at 388.
86. *Byrne* v. *Armstrong* (1899) 25 V.L.R. 126 at 127-128.
87. (1884) 10 V.L.R.(L.) 279. Observation of Sir Gerard Brennan, "The Judiciary", in "Law Politics and Public Life" – The George Higinbotham Centenary Conference, Melbourne, 27 November 1992, 3.
88. (1884) 10 V.L.R.(L.) at 286.
89. An English visitor remarked that "the Yarra is a foul stream, brown in repose, and the colour of ink when stirred up, and smelling horribly all the time" – Harold Finch-Hatton, *Advance Australia* (London 1885), 341.
90. (1884) 10 V.L.R.(L.) at 284.
91. At 285-286.
92. *Halsbury's Laws of England* Vol. 43 (4th edn London 1983), *s.v.* "Shipping and Navigation", § 943.
93. (1881) 7 V.L.R.(L.) 488.
94. At 491.
95. At 498.
96. Above, text following n. 76.
97. (1881) 7 V.L.R.(L.) 4.
98. At 6.
99. At 6-7.
100. (1882) 8 V.L.R.(L.) 256.
101. At 261, 263.
102. At 264.
103. At 257.
104. At 267.
105. (1881) 7 V.L.R.(L.) 280 at 291. He substantially reiterated that view in *Emerald Hill Corporation* v. *Ford* (1883) 9 V.L.R.(L.) 351 at 352-353, but he did not extend it to road bridges – *Coad* v. *St Arnaud Corporation* (1886) 12 V.L.R. 162. For a similar opinion concerning access to railway stations – *Langton* v. *Board of Land & Works* (1880) 6 V.L.R.(L.) 316 at 323, and *cf Victorian Woollen & Cloth Manufacturing Co. (Ltd)* v. *Board of Land & Works* (1881) 7 V.L.R.(L.) 461 at 467.
106. (1883) 9 V.L.R.(L.) 435 at 440. *Cf* his strict views on the responsibilities of Councils, in entering into contracts, to protect the interests of their ratepayers – *Richmond Corporation* v. *Edwards* (1883) 9 V.L.R.(L.) 348 at 350.
107. (1885) 11 V.L.R. 743 at 746.
108. *Id.*, 785.
109. At 791.
110. At 792.
111. (1880) 6 V.L.R.(L.) 329.
112. At 333.
113. At 333-334. For Higinbotham's later protest against "the serious inconvenience likely to arise from the existence within the Port limits of several jurisdictions for different purposes – *Beaver* v. *Williamstown Justices* (1883) 9 V.L.R.(L.) 454 at 456-457.
114. (1880) 6 V.L.R.(L.) at 334.
115. (1881) 7 V.L.R.(L.) 248.
116. At 255.
117. At 261, 263.
118. At 265.

119. Above, text to n. 111.
120. At 333.
121. (1876) 2 Ex.D. 63 at 160.
122. *Legislative, Executive and Judicial Powers in Australia* (5th edn Sydney 1976), 67. Victoria never was a "Dominion" and lacked power to require its courts to implement domestic laws of purportedly extraterritorial operation.
123. And *see Bonser* v. *La Macchia* (1969) 122 C.L.R. 177 at 219 (*per* Windeyer, J.).
124. (1881) 7 V.L.R.(L.) 113 at 123.
125. At 119.
126. Above, at 133.
127. *Lee* v. *Bude & Torrington Junction Railway Co.* (1871) L.R. 6 C.P. 582.
128. (1886) 12 V.L.R. 604.
129. At 610.
130. For a similar examination of extraterritoriality in relation to the Post Office, *see Spitzel* v. *Becxx* (1890) 16 V.L.R. 661 (*per* Hood, J.).
131. (1886) 12 V.L.R. at 608.
132. At 609.
133. In, for example, *In re Thoneman* (1887) 13 V.L.R. 204 at 213; *Brooks, Robinson & Co.* v. *Howard Smith & Sons* (1890) 16 V.L.R. 245 at 250.

Chapter 8

1. *See* generally, J.M. Bennett, *Lives of the Australian Chief Justices – Sir William Stawell* (Sydney 2004), 178-179.
2. 18 September 1886, 9.
3. The position was otherwise in Tasmania where the relatively small profession was conducive to judicial promotion. Between 1870 and 1914 Sir Francis Smith, Sir William Dobson and Sir John Dodds were successive Chief Justices, each having been promoted from a puisne judgeship.
4. *See* also Ch. 10, text following n. 56; and *see* generally, J.M. Bennett, "The Royal Prerogative of Mercy" (2007) 81 *Australian Law Journal* 35.
5. Higinbotham to the Attorney-General, 10 May 1884, enclosure Stawell to the Earl of Derby, 16 June 1884, C.O. 309/127, f. 54.
6. *Ibid*. The Colonial Office dissented, minuting that "Any power or prerogative which the Crown exercised over the colony before the Constitution Act, and which are not by that Act vested in the Governor in Council or the Col[onial] Legislature, still remain in the Crown" (C.O. 309/127 at f. 52).
7. *Op. et loc. cit.* n. 5.
8. *Ibid*.
9. Kerferd to Higinbotham, 16 May 1884, *ibid*.
10. Kerferd to Higinbotham, 27, 30 May 1884, *ibid*.
11. C.O. 309/127, f. 54 at f. 54a: the Colonial Office also agreed with the Attorney-General, minutes at f. 52.
12. *Id.*, at ff. 51, 52.
13. At f. 52a.
14. At f. 53a.
15. Higinbotham to Kerferd, 21 December 1885, published *Argus*, 9 January 1886, 10.
16. Morris, 259-260.

17. 14 May 1886 (repeated in his letter of 16 September cited at n. 19).
18. Wrixon to Higinbotham, 10 September 1886, C.O. 309/130, f. 310.
19. Higinbotham to Wrixon, 13 September 1886, *ibid.*
20. Memo for the Attorney-General, 17 September 1886; advice of 23 September 1886, C.O. 309/130, f. 304 and at f. 297a.
21. *See* also Ch. 10, text to and following n. 87.
22. Memo for the Premier, 22 September 1886, C.O. 309/130, f. 308 at f. 309.
23. *Argus*, 25 September 1886, 9; *Age*, 25 September 1886, 9.
24. 20 October 1886, 649.
25. 9 October 1886, 747.
26. 7 October 1886, 169.
27. J.A. La Nauze and R.M. Crawford (eds), Alfred Deakin, *The Crisis in Victorian Politics, 1879-1881* (Melbourne 1957), 22. *See* also Ch. 7, text to n. 33.
28. "A Dream of Fair Judges", quoted Dean, 310.
29. *See* generally Ch. 10.
30. (1972) 4 *A.D.B.* 394.
31. *Ah Chin* v. *Thiel* (1887) 13 V.L.R. 485 at 486.
32. *R.* v. *Birkett* (1890) 16 V.L.R. 398 at 400.
33. *See* generally, J.M. Bennett, *Lives of the Australian Chief Justices – Sir Henry Wrenfordsley* (Sydney 2004).
34. (1888) 15 V.L.R. 94 at 109.
35. At 106-107.
36. R. de B. Griffith, Q.C., in Dean, 292.
37. *In re Dakin* (1887) 13 V.L.R. 522.
38. At 523.
39. At 524.
40. At 525.
41. (1873) L.R. 9 Q.B. 230, 241.
42. (1887) 13 V.L.R. at 526.
43. At 528.
44. At 538, 529, respectively.
45. *Op. cit.* n. 41, at 233.
46. (1887) 13 V.L.R. at 535.
47. At 537.
48. At 544.
49. At 547.
50. (1889) 15 V.L.R. 402.
51. Quoted at 406.
52. At 414.
53. At 406-407.
54. At 415, 416.
55. (1891) 17 V.L.R. 391.
56. At 393, 394.
57. At 396.
58. At 401.
59. At 402-403.
60. At 400.
61. At 400-401.
62. (1887) 13 V.L.R. 708.
63. At 709.
64. (1890) 16 V.L.R. 501 at 502.

65. (1889) 15 V.L.R. 163 at 169.
66. A. Garran, "Are Victorian Judicial Appointments Valid?" (1932) 6 *Australian Law Journal*, 123 at 124.
67. (1889) 15 V.L.R. 40.
68. At 54. It was common, in those days of a small complement of judges, for a trial judge to sit as a member of the Full Court entertaining further proceedings.
69. At 48, 49.
70. At 53, 51, respectively.
71. At 42.
72. At 48, 44, respectively.
73. At 46-47.
74. At 47-48.
75. (1887) 13 V.L.R. 37.
76. At 38, 40.
77. *In re Merry* (1888) 14 V.L.R. 176.
78. At 185, 186.
79. H.J. Gibbney and Ann G. Smith, *A Biographical Register 1788-1939* (Vol. II Canberra 1987), 308.
80. The *County Court Judges Tenure of Office Act* 1884.
81. *Trench* v. *The Queen* (1887) 13 V.L.R. 13, at 15.
82. At 17.
83. At 19, 20.
84. (1892) 18 V.L.R. 282.
85. At 286, 287.
86. (1887) 13 V.L.R. 491.
87. At 494.
88. At 496.
89. (1890) 16 V.L.R. 607.
90. (1808) 15 Ves. 248.
91. (1890) 16 V.L.R. at 610.
92. (1891) 17 V.L.R. 178.
93. At 181.
94. (1888) 14 V.L.R. 301.
95. At 303.
96. At 304, 305.
97. At 305, 306.
98. (1891) 17 V.L.R. 364.
99. At 367.
100. At 368.
101. At 366.
102. (1889) 15 V.L.R. 154.
103. At 161, 162.
104. At 160.
105. *Albrecht* v. *Patterson* (1886) 12 V.L.R. 821 at 826 – a dissenting judgement.
106. (1886) 13 V.L.R. 268.
107. At 286.
108. At 292.
109. At 278-279, 281.
110. At 287-288. Holroyd, on the other hand, held that the preliminary phrase was "prohibitive" (at 290).
111. At 283-284.

112. At 286.
113. (1888) 14 V.L.R. 77.
114. At 82, 83.
115. (1888) 14 V.L.R. 567.
116. At 582.
117. At 577.
118. (1888) 14 V.L.R. 748; (1889) 15 V.L.R. 761.
119. (1888) 14 V.L.R. at 757, 755, respectively.
120. (1889) 15 V.L.R. at 763, 765.
121. At 772-773.
122. At 770-771.
123. At 772.
124. Generally, Paul Finn, *Law and Government in Colonial Australia* (Melbourne 1987), 110.
125. (1891) 17 V.L.R. 560.
126. At 582, 584.
127. At 586, 588-590.
128. (1890) 16 V.L.R. 555.
129. (1891) 17 V.L.R. at 571.
130. At 575.
131. (1933) 50 C.L.R. 154.
132. At 163.
133. At 177.
134. At 180.
135. (1888) 15 V.L.R. 190.
136. At 199-200, 301.
137. At 203, 204.
138. At 197. *Note* the modern extension of this in *Victorian Railways Commissioners* v. *Seal* [1966] V.R. 107.
139. (1892) 18 V.L.R. 250.
140. At 257, 258.
141. At 260-261.
142. At 255.
143. At 263, 264.
144. At 265.
145. (1887) 13 V.L.R. 3511.
146. At 357.
147. (1887) 14 V.L.R. 1.
148. At 8.
149. At 6.
150. At 7.
151. *Ibid.*
152. (1890) 16 V.L.R. 591.
153. At 594.
154. At 595.
155. At 594.

Chapter 9

1. Bailey, 395 at 397.
2. Generally, Myra Willard, *History of the White Australia Policy* (Melbourne 1923), 82-83; J.M. Bennett, *Colonial Law Lords* (Sydney 2006), 27-43.

3.   Bennett, *ibid.*, 30-31
4.   *Ex parte Lo Pak* (1888) 9 N.S.W.L.R.(L.) 221 at 235.
5.   (1888) 14 V.L.R. 349.
6.   At 413.
7.   At 415.
8.   At 416.
9.   At 419.
10. *Ibid.*
11. At 426-427, 428, 429.
12. At 434.
13. At 441-442.
14. *Egan* v. *Willis* (1998) 195 C.L.R. 424 at 451 (*per* Gaudron, Gummow and Hayne, JJ.): *cf* Anne Twomey, *The Constitution of New South Wales* (Sydney 2005), 26-28.
15. "The Responsible Government Question in Victoria, South Australia and Tasmania, 1851-1856" (1978) 63 *Journal of the Royal Australian Historical Society*, at 221. For a more detailed commentary – H.V. Evatt, *The Royal Prerogative* (Sydney 1987), Ch. II.
16. (1888) 14 V.L.R. at 385.
17. At 387.
18. *Ibid.*, and at 388, 396.
19. At 391.
20. At 392-393.
21. At 408, n. (e).
22. At 416, 417, 418, 419.
23. At 428.
24. At 434.
25. At 442.
26. Zelman Cowen, *Sir John Latham and Other Papers* (Melbourne 1965), 121.
27. (1888) 14 V.L.R. at 403, 404.
28. A.B. Keith, *Responsible Government in the Dominions* (Vol. I, 2nd edn Oxford 1928), 51, contended that "this assertion … was historically without foundation" in its premise that colonial self-government rested wholly on statute and not on common law. And *note* K.C. Wheare, *The Statute of Westminster and Dominion Status* (Oxford 1942), 49.
29. (1888) 14 V.L.R. at 398.
30. At 374-375.
31. At 378.
32. At 381.
33. At 379, 395-396, 397.
34. At 396, 397.
35. At 376.
36. At 384.
37. At 385.
38. At 393.
39. Geoffrey Serle, *The Rush to be Rich* (Melbourne 1974 edn), 303.
40. *Musgrove* v. *Toy* [1891] A.C. 272; (1891) 60 L.J.P.C. 28.
41. 11 June 1888, 5.
42. [1891] A.C. at 283. Evatt, *op. cit.* n. 15, at 99-100, energetically criticized the Board for depreciating Higinbotham's decision – "a perfectly straightforward judgment dealing in perhaps clearer and more straightforward terms with the important questions arising for decision than

that of Kerferd J". But the question remains, how relevant was that straightforward decision, and the answer necessarily is that it was a gratuitous excursus from the real points at issue.

43.   [1891] A.C. at 281.

44.   At 283. That continues to be cited as authority for the proposition that "at common law, an alien friend had no legal right to enter British territory", *Halsbury's Laws of England* (4th edn, Vol. 4 London 1973), *s.v.* "British Nationality", § 951, n. 1.

45.   As Professor Keith remarked, *op. cit.* n. 28, 116, "the Privy Council … were very careful to avoid answering any of the important points raised".

Chapter 10

1.   C.O. 448/2, f. 504.

2.   At f. 504a.

3.   Darley was made a Knight Bachelor in 1887 but was not appointed K.C.M.G. until 1897 – (1972) 4 *A.D.B.* at 19.

4.   C.O. 448/2 at f. 502. Julian Emanuel Salomons (later Sir Julian) was not knighted during his brief term as nominal Chief Justice of New South Wales in 1886, nor was he sworn in to the office.

5.   A. Patchett Martin, *Australia and the Empire* (Edinburgh 1889), claimed to have heard Higinbotham denounce knighthoods with "intense bitterness … [he] declared of these knighthoods that it was 'impossible to discriminate their relative baseness'". (1972) 4 *A.D.B.* at 396. Geoffrey Serle, *The Rush to be Rich* (Melbourne 1974 edn), 219. The *Bulletin* (Sydney), 11 October 1890, 7, characterized Higinbotham as "one of the very few public men in [Victoria] who has not deserved the infamy of a K.C.M.G.-ship". England's *Daily Chronicle* (January 1893, Higinbotham Papers) correctly pointed out that Higinbotham's refusal of a knighthood "prevented a similar honour being paid to any of the puisne judges, much, perhaps, to the mortification of their wives".

6.   28 February 1887, published in *Argus*, 16 February 1889, 5; *Australasian*, 23 February 1889, 424.

7.   *Ibid.*

8.   7 January 1893, 29.

9.   1 November 1886, quoted (1956) 29 *Australian Law Journal*, at 710, n. 15.

10.   Morris, 282; Turner, 265.

11.   Carnarvon's Diary for 1888 (B.L. Add MSS60930), 27 January 1888, p. 13a. Carnarvon had formed a similar impression at a lunch held by Higinbotham as President of the Exhibition Commission in November 1887, writing (Carnarvon's Diary for 1887 (B.L. Add MSS60929) 26 November 1887, p. 74a), "The Ch Justice very amiable and interesting. He drove me home. Our conservation turned much on the Melbourne workmen and the 8 hours system & the general condition of the class. He is one of the remarkable figures here in Victoria – very popular with a large class & having since his fiery days conciliated a large number of the educated people".

12.   *Australasian*, 12 May 1888, 1041.

13.   Turner, 267.

14.   (1976) 6 *A.D.B.* at 88. The Exhibition, budgeted to cost £25,000, in fact required nearly £240,000, prompting the visiting Sir Henry Parkes to

declare his delight that it had been held in Victoria "because it would be attended by a loss which New South Wales could not well bear", *Argus*, 4 January 1889, 4. For the minutes relating to Sargood's appointment, and a prolonged exchange of letters between him and Higinbotham, P.R.O. file L5550.

15. *Argus*, 2 January 1893, 6; Turner, 268; *Australasian*, 12 May 1888, 1041.
16. *Argus*, 2 August 1888, 7.
17. Serle, *op. cit.* n. 5, 286; Turner, 266. For a similar ecclesiastical tiff, C.M.H. Clark, *A History of Australia* (Vol. 5 Melbourne 1981), 13.
18. Below, text following n. 86.
19. *Age*, 3 August 1887, 7.
20. *Mirror* (Melbourne), 5 October 1888, 4.
21. P. A. Jacobs, *Famous Australian Trials* (2nd edn Melbourne 1943), 127.
22. *Id.*, 126.
23. *Ibid.* The *Weekly Times* (Melbourne), 7 January 1893, 22, reported that "on these occasions the serious face of the grave man disappeared. His judicial bearing thawed, and he was all smiles and sociability. He had that charm of manner that makes one feel instinctively at ease and talking to a kindly friend".
24. Morris, at 320, conceded the fact: "Early in life he came to the conclusion that ridicule was wrong. It hurt the feelings of others, and therefore should be discouraged. A near relative remarked that when Higinbotham heard a joke he looked all round it to see that no one was hurt before he laughed. When subjected to that treatment humour evaporates". Archbishop F.F. Goe (Higinbotham Papers, letter to Morris, 31 July 1895) found it "hard to believe that the Judge had not the gift of humour", and distinguished humour from ridicule. Charles Bright (*The Cosmos Magazine*, 31 May 1895, 461 at 464) wrote: "It has often been asserted that Mr Higinbotham was lacking in all sense of humour. I scarcely think that this is a just characterisation. That his faculty of humour was held in strict restraint, like every other impulse of his comprehensive nature, is doubtless true".
25. Higinbotham Interview (1975).
26. C.O. 309/130, f. 295.
27. At f. 293a.
28. At f. 294a.
29. Holland to Loch, 21 November 1886, C.O. 309/130, f. 312.
30. 28 February 1887, C.O. 309/131, f. 730. This is the printed text of the letter to which Loch added marginalia in manuscript. For convenience of reference the numbered pages of that text are cited here. The exchange of correspondence was published, at Higinbotham's instigation, in the *Argus*, 16 February 1889, 5-6 (copied at C.O. 309/134, from f. 142) and the *Age*, 16 February 1889, 10. Some of the material appeared in the *Australasian*, 23 February 1889, 423-424. Morris, at 209, published Higinbotham's letter of 28 February 1887 because, so he said, at 201, "no copy of the number of the newspaper in which it was printed can now be procured".
31. Printed text at 2.
32. *Id.*, at 1-2.
33. They had been changed as recently as 1879, though not in the way Higinbotham desired – *see* Ch. 6, text to n. 88.
34. Printed text at 5.

35. *Id.*, at 8.
36. *Ibid.*
37. Printed text at 11. This comment was directed particularly at the British Government's failure to support Australian proposals for annexation of some Pacific islands – *see* further, Ch. 11, text following n. 77.
38. Printed text at 8. *Note* also, Gavan McCormack, "Victorian Governors and Responsible Government" (M.A. thesis, University of Melbourne 1962), 190.
39. Advice of 31 January 1887, C.O. 309/131 at f. 727. Wrixon's view reflected that of the Colonial Office, Henry L. Hall, *The Colonial Office – A History* (London 1937), 111-112.
40. Advice of 31 January 1887, *loc. cit.* n. 39.
41. He thought the same of cl. 7 (Governor entitled to act contrary to advice of Executive Council); and cl. 6 (Governor entitled at his discretion not to consult Executive Council) as being "alien to the Constitution".
42. Serle, *op. cit.* n. 5, 304, note *.
43. Higinbotham to Knutsford, 26 May 1888, published in *Argus*, 16 February 1889, 5.
44. *Ibid.*
45. Henry L. Hall, *Australia and England* (London 1934), correctly concluded that "to speak of sinister and clandestine policy as late as 1888 (or indeed at any period) was absurd".
46. Minutes to Loch to Holland, (confidential) 4 August 1887, C.O. 309/131, f. 230 at f. 231a.
47. At f. 231.
48. Knutsford to Higinbotham, 12 July 1888, published in *Argus*, 16 February 1889, 5.
49. Below, text following n. 94.
50. Higinbotham to Knutsford, 20 August 1888, published in *Argus*, 16 February 1889, 5.
51. 16 February 1889, 6; and 18 February 1889, 4. The *Australasian*, 23 February 1889, 405, echoed the criticism, writing, "the Chief Justice is still engaged in combating some imaginary grievance that was never really proved to exist … [The] Queen's Instructions, to which [he] objects, are virtually obsolete. Were they to be interpreted theoretically and literally, they would be unworkable. But … no attempt is made to work them, and … no friction has been caused by them". Higinbotham, however, remained unrepentant, writing to Shiels (William Shiels Papers, La Trobe Library, Melbourne, MS 8730, Box 945/26), 16 December 1889, renewing his condemnation of Downing Street's "illegal intervention in our domestic affairs" and proposing virtual rebellion – "Open resistance to such claims by the Imperial Government would be, in my opinion, the only legitimate mode of performing an imperative duty devolving in such a case upon the Colonial Legislature & Her Majesty's Colonial Government".
52. 18 February 1889, 4.
53. 18 February 1889, 4; 19 February 1889, 4.
54. Minute paper, C.O. 309/134 at ff. 139, 136 respectively.
55. *Id.*, at f. 139.
56. Loch to Holland, 29 September 1887 and enclosure, C.O. 309/131, f. 340. *Note* the earlier cases of Morgan and Morrell, Ch. 8, text following nn. 4, 15.

57. Wrixon to Higinbotham, 15 September 1887, Crown Law Department Papers, P.R.O. 87/5108.
58. Higinbotham to Wrixon, 17 September 1887, Crown Law Department Papers, P.R.O. 87/5107A.
59. *Ibid.*
60. *Ibid.*
61. *Ibid.*
62. Draft, Wrixon to Higinbotham, undated, Crown Law Department Papers, P.R.O. 87/5108.
63. Memorandum, Loch to Wrixon, "September 1887", *ibid.*
64. *Ibid.*
65. 20 September 1887, Crown Law Department Papers, P.R.O. 87/4894.
66. *Ibid.* Mepham's sentence was commuted to life imprisonment on a ministerial recommendation of 28 September 1887: enclosure in Loch to Holland, 29 September 1887, C.O. 309/131, f. 340 at f. 341.
67. Hall, *op. et loc. cit.* n. 45.
68. C.O. 234/49, f. 147. B.H. McPherson, *The Supreme Court of Queensland* (Sydney 1989), 119 and sources there cited. For McIlwraith, (1974) 5 *A.D.B.* 161.
69. McIlwraith to Musgrave, 9 August 1888, C.O. 234/49 at ff. 163, 163a.
70. (1974) 5 *A.D.B.* 324.
71. C.O. 234/49, f. 147 at f. 147a. *Note* the view of H.V. Evatt, *The Royal Prerogative* (Sydney 1987), 119, that early colonial administrations shirked responsibility on the exercise of the prerogative of pardon, preferring to leave the Governor to be answerable for what was done or not done.
72. C.O. 234/49, at f. 152; and *note id.,* at ff. 197-238a.
73. The circumstances are reviewed in detail in A.B. Keith, *Responsible Government in the Dominions* (Vol. 3, 1st edn, Oxford 1912), 1407-1411.
74. Minutes to C.O. 209/251, f. 42 at f. 42a.
75. Keith, *op. cit.* n. 73 (Vol. 1, 2nd edn, Oxford 1928), 110-113; A.B. Keith, *The Sovereignty of the British Dominions* (London 1929), 48-49.
76. *The Compact Edition of the Dictionary of National Biography* (Oxford 1975), 2520. On one view his methods had not been gentle: he became "a thorn in the side of the Colonial Office", Hall, *op. cit.* n. 39, 223.
77. *Op. cit.* n. 74, at f. 43a.
78. Bailey, at 401.
79. *Op. cit.* n. 74, at f. 44a.
80. John Quick and R.R. Garran, *The Annotated Constitution of the Australian Commonwealth* (Sydney 1901), 398. Even then, they were purposely vague in some respects, R.D. Lumb, *The Constitutions of the Australian States* (2nd edn St Lucia 1963), 77.
81. D.H. Rankin, "George Higinbotham" (1956) 27 *Victorian Historical Magazine*, 41 at 54. Vance Palmer, *National Portraits* (3rd edn Melbourne 1960), 88.
82. (1972) 4 *A.D.B.* at 394.
83. Minute to C.O. 209/251, f. 42.
84. *See* n. 11 above. There was some suggestion that he once attended a conference at Albury. As to his Tasmanian visit, *Australasian*, 3 January 1874, 20.
85. R.B. Pugh, *The Records of the Colonial and Dominions Offices* (London 1964), 8.

86. Minute to C.O. 309/120, f. 185 at f. 185a. The ensuing letter, of 10 November 1879, was slightly differently worded, *id.*, f. 194 at f. 196.

87. Loch to Stanhope, 30 September 1886, C.O. 309/130, f. 296 at f. 298a.

88. At f. 299a.

89. At f. 293.

90. "Questions Put to The Attorney-General of Victoria", Crown Law Department Papers, P.R.O. 87/5108.

91. *Ibid.*

92. Stephen to Loch, 7 February 1887, *ibid.*

93. Loch to Higinbotham, 8 March 1888, C.O. 309/132, f. 169 at f. 169a. Higinbotham caused this and the ensuing exchange of letters to be published in the *Argus*, 16 February 1889, 5-6.

94. Higinbotham to Loch, 12 March 1888, C.O. 309/132, f. 173 at f. 177. The Colonial Office remarked in the minutes (at f. 165) on Higinbotham's "holding such peculiar views of his duty to the Crown".

95. Knutsford to Loch, 30 April 1888 (confidential), C.O. 309/133, f. 413; McCaughey, 260.

96. Loch to Knutsford, 26 October 1888 (secret), C.O. 309/132, f. 519 at ff. 521a, 522a.

97. Report of Richard Webster and Edward Clarke, 26 January 1888, C.O. 309/133, f. 376.

98. Knutsford to Loch, 23 July 1888, published *Argus*, 16 February 1889, 5: and that was in spite of Herbert's opinion (C.O. 309/132 at f. 518) that Higinbotham had disqualified himself by declaring "his inability to accept the conditions under which the appointment is held".

99. Knutsford to Loch, 23 July 1888 (confidential), C.O. 309/133, f. 447.

100. Higinbotham to Loch, 10 November 1888, published *Argus*, 16 February 1889, 6.

101. Knutsford to Loch, 14 December 1888 and Loch to Higinbotham, 13 December 1888, published *Argus, ibid.*

102. Higinbotham to Loch, *ibid.*

103. The catalyst of the *Colonial Laws Validity Act* 1865 (Imp.), he having detected "illegality" in most of South Australia's statutes – (1969) 3 *A.D.B.* 194; R.M. Hague, *History of the Law in South Australia 1837-1867* (Adelaide 2005, from a 1936 manuscript), Vol. 1, Ch. 5.

104. Archibald Michie, Q.C., in the *Argus*, 22 February 1889, 5.

105. *Id.*, 16 February 1889, 5-6.

106. Minute paper, C.O. 309/134, f. 213 at f. 215a. A dormant commission naming the President of the Legislative Council was enclosed with despatch Knutsford to Loch, 23 July 1888, C.O. 309/133, f. 448. Knutsford had previously confided to the minutes his doubts "whether the C.J. with his peculiar views could be allowed to administer the Govt", C.O. 309/133, f. 369 at f. 373a.

107. "Our Governors and the Home Office" (1889-1890) 2 *The Centennial Magazine*, 946. "Constitutionalist", the author of *Responsible Government: What is it?* (Sydney 1872), was identified by the Dixson Library, Sydney, as Sir Henry Parkes – John Alexander Ferguson, *Bibliography of Australia* (Vol. V Canberra 1977), 693, §8603.

108. *The Centennial Magazine, id.*, at 946-947, 950.

109. *Argus*, 22 February 1889, 5. Challenged with the same point in Parliament in 1875, Higinbotham merely replied, "There are many things I ought to have done, and there are many things which I ought not to have done that I have done" (1875) XXI *V.P.D.* 508.

110. *Argus*, *ibid.*
111. *The King and His Dominion Governors* (2nd edn Melbourne 1967), 125.
112. *Op. cit.* n. 97, at f. 392.
113. Bailey, 397.
114. Serle, *op. cit.* n. 5, 304.
115. Minute paper to C.O. 309/133, f. 420.
116. Higinbotham to Crisp (private), 12 January 1892, Christopher Crisp Papers (N.L. MS743), 354 at 355, italics added: published posthumously in *Bacchus Marsh Express*, 7 January 1893, 2.

Chapter 11

1. Lord Scarman, *Law Reform – The New Pattern* (London 1968), 20.
2. (1864) X *V.H.* 91.
3. Moreover, "amendment was patched on to amendment until even professional persons were puzzled to say what was the law", Donald Mackinnon in Morris, 289.
4. (1862) IX *V.H.* 44; (1864) X *V.H.* 18; *Argus*, 2 December 1864, 6.
5. "He thought it was a work within the compass of the labour of a few minds to effect the reduction of this body of law to something like orderly arrangement" (1864) X *V.H.* 20.
6. *Ibid.*, and at 89. J.D. Wood, *id.*, at 88, thought "the arrangement … susceptible of great improvement".
7. *Argus*, 2 December 1864, 6.
8. (1914) 1 *V. & P. (L.A.)*, 399.
9. (1864) XI *V.H.* 46. As Higinbotham conceded (1864) X *V.H.* 89, "He did not flatter himself that [the Bills] were free from errors; and it was impossible that a series of bills dealing as they did, with the whole statute law could be free from error".
10. *Argus*, 2 December 1864, 6.
11. (1864) XI *V.H.* 27.
12. (1864) X *V.H.* 20.
13. *Id.*, 19.
14. For the methods employed to see the 1860s work to completion, and thereafter, Mackinnon in Morris, 290-292.
15. Chapter 4, text following n. 18.
16. (1865) XI *V.H.* 797-798.
17. *Argus*, 12 June 1890, 9.
18. (1864) X *V.H.* 20. Professor Hearn protested, in 1879, that Higinbotham's consolidation was "a work of which the magnitude and the success have never been properly appreciated" (1879) 4 *Melbourne Review*, 237.
19. For the circumstances, Mackinnon in Morris, 293; J.A. Gurner, *Life's Panorama* (Melbourne 1930), 266.
20. (1986) 10 *A.D.B.* at 313; his account of the undertaking appears in Morris, Ch. XXVII.
21. *Argus*, 2 January 1893, 6.
22. *Id.*, 12 June 1890, 9; and *ibid.*, 6, "The Consolidation of the Law".
23. *Id.*, 24 October 1890, 9.
24. *Age*, 24 October 1890, 7.
25. Morris, 294.
26. *Id.*, Ch. XXVIII, and at 299.

27. (1888) 1 *V. & P. (L.A.)*, paper D5, 13.
28. Quoted, Morris, 301.
29. Leighton Journal, 7.
30. *Australasian*, 11 March 1871, 308.
31. To Richard Richardson, 6 April 1885, quoted, Morris, 204 at 207, 208.
32. Manuscript notes for speech (January 1893), Clark Papers, Morris Miller Library, University of Tasmania, Hobart.
33. 8 March 1891, Clark Papers, *ibid*.
34. *Ibid*.
35. *Ibid*.
36. Higinbotham to Deakin, 4 April 1891, Deakin Papers (N.L. MS 1540/11/7-8). His one concession was that, "the title, 'Commonwealth', was at first startling but it improves as it becomes familiar, and I now like it".
37. Joel, II, 28.
38. Alfred Deakin (ed. Herbert Brookes), *The Federal Story* (Melbourne 1944), 8.
39. 7 January 1893, 2.
40. Morris, 232.
41. (1864) X *V.H.* 293. Those sentiments were not unique to him – *note*, for example, Gwyneth M. Dow, "Political Factions and Education in Victoria, 1857-8" (1971) 6 *Journal of Religious History*, 246 at 249-250.
42. In Morris, 155-156.
43. *Id*., 145.
44. Clauses 3, 5.
45. Clauses 16, 14 and 10 respectively.
46. (1972) 4 *A.D.B.* at 391.
47. Dow, 109.
48. Higinbotham to Parkes, 17 June 1867, Letters From Public Men of Australia (M.L. A68), 574. He did not abandon his views, urging upon the Legislative Assembly in 1869 that "the only course left for improving upon the present system was to establish a system of secular education solely, and free from the element of religious instruction" – *Age*, 2 September 1869, 2. He later strove to advance purely secular education in Brighton, *id*., 15 January 1870, 2.
49. Quoted, Dow, 134.
50. *Australasian*, 11 March 1871, 308.
51. Dow, 10; A. de Q. Robin, *Charles Perry Bishop of Melbourne* (Nedlands 1967), 107-111, 135.
52. Morris, 322.
53. *Ibid*., and *cf* Dow, 7.
54. (1976) 6 *A.D.B.* 208.
55. Published as a pamphlet (Melbourne 1883) from the transcript in the *Argus*, 2 August 1883, 9-10.
56. Pamphlet, *id*., 3.
57. *Id*., 4-5.
58. *Id*., 11.
59. *Id*., 12-13, 16.
60. *Id*., 18.
61. *Id*., 19.
62. *Ibid*.
63. *Id*., 20, 21, 24.

64. Sir Robert Garran, *Prosper the Commonwealth* (Sydney 1958), 51. The *Australasian*, 7 January 1893, 29, pointed out that the attitude of the church proved to demonstration the truth of Higinbotham's submissions: had the lecture been delivered in, say, the Town Hall, it would have been "criticised and forgotten". It also claimed that those submissions were unoriginal – "there was nothing that he said that had not been said and written by scores of magazine writers and scientific speakers".

65. *Address Delivered in Connection with the Opening of the New Unitarian Church* (Melbourne 1887), 8. The historian Henry Gyles Turner was chairman.

66. *Id.*, 10.

67. *Mr Justice Higinbotham on the Orthodox Faith* (Melbourne 1887), 23.

68. *Ibid.*

69. Morris described the contributor as "one who knew him well" (at 324) and quoted much of *The Inquirer's* article. As the journal attributed its information to a "relative" of Higinbotham, it is unlikely that the source was anyone but Morris himself.

70. 22 April 1893.

71. (1972) 4 *A.D.B.* at 396.

72. (1866) 3 W.W. & a'B. (L.) 133.

73. At 135, 136.

74. (1868) VI *V.P.D.* 623, 657, 875-878.

75. Higinbotham to Peck, n.d., published *id.*, at 875.

76. *Argus*, 10 September 1868, 4.

77. The more so, as J. A. Froude, *Oceana* (London 1886 edn), 137, recorded that "the language which I heard and read during the New Guinea excitement" convinced him that Victorians were "impulsive, susceptible and easily offended".

78. 13 June 1859, 4.

79. *Op. cit.* n. 31, 204, 205.

80. Roger C. Thompson, *Australian Imperialism in the Pacific* (Melbourne 1980), 71. And *note* Geoffrey Serle, *The Rush to be Rich* (Melbourne 1974 edn), 183-184.

81. *Op. cit.* n. 31, 205-206.

82. C.O. 309/131, f. 370, published *Argus*, 16 February 1889, 5-6.

83. *Op. cit.* n. 31, 209.

84. 8 September 1857,

85. *See* Ch. 7, text following n. 97 and Ch. 8, text following notes 145 and 147.

86. *Note* Dow, 20; and the quotation from Carnarvon's Diary, above, Ch. 10, n. 11.

87. 11 September 1891, La Trobe Library, Melbourne, Box 136/3, item H17572.

88. Quoted (1972) 4 *A.D.B.* at 396.

89. Higinbotham to C. H. Pearson, 20 June 1882, Pearson Papers, La Trobe Library, Melbourne, MS 7371, Box 440/1a.

90. (1974) 5 *A.D.B.* at 373.

91. (1972) 4 *A.D.B.* 93.

92. The letter was published in the *Argus*, 2 January 1893, 6.

93. *Bulletin* (Sydney), 11 October 1890, 11.

94. 29 November 1890, 1037.

95. "Price Warung" (William Astley), *Bulletin* (Sydney), 7 January 1893, 9.
96. Undated cutting, Higinbotham Papers: reiterated even more strenuously in *Argus*, 3 October 1890, 4-5; 4 October 1890, 7; 6 October 1890, 4-5; 7 October 1890, 9; and *note* letter by J. Dennistoun Wood, *id.*, 9 October 1890, 10.
97. 11 October 1890, 7.
98. Commencing 31 August 1899, 2.
99. 14 September 1899, 2. *See* also Ch. 4, text to n. 25.
100. Quoted, *Tocsin*, 5 October 1899, 7, from (1869) VII *V.P.D.* 784-785.
101. *Age*, 7 February 1893, 6; 15 April 1893, 10.
102. Unidentified press cutting, April 1893, Higinbotham Papers.
103. Dow, 44, n. 6; *Age*, 17 September 1990, 5; Sir Ninian Stephen, "George Higinbotham", Daniel Mannix Memorial Lecture, University of Melbourne, 13 September 1983, N.L. MS 7738, 37-38. Dr Serle observed (*op. cit.* n. 80, 32) that Higinbotham "stood out … such was his reputation as a democrat, as the idol of the trade union movement".
104. *Illustrated Australian News*, 1 February 1893, 10; *Talbot Leader*, 4 January 1893, 2. As to payment of Members of Parliament, *note* (1865) XI *V.H.* 374-375, (1867) IV *V.P.D.* 1730.
105. *Weekly Times* (Melbourne), 7 January 1893, 22; *Ballarat Star*, 3 January 1893, 2; *Bacchus Marsh Express*, 7 January 1893, 2.
106. *Weekly Times* (Melbourne), 7 January 1893, 22; J. L. Forde, *The Story of the Bar of Victoria* (Melbourne n.d.), 189.
107. *Argus*, 2 January 1893, 5; Morris, 308.
108. 3 January 1893, 4.
109. *Illustrated Australian News*, 1 February 1893, 10; *Bendigo Evening News*, 3 January 1893, 2.
110. On one account, not corroborated in the contemporary press, the trade unionist and long standing friend Benjamin Douglass also attended – (1972) 4 *A.D.B.* 93
111. Unidentified press cuttings, Higinbotham Papers; *Illustrated Australian News*, 1 February 1893, 10. The *Herald* (Melbourne), 5 January 1893, 4, expressed outrage that Higinbotham's wishes had not been respected.
112. The full text of the will was published in the *Australasian*, 4 February 1893, 216. There was no provision for a supposedly lunatic brother (Stuart Macintyre, *A Colonial Liberalism* (Oxford 1991), 221), though gossip about such a relative had long circulated, Leighton Journal, 5.
113. Unidentified press cutting, Higinbotham Papers.
114 *Argus*, 22 December 1910, 7.
115. For example, *Maffra Spectator*, 5 January 1893, 3; *Hamilton Spectator*, 3 January 1893, 3; *Inglewood Advertiser*, 3 January 1893, 3.
116. 2 January 1893, 5-6.
117. *Id.*, 4.
118. *Ibid*.
119. 2 January 1893, 4; *id.*, 2 January 1893, 5-6; and *note* editorial, 3 January 1893, 4.
120. 2 January 1893, 2.
121. 7 January 1893, 20.
122. 7 January 1893, 21.
123. 1 February 1893, 10.
124. 14 January 1893, 87.
125. 7 January 1893, 16.

126. 2 January 1893, 4.
127. 7 January 1893, 2.
128. 3 January 1893, 2.
129. 6 January 1893, 3.
130. 5 January 1893, 3.
131. 2 January 1893, 2.
132. *South Australian Register*, 2 January 1893, 4.
133. 21 January 1893, 134. Sydney's *Law Chronicle*, 1 January 1893, 125, reviewed his legal career. William Astley was infuriated by the terse Sydney obituaries – "they revealed nothing so much as the provincialised character of our journalism", 2 January 1893, William Astley Papers, Dixson Library, State Library of New South Wales, MS Q513, 137.
134. 2 January 1893, 4.
135. 2 January 1893, 5.
136. 2 January 1893, 5.
137. *Argus*, 9 January 1893, 5; 10 January 1893, 5. Williams' churlish letter of 7 January 1893 to the *Argus* is reproduced in Dean, 153-154.
138. Unidentified press cutting, Higinbotham Papers.
139. *Argus*, 5 January 1893, 6.
140. *Id.*, 11 January 1893, 9.
141. *Ibid.*
142. *Mercury* (Hobart), 28 July 1893, 3.
143. *Op. et loc. cit.* n. 32.
144. 27 June 1867, 201.
145. 15 August 1867, 52-53.
146. 10 August 1865, 53. The "St Georgey" cartoon is reproduced in this book.
147. Paul Finn, *Law and Government in Colonial Australia* (Melbourne 1987), 84. A somewhat similar approach, but in another context, was H.G. Turner's depiction of Higinbotham as "certainly the most striking figure in Victorian politics", leaving open the question whether "striking" was a good or a bad quality of conspicuousness – Turner, 139.
148. *Op. et loc. cit.* n. 65.
149. *Argus*, 11 January 1893, 9.

Index

a'Beckett, Sir Thomas (J,), 162, 165, 175, 176, 181-182, 183, 186, 193-194, 197
a'Beckett, Sir William (C.J.), 15, 16, 18, 60, 121, 152, 240
Acts

Victoria

Administration of Justice Act 1885, 170
Ammunition Factory Act 1889, 171-172
Audit Act, 92
Boroughs Statute 1869, 141-142, 177
Chinese Act 1881, 192, 197
Chinese Immigrants' Statute, 1865, 192
Common Law Practice Statute 1864, 169
Common Schools Act 1862, 235
Constitution Act 1855, 77, 78, 92, 93, 110, 112, 122, 147, 194, 195, 196, 198, 225, 259
Conveyancers Act 1863, 56
County Court Statute 1869, 137
County Court Act 1890, 172
Crimes Act 1890, 173
Crown Remedies & Liabilities Act 1865, 79, 83, 89, 92, 170
Electoral Act 1863, 70
Employers' Liability Act 1886, 188
Explosives Act 1890, 171
Health Amendment Act (No. 310), 136
Imprisonment for Debt Act (No. 284), 173-174
Judicature Act 1883, 173
Land Act 1862, 54-55, 71, 72-73, 75, 76
Land Act Amendment Act, 229
Lands Compensation Statute 1869, 137
Local Government Act 1874, 177, 178, 179, 180, 182, 229
Married Women's Property Act 1870, 135
Matrimonial Causes Act 1864, 44
Municipalities Act, 229
Passengers, Harbours & Navigation Act 1865, 147-149
Police Offences Act 1865, 242
Police Offences Act 1890, 174
Post Office Act 1883, 151
Real Property Act 1862, 56, 60
Road Act 1852, 39
Shires Statute 1869, 177
Stamp Duties Act 1879, 138, 175-176
"Statute of Frauds", 132
Supreme Court (Administration) Act 1852, 61, 169

England, Imperial and U.K.
Australian Courts Act 1828, 140
British North America Act 1867, 117
County Courts Act 1850, 137
Employers' Liability Act 1880, 139
Foreign Enlistment Act 1819, 68
Merchant Shipping Act 1854, 148, 149
Statute of Westminster 1931, 19, 150
Sunday Observance Act 1780, 140
Territorial Waters Jurisdiction Act 1878, 150
Adamson, Travers, 227
Afghan, The, 192-197
Aisbett v. *City of Camberwell* (1933), 184
Alcock v. *Fergie* (1867) 91-92
Alfred, Duke of Edinburgh, 90
Anderson v. *Robertson* (1882), 144-145
Ashley, A.E.M., 155
Astley, William, 20, 115, 257
Atkins v. *Walsh* (1885), 146
Australian Club (Melbourne), 206
Bailey v. *Port Melbourne Corporation* (1888), 179-180
Bailey, Prof. (Sir) Kenneth, 69, 113, 116
Ballarat, 11, 12, 68, 174-175, 189
Bar, Victorian, 37-38, 41-42, 60
Barkly, Governor Sir Henry, 52-53, 112
Barry, Sir Redmond (J.), 15, 25, 60, 91, 121, 122, 130, 148, 152, 242
Becke v. *Smith* (1836), 172
Belmore, Earl of, 117
Bergin v. *Cohen* (1866), 242
Berry, (Sir) Graham, 98-99, 122, 123, 127
Billing, R. A., 91
"Blackbirding", 244
Blair, David, 236
Blake, Edward, 111, 117, 118-119, 120, 218
Blanchard, William, 68
Boothby, Benjamin (J.), 223
Box, J. B., 140, 160-161
Boyne, Battle of, 1-2
Bramston, (Sir) John, 127, 208, 213
Bramwell, Baron G.W.W. (L.J.), 132
Brett v. *Slater* (1888), 179, 183
Brighton, 13, 14, 46, 47, 55, 72, 83, 90, 97, 127, 238, 249
    Free Library, 48
    Mechanics' Institute, 48
    Volunteer Rifle Corps, 48
Briseis, The, 7, 11
Britannia, The, 250
Brodribb, W. A., 47, 48

Brougham, Catherine, 5-6
Brougham, Lord, 22
Brown v. *Board of Land & Works* (1885), 138, 143, 144
Brown, Capt. J. R., 7
Buckingham, Third Duke, 90, 93, 101
Bunny, B. F., 18
Burtt, J. G., 47
Cairns, Sir Hugh (L.C.), 101
Callaghan, Thomas, 227
Callan, Dr, 50
Cameron v. *Kyte* (1835), 109
Campbell v. *Kerr* (1886), 140
Canada, constitutional position, 117, 118, 119, 207, 211, 217-218
Canterbury, Viscount – *see* Manners-Sutton
"Canvas Town", 11
Cape Colony, 28, 112, 223
Cardwell, (Viscount) Edward, 81-82, 86, 87, 88, 233
Carey, Brig-General G. J., 87
Carnarvon, Fourth Earl, 88, 101, 112, 114, 118, 119, 120, 204
Carslake v. *Caulfield Shire Council* (1891), 182-183, 184
Cary, Henry, 227
Casey, J. J., 169
Centennial International Exhibition (Melbourne 1888), 205-206
"Chancery Lane" (Melbourne), 36
Chapman, H. S., 17, 18, 27, 57
China, Emperor of, 200
Chitty, Joseph, 7
Clark, A. I., 233, 256
Clarke, W. J., 48
Cockburn, Sir Alexander (L.C.J.), 149, 161
Collins v. *Munro* (1887), 188
Colonial Office – *see* Higinbotham, George
Conveyancers, 56
Cope, Edward, 64
Cope, T. S., 147
Coriolanus, 46, 48
Cowper, (Sir) Charles, 23
Crisp, Christopher, 226, 234, 253, 257
Crown, prerogatives of, 53, 109-111, 117-118, 153-155, 203, 209, 210, 214-217
Cussen, (Sir) Leo (J.), 159, 228
Dakin, T. E., 160-161
Daly, In re (1889), 163
Daly, A.D.J., 163-164
Darley, (Sir) Frederick (C.J.), 3-4, 192-193, 202
Darley, Revd J. R., 3-4
Darling, Governor Sir Charles, 58, 60-61, 67-70, 71, 77-78, 79-83, 85-86, 88, 94, 100-101, 106, 113, 225

Darling, Elizabeth (Lady), proposed gratuity to, 87-91, 94
Darling, Sir Ralph, 79
Davey, Sir Horace, 200
Davidson v. *Wright* (1887), 187-188
Davies v. *Herbert* (1885), 138
"Deadlock", parliamentary, 78-82, 84-85, 88, 89, 97, 122
Deakin, Alfred, 44, 45, 90, 128, 129, 156, 158, 200, 204, 219, 233, 234, 246, 257
Dean, Sir Arthur (J.), 13
Denison, Sir William, 23
Derby, Fifteenth Earl, 155
Dickens, Charles, 5
Dill, George, 65
Disraeli, Benjamin, 6
Dixon, (Sir) Owen (C.J.), 184
Dobbin, James and Jane, 2
Dodds v. *Berwick Corporation* (1885), 146
Donaldson, (Sir) Stuart, 23
Douglass, Benjamin, 247
Dow, G. M., 235
Duffy, (Sir) Charles Gavan, 4, 26, 27, 49-50, 71
Duffy, (Sir) Frank Gavan (C.J.), 91, 129, 158, 159
East Bourke Boroughs, 98
Ebden, C. H., 46
Ebsworth, In re; ex parte Tompsitt (1891), 164-165
Ebsworth, A. M., 164
Education, Royal Commission on, 57, 235-238
   see also Higinbotham, George
Eggleston, (Sir) Frederick (J.), 116
Ellis v. *Bourke* (1889), 166
Emerald Hill, 11, 13, 46, 122
Erle, Sir William (C.J.), 132
Evans, Dr G. S., 53
Evatt, Dr H. V. (J.), 44, 110-111, 184, 225
Federation (Australian), 97, 217, 218, 230, 232-235, 253-254
Fellows, T. H. (J.), 16, 17, 41, 46, 57, 80, 85, 89, 91, 94, 121, 127
Fergusson v. *United Steamship Co.* (1884), 141-142
Ferrier v. *Owen* (1856), 14-15
Fiji, 244
Fink, Theodore, 38, 40
Fitzgerald, J. L. *see* Foster
Fitzroy Local Board of Health v. *Howell* (1881), 136-137
Fleming v. *Essendon Borough* (1890), 166
Forbes, Sir Francis (C.J.), 259
Forde, J. L., 2-3, 64, 127
Foster, J.L.F.V., 10, 26, 116, 250
Francis, J. G., 98, 121, 122, 123, 238
Free Trade – *see* Protection and Free Trade

Free Trade Association, 76, 84
Gardiner, Frank, 118
Garran, Dr Andrew, 240
George, Hugh, 65-67
Gillies, Duncan, 44, 156, 200, 204, 231
Gladstone, W. E., 6
Glass, Hugh, 95-97
Goe, Archbishop F. F., 8
Goldfields, Victorian, 10-12, 191
Goold, Bishop J. A., 236
Gosman, Revd Alexander, 241
Governor, constitutional position of Victorian, 53, 94, 98, 101, 102, 108-111, 112, 153, 193, 198, 199, 203, 209, 215, 217, 219, 220-221, 222, 224, 225
    instructions to, claimed illegality of, 53, 94-95, 102, 111, 112-113, 124, 153-154, 156-157, 207, 208, 209, 211-212, 215, 218-219, 222, 225, 226
Grant, J. M., 75
Gray, M. W., 20
Greeves, A.F.A., 26
Grey, Third Earl, 27
Griffith, C. J., 25
Griffith, Sir Samuel (C.J.), 233, 259
Gurner, J. A., 58
Haines, W. C., 29
Hanson, Sir Richard (C.J.), 259
Harding v. *Board of Land & Works* (1882), 137
Hare, Thomas, 52
Harnett v. *Wilson* (1856), 18
Harris, W. G., 91
Hartle v. *Campbell* (1886), 151
Heales, Richard, 47, 52, 71, 235
Hearn, Prof. W. E., 91, 228-229, 231-232
Helms v. *Munro & Co. Ltd* (1890), 189-190
Herbert, Sir Robert, 155, 202, 207-208, 211, 213-214, 217, 218, 219
Hickling v. *Todd* (1889), 175-176
Higgins, H. B. (J.), 44-45, 159
Higinbotham, derivation of name, 1-2
Higinbotham, Andrew, 2
Higinbotham, Edward (son of George), 1, 2, 36
Higinbotham, George
    ancestry, parentage and birth, 1, 2, 3, 4
    schooling, 3-4
    university education, 4-6
    physical features, 128-129, 158
    English journalist and law reporter, 6, 11
    call to English Bar, 7
    migration to Victoria, 7, 10-11

Higinbotham, George (*cont*)
  marriage, homes and family, 6, 11, 12, 18, 35-36, 206, 207, 249
  charitable gifts, 8, 19, 48, 206-207, 247-248
  recreations, 6, 41, 48
  Argus (Melbourne), editor of, 13, 18-34, 46, 244
  radical tendencies, 3, 20, 22, 46, 47, 106, 113, 203, 245, 247, 248
  health, 36, 230, 249
  death and burial, 249-250
  will and bequests, 250
  obituaries and eulogies, 250-256
  private papers destroyed, 7-9
  statue of, 248
  his "disciples", 43-45
  character assessed, 1, 3, 12, 19, 33, 45, 48, 57, 58, 64, 86, 93, 106,
      115-116, 128, 129, 130, 191, 201, 210, 213, 218-219, 220, 237, 240,
      250-259
  his views on –
      "society", 12-13, 43, 73
      its "wealthy lower orders", 73
      party government, 21, 22-28, 29, 31, 32, 47, 77, 84
      coalition government, 52
      republican government, 106-107
      electoral equality, 29-33, 52, 99
      parliamentary privileges and procedure, 6, 25, 49-52, 53, 58-59,
          64-67, 95-97
      parliamentary select committees, 50
      payment of Members of Parliament, 51
      British monarchy, 41, 94, 106, 202
      Colonial Office "interference", 21, 57, 69, 86-87, 91, 93, 94-95,
          97, 98, 100-120, 123, 154, 191, 199, 200, 201, 202, 209, 211-212,
          220, 233, 243, 244-245, 251
      colonial magistracy, 39, 59,
      women's status, 12-13, 39, 44, 59, 252
      religion, 1, 4, 236, 237, 238-241
      education, 3, 47, 55, 57, 97, 235-238
      immigration, 47, 55
      squatters and the land laws, 47, 54-55, 57, 71, 72, 73-74, 76, 97
      labour organizations, 246-248
      gambling and lotteries, 241-243
      and see Crown, prerogatives of; Federation; Governor, consti-
          tutional position; Statute law consolidation
  Political career, 1, 19, 21, 45-48, 49-99
  Attorney-General, 37, 40, 41-42, 56-95, 106, 125, 227-229, 236, 242-
      243, 257-258
  Judges "officers in his Department", 60-64, 122, 155, 215, 224
  Legislative Council, contests with, 56, 61-62, 70-74, 75-91, 113, 116,
      259
  Supply, government without, 76, 79-82, 84-86

"Resolutions" of 1869, 102-120, 215
Vice-President, Board of Land & Works, 42, 95
self-confidence in own opinions, 55, 57, 58, 72, 93
Legal career
Victorian Bar, admission to and practice at, 12, 13-18, 35, 42-43, 48
appointment as Solicitor-General canvassed, 18
Melbourne Bar chambers, 36-37
declined silk, 41, 203
demeanour of, as counsel, 37, 45
specialized at common law, 37, 38
fees, modesty of, 40-41, 206
As Puisne Judge, 121-151
appointed and took seat, 126, 127
stipulated conditions for own appointment, 123-124, 125, 126, 153, 214
political views retained, 125, 154
judicial methodology, 130-134, 137-138, 142-143, 147
prolixity in judgement, 128-129, 130
prerogative of mercy, attitude to, 124, 153-154
As Chief Justice, 3, 100, 115, 119, 128, 131, 141, 152-259
precedence, 205-206
Lieut-Governor, not appointed as, 157, 206, 212, 220-222, 224
political position, 159, 210-211, 213, 219-220, 226, 243-248
knighthood declined, 158, 202-203, 251
judicial traditions maintained, 203-204, 205-206
pragmatic views, adoption of, 158-159
salary, disposal of, 206-207
thanked by Parliament, 231-232
see also Centennial International Exhibition; Statute law consolidation
Higinbotham, Henry (grandfather of George), 2
Higinbotham, Henry (father of George), 2-3, 7
Higinbotham, Henry (brother of George), 7
Higinbotham, Jane (sister of George), 250
Higinbotham, Margaret (wife of George), 12-13, 35, 36, 238, 250
Higinbotham, Quartermaster Thomas, 1, 2
Higinbotham, Sarah (mother of George), 3
Higinbotham, Thomas (brother of George), 1, 3, 13, 35, 121
Hill v. *Bigge* (1841), 109
Hitchins v. *Borough of Port Melbourne* (1888: 1889), 180-182
Hodges, (Sir) Henry (J.), 37, 160, 167, 172, 182-183, 255
Holland, Sir Henry, 203, 208, 210, 211-213, 218, 222, 224, 245
Holroyd, (Sir) Edward (J.), 121, 129, 130, 135, 145, 147, 151, 162-163, 167, 168, 179, 180, 181, 182, 185, 186-187, 193-195, 196
Hood, Sir Joseph (J.), 165, 183
Hooper, Dr Dunbar, 249
Hopetoun, Earl of (Governor), 223-224

Interpretation, of statutes and instruments, 134-141, 171-176
    legislative history, resort to, 135-138, 183, 194, 195-196
Ireland, R. D., 17, 51, 56, 57, 67, 91, 228
Isaacs, (Sir) Isaac (J.), 57, 255
James II, King of England, 2
Jervois, Sir William, 119
Keith, Prof. A. B., 110, 113
Kelly, Edward ("Ned"), 126
Kelly, W. H., 35, 48
Kerferd, G. B. (J.), 98, 124, 130, 153, 154, 155, 156, 157, 167-168, 176,
    177, 179, 182, 196, 197, 200
Kimberley, First Earl, 127
King v. *Victorian Railways Commissioners* (1892), 186-187
King's Inns, Dublin, 7
Kitt, Benjamin, 216-217
Knox, B. A., 104
Knutsford, Viscount, *see* Holland
La Trobe, Lieut-Governor C. J., 18
Law Society, 56
Lawes, Henry, 41
Legislative Council
    constitution of, 54, 70, 73, 75
    Higinbotham's contests with, 57, 61-62, 70-74, 75-99, 123
Leighton, Stanley, 232
Lester v. *Garland* (1808), 172
Levey v. *Azzopardi* (1887), 172
Levey, G. C., 63, 64, 66
Levi, Nathaniel, 67
Lilley, Sir Charles (C.J.), 152, 259
Lincoln's Inn, London, 7
Litton v. *Thornton* (1881), 143-144
Local government, legal liability of local authorities, 145-147, 176-184
Loch, Governor Sir Henry, 101, 155, 157, 202, 207, 208, 209, 213, 215,
    220-222, 223
Lords, House of, on colonial policy, 100-101, 106
Lowe, Robert, 116
Lyon, Commander, 250
Macartney, Revd H. B., 5
McCulloch, (Sir) James, 41, 42, 44, 65-67, 70, 72, 76, 77, 79, 81, 83, 85,
    86, 88-90, 93, 95, 98, 99, 108, 122, 224, 237
McDonald v. *Shire of Coburg* (1886), 177-178, 180
McFarland, John, 143
McHugh v. *Robertson* (1885), 140
McIlwraith, Sir Thomas, 216, 244
Macintyre, Prof. Stuart, 25
Mackay, F. H., 230
Mackay, Dr George, 18, 91, 227
Mackinnon, Donald, 230, 231

Mackinnon, Lauchlan, 62
MacPherson, J. A., 102, 108
McTiernan, Sir Edward (J.), 184
McVea v. *Pasquan* (1882), 131
Madden, (Sir) John (C.J.), 141, 158, 159, 160-161, 170, 190, 255
Manners-Sutton, Governor Sir John (Viscount Canterbury), 88-94, 108, 225
Maritime Strike (1890), 247-248, 257
Martin, Sir James (C.J.), 116, 118, 259
Martley, J. F., 50-51
Matthews v. *Muttlebury* (1863), 40
Mepham, Bridget, 214, 216
Merivale, Herman, 104
Michie, (Sir) Archibald, 11, 12, 16, 17, 18, 41, 57, 68, 81, 83, 224-225
Michie's Building, 36-37
Mill, J. S., 70
Miller v. *Campbell* (1886), 151
Mitchell v. *Watson* (1880), 132
Molesworth v. *Molesworth* (1862), 39
Molesworth, Sir Robert (J.), 39-40, 121, 130, 140, 153, 157, 175, 183
Montford, Paul, 248
Moore, John, 41
Morgan, Henry, 153-154
Morning Chronicle (London), 6, 18
Morrell, Freeland, 156
Morris, Prof. E. E., 5, 8-9, 11, 13, 41, 86, 121, 156, 204, 235, 238, 241, 248, 249, 257
Munro, James, 219
Murphy v. *Lee* (1891), 174-175
Murphy, (Sir) Francis, 25, 65, 77, 85
Musgrave, Sir Anthony, 216-217
Muttlebury, Malleson & England, 40
Negligence, principles of, 138-139, 141-147, 184-190
    contributory negligence, 144, 147, 187-189
    fellow servants in common employment, 138-139
    volunteer, position of, 189
Nelson, The, 204
New Caledonia, 244
New Guinea, 244-245
New Zealand
    Higinbotham's possible removal to, 64
    death sentences commuted in, 217, 218
Nicholson, William, 50
Nixon, Anne, 2
Normanby, Marquis of (Governor), 127, 155
Nutt & Murphy, 91
Oakden v. *Gibbs* (1882), 134
O'Connor v. *Hotham Corporation* (1883), 146

O'Loghlen, Sir Bryan, 127, 231
Ormond, Francis, 246
O'Shanassy v. *Symons* (1856), 16
O'Shanassy, (Sir) John, 26-27, 48, 49-50, 56, 70, 71, 77, 85
Pacific Ocean policies, 243-245
Palmer, Vance, 257
Parkes, (Sir) Henry, 18, 33, 117, 192-193, 224, 233
"Parliamentary supremacy", concept of, 130-131, 133
Parsons, Thomas, 37-38
Patterson v. *O'Brien* (1856), 16
Pearson, C. H., 44, 156
Peck, Hugh, 242-243
Perry, Bishop Charles, 238
Piddington, A.B., 123-124
Piggott, Gerald, 249
Playford v. *Brown* (1880), 137
Pohlman, R. W., 12
Point Lonsdale, 147
Point Nepean, 50, 147
Prerogative, royal, – *see* Crown, prerogatives of
Press, newspaper, liberty of, 64-67
Privy Council, appeals to or advice of, 109-111, 115, 130-131, 200-201
Protection and Free Trade, 23, 76, 79, 83, 97
Punch v. *Ainslie* (1854), 12
Purves, J. L., 127
Puseley, Daniel, 20
Quick, Dr John, 166
R. v. *Call; ex parte Murphy* (1881), 150-151
R. v. Casey; ex parte Lodge (1887), 169
R. v. *Fitzgerald* (1889), 167-168
R. v. *Henson; ex parte Bond* (1888), 173
R. v. *Keyn (The Franconia)* (1876), 149-150
R. v. *Melbourne & Mt Alexander Railway Co.* (1856), 15
R. v. *Morton* (1891), 173
R. v. *Pearson; ex parte Smith* (1880), 147-148, 149
R. v. *Strickland; ex parte King* (1887), 166
Reid, Sir George, 3-4
Renison v. *Keighran* (1884), 135
Responsible Government, 21, 23-24, 26, 28, 46, 57, 61, 72, 79, 94, 102, 103, 116, 117, 120, 152, 195-197, 209, 210, 213, 214-215, 216, 217, 218, 259
Rich, Sir George (J.), 184
Richardson, Richard, 125
Roads, laws relating to – *see* Local Government
Robinson v. *Bonfield* (1862), 39
Robinson, Sir Hercules, 117-118
Robinson, Sir William, 223
Rogers, Sir Frederic, 83, 103-105, 113-115, 119, 120, 212

Ross, J. T., 246
Royal prerogative – *see* Crown, prerogatives of
Royal School, Dungannon, 3
Rusden, G. W., 66, 70, 79
Rutledge, J. Y., 4
St Kilda, 12, 83, 94
Salisbury, Marquis of, 101, 200
Sargood, F. T., 205
Schomberg, Frederick, Duke of, 1-2
Scott v. *Collingwood Corporation* (1881), 145-146
Serle, Dr G., 11, 20
Service, James, 11, 46, 122, 123, 125, 126, 127, 153, 156, 255
Sewell, Dr R. C., 17
Shenandoah, C.S.S., 67-70
Shiels, William, 44, 129, 255-256, 259
Skipworth's Case (1873), 161, 162
Slade v. *Victorian Railways Commissioners* (1888), 185-186
Sladen, (Sir) Charles, 42, 94
Smith v. *Robertson* (1882), 144-145
Smith, G. P., 43, 242
Smith, Dr L. L., 51
South Melbourne, 11, 35
South Yarra, Higinbotham's last residence, 249
"Sovereignty", how understood, 53, 108-111, 147, 149, 192-193, 194, 195, 197-200, 216, 234
Stanhope, Edward, 207, 208
Stanley, Lord, 116
Starke, Sir Hayden (J.), 184
Statute law consolidation, 57, 60, 61, 71, 173, 227-232
Statutes – *see also* Acts
    codification of, proposed, 228, 231-232
    extraterritorial operation of, 147-151
Staughton v. *Tulloch* (1856), 17
Stawell, Mary Frances Elizabeth (Lady), 125
Stawell, Sir William (C.J.), 17, 57, 58, 61, 70, 91-92, 95, 96, 98, 116, 121, 125, 130, 132, 133, 134, 135, 136, 137, 144, 145, 148, 149, 150, 151, 152, 153, 155, 156, 157, 158, 159, 168, 190, 195, 220, 238, 242, 250, 259
Stephen, Sir Alfred (C.J.), 60, 220-221, 259
Stephen, Sir George, 18
Stephen, J. W. (J.), 41, 84, 121, 129, 130, 132, 136, 144, 148, 152-153, 238
Stevenson v. *The Queen* (1865), 82-83
Stretch, Revd J. F., 249
Strong, Revd Charles, 238-239
Supple, G. H., 42-43
Supply, government without, 79-83, 91-93, 113, 125
Supreme Court, relationship between parliamentary and curial powers, 130-131
    summary jurisdiction, 162-163

Supreme Court (*cont*)
    seal of, 169-170
Supreme Court House, Melbourne, 59-60, 160
Supreme Court Judges
    accountability to Attorney-General, 60-64
    appointment as Executive Councillors canvassed, 204
"Tacking" of legislation, 77-78
Tarring, Sir Charles, 109, 110
Tasmania, Higinbotham's visit to, 36, 219
Tobin v. *Melbourne Corporation* (1881), 142-143
Todd, Dr Alpheus, 100-101, 111
Tompsitt, H. T., 164
Toy v. *Musgrove* (1888), 159, 183, 191-201, 259
Trench, R. Le P., 170-171
Trinity College, Dublin, 1, 3, 4, 5, 6, 28, 43, 101
"Tullymaglowny", Ireland, 1-2, 7
Turner, H. G., 58, 71, 90, 98, 122-123
Unitarian Church, 240-241
United States and American influences, 28, 32, 67-70, 115, 187
Urquhart, George, 62
Verdon, (Sir) George, 77, 228
Victoria Steam Navigation Board (In re); ex parte Allen (1881), 148-149
Walshe, J. S., 42-43
Warburton v. *Alston* (1888), 159
Ward, Prof. J. M., 195
"Warrain", Brighton, 35-36
Washington, George, 3, 257
Watson v. *Issell* (1890), 172
Way, Sir Samuel (C.J.), 220-221
Webb, G.H.F. (J.), 130, 177, 181, 182, 190, 193
Wentworth, W. C., 115, 116, 257
Whipham, T. W., 18
Whitney v. *Footscray Justices* (1892), 171-172
Willes, Sir John (C.J.), 151
William III, King (William of Orange), 1-2
Williams, Sir Edward (J.), 15, 25, 62-64, 121, 147, 242, 248
Williams, (Sir) Hartley (J.), 129, 130, 137, 138, 151, 162, 163, 167, 178, 180, 181, 182, 185, 187, 189, 193-194, 196, 199-200, 255
Wilson, Edward, 18-21, 29-33, 62
Wilson, Joseph, 3
Winter, In re (1889), 163-164
Wood, J. D., 18, 27, 41, 51, 56
Working Men's College, Melbourne, 246-247
Wrenfordsley, Sir Henry, 159, 193-195, 197
Wrixon, (Sir) Henry, 43-44, 156, 157, 200, 207, 208, 210, 214-215, 220-221, 226, 230
Wynes, Dr W. A., 150
Yarra River, 141-142